The American South

The American South

SEVEN BOOKS SUGGESTED
FOR REPRINTING BY
C. VANN WOODWARD

G. W. Dyer
Democracy in the South Before the Civil War. 1905

D. R. Hundley
Social Relations in Our Southern States. 1860

Charles H. Otken
*The Ills of the South, Or, Related Causes Hostile
to the General Prosperity of the Southern People.*
1894

Robert Royal Russel
Economic Aspects of Southern Sectionalism, 1840–1861.
1923

Robert Somers
The Southern States Since the War, 1870–1. 1871

D. Augustus Straker
The New South Investigated. 1888

Richard Taylor
*Destruction and Reconstruction: Personal Experiences
of the Late War.* 1879

ECONOMIC ASPECTS OF SOUTHERN SECTIONALISM, 1840-1861

BY

ROBERT ROYAL RUSSEL

ARNO PRESS

A NEW YORK TIMES COMPANY

New York ☆ 1973

Reprint Edition 1973 by Arno Press Inc.

Reprinted from a copy in
  The University of Illinois Library

The American South
ISBN for complete set: 0-405-05058-5

Manufactured in the United States of America

——◆——

Library of Congress Cataloging in Publication Data

Russel, Robert Royal, 1890-
    Economic aspects of Southern sectionalism, 1840-1861.

    (The American South)
    Thesis--University of Illinois, 1922.
    Reprint of the 1924 (thesis) ed. published by the
University of Illinois, Urbana, which was originally
issued as v. 11, no. 1.and 2 of the University of
Illinois studies in the social sciences.
    Bibliography: p.
    1.   Southern States--Economic conditions.
2. Southern States--Politics and government--1775-
1865. I. Title. II. Series. III. Series: Illinois.
University. Illinois studies in the social sciences,
v. 11, no. 1,2.
    HC107A13R8   1973   330.9'75'03   72-11346
    ISBN 0-405-05062-3

ECONOMIC ASPECTS OF SOUTHERN SECTIONALISM, 1840-1861

BY

ROBERT ROYAL RUSSEL
A.B. McPherson College, 1914
A.M. University of Kansas, 1915

———————

THESIS

SUBMITTED IN PARTIAL FULFILLMENT OF THE REQUIREMENTS
FOR THE DEGREE OF DOCTOR OF PHILOSOPHY IN HISTORY
IN THE GRADUATE SCHOOL OF THE UNIVERSITY
OF ILLINOIS, 1922

Reprinted from the UNIVERSITY OF ILLINOIS STUDIES IN THE SOCIAL SCIENCES,
Vol. XI, number 1, pages 1 to 325.

To My Father and Mother

TABLE OF CONTENTS

PREFACE

The object of this monograph is to attempt to evaluate some of the causes for the secession of our Southern states which, to me, seem generally to have been underestimated. Lack of time has prevented the utilization of much available newspaper, pamphlet, and manuscript material of considerable value; but great confidence is felt that the evidence is typical, if not exhaustive. The work deals with matters which even today in a measure arouse the passions or prejudices of men; the greatest effort has been made, therefore, to preserve a detached point of view. A better contemporary understanding of the economic relations of the sections before 1861 might have moderated the bitterness of the sectional controversy; a better understanding of them even now would soften its memories.

The subject of this study was suggested to me while I was preparing a master's thesis on the subject "Early Projects for a Railroad to the Pacific" under the direction of Professor F. H. Hodder, of the University of Kansas. The preparation of the study was begun in 1916 under the supervision of Professors E. B. Greene and A. C. Cole and completed under the supervision of Professor T. C. Pease, of the University of Illinois. I am indebted to each of these men for very valuable criticisms and suggestions. I have used the works of many men who have written on related subjects, and am under greater obligations to them than citations in the footnotes or bibliography can indicate. The materials used in the preparation of this monograph were found, with few exceptions, either in the Library of the University of Illinois, the Library of Congress, or the Library of the University of Chicago. To the officials and staffs of these institutions, I am grateful for much assistance and many courtesies.

ROBERT R. RUSSEL.

INTRODUCTION

THE BASES OF SOUTHERN SECTIONALISM

The most significant fact of American history from about 1820 to 1875, at least, was sectionalism. The section which was at all times most clearly defined was the *South*. The term *South*, however, did not have the same connotation at all times and to all men. Until about 1845 the term *South* was commonly applied only to the South Atlantic states. The states of the lower Mississippi valley were gradually brought under the term as their economic and social organization and general conditions approximated those in the old South and differentiated from those of the states of the upper part of the valley, for Southern sectionalism had bases in several distinctive features besides latitude.

Foremost of these was the existence of slavery. For reasons chiefly geographical, slavery had never flourished in colonial days above Mason and Dixon's Line as it had below it, and the institution had been abolished there during or shortly after the Revolutionary War. Into the Old Northwest, slavery had not been extended; while into Kentucky and Missouri and the region to the south it had been carried in the same form as in the South Atlantic states. To be sure, the slave population was not evenly distributed throughout the South. The great majority of the slaves were concentrated in the so-called black belts, which corresponded roughly to the areas best adapted to the cultivation of cotton, tobacco, sugar cane, rice, and hemp, and the concentration became more pronounced as the Civil War approached. Outside the black belts the South was upon an essentially free-labor basis. Within the black belts the plantation predominated over the farm; outside, the farm prevailed. But the slaveholding planters were the dominant element in Southern society, and the people of the farming districts had interest in slavery in that they found markets for their surplus products chiefly in the planting regions. The institution of slavery came to be regarded as absolutely essential to Southern prosperity. Consequently Southern men defended it as right, shaped their political policies to protect it and secure its extension, and demanded that attacks upon it cease.

There was basis for sectionalism, also, in divergent economic interests and conditions. To what extent the divergence was due to geography, to what extent due to other factors, including social organization, it is not necessary here to inquire. The Southern states, however, were engaged largely in the production of a few great staples—cotton, tobacco, and sugar—not produced in other states of the Union. Of these staples only a small proportion was consumed at home; much the greater part was exported either to the North or to Europe. The portion exported abroad constituted considerably more than half the nation's total exports. Manufacturing and mining had made, and were making during the period under survey, little progress in the South compared with the same industries in other sections; the exports of the South were exchanged in part for agricultural products of the West but chiefly for manufactured goods of the East or Europe. The ocean commerce of the South, whether coastwise or foreign, was carried almost altogether in Northern or European vessels; foreign goods for Southern consumption came largely by way of Northern ports. Only a small percentage of the Southern population was urban; the cities and towns of the section were few and small compared with those of the East or even those of the growing Northwest. The banking capital of the country was largely concentrated in the East; the South was not financially independent.

Divergent economic interests of the sections led to the advocacy of different policies, on the part of the Federal government, as regards tariff, taxation, navigation laws, and the amount and objects of government expenditures. The disparity of the sections in industry and commerce was to many Southerners an evidence of lack of prosperity in the South commensurate with that of the North, and, consequently, was a cause of dissatisfaction, and was galling to Southern pride. The causes of Southern "decline" were sought for; it was variously attributed to geography and climate, qualities of the people, misdirection of private enterprise, mistaken policies of the state and local governments, and the unequal operation of the Federal government, but not, generally, to slavery. Remedies were proposed, corresponding roughly to the causes, as analyzed.

Other bases for sectionalism were of much less importance. Because of early conditions of settlement, and especially because later immigration was mostly into the non-slaveholding states, there were slight differences in the racial types of the sections. The sparsity of population and the social organization in the South were accountable for backwardness in general education and cultural development. Early conditions of settlement, agricultural pursuits, slavery and the plantation system, and sparsity of population largely explain the variation from other sections in political ideals and methods.

It is the purpose of this study to attempt to discover to what extent Southern sectionalism had its basis in divergent economic interests and conditions. The study is primarily a study of public opinion. It will require an examination of the opinions of Southern men as to the divergence of economic interests and the extent of the disparity of economic development in the sections, the causes of such disparity, and the proper remedies therefor. Actual economic conditions and changes will be described and explained only in so far as such description and explanation are essential to an understanding of Southern public opinion. It is hoped, however, that incidentally some additional light may be thrown upon the economic status of the ante-bellum South, and that some conclusions may be drawn as to the justification for Southern discontent. Frequent references will of necessity be made to the sectional quarrel over slavery, and the attempt will be made to maintain proper proportion between the minor aspects of sectionalism herein treated and the major issue of the sectional struggle.

In seeking to analyze Southern opinion relative to the matters mentioned above, several movements in behalf of the economic regeneration of the South will be described, and the accompanying discussion examined. Evidence of economic discontent can be found in the discussion of some of the outstanding political questions of the day, and such bodies of discussion will, therefore, be analyzed. In the years 1837-1839, a number of direct trade conventions held in the South Atlantic states gave earnest consideration to direct trade with Europe as a remedy for Southern decline. During the 1840s, especially the latter half of the decade, there was much discussion of the practicability and desirability of developing manufactures, especially cotton manufactures. The political crisis of the years 1847-1852 furnished the occasion for considerable consideration of the economic relations of the sections. During the 1850s, direct trade with Europe was almost constantly a subject before the public. Between 1852 and 1859, a series of Southern commercial conventions, whose original object was to devise measures for effecting the economic regeneration of the section, met in various cities of the South. The tariff question was not dead during the period studied, and during the 1850s policies of state and local protection of industry were proposed and discussed. The agitation of the late fifties in behalf of secession, as well as the movement for the revival of the foreign slave trade of the same period, gave evidence of discontent with the economic position of the South. Finally, every phase of Southern sectionalism was brought out by the actual dissolution of the Union and the necessity of inaugurating Confederate governmental policies. Time and the scope of this work have not permitted adequate consideration of the sectional aspects of two important problems of the ante-bellum South, namely, the building of railroads, especially into the Northwest and to the Pacific, and the establishment of a satisfactory banking and credit system.[1] It is not believed that the omissions will vitiate the conclusions reached in any material degree. The period covered by this study has been rather arbitrarily limited.

[1]"Early Projects for a Pacific Railroad" was the subject of an unpublished master's thesis of the author.

CHAPTER I

AGITATION IN BEHALF OF DIRECT TRADE WITH EUROPE, 1837-1839

In colonial days the exports and imports of the Southern colonies compared very favorably in amount with those of the Northern; but shortly after independence from Great Britain was achieved, it became apparent that the importing business of the nation was being concentrated in Northern ports. As the years went by the concentration became more and more pronounced. While the exports of the staple producing states grew at a phenomenal rate, the value of the imports into Southern ports remained almost stationary or grew very slowly. This was particularly true in the case of the Atlantic ports. In the case of New Orleans, for long almost the sole outlet for the commerce of the rapidly filling Mississippi valley, there was early in the last century phenomenal increase in both exports and imports; but after about 1835 the latter increased very slowly, while the former continued to grow at the same remarkable rate. Prior to the Civil War the imports of the Northern states greatly exceeded their exports. In the Southern states the reverse was the case. A comparison of the exports from all Southern ports with those from all Northern ports shows that after about 1830 the former always exceeded, and sometimes greatly exceeded, the latter. The imports of the Southern ports, however, were only a fraction of the imports of Northern ports, and became proportionally less as the years went by.[1] If the growing superiority of the North in population be remembered, and the comparison be made on the basis of population, the disparity is still striking. It indicates that either the people of the South did not consume their proportionate share of the nation's imports, or that Northern merchants imported largely on Southern account, or both.

A study of the growth of population of Northern and Southern seaports likewise reveals a growing disparity in favor of the former.[2] The ante-bellum South had no large and growing ports except New Orleans and Baltimore, the latter of which was on the line between the two sections.

[1]See Appendix, Table I.
[2]See Appendix, Table II.

The available statistics of the shipping built or owned in the two sections again reveals a disparity in favor of the North as great or greater than that in the value of imports or the population of the seaports. If the comparison be limited to vessels engaged in the foreign trade, it is even more to the advantage of the North.[3] These facts would seem to indicate that the foreign commerce of the Southern states was carried largely in Northern or foreign vessels, and that the coasting trade of the South, if large, must have been conducted largely in Northern vessels.

The comparative growth of Northern and Southern seaports, the tendency to concentration of the importing business of the United States in Northern cities, especially New York, and the disparity between the shipping industries of the two sections, in short the "commercial dependence" of the South upon the North, were matters which received considerable attention in the antebellum South, not only from citizens of the seaports themselves but from the section as a whole. Southern men quite generally looked upon commercial dependence as an evidence of the failure of the South to prosper as it should. They gave consideration to the relation of commercial dependence to the comparatively slow accumulation of mobile capital in the South and to the inadequacy of credit facilities, because of which they were handicapped in their efforts to construct internal improvements and to develop the varied resources of the section. They canvassed commercial dependence as a cause for the slower increase of population in the South than in the North—a matter of much concern because of its bearing upon the sectional struggle over slavery. The causes of commercial dependence were sought, therefore, and efforts were made to devise and apply remedies.

The whole subject was first thoroughly discussed, and the first efforts made to effect a revolution in the manner of conducting Southern commerce, by a number of direct trade conventions which met in Georgia, South Carolina, and Virginia in 1837, 1838, and 1839.

The direct trade convention originated in Georgia. While the financial crash of 1837 deranged the currency and the exchange and credit operations of the country, it seems not to have affected the old South as disastrously at first as it did other sections of

[3]See Appendix, Table III.

the Union.[4] It was seized upon as affording a good opportunity for attempting to effect the establishment of direct trade and a change in the method of marketing cotton. With these objects in view, William Dearing and other gentlemen, of Athens, issued a call for a convention to meet in Augusta in October, 1837.[5] The call stated that a crisis had arrived in the commercial affairs of the South and Southwest, "the most favorable that has occurred since the formation of the American government, to attempt a new organization of our commercial relations with Europe."[6] The first Augusta convention was followed in April and October, 1838, by a second and a third and, in April, 1839, by a fourth, in Charleston.

Each of this series of conventions was composed of from one hundred to two hundred delegates, elected by local meetings. The great majority in each case was from Georgia and South Carolina, but there were scattering representatives from North Carolina, Tennessee, Alabama, and Florida Territory, and an attempt was made to enlist as many Southern states as possible. Although the state rights, anti-tariff men gave tone to the proceedings, the conventions were bi-partisan in composition; they were not got up for partisan purposes, and party politics played a minor part in their deliberations. Among the delegates were bankers, merchants, and planters, as well as men active in politics. The lists of delegates included such well known names as Robert Y. Hayne, A. P. Hayne, George McDuffie, James Hamilton, Ker Boyce, James Gadsden, Colonel Blanding, F. H. Elmore, H. S. Legaré, J. H. Hammond, J. E. and J. A. Calhoun, Chancellor Harper, and C. G. Memminger, of South Carolina, Thomas Butler King, A. H. Stephens, George W. Crawford, J. M. Berrien, G. B. Lamar, Judge A. B. Longstreet, and Joseph H. Lumpkin, of Georgia, A. J. Pickett, of Alabama, and Spencer Jarnaghin, of Tennessee. John C. Calhoun was not present in any of these conventions, but their purposes met with his approval.[7] The presence and active participation of such men are sufficient to indicate the deep interest in the

[4]Charleston *Courier*, Oct. 7, 1837.

[5]*Niles' Register*, LV, 43, 189. The delegates of the third Augusta convention presented William Dearing with a silver cup in recognition of his part in inaugurating the direct trade conventions.

[6]Charleston *Courier*, Aug. 14, 1837.

[7]Calhoun to Sidney Breese, July 27, 1839, *Calhoun Correspondence*.

objects of the conventions. Numerous local meetings and the accompanying press discussion give testimony to the same effect. In addition to the debates and resolutions and the newspaper comments, the views, objects, and plans of the conventions were set forth in several quite able addresses and reports. The report from the committee of twenty-one of the first convention was read by George McDuffie, chairman.[8] He was made chairman of a committee to address the people of the South and Southwest upon the objects of the convention, and wrote the address.[9] At the second convention the report of the general committee was read by Robert Y. Hayne, chairman, and a committee, of which A. B. Longstreet was appointed chairman, was instructed to prepare an address to the people.[10] At the Charleston meeting, Robert Y. Hayne read a report upon direct trade, which he had prepared, and which was adopted by the convention;[11] F. H. Elmore read a report from another committee, composed chiefly of merchants from interior towns.[12]

Three delegates from Norfolk, Virginia, attended the second Augusta convention and took a prominent part in its proceedings. As a result of growing interest, a direct trade convention was called to meet in Richmond in June, 1838. This meeting was followed by another in Norfolk in November. Besides these two large conventions there were a number of more local gatherings which discussed the same subjects. The great majority of the delegates at Richmond and Norfolk were from Virginia, but several came from North Carolina. These gatherings were bi-partisan in composition, as were those in Georgia and South Carolina, but they did not succeed so well in keeping partisan politics out of the proceedings. Among the delegates were such prominent men as John S. Millson, J. M. Botts, James Caskie, Francis Mallory, Edmund Ruffin, Myer Myers, and W. C. Flournoy. At Norfolk, John Tyler presided. These conventions, too, left sev-

<hr/>

[8]Charleston *Courier*, Oct. 24, 1837.
[9]*DeBow's Review*, IV, 208 ff.
[10]Report is in Savannah *Daily Republican*, April 6, 9, 19, 1838. The address is in the Charleston *Mercury*, Aug. 11, 1838; *DeBow's Review*, XIII, 477-93; *Niles' Register*, LV, 40 f.
[11]DeBow, *Industrial Resources of the South and West*, III, 92-111.
[12]*DeBow's Review*, IV, 493-502; DeBow, *Industrial Resources*, etc., III, 111-116.

eral ably written reports, notably, the report of the committee on commerce of the Richmond convention,[13] a report prepared and submitted to the same convention by Francis Mallory but withdrawn because of the opposition it encountered,[14] and the report of the general committee of the Norfolk convention, read by John S. Millson.[15]

There was substantial agreement in all of the conventions in regard to the manner in which Southern commerce was conducted, the evils attendant thereon, and the benefits to follow the establishment of direct trade with Europe. The staple growing states were described as being in a "state of commercial dependence, scarcely less reproachful to their industry and enterprise than it is incompatible with their substantial prosperity."[16] What would be more natural than that those who furnished the nation's exports should also receive its imports? Yet, while the South furnished two-thirds of the exports, she received directly only one-tenth of the imports of the United States. Francis Mallory estimated that nine-tenths of the exports went directly to Europe, while five-sevenths of the imports from abroad came indirectly by way of Northern seaports. The direct imports of Charleston were said to have amounted to several millions in 1807; by 1833 they had dwindled to one-half million; since that time they had gradually increased, but were still insignificant.[17] The same was said to be true of Virginia. At the time of the Revolution exports and imports had been equal; from that time to 1831 imports had steadily declined; since 1831 there had been some, though not marked, improvement.[18] Though Southern exports went directly to Europe, the business was not conducted by home merchants, but chiefly by agents of Northern and English firms. Southern

[13]Richmond *Enquirer*, June 22, 1838.

[14]*Ibid.*, June 26, 1838; June 19. Mallory's report may be found in pamphlet form also.

[15]*Ibid.*, Nov. 30, 1838. In addition to the reports already mentioned, were a "Report on Manufactures" and a "Supplementary Report on Manufactures," both adopted by the Richmond convention. *Ibid.*, June 26, 1838.

[16]Charleston *Courier*, Oct. 24, 1837, report of the general committee of the first Augusta convention.

[17]Savannah *Daily Republican*, April 7, 1838, report of the general committee of the second Augusta convention.

[18]Richmond *Enquirer*, June 26, 1838, Mallory's report.

seaports were described as mere appendages of Northern seaports, "places where their agents and factors do business, and
who, having but little local interest, withdraw from them after a
few years residence, with all their gains, to swell the wealth of
the place of their early affection and attachment."[19] In Virginia,
Northern steamboats often went up the rivers buying and selling
directly to the farmers, the lumbermen, and the country merchants; the cargoes were paid for by bills on New York, and the
money never entered Virginia. Interior merchants purchased their
stocks in New York, Philadelphia, or Baltimore without the intervention of jobbers in Southern ports.[20]

The profits Northern merchants and shippers made from conducting Southern commerce were believed to be very great and to
account in large measure for the prosperity of Northern cities,
while the loss of those profits explained the impoverishment of the
cities of the South. The address issued by the second Augusta
convention, after estimating at $630,000,000 the duties paid by
the Southern states since the establishment of the Constitution of
the United States, continued:

If we suppose the value of the goods upon which the six hundred and thirty millions of duties were levied, to have been but
four times the value of the duties, it amounted to $2,500,000,000.
How were these goods brought to this country and distributed?
The northern merchant has come hither and bought from the
southern planter produce of equal value, abating from the price
all the expenses, direct and incidental, of transportation. He has
insured them in northern offices, and shipped them abroad in his
own vessels—exchanged them at a small profit for foreign merchandise—brought it home—paid one-fourth its value to the government—added that amount and all the expenses of importation,
and fifteen to twenty per cent. for his profits, to the price, and
exposed it for sale. The southern merchant has now gone to him
—lingered the summer through at heavy expense—bought a portion of the goods, reshipped them in northern vessels to southern
ports—added twenty-five per cent. more to the price, to cover his
expenses and profits—and sold them to the southern planter. All
the disbursements made in this process, save such as are made
abroad, are among northern men; all the profits, save the southern merchant's, are made by northern men ... Every item in the
endless catalogue of charges, except the government dues, may be
considered a voluntary tribute from the citizens of the south to

[19]Richmond *Enquirer*, June 26, 1838, Mallory's report.
[20]*Ibid.*

their brethren of the north; for they would all have gone to our own people, had we done our own exporting and importing.[21]

At Charleston, Robert Y. Hayne quoted a report of a committee of the Alabama Legislature in which it was estimated that over one-third the price of cotton went to New York agents and shippers. Hayne himself was content to put the tolls at 10 or 15 per cent.[22] George McDuffie thought the "voluntary tribute" paid annually to the North for carrying Southern commerce amounted to $10,000,000.[23] A Virginia delegate said the state could save $1,000,000 annually by importing directly.[24] But this direct annual drain was not the only loss occasioned the Southern people; there were also the "consequential losses," that is, the capital which would have accumulated had the South conducted her own commerce. Commercial dependence had operated to prevent the accumulation of capital in the South, and the deficiency of capital had handicapped enterprise.

The greatness of New York City was pictured—all said to have been built upon Southern staples and Southern trade. "You hold the element," ran the address of one of these conventions, "from which he derives his strength, and you have only to withdraw it to make him as subservient to you, as you now are to him. You have but to speak the word, and his empire is transferred to your own soil, and his sovereignty to the sons of that soil."[25] But the benefits were not confined to New York; the virtual monopoly of Southern commerce had "either directly or indirectly made the whole of the North and Northwest what they are," according to the call of the first Augusta convention.[26] Because of it, "the one people has risen like the rocket, and the other has fallen like its stick—their positions must have been reversed, if the southern people had maintained their foreign trade."[27] Glowing descriptions were given of the prosperity of Southern states and cities after direct trade should be restored. Were direct trade established, according to the address calling the second Augusta convention, "there would be an end to the unequal barter of which

[21]*Niles' Register*, LV, 41.

[22]DeBow, *Industrial Resources*, III, 93.

[23]Charleston *Courier*, Oct. 24, 1837, report, first Augusta convention.

[24]Richmond *Enquirer*, June 15, 1838.

[25]*Niles' Register*, LV, 43, second Augusta convention.

[26]Charleston *Courier*, Aug. 14, 1837.

[27]*Niles' Register*, LV, 42.

we have spoken. The doleful cry for northern funds would be hushed. The speculators upon southern distress would cease. The disorders of the currency would be healed. The relation of the commercial agency would be changed. They would be acquaintances and friends, identical in feeling and interest; enjoying mutual confidence, and interchanging mutual favors . . . . The fountain and the streams of commerce lying all within our land, would enrich it to an extent that none can foresee. Our works of internal improvement would receive a new and ever-accelerating impetus. Our drooping cities would be revived—our creeping commerce winged; and all the blessings, physical, moral, and intellectual, which invariably accompany affluence and independence, would be ours."[28]

In regard to the causes for the "decline" of the shipping and the import trade of Southern ports, the conventions exhibited differences of opinion. First, there was the view that for many years the North had possessed great advantages over the South for these lines of business by reason of its superior wealth and larger accumulations of capital. Not only must ship owners and importers be men of large capital, but they must have the backing of wealthy communities.

And men of the South Carolina school, the followers of Calhoun and McDuffie, who predominated in the Augusta and Charleston conventions, were ready with explanations for the more rapid accumulation of capital in the North than in the South. It was, they said, because of the unequal operation of the Federal government. The tariffs had long enriched the manufacturing sections at the expense of the agricultural. Furthermore, while the people of the South had paid their proportionate share of the Federal revenues, these revenues had been disbursed chiefly in the Northern cities, and this process, going on year after year, had transferred a staggering total from the one section to the other. A minority report in the Richmond convention rehearsed the old story of the assumption of the state debts by the Federal government and the refunding of the national debt carried out under the guidance of Alexander Hamilton. The refunded debt had been distributed between the North and South in the ratio of three to one, and, because of this inequality of distribution, had acted as a mortgage

[28] *Niles' Register*, LV, 43. Cf. Richmond *Enquirer*, June 26, 1838.

of the one section upon the other, great sums having been transferred from the South to the North in the form of interest paid
to Northern bond holders from the common treasury.[29] It was
claimed, also, by men in these conventions, that for long the funds
of the Federal government had been deposited almost altogether
in Northern banks, thus giving Northern business men a decided
advantage over Southern in the ability to secure financial assistance. Those who held these views of the causes of Southern decline saw basis for hope for revival in the gradual reduction of the
tariff, according to the provisions of the Compromise Tariff law of
1833, the recent extinguishment of the national debt, the destruction of the United States Bank, and the evidence of a new policy
in distributing deposits of the public funds.

Another alleged cause for Southern commercial dependence,
closely related to the one just mentioned, was the inadequacy of
credit facilities. An examination, however cursory, of business
methods in the South in that period makes it clear that a successful importing firm would have to command very great resources
of capital or credit or both. It was proverbial that the planters
lived each year upon the prospective income from the next year's
crop. The country merchants, who extended them long credit,
could not buy, therefore, except on long time. Importers, who
bought on sixty or ninety days time, had to sell to the merchants
upon from six to twelve or sixteen months. Country merchants
were sometimes unwilling to give negotiable notes; they considered a request to do so a reflection upon their business integrity.[30]
Southern importers and jobbers did not, unaided, possess the
means, and Southern banks were unable to lend them sufficient
support, to enable them to extend to retail merchants the long
credits which the latter received in the North.

A correspondent of the Charleston *Courier* attributed the loss
of foreign trade to the fact that country merchants began to buy
of Northern jobbers because of the longer credits obtained.[31]
Robert Y. Hayne enumerated long credits as one of the causes of
the decline of Southern commerce.[32] McDuffie said he confidently

[29]Richmond *Enquirer*, June 26, 1838, Mallory's report.
[30]*Ibid.*, June 22, 1838, remarks of Mr. James and Mr. Caskie; June 26, 1838,
Mallory's report.
[31]Oct. 17, 1837.
[32]DeBow, *Industrial Resources*, III, 98.

believed that, if the planters would "adopt the system of expend-
ing, in the current year, the income of the year preceding . . . .
it would dispense with one-half of the capital that would otherwise
be necessary for carrying on our foreign commerce by a system of
direct importation."[33] One of the questions dividing public opinion
in Virginia in that period was the policy of authorizing an increase
of bank capital in the state. It was the subject of animated debates in both the Richmond and the Norfolk conventions. Those
favoring the increase thought the unwise policy of the legislature
in refusing the authorization largely responsible for the decline of
direct trade in Virginia.

It is to the credit of the men of these conventions that they
recognized other causes for Southern commercial dependence
than the action or non-action of the Federal and state governments. They recognized that agriculture had in the past proved
more attractive to capital than the shipping or mercantile business;
land and negroes had been considered the best investments. The
existence of a prejudice against other pursuits than agriculture and
the professions was admitted. Some were willing to credit the people of the North with habits of industry not possessed by their own
people and with superior commercial enterprise; they spoke of the
"voluntary tribute" which the South paid the North. The able report of the general committee of the Norfolk convention, read by
John S. Millson, traced the decline of Virginia's foreign commerce
to a very early date. Before the Revolution, the report said, business was conducted by British capitalists, and even then the resident merchants were foreigners. At the time of the Revolution,
British capital was withdrawn. True, the same thing happened in
the North, but to a less degree, and the North was better prepared to take the place left by the British. Furthermore, agriculture became unprofitable in the North at an earlier day than in the
South, and capital had been diverted to other industries. The
committee further candidly admitted that "the decline of a considerable portion of our foreign import trade may be accounted
for in the fact that we now derive from the Northern states
many of those articles that we formerly imported from abroad."
Such a diversion of trade was not a subject for regret.[34] A committee in the Charleston convention likewise reported that the

[33]*DeBow's Review*, IV, 221.
[34]Richmond *Enquirer*, Nov. 30, 1838.

consumption of domestic goods had increased greatly, was still increasing, and was estimated by merchants to extend already to
one-third of the whole consumption. The committee believed,
however, that the quantity of foreign goods consumed in the South
was sufficient to justify merchants in Southern seaports embarking
in the importing business and to enable them to compete with
Northern importers, who, of course, supplied a larger demand.[35]

It was generally denied that Northern seaports possessed any
natural or physical advantages over Southern seaports for conducting foreign commerce. The direct course of trade was the
natural course, and the indirect the unnatural. Direct trade would
save one set of jobbers' profits, the cost of shipping coastwise, the
difference between the discount of Southern notes in New York
and Charleston (or the cost of whatever other mode of payment
was employed), and the expenses retail merchants incurred in going North to lay in their stocks. Southern harbors were said to be
as good as Northern. However that may be, it is certain that
ocean going vessels entered Southern harbors to receive their exports. These ships often came in ballast, and, it was reasonably
argued, would be willing to carry imports at low freights. Shipping was considered adequate, though there was recognition that
regular packet lines were needed.[36] The South was said to have
timber for ship-building; but, in the thirties, not much was said
about the desirability of promoting ship-building or ship-owning:
the big object was to save the "importers' profits." Now and then
someone suggested that the importing business in Southern cities
was rendered precarious by visits of yellow, or "strangers'," fever;
but residents of the South were generally ready to defend their
coast cities against the prevalent belief that they were unhealthy.[37]

Various plans and measures were suggested for promoting
direct importations of foreign goods. Some were intended to overcome the obstacle to direct trade which lay in the lack of mercan-

[35]*DeBow's Review*, IV, 495, Elmore's report.

[36]It is a rather significant commentary, however, that much of the import
trade of Charleston was made by her own merchants through New York, the
goods being transhipped there. *DeBow's Review*, IV, 499.

[37]DeBow, *Industrial Resources*, III, 98; Buckingham, *Slave States of America*, I, 67 ff. In 1838, Charleston experienced the most costly epidemic of yellow
fever of her history to that time. The severity of the epidemic was partly due
to the conditions resulting from the great fire earlier in the same year. Charleston
Mercury, Sept. 13, Oct. 26, 1838; *Niles' Register*, LV, 52, 161.

tile houses with sufficient capital to enable them to embark in the importing business. The first Augusta convention took the view that, while individual merchants were not possessed of resources necessary, the requisite capital could be got together by associations of individuals, and to that end it appointed a committee to memorialize the state legislatures in behalf of limited co-partnership laws. In response to the committee's memorials the legislatures of Virginia, South Carolina, Georgia, Alabama, Tennessee, and Florida Territory enacted the desired legislation, and subsequent conventions urged men of means to avail themselves of the opportunity thus afforded.[38] The opinion was expressed that there was an overproduction of cotton in the South, and that planters could profitably invest a portion of the proceeds of their crops otherwise than in land and negroes. If for a few years the planters would apply one-half their net income to commerce, abundant capital would be supplied to conduct the whole foreign commerce.[39] This suggestion, however, could not carry great weight, for, though subject to fluctuation, it was not until 1839 that there was a marked decline in cotton prices, and the average for the years 1835 to 1839 was fourteen cents, a higher average than that of any equal period since 1820 to 1824.[40] The question of capital, it was considered, would be a serious one only while the revolution in trade was being effected, for, once established, the profits of direct importations would supply the capital requisite for their continuance.[41]

Other recommendations of the direct trade conventions dealt with the great obstacle to direct trade which lay in the inadequacy of credit facilities in the South. The second Augusta convention was especially detailed in its recommendations. It requested banks to form European connections that they might be able to assist importers with letters of credit. It recommended that the banks in the seaports discount paper from the interior for the

[38]Savannah *Daily Republican*, April 6, 10, 1838; *Niles' Register*, LV, 43, 189. The Charleston convention adopted a resolution directing the chairman to appoint and designate the spheres of committees whose duty it should be to call meetings of the people and recommend to them to invest a portion of their surplus capital in limited partnerships with merchants in trading centers and towns of their respective states. Charleston *Courier*, April 19, 1839.
[39]*Ibid.*, Oct. 24, 1837; *DeBow's Review*, IV, 222.
[40]Donnell, E. J., *History of Cotton, passim*.
[41]Savannah *Daily Republican*, April 10, 1838.

importing merchants—paper for longer periods than six months as well as for shorter periods. The banks of the interior were requested to cooperate by collecting and remitting the proceeds of such paper to the coast with as little delay as possible. "It is not to be concealed that without the aid and support of the banks, the difficulties in our way will be greatly multiplied. It will depend upon them, in great measure, to determine the fate of our great measure."[42] The banks had suspended specie payment in May, 1837, and were beset with great difficulties. The convention devised a plan for equalizing the domestic exchanges and keeping up the credit of the banks during the period of suspension. In substance the plan was that the banks of the principal Southern cities receive each other's notes and adopt some sort of a clearing house system, and that other banks maintain the value of their notes and keep down the rates of exchange by redeeming their notes at the seaports. A committee was appointed to urge the banks to adopt the plan.[43] The plan had good points, but was too complicated to be adopted at the time. The banks did make a more or less concerted effort to resume specie payments in 1838, but after a few months were again forced to suspend, in October, 1839. The Virginia conventions contented themselves, after hot discussions, with passing resolutions asking the legislatures of Virginia and North Carolina to authorize increases of banking capital.[44]

Many other suggestions designed to promote direct importations were made. Individual citizens were urged to be more enterprising. It was declared a sacred duty to buy of those merchants who traded directly in preference to those who bought foreign goods from Northern jobbers. Interior merchants were requested not to go North for their stocks until they had investigated the possibilities of making their purchases in their own seaports. A local Virginia convention, in 1838, recommended the organization of an association of retail merchants pledged to deal, after September 1, 1839, with the importing merchants of Virginia cities only, "provided those merchants would sell as cheaply as the Northern merchants;" and sixty or seventy citizens actually signed a pledge not

[42]Savannah *Daily Republican*, April 10, 1838.
[43]*Ibid.*, April 6, 1838.
[44]Richmond *Enquirer*, June 19, Nov. 23, 1838. These states did not have free banking laws at that time.

to patronize any merchant who would not join the association.[45]
The pledge system was advocated in the Norfolk convention, but
the convention refused to recommend it.[46] Complaint was made
that the tax laws of the states descriminated against commercial
capital in favor of land and slaves.[47] Some Southern states and
cities taxed sales; port and wharf charges and fees were said to be
too high.[48] The Charleston convention adopted a resolution requesting the state legislatures to repeal discriminatory taxes.[49]
A motion introduced at Norfolk to ask the Legislature of Virginia
to exempt direct imports from taxation was defeated.[50] The
prejudices of the people against mercantile pursuits were deplored: "The commercial class must be elevated in public opinion
to the rank in society which properly belongs to it." It was
recognized as an evil that the great majority of the merchants,
commission merchants, and factors in all the seaport cities of the
South (and interior towns too, for that matter) were either
Northerners or naturalized citizens. Commercial education was
recommended to train Southern youth to enter the field. Robert
Y. Hayne advanced to his son, William C., the capital necessary
to enter into a partnership with one of the old importers of Charleston. His purpose, he wrote, was to "try what can be done to
rear up a young brood of Carolina merchants, which I believe to
be indispensable to put our Southern America on a right footing."[51] Manufacturers and exporters of foreign countries were
asked to establish agencies in Southern cities for selling their
goods, as they had done in New York and other Northern seaports.
The Norfolk convention considered this quite important; it appointed a committee of seven to get in communication with
European firms.[52]

[45]Richmond *Enquirer*, Nov. 13, 1838, account of a meeting in Elizabeth City
County, Oct. 6, 1838.
[46]*Ibid.*, Nov. 20, 1838.
[47]Charleston *Courier*, April 17, 1839, "Report on the Taxation of Commercial Capital," submitted by Mitchell King in the Charleston convention.
[48]*DeBow's Review*, IV, 498.
[49]Charleston *Courier*, April 19, 1839.
[50]Richmond *Enquirer*, Nov. 23, 1838.
[51]Hayne to J. H. Hammond, Jan. 18, 1839, *J. H. Hammond Papers.*
[52]DeBow, *Industrial Resources*, III, 100; Richmond *Enquirer*, Nov. 20, 30,
1838. Early in 1839, George McDuffie was in England in the interest of a plan
of his own "to form associations of from twenty to thirty planters to buy directly

The direct trade movement of these years was very closely related to efforts being made in the South Atlantic states to establish connections by railroads or canals with the Ohio valley. South Carolinians were the chief promoters of a great project, which ultimately had to be abandoned, to build the "Louisville, Cincinnati, and Charleston Railroad."[53] The State of Georgia had undertaken the construction of a trunk line, the Western and Atlantic, from Atlanta to the Tennessee river.[54] Virginia had chartered the James River and Kanawha Canal Company, which, as the name indicates, was intended to provide continuous water communication between the seaboard and the Ohio.[55] All of the direct trade conventions very heartily endorsed these projects for connecting the South and West as most promising measures for securing direct trade. The West sold to the South, it was said; if it could also buy in the South, such a demand for goods would be created in Southern seaports that there could no longer be any question of their ability to import directly. "We must contend for the commerce of the West," read Mallory's report, "the section that gets that commerce will get the commerce of the country." A resolution adopted by the Norfolk convention declared internal improvements to be the foundation of an import trade.[56] The general committee of the Second Augusta convention said that direct trade was inseparably connected with the extension of intercourse to the West. "And when the great West shall find a market and receive their supplies through the seaports of the South, a demand will be furnished, the extent and value of which *cannot* be too largely estimated."[57] Calhoun, who took a deep interest in both projects, believed that direct trade could not be es-

from English manufacturers without commissions or profits to agents, factors, or merchants except a small commission to Liverpool houses selected to sell the planters' cotton and send their orders to the manufacturers." He believed the planters could save 25 per cent upon their purchases in this way. McDuffie to J. H. Hammond, March 31, 1839 (Manchester, England), *J. H. Hammond Papers.*

[53]This project is discussed at length in U. B. Phillips, *History of Transportation in the Eastern Cotton Belt*, ch. IV; and T. D. Jervey, *Robert Y. Hayne and His Times.*

[54]Phillips *op. cit.*, ch. VII.

[55]Ambler, *Sectionalism in Virginia from 1776 to1861*, p. 182.

[56]Richmond *Enquirer*, Nov. 20, 23, 1838.

[57]Savannah *Republican*, April 9, 1838.

tablished until railroads had been extended to the West.[58] On the other hand, discussion of the establishment of direct trade with Europe would stimulate interest in projects for connecting the seaboard and the Ohio valley. Many of the members of the direct trade conventions were closely associated with the internal improvement projects, and, though it would be inaccurate to say that the former were got up to give impetus to the latter, that was undoubtedly one of the objects of the conventions. The relation was made very clear in the message of Mayor Pinckney, of Charleston, August, 1838. During the previous year, he said, Charleston had held meetings, "giving a decided impetus to those great enterprises, the Cincinnati railroad and a direct trade with Europe, of which the latter will supply the former with its life blood, and of which the united operation will assuredly achieve the commercial independence of the South, and, with it, the permanent prosperity of our beloved city."[59]

Although the money panic of 1837 was the occasion for the convening of conventions which proposed to attempt to change the course of Southern trade, the movement cannot be considered the outgrowth of depressed economic conditions. In 1837 and 1838, it was believed that business had received only a temporary, although sharp, check, and that enterprise would soon be in full swing once more. As were the rapid building of railroads, canals, and turnpikes, the direct trade movement was a manifestation of the spirit of progress and enterprise which had seized upon East, West, and South alike. The movement came to a temporary close when general stagnation of business settled upon the country in 1839 and continued for several years thereafter.[60]

It is noteworthy that these direct trade conventions were concerned almost exclusively with economic conditions and means for improving them. The slavery question, which was being given considerable prominence about this time both in Congress and out

[58]Calhoun to Sidney Breese, July 27, 1839; to James Edward Calhoun, Nov. 1, 1841, *Calhoun Correspondence.*

[59]*Report; Containing a Review of the Proceedings of the City Authorities from the 4th of Sept., 1837. By Henry L. Pinckney, Mayor.*

[60]The Charleston convention adjourned to meet in Macon, Georgia, in May, 1840; the meeting did not occur. The Norfolk convention arranged for another to meet in Raleigh, North Carolina, in November, 1839; there is no record of the meeting of the convention.

by reason of the debates in Congress upon the exclusion of abolition literature from the mails and the treatment of abolition petitions in Congress, was rarely mentioned. A decade later no direct trade convention could be held, no plan for achieving commercial independence proposed, nor, for that matter, for erecting a cotton mill, building a railroad, opening a mine, or in any way promoting the material progress of the South, without consideration of, or due advertance to, its relation to the sectional struggle over slavery and the extension thereof. The argument would then without fail be advanced that the South must develop her strength and resources and achieve commercial and industrial independence in order to be prepared to defend her rights and honor in the Union, or, if worst came to worst, her independence out of it. George McDuffie did indeed allude to the existence of causes, tariff and slavery, which made the dismemberment of the confederacy "one of the possible contingencies for which it is the part of wisdom to provide";[61] but as yet such considerations were very infrequently advanced, at least in public. The direct trade conventions of the thirties were in the main what they purported to be, namely, bona fide efforts on the part of Southern men to promote the prosperity and progress of their states and section and, particularly, their seaports.

Several reasons may be advanced to explain the comparatively little interest displayed in the direct trade movement outside the three states of Georgia, South Carolina, and Virginia. North Carolina had no seaport which was considered to have the requisite natural advantages for becoming a great Southern emporium. Most of her exports and imports were made by way of Virginia and South Carolina. Her population was conservative and comparatively devoid of state pride. Alabama and Louisiana had seaports in Mobile and New Orleans. Both states were young, and were growing rapidly in population. Their agriculture had been prosperous. Just before the financial panic of 1837, both had enjoyed several years of speculative prosperity, which had been fully shared by Mobile and New Orleans. The rapidly growing population of the two towns consisted largely of immigrants from the North of Europe; civic pride had not yet developed. The crash of 1837 was more severe in the Southwest than in the older

Southern states, and the time was not auspicious for interest in any new movements.

The direct trade conventions accomplished no tangible results in the way of changing the course of Southern commerce. They afford evidence of discontent in the older states of the South with their material progress. They show that the belief was held, and no doubt they contributed to its spread, that commercial dependence was an evidence and, at the same time, a cause of "Southern decline." It is unnecessary to point out the common element in the view that the East was being enriched at the expense of the South because of the commercial vassalage of the latter and the quite prevalent belief that the operation of the Federal government had been unequal in its effects upon the material progress of the two sections. The direct trade conventions were another manifestation of the economic discontent of which evidence had been given during the nullification controversy.

CHAPTER II
MOVEMENT FOR THE DIVERSIFICATION
OF INDUSTRY, 1840-1852

The industrial revolution was not well under way in the South until almost a generation after the Civil War. While the ante-bellum South was not completely devoid of manufacturing and mining, the progress of those industries did not keep pace with the progress of agriculture. Southern industry was no more diversified in 1860 than in the earlier decades of the century. In this respect the South presented a contrast to the North, where the industrial revolution was proceeding apace. Elsewhere in this thesis statistics are given which illustrate the comparative industrial progress of the sections.

During the 1840s, Southern agriculture suffered a long and quite severe depression. During the same period cotton factories were being established at a more rapid rate than in the decades immediately preceding or following, and there was unusual progress in a few other lines of industry. The profits of manufacturers seem to have been large in comparison with those of planters. These conditions were chiefly responsible for the beginning of a more or less organized agitation in favor of the establishment of manufactures. As the agitation developed, social and political arguments were adduced to support the economic. The arguments of the proponents of diversified industry did not go uncontroverted, however. The history and analysis of this discussion shed light upon the subject of economic discontent in the South before the Civil War. An essential similarity will be noted between some of the ideas at the basis of the agitation in behalf of manufactures and ideas which animated the direct trade movement described in the preceding chapter.

The decade 1840-1850 brought the severest depression to agriculture, particularly to cotton culture, that the South experienced prior to the Civil War. During the preceding decade cotton prices had averaged 12.6 cents, and the industry was profitable. During the 1840s, however, the average price was about 8 cents, and the cotton planters were greatly disheartened. The decade opened with cotton between 8 and 9 cents; the following year prices were slightly higher; but after 1841 prices steadily declined until middling upland sold for 5 cents in New York, January 1, 1845, the lowest price ever paid for American cotton.[1] A contributor to the *Southern Quarterly Review* wrote: "At no period of our history, from the year 1781, has a greater gloom been cast over the agricultural prospects of South Carolina, than at the present time."[2] John C. Calhoun wrote his son-in-law: "Cotton still continues to fall. Its average price may be said to be about 4 cents per pound. The effect will be ruinous in the South, and will rouse the feeling of the whole section."[3] For years, 1845 was remembered as the year of the great cotton crisis. The depression in agriculture was not confined to the cotton belt. Edmund Ruffin wrote from Virginia that prices were so low that agriculture could scarcely live.[4] Similar reports came from the Northwest, which still depended largely upon the cotton belt for a market for grain, pork and bacon, and live stock. The replies to Secretary of the Treasury Walker's circular (1845) requesting information upon which to base recommendations for a revision of the tariff, even after due allowance has been made for partisan bias, testify to the low state of agriculture in the South and West.[5] A North Carolinian reported that for three years the profits of agriculture in his state had not been more than 3 per cent, because of poor crops and low prices; horses and mules were imported from Ohio, Indiana, Kentucky, Tennessee, and western Virginia, and prices were one-third lower than they had been during the ten years preceding. Similar replies came from South Carolina, Georgia, and Alabama. Replies from Ohio, Indiana, Illinois, and Missouri represented the profits of agriculture to be from 2 to 5 per cent. Scarcely a response was optimistic about the outlook for agriculture.

The grain growing states were the first to experience a revival of prosperity. In 1846, the crop failure in Ireland and large deficiencies in Great Britain and in many parts of the Continent

[1]C. F. M'Cay, "The Cotton Trade from 1825-1850," in *Hunt's Merchants' Magazine*, XXIII, 595-604; E. J. Donnell, *History of Cotton, passim;* M. B. Hammond, *The Cotton Industry.*
[2]VIII, 118 (July, 1845).
[3]Calhoun to Thomas G. Clemson, Dec. 27, 1844, *Calhoun Correspondence.*
[4]Ruffin to Hammond, May 17, 1845, *J. H. Hammond Papers.*
[5]*Exec. Docs.,* 29 Cong., 1 Sess., II, No. 5. A digest of the replies is in *DeBow's Review,* VI, 285-304.

created an extraordinary demand for foodstuffs, which, together
with the repeal of the English Corn Laws the same year, led to a
remarkable increase in the exports of provisions from America
in that and the following year.[6] Other factors soon contributed to
the revival, and Western agriculture entered upon a period of
remarkable prosperity, unbroken until 1857.[7] The revival of prosperity in the cotton industry was delayed for two or three years.
The crop of 1846 was short, while the very conditions which
caused a great increase in the prices of provisions prevented a
considerable rise in the price. It was a saying in the South that
dear bread in Europe meant cheap cotton. The crops of 1847 and
1848 were large, but breadstuffs continued high in Great Britain,
Europe, in 1848, was in revolution, and cotton prices remained
low. In the fall of 1849, however, cotton was high. Pacification of
Europe, revival of business in France, fine harvests and consequent cheap bread in England, the exhaustion of old stocks of raw
cotton, and the belief that the new crop was short, caused the season to open with cotton at 9.5 to 11.5 cents at New Orleans. The
average for the year was between 11 and 12 cents, and the price
was maintained the following year. Though the price fell again
in 1851-1852, it never again, before the war, fell to the level of the
1840s. The average price for the decade 1850-1860 was 10.6 cents.[8]

As cotton prices fell the older cotton states were the first to find
its culture unprofitable. Their lands could not compete on equal
terms with the newer lands of the Southwest; they faced not only
reduced prices and diminished returns but also loss of population through emigration. As early as 1841, J. H. Hammond, of
South Carolina, in an address before the State Agricultural Society, showed a thorough grasp of the situation and proposed the
remedies which were so fully discussed during the following

[6]Census of 1860, *Agriculture*, cxli.

[7]Other factors were the construction of railroads and canals connecting the
East and the Northwest and the development of the Eastern market.

[8]Donnell, *History of Cotton, passim*. Donnell's annual reviews of the cotton
trade were taken from the New Orleans *Price Current*. His statistics were from
the New York *Shipping List*. I have also used C. F. M'Cay's annual reviews of
the cotton trade, which appeared regularly for several years in the December
numbers of *Hunt's Merchants' Magazine*. See also *DeBow's Review*, XXVII, 106,
for cotton prices.

years.[9] In the past, he said, the production of cotton could not keep pace with the demand, but now production promised to outrun consumption. Already the price had been forced down to a figure, 8 cents, at which cotton culture in South Carolina was profitable only on the richest soils. As remedies, Hammond proposed, first, improved methods of cultivation and diversification of agriculture. The planters must grow grain in sufficient quantities to supply the home demand; they must raise live stock and save the "immense sums which are annually drawn from us in exchange for mules, horses, cattle, hogs, sheep, and even poultry." Tobacco, indigo, sugar cane, and grapes might be introduced. But these remedies would not suffice; capital must be diverted from agriculture to other pursuits. The state had mineral resources which could be developed. "Already furnaces, forges, bloomeries, and rolling mills have been put in operation with every prospect of success at no distant day." He hoped coal would be found near the iron. Manufactures might be developed. The state possessed splendid resources of water-power. A beginning had already been made in cotton manufacture. Manufactures should not be fostered by legislation at the expense of other industries; but where they grew up spontaneously they were undoubtedly a great blessing— increasing population, providing a home market for agriculture, and saving large sums which otherwise would be sent out of the state. An industrial revolution was inevitable, and the change could be effected with less anxiety and loss if begun early and conducted judiciously. Hammond regretted the revolution in industry and in "manners and probably the entire structure of our social system" which the failure of the old system was likely to occasion, but saw no grounds for apprehension.

In the following years the discussion increased in volume. The Charleston *Patriot* published, in 1842, a series of articles in which it was maintained that there was an overproduction of cotton and the people of South Carolina were urged to abandon in part the raising of that staple and turn their attention to manufacturing.[10]

[9]File 20,219, *J. H. Hammond Papers*. It is worthy of note that Hammond had been a nullifier in 1832; as governor, in 1844, he was ready to lead his state in separate resistance to the Tariff of 1842; and shortly after he wrote the famous *Letters on Southern Slavery, Addressed to Thomas Clarkson, Esquire*.

[10]*Niles' Register*, LXII, 71.

Georgia newspapers were recommending to their people to do the same.[11] Professor M'Cay, of the University of Georgia, who for many years reviewed the cotton trade for *Hunt's Merchants' Magazine*, warned planters that production was outrunning consumption.[12] In February, 1845, a convention of cotton planters was held in Montgomery, Alabama, to organize the planters of the cotton belt for the purpose of limiting production and forcing prices up.[13] The committee on agriculture of the Southwestern Convention, at Memphis, in 1845, complained that interest in agricultural improvement had given way to interest in internal improvements and politics, and that there was an overproduction of cotton. The committee recommended that planters grow less cotton and produce their own bread and meat; that scientific agriculture be encouraged by the establishment of agricultural societies and agricultural journals, and by state legislatures; and that capital be diverted from cotton planting to manufacturing.[14] There was still talk, however, of possible competition from India if prices should rise,[15] and the low prices were frequently attributed to speculation in cotton and to a combination of English factors with the Manchester buyers.[16]

It was in South Carolina that a serious attempt to arouse the public mind in favor of the diversification of industry was first made. The situation there was unusual. Not only was the depression in the cotton industry most severely felt, but the peculiar political bias of a large element threatened, in 1844 and 1845, to lead to another crisis similar to that of 1832 and 1833. When the Tariff of 1842 was enacted, the South Carolina Legislature had been content to pass resolutions denouncing it and declaring that it would be endured as long as there was hope of repeal by the Democratic party after the next election.[17] In the next Congress, 1843-1845, the Democrats were in the majority in the House; but an attempt to revise the tariff, by the McKay bill, was defeated,

[11]*Niles' Register*, loc. cit.
[12]*Hunt's Merchants' Magazine*, IX, 523.
[13]*Niles' Register*, LXVIII, 4.
[14]*Journal of the Proceedings of the Southwestern Convention began and held at the city of Memphis on the 12th of November, 1845*, pp. 41-55.
[15]Donnell, *History of Cotton*, 276.
[16]New Orleans *Bee*, Mar. 2, 1844; *Niles' Register*, LXVI, 38.
[17]*Ibid.*, LXIII, 232-235, 344-345.

May, 1844, by an alliance of twenty-seven Northern Democrats
with the Whigs.[18] This desertion by Northern Democrats and,
shortly thereafter, the publication of the celebrated "Kane Letter," in which the Democratic candidate for the presidency clever-
ly "straddled" the tariff question,[19] caused many in South Carolina to abandon hope of relief from the burdens of the tariff
through the instrumentality of the Democratic party. Meanwhile,
the blocking of the annexation of Texas by representatives from
the non-slaveholding states had occasioned the cry of "Texas or
disunion" in South Carolina and other Southern states. Under
these circumstances a group of South Carolina politicians, led by
R. B. Rhett, Armistead Burt, and I. E. Holmes, with the support
of the Charleston *Mercury* and several other papers of like stripe,
and the sympathy of Governor J. H. Hammond, George McDuffie,
and Langdon Cheves, declared, in the summer of 1844, for state
resistance to the Tariff of 1842 and attempted to lead the state
to adopt that policy.[20] It was with some difficulty that John C.
Calhoun, F. H. Elmore, and other leaders checked the "Bluffton
Movement," as it was termed, and caused saner counsels to prevail.[21] Governor Hammond, indeed, in his message to the Legislature, November 26, 1844, arraigned the tariff, expressed the
opinion that no relief could be expected from the incoming Polk

[18]*Cong. Globe*, 28 Cong., 1 Sess., 622.

[19]*National Intelligencer*, July 25, 1844.

[20]I. E. Holmes to Hammond, July 23, 1844, *J. H. Hammond Papers*; Hammond to Capt. R. J. Colcock, Sept. 12, 1844 (asking for the plans of the Citadel);
George McDuffie to Hammond, Sept. 22, 1844; General James Hamilton to Hammond, Oct. 4, 1844; R. B. Rhett to Hunter, August 30, 1844, *Correspondence of
R. M. T. Hunter*; Charleston *Mercury*, Aug. 8, 1844, an account of the dinner
given to R. B. Rhett at Bluffton, July 31, 1844, where the movement was
launched and whence it got its name; *ibid.*, Aug. 9, editorial, "Our Position and
Our Pledges" (by A. J. Stuart, senior editor); *Niles' Register*, LXVI, 369, quoting letter from I. E. Holmes to the Charleston *Mercury*; *ibid.*, LXVII, 49, quoting letter from Judge Langdon Cheves to the Charleston *Mercury*. Cf. Stephen-
son, *Texas and the Mexican War*, ch. IX.

[21]F. H. Elmore to Calhoun, Aug. 26, 1844, *Calhoun Correspondence*. "The
excitement in a portion of Carolina .... has gradually subsided, and will give no
further trouble. I had to act with great delicacy, but at the same time firmness
in relation to it." Calhoun to Francis Wharton, Sept. 17, 1844, *Calhoun Correspondence*. Cf. James A. Seddon to Hunter, Aug. 19, 22, 1844, *Correspondence
of R. M. T. Hunter*; *Niles' Register*, LXVI, 434, account of the big Charleston
meeting of Aug. 19, 1844.

administration, and urged the Legislature to take such measures as would at an early day bring all the state's "moral, constitutional, and, if necessary, physical resources, in direct array against a policy which has never been checked but by her interposition."[22] But the Legislature tabled all resolutions for resistance, and by a large majority voted confidence in the Democratic party. This action was taken just after the notorious Twenty-first Rule of the House, prohibiting the receiving of abolition petitions, had been defeated at Washington.[23] The leaders of the Bluffton movement credited their defeat to the presidential aspirations of John C. Calhoun, and complained very bitterly of what they termed his desertion.[24]

The resistance faction, as well as many anti-tariff men who still placed reliance in the Democratic party, attributed the crisis in the cotton industry to the tariff. They thought the view that there was an overproduction of cotton unworthy of consideration.[25] England, they said, could not consume cotton because the Tariff of 1842 had deprived her of the American market for manfactured goods. I. E. Holmes professed to believe that the operation of the tariff would in a few years render cotton planting entirely profitless, and that no other industry could be found to which labor could profitably be turned.[26] Rhett and McDuffie warned tariff men in Congress that South Carolina might be "driven" to manufacture for herself.[27] Calhoun wrote: "The pressure of the Tariff begins to be *felt*, and understood, which will lead to its overthrow, either through Congress or the separate action of the South."[28]

---

[22]*Niles' Register*, LXVII, 227 ff.

[23]Hammond to McDuffie, Dec. 27, 1844, *J. H. Hammond Papers*; F. W. Pickens to Calhoun, Dec. 28, 1844, *Calhoun Correspondence; Niles' Register*, LXVIII, 347 (Aug. 16, 1845), quoting from the Charleston *Mercury* a letter from "Bluffton Politician," dated on the anniversary of the Bluffton dinner; *Cong. Globe*, 28 Cong. 2 Sess., 7.

[24]Hammond to McDuffie, Dec. 27, 1844, *J. H. Hammond Papers*.

[25]Letter of Judge John P. King, Charleston *Mercury*, Nov. 5, 1844.

[26]*Niles' Register*, LXVI, 369, quoting the Charleston *Mercury; National Intelligencer*, Aug. 6, 1844.

[27]*Cong. Globe*, 28 Cong., 1 Sess., 612; Appx. 108, 658; *Hunt's Merchants' Magazine*, X, 406.

[28]Calhoun to Thomas G. Clemson, Dec. 27, 1844, *Calhoun Correspondence*.

Against these convictions, the Whigs and many Democrats took issue. The Charleston *Courier* declared without equivocation for a moderate tariff.[29] A pamphleteer, replying to a letter of Judge Langdon Cheves, declared that free trade would not save the state. The ruin of the state was due to the lack of stimulus which manufactures would give to agriculture and commerce; and it was the hostility of politicians which prevented manufactures from being established.[30] R. W. Roper, a rich planter, generally aligned in politics with the Hammond or anti-machine faction of the Democratic party, came out for the policy of encouraging domestic manufactures as an amelioration of the tariff. In an address before the State Agricultural Society, in November, 1844, he traced the depression in the cotton industry to overproduction, and declared for diversified agriculture and the encouragement of manufactures and commerce, not only as a remedy for economic ills but also as a means of becoming independent of the North. "As long," he said, "as we are tributaries, dependent on foreign labor and skill for food, clothing, and countless necessaries of life, we are in thraldom."[31] Roper's address was vigorously attacked in a series of articles in the Charleston *Mercury* under the caption, "Shall we continue to plant and increase the overgrowth of cotton? Or shall we become manufacturers of cotton stuffs?" In the opinion of the author of these articles, there was no overproduction of cotton; but the ills of the South came from overtaxation. South Carolina, he said, could not develop diversified industry with her system of labor, and it was not desirable that she should.[32]

Late in the year 1844, there appeared a series of articles headed *Essays on Domestic Industry; or an Inquiry into the Expediency of Establishing Cotton Manufactures in South Carolina,* by William Gregg, of South Carolina. The articles first appeared in the Charleston *Courier.* Upon request they were reprinted in pamphlet form. They attracted wide attention throughout the South, being republished in nearly all the newspapers of Georgia, Ala-

---

[29]Quoted in the *National Intelligencer,* Aug. 6, 1844.

[30]*A Reply to the Letter of the Hon. Langdon Cheves. By a Southerner.*

[31]Roper to Hammond, Oct. 28, 1844, *J. H. Hammond Papers; Niles' Register,* LXVIII, 103, 120. The address was reviewed in the *So. Quar. Rev.,* VIII, 118-148 (July, 1845).

[32]*Niles' Register,* LXVIII, 54, 103, 120.

bama, and other states.[33] They constituted the most elaborate argument for the diversification of Southern industry that appeared before the Civil War. Already a cotton manufacturer, Gregg later increased his interests. He was known until after the Civil War as the most successful cotton manufacturer in the Southern states and the ablest advocate of the policy of developing manufactures in that section.[34]

Gregg described the depressed condition of agriculture in the state and the tendency of capital and enterprise to migrate to more fertile lands. The causes lay not in the tariff but in lack of energy on the part of the people, want of diversified agriculture, and dependence upon the North for numerous articles of manufacture which might be produced at home. He called attention to the rapid progress then being made in cotton manufacturing in the neighboring states of Georgia and North Carolina and advised the people of South Carolina to emulate the example. He showed that the requisite capital was available. As for a labor supply, slaves could be used, and in many respects would be preferable to whites; but he did not overlook the possibility of employing the thousands of poor whites, who as a class were an unproductive element in society. Later he became an earnest advocate of the employment of this class both on economic and philanthropic grounds. Gregg understood the difficulties which infant industries would have to meet. He, therefore, advised the establishment of factories by joint stock companies rather than by individuals, and confinement for several years to the manufacture of only coarse goods, thus taking fullest advantage of the ability of Southern mills to command cheaper raw materials than Northern mills. It seemed politic not to antagonize unduly the anti-protectionist sentiment of South Carolina: Gregg assured his readers that no laws would be asked for the protection of the enterprises in which it was proposed to embark. He did not believe that manufactures would ever predominate over agriculture in the state; and those who advocated diversification did not wish such a result, he said.

[33]*DeBow's Review*, X, 349. The essays are, in a somewhat abridged form, in *DeBow's Review*, VIII, 134-46; also in the appendix of D. A. Tompkins, *Cotton Mill, Commercial Features, A Text-Book for the Use of Textile Schools*, etc. (Charlotte, N. C., 1879).

[34]*DeBow's Review*, X, 348-52, a short sketch of Gregg's career.

At the next session of the South Carolina Legislature, November, 1845, charters for several companies to erect cotton factories were applied for. At the time corporations were somewhat unpopular in the South, and opposition was met. Gregg thereupon wrote a pamphlet entitled *An Inquiry into the Expediency of Granting Charters of Incorporation for Manufacturing Purposes in South Carolina*. Copies were distributed among the members of the Legislature. After a sharp struggle the charters were granted by large majorities.[35] The Graniteville company, in which Gregg was a large stockholder, was one of those chartered. Only the most substantial citizens were permitted to take stock.[36] Gregg was made manager; the factory was soon built and put in successful operation. He was allowed to carry into practice his philanthropic ideas in regard to the poor whites. Cottages were built and rented to the operatives, free and compulsory education established, a church constructed, and intemperance forbidden. No negroes were employed. The factory was one of the few in the South that continued to pay dividends during the hard years of 1850-1854.[37]

Many others, following the publication of Gregg's essays, came forward to advocate the diversification of Southern industry, particularly by the erection of cotton factories near the cotton fields. Governor Crawford, of Georgia, urged the Legislature to adopt some plan to restore the fertility of the soil and foster manufactures.[38] The Tennessee House of Representatives appointed a select committee to report on manufacturing resources.[39] The state of Alabama engaged Mr. Tuomy, professor in the State University, to make a survey of the mineral resources of the state.[40] The Richmond *Whig* published, in 1846, the *Letters from the Hon. Abbott Lawrence to the Hon. William C. Rives of Virginia*, which, while primarily a plea against the repeal of the tariff, hailed the movement in the South for diversification of industry,

[35] *DeBow's Review*, X, 351.
[36] Ker Boyce to Hammond, Dec. 12, 1845, *J. H. Hammond Papers*.
[37] *DeBow's Review*, X, 351; XVIII, 789 f.; *Hunt's Merchants' Magazine*, XXI, 671. Cf. Ingle, *Southern Sidelights*, 85.
[38] *Niles' Register*, LXIX, 162.
[39] *Ibid.*, LXIX, 400.
[40] *DeBow's Review*, IV, 404. Tuomy later became state geologist and issued his *First Annual Report*, 1850.

and urged the people of Virginia to manufacture and develop the state's mineral resources.[41] *DeBow's Review,* the first number of which appeared in January, 1846, lent its influence to the cause.[42] Numerous articles in that journal testify to the growing conviction that there was an overproduction of cotton, and that the South should diversify agriculture and divert capital to other industries. In South Carolina, 1849, an organization styled the "South Carolina Institute for the Promotion of Art, Mechanical Ingenuity, and Industry" was formed. This organization was a direct outgrowth of the movement for diversification of Southern industry.[43]

The interest in cotton manufactures spread to the Ohio valley. One of the most active advocates was Hamilton Smith, a wealthy lawyer and business man of Louisville, Kentucky, who had acquired large holdings in coal lands near Cannelton, Indiana. In 1847, he wrote a series of articles for the *Louisville Journal* demonstrating the advantages of coal over water power in cotton factories, and the advantage of the Ohio valley over the East as a seat for such factories by reason of proximity to the cotton fields. His articles were widely copied in Southern and Western newspapers, and some of his letters were inserted in the Manchester, England, *Guardian.* In the following year, Smith and several other public spirited citizens of Kentucky, Indiana, Mississippi, and Louisiana, being desirous of proving their faith by works, organized a company which constructed a model factory at Cannelton. Charles T. James of Rhode Island, the most successful builder of steam cotton factories in the United States, became interested in the project, and superintended the erection of the factory. A journal, the *Cannelton Economist,* was established to conduct a campaign in the behalf of manufactures.[44]

The agitation in behalf of building cotton factories received encouragement from the fact that considerable capital was actually being invested in the new branch of industry and seemed to be

[41]Also published as a pamphlet, 1846.

[42]I, 5. In the number for Nov., 1847, a Department of Domestic Manufactures was begun, which was continued with few interruptions for several years.

[43]*DeBow's Review,* VIII, 276; XI, 123.

[44]*Ibid.,* XI, 90 f.; VI, 75 ff.; VIII, 456-61; *Western Journal and Civilian,* II, 139; Hamilton Smith, *The Relative Cost of Steam and Water Power, the Illinois Coal Fields, and the Advantages Offered by the West, particularly on the Lower Ohio, for Manufactures.*

yielding good profits. All through the 1840s, the journals of the
South recorded at frequent intervals the establishment of factories, especially cotton factories, in that section. In 1843, the Baltimore *American* stated that in North Carolina a revolution had
been effected in the trade of cotton yarns within a few years.[45]
Niles' Register, in 1845, remarked the number of cotton factories
being erected alongside the cotton fields, and prophesied that in a
few years the Southern states would supply coarse cotton clothing
for millions.[46] In the tariff debates of 1844 and 1846, congressmen
from North Carolina and Georgia, particularly, invited attention
to the rapid development of cotton and other manufactures in
their states.[47] The numerous acts incorporating manufacturing
companies passed during these years by the legislatures of states
which had not yet enacted general incorporation laws would seem
to testify to a development of manufacturing. During the last few
years of the decade and the first few years of the next, the accounts of new factories, built or in process of building, became
more and more frequent; and the development began to attract
notice in the North. Said *Hunt's Merchants' Magazine,* 1850:
"We seldom take up a paper published in the Southern and
Western States of the Union, that does not contain some new development of their manufacturing enterprise."[48]

By 1849 the movement to "bring the spindles to the cotton" had
become popular in all quarters of the South. According to *De-
Bow's Review,* every month added more and more to the interest
shown in manufactures.[49] The next year Hamilton Smith wrote:
"...for the last two years, one of the most prominent topics of discussion in the newspapers of the South and West has been, not
whether cotton mills could or could not be operated at home, but
when, where and by whom, they should be put in operation."[50]

[45]Quoted in *Niles' Register,* LXIV, 272.
[46]*Ibid.,* LXVIII, 87, April 12.
[47]*Cong. Globe,* 28 Cong., 1 Sess., Appx., 598, Cobb, of Ga., in the House; 28
Cong., 1 Sess., Appx., 108, McDuffie, of S. C., in the Senate; 28 Cong., 1 Sess.,
512, Berrien, of Ga., in the Senate.
[48]XXIII, 247. Cf. XVIII, 227. "The progress of manufacturing industry at
the South and West has been very rapid in the past two years." *Ibid.,* XXII,
646, (1850).
[49]VII, 454.
[50]*DeBow's Review,* VIII, 550.

The people of the South became firmly convinced that their section had rare advantages for the manufacture of cotton goods, and could compete successfully with New England. Statements were frequently made and rarely contradicted that mills already in operation were earning profits of from 15 to 20 per cent. The representations of Gregg, Hamilton Smith, and others, relative to the advantages possessed by the South, seemed sound. The most authoritative statements were those of General Charles T. James, of Rhode Island. James claimed to have superintended the erection of more than one-eighth of the cotton spindles in the United States. He had shown his faith in the South and West by taking stock in the steam factory at Charleston, South Carolina, and the one at Cannelton, Indiana.[51] Leaders in the diversification movement appealed to him to give information which might help to arouse interest and educate the people in the subject. In response he wrote, in 1849, a pamphlet entitled, *Practical Hints on the Comparative Cost and Productiveness of the Culture of Cotton and the Cost and Productiveness of its Manufacture*, etc.[52] The pamphlet was widely read and quoted, as were a number of articles which he wrote. He compared the great profits of cotton manufacturers with planters' profits; undertook to demonstrate the superiority of steam-power, which the South must use, over water-power; and dwelt upon the advantages the South possessed in having fresh raw material at hand and the saving in freight charges to be effected by establishing the factories near the fields. He gave the assurance that no great reserve of capital was necessary to embark in the business. Factories could be started on credit, and capital would accumulate—just as had been the case in New England. No fears need be entertained in regard to labor supply: if the factories should be opened, the labor and skill would be at hand. The South would not experience the difficulties in effecting this revolution in its industry which New England had encountered thirty years before; for she could start with the best machinery, and could avoid the mistakes made in the North.

James's statements were violently attacked in the New England press.[53] A warm debate was conducted by James and Amos A.

---

[51] *DeBow's Review*, IX, 671 ff.; *Hunt's Merchants' Magazine*, XXII, 311, 455.

[52] Published also in *DeBow's Review*, VII, 173-6, 370-2; VIII, 307-11, 462-6, 556-60. The substance is in *Hunt's Merchants' Magazine*, XXI, 492-502.

[53] *DeBow's Review*, IX, 558, quoting the New York *Herald*.

Lawrence, a prominent Massachusetts cotton manufacturer, through the columns of *Hunt's Merchants' Magazine*. Lawrence said the South could not manufacture because she lacked capital, and factories could not be successful if built with borrowed money. He contended that James had underestimated the profits of cotton planters and overestimated those of cotton manufacturers. He controverted James's statements in regard to the superiority of steam-power over water-power. William Gregg and Hamilton Smith joined in the controversy in support of James.[54] The Southern press thought Lawrence's articles were dictated by self-interest, and that James had completely prostrated his reviewer. The New England manufacturers were represented as being hostile to the new enterprises in the South. James himself wrote: "For years the Northern press has been loud and frequent in recommendations to the South, to enter the field of enterprise, and manufacture her own staple.....During the time, however, the manufacturers have uttered no note of encouragement."[55]

But the wide spread interest manifested in manufacturing during these years and the welcome given every evidence of industrial enterprise were not due solely to the prevalent belief that there was an overproduction of cotton, and that spinning the yarn and weaving the cloth would yield a higher profit upon capital invested than did the production of the raw material. Manufactures were approved as promising an avenue of escape from an ill balanced economic system and its attendant evils, social and political.

In the first place, home manufactures would free the South from dependence upon the North for numerous articles which might be produced at home; just as diversified agriculture would free it from dependence upon the West for horses, mules, pork, and bacon; or as direct trade would free it from commercial dependence upon the East. Dependence upon other sections of the Union was felt to be "degrading vassalage," a subject for mortification and humiliation, and because of it the North was being enriched and the South impoverished.

[54] *Hunt's Merchants' Magazine*, XXI, 628-33; XXII, 26-35, 184-94, 290-311, 107-8; XXIII, 342-3; *DeBow's Review*, VIII, 550-55; IX, 674-75.
[55] *Hunt's Merchants' Magazine*, XXII, 309.

Northern men were constantly boasting of the superiority of their section of the Union; every foreign traveler drew a picture of contrast. The wealth and population of the North, the size, prosperity, and attractiveness of its cities and towns, the mileage, cost, and efficiency of the railroads and canals, the manufactures and mines, ships and shipping, the farms, the price of land and the methods of agriculture, the homes, shops, and places of amusement, the schools and colleges, number of students and percentage of illiteracy, newspapers and their circulation, the development of literature and art—all were contrasted with those of the South, and almost invariably to the advantage of the North. It was pointed out that Southerners depended upon Northern shipping, bought Northern manufactured goods, flocked to Northern watering places, sent their sons to Northern colleges, and read Northern literature. The conclusion was that the North had reached a higher degree of civilization, prosperity, and comfort. The disparity was generally credited to superior industry and enterprise in the North and to the blighting effects of slavery in the South.

Southern people admitted the contrast—it was impossible not to do so. They generally, by no means without exception, admitted that the North was more prosperous. When John Forsyth, in his lecture on "The North and the South," asked the question, "Why is it that the North has so far outstripped the South in commerce, the growth of its cities, internal development, and the arts of living?"[56] he but made an admission that Southerners commonly made. J. H. Hammond wrote: "It has so often been asserted, that in population and its ratio of increase, in wealth, aggregate and average and the facility of its accumulation, in industry, intelligence and enterprise the North is vastly in advance of the South, and by consequence that it is the strong and protecting, while the South is the weak and dependent section—all these things have been so long and so generally asserted in the South as well as the North, that they have gained almost universal credence."[57]

[56]*DeBow's Review*, XVII, 365.
[57]*Southern Quarterly Review*, XV, 275. Cf. J. H. Hammond to Wm. Gilmore Simms, Mar. 9, 20, 23, Apr. 6, 1849. *J. H. Hammond Papers.*

Now the superiority of the North in these respects was not to be viewed with equanimity in any case by the loyal and progressive Southerner; and his discontent was augmented because of his belief that the North was prospering at the expense of the South. The feeling of a large element in the South in regard to the matter is well illustrated by the following typical quotation from an Alabama newspaper:

At present, the North fattens and grows rich upon the South. We depend upon it for our entire supplies. We purchase all our luxuries and necessaries from the North . . . . With us, every branch and pursuit in life, every trade, profession, and occupation, is dependent upon the North; for instance, the Northerners abuse and denounce slavery and slaveholders, yet our slaves are clothed with Northern manufactured goods, have Northern hats and shoes, work with Northern hoes, ploughs, and other implements, are chastised with a Northern-made instrument, are working for Northern more than Southern profit. The slaveholder dresses in Northern goods, rides in a Northern saddle, ... sports his Northern carriage, patronizes Northern newspapers, drinks Northern liquors, reads Northern books, spends his money at Northern watering-places, ... The aggressive acts upon his rights and his property arouse his resentment—and on Northern-made paper, with a Northern pen, with Northern ink, he resolves and re-resolves in regard to his rights! In Northern vessels his products are carried to market, his cotton is ginned with Northern gins, his sugar is crushed and preserved by Northern machinery; his rivers are navigated by Northern steamboats, his mails are carried in Northern stages, his negroes are fed with Northern bacon, beef, flour, and corn; his land is cleared with a Northern axe, and a Yankee clock sits upon his mantel-piece; his floor is swept by a Northern broom, and is covered with a Northern carpet; and his wife dresses herself in a Northern looking-glass; . . . his son is educated at a Northern college, his daughter receives the finishing polish at a Northern seminary; his doctor graduates at a Northern medical college, his schools are supplied with Northern teachers, and he is furnished with Northern inventions and notions.[58]

Some of those who preached diversification of industry not only affirmed, as did the anti-tariff men for that matter, that the North was growing prosperous, wealthy, and powerful at the South's expense, but demonstrated why it would continue to do so as long as the latter persevered in her unwise application of labor. They

---

[58]Quoted in F. A. P. Barnard, *An Oration Delivered before the Citizens of Tuscaloosa, Alabama, July 4th, 1851*, p. 12.

laid down the general propositions that an agricultural people is always exploited by an industrial people, and that wealth tends to flow toward industrial centers. In the opinion of M. Tarver, it was because she parted with her staples at prime cost and purchased almost all of her necessary supplies from abroad at cost plus profits, that the South was "growing poorer while the rest of the world is growing rich, for it is easy for the world to enrich itself from such a customer on such terms."[59] Governor J. H. Hammond, who in his address before the South Carolina Institute set himself the task of showing philosophically why a people of one occupation can never attain prosperity and influence, thought one industry was not enough to absorb all the genius and draw out all the energies of a people.[60] According to the Richmond *Enquirer*, "commercial and manufacturing nations levy a heavier tax on their dependents than any despot ever exacted from subject provinces. Labor employed in commerce or manufactures, in the general, pays three or four times as much as farming labor, and in the exchange of one for the other, the farmer gives the manufacturer three or four hours' labor for one."[61] Similar was the reasoning of F. A. P. Barnard, of Alabama State University: The kinds of labor in which the element of skill most predominates are the most productive. Therefore, the wealth of a people depends as much upon the direction given to labor as upon the amount of labor employed. An agricultural people might be rich, though only in the case Nature is lavish in her bounties; but "riches thus bestowed, while the means of greater riches remain unemployed, will never give contentment."[62]

But no matter how the North reaped profit from Southern industry, there could be no doubt of the advantages of retaining the profit at home. Everything that manufactures had done for the North and for England they would do for the South. Her stagnant cities would grow, and new ones spring into existence.

[59]*DeBow's Review*, III, 203.

[60]*Ibid.*, VIII, 503 ff. Cf. Hammond to William Gilmore Simms, Dec. 20, 1849. *J. H. Hammond Papers*.

[61]Quoted in *DeBow's Review*, XX, 392. See also Fitzhugh, *Sociology for the South*, ch. XIV, "Exclusive Agriculture," and ch. XVIII, "Head-work and Hand-work."

[62]*Oration Delivered before the Citizens of Tuscaloosa, Alabama, July 4th, 1861*, p. 16 f.

Surplus capital no longer would be under the necessity of seeking investment elsewhere. Railroads would be built, and steamships launched upon the rivers; dykes would be built, and marshes drained; capital would be forthcoming to develop the mineral resources which the people of the South were beginning to realize she possessed. For the planter and the farmer a *home market* would be provided, not subject to the fluctuations of the foreign market. Diversified agriculture would be stimulated; the planter would no longer have to resort to distant states for his mules, pork, corn, and hay.[63]

Nor did the proponents of diversification neglect to depict the social benefits to come with new industries. With the development of manufactures, towns and villages would spring up among the scattered population. More and better schools could be established; for the chief cause of backwardness in educational progress in the South was the sparsity of population. Churches could be brought within the reach of a greater number. Colleges could be supported at home, and Southern parents would no longer be under the necessity of sending their sons North for a good college training. With the increased wealth and population which manufactures would bring, the South could adequately support her own press and literature. Said Hammond, after having given a glowing description of the revivifying effects of manufactures upon his state: "I am not conjuring up ideal visions to excite the imagination. All these things have actually been done. They have been, in our own times, and under our own eyes, carried out and made legible, living, self-multiplying and giant-growing *facts* in Old England and New England; and they have been mainly accomplished by the incalculable profits which their genius and enterprise have realized on the product of *our labor*."[64]

But the prophets of a new order met prejudices against manufactures which they could not wholly dispel. Politicians had too often described the cities and factory towns of the North as hotbeds of poverty, ignorance, vice, crime, and unreligion, the seats of abolition and the numerous *isms* with which the land was

---

[63]The best examples of the home market argument are in Barnard, *op. cit.*, and an article, "Should the Loom Come to the Cotton, or the Cotton Go to the Loom?" *Western Journal and Civilian*, I, 319-332.

[64]*DeBow's Review*, VIII, 516. See also Fitzhugh, *Sociology for the South*, chs. XII-XV.

afflicted. Manufactures had been too frequently described as incompatible with liberty, freedom, culture, and virtue, and agriculture glorified as the only industry capable of producing a
liberty-loving and chivalrous race.[65] Often the proponents of diversification considered it necessary to give the assurance that no
large towns, but only villages, would be created, and that there
was no danger of manufactures ever predominating over agriculture in the planting states.[66] Too, it must be noted, there was a
feeling all too prevalent in the South that manual labor, and particularly mechanical labor, was degrading and beneath the dignity
of white men. Young men of intelligence and ability, who might
have become skilled mechanics, managers, or superintendents of
factories, felt that they would lose caste by entering a cotton factory. Such employment was less becoming gentlemen than agriculture, the professions, or even the mercantile business. The dignity of labor had to be proclaimed. Few more scathing denuncia-
tions of Southern social standards, as well as of the inertia,
lethargy, and lack of foresight of Southern men, can be found
than some of those uttered by Southern men who were trying to
point the path of progress and urge their people along it.[67]

One argument in behalf of manufactures by no means infrequently used was that they would give employment to the "poor
whites." The poor whites were the non-slaveholding whites of the
black belts, the hill country, and the pine barrens. Some of them,
upon worn out and abandoned plantations or their small hill
farms, engaged in agriculture in feeble competition with the
planters. Others obtained a precarious subsistence by doing occasional jobs for the planters, by hunting and fishing, by begging
or stealing from the slaveholders, or by trading with the slaves
and inducing them to plunder for their benefit. They were not
employed by the planters to work in the cotton fields, and would
have been unwilling to work with the slaves had opportunity been
afforded them. As a class they produced less than they consumed,

[65]*DeBow's Review*, VIII, 508; XI, 127; XII, 49; XVII, 178; *So. Quar. Rev.*,
VIII, 142.
[66]*DeBow's Review*, VIII, 522; XI, 130-132.
[67]*So. Lit. Mess.*, XX, 513-28 (Sept., 1854); *So. Quar. Rev.*, VIII, 460 ff.;
DeBow's Review, VIII, 134, 506; XVII, 363; XIX, 614; XXIV, 383; Barnard,
op. cit., 23; Aaron V. Brown, *Speeches, Congressional and Political, and other
Writings*, 668.

and, therefore, were a burden upon society. Their ignorance was as general as their poverty; vice and crime were common among them. Their number is difficult to estimate. In 1849, Governor Hammond estimated at 50,000 the number of those in South Carolina whose industry was not "adequate to procure them, honestly, such support as every white person in this country is, and feels himself entitled to."[68] William Gregg put the number at 125,000, more than one-third of the white population of the state.[69] The number in other Southern states was probably somewhat less in proportion to population. Charles T. James said there were thousands of poor whites.[70] James Martin, of northern Alabama, spoke of a "large poor population, almost totally without employment."[71] *Hunt's Merchants' Magazine* referred to them as a "mass of unemployed white labor."[72]

Many of the advocates of manufactures believed the employment of this class of unfortunates desirable from every viewpoint. They were said to be more than glad to avail themselves of the opportunity to work, even at most moderate wages, at labor deemed respectable for white persons; and, when so employed, to quickly assume the industrious habits of Northern operatives. By employment in factories, they would be brought together in villages, where the influence of church and school could reach them. In this way and only in this way could they be elevated to a state of comparative comfort and independence and social responsibility. From the viewpoint of the prosperity and power of the community at large, the employment of the poor whites would be of incalculable benefit: it would transform thousands of them into productive citizens and enormously increase the wealth of the region. The number of this class in some states was said to be sufficient to work up into goods all the cotton grown therein. This product would be a clear gain; for the employment of the poor whites in factories would withdraw little or no labor from the production of the raw material. How, it was asked, could the South keep pace with the North in the race for power and wealth,

[68]*DeBow's Review*, VIII, 518.
[69]*Ibid.*, XI, 133.
[70]*Ibid.*, VIII, 558.
[71]*Ibid.*, XXIV, 383.
[72]XXII, 649.

when so large a part of the total possible labor force was comparatively idle?[73]

Many thoughtful Southerners regretted that so much of the capital, enterprise, and intelligence in the South was employed in directing slave labor to the almost complete neglect of a large part of the white population.[74] Thomas P. Devereaux, a large slaveholder of North Carolina, thought it the great evil of slavery, that it rendered a mass of white producing ability more than unproductive; and there is evidence indicating that many shared his opinion.[75] But whether slavery was responsible for the existence of the poor white class or not, its opponents in the North and elsewhere charged it with that responsibility, and it would seem that the defenders of the institution should have welcomed every opportunity for remedying the evil and proving the charge unfounded. Too many slaveholders, however, opposed manufactures on the very ground that they would aid in developing a class consciousness among white labor, which would be hostile to slavery.

In fact, it was already evident that such a class consciousness was developing, particularly in the cities and towns. It manifested itself in a movement to drive the slaves from the cities and from mechanical employments, and restrict them to agriculture. In 1849, C. G. Memminger wrote Hammond that the opinion was gaining ground in Charleston and even in the low country, that slaves should be excluded from mechanical pursuits, and their places filled by whites; and that there would soon be a formidable party on the subject.[76] Several years earlier, a bill had been drafted and presented to the North Carolina Legislature to limit the employment of slaves in mechanical callings, but had been met and defeated by the objection that it interfered with the rights of the slave owners; an act of the Georgia Legislature, December 27, 1845, forbade negro mechanics to make contracts.[77] In the cities there was constant friction between the white stevedores, porters,

[73]See notes 68-72.

[74]*DeBow's Review*, XI, 135.

[75]Devereaux to Hammond, April 17, 1850, *J. H. Hammond Papers*. Cf. *So. Quar. Rev.*, VIII, 449 ff.; XXVI, 446.

[76]Memminger to Hammond, April 28, 1849, *J. H. Hammond Papers*.

[77]Devereaux to Hammond, April 17, 1850, *ibid*.

draymen, and mechanics and the negroes. [78] Everywhere there was opposition to slaves learning trades.[79]

The slaveholders feared this self-assertion of white labor; for, as Memminger put it, were the negro mechanics and operatives driven from the cities, whites would take their places, everyone would have a vote, and all would be abolitionists. Those urging manufactures, he thought, were aiding and abetting the free labor party, which was the only one from which danger to slavery was to be apprehended.[80] General A. H. Brisbane, who was leading in the agitation in behalf of manufactures in South Carolina, and who was instrumental in founding a mechanics' institute in Charleston, complained of the opposition he met at every turn from the slaveholders of Charleston and the seaboard.[81]

On the other hand, some slaveholders thought more danger was to be apprehended from the poor whites under existing conditions than if they should be brought together in cotton factories with constant employment and adequate remuneration. In the latter case, they would see that their occupation depended upon the preservation of a system necessary for the production of cotton. In the opinion of Thomas P. Devereaux, if a notion should arise among the poor whites that slavery barred their way to the full enjoyment of the fruits of their labor, deprived them of a market for their produce, and hindered the advancement of their children, the slaveholders would have an enemy in their midst far more to be feared than abolition preachers.[82] Brisbane believed it better for white labor to develop in the South, where it could see its dependence upon black labor, than in the North, where it could not, and would, therefore, be the fanatical enemy of slavery.

Over against the discussion of the desirability of providing employment for the poor whites must be set the discussion of the

---

[78]*DeBow's Review*, XXVI, 600, extract from the *Report of the Committee on Negro Population of the South Carolina Legislature; ibid.,* XXX, 67-77.

[79]F. L. Olmsted, *Cotton Kingdom,* II, 98; Lyell, *A Second Visit to the United States,* II, 36, 81-83. And see below, pp. 218-220.

[80]Memminger to Hammond, April 28, 1849, *J. H. Hammond Papers.*

[81]Brisbane to Hammond, Oct. 8, 1849, *ibid.;* cf. Gregg to Hammond, Dec. 1, 1848.

[82]Devereaux to Hammond, April 17, 1850, *ibid.* Cf. W. B. Hodgson, of Georgia, to Hammond, Nov. 20, 1850, *ibid.; So. Quar. Rev.,* XXVI, 447; *DeBow's Review,* III, 188; VIII, 25. See also Fitzhugh, *Sociology for the South,* 147.

practicability of employing slaves in factories. During the period of overproduction of cotton there was a belief that slave labor engaged in producing the staple was redundant, and that it was desirable to divert some of it to other industries. The division of slave labor between the factory and the field would increase the profits of agriculture and enhance the value of slaves.[83] Slave labor was tried in several cotton factories, notably the DeKalb and the Saluda factory, both of South Carolina, and the alleged success of the experiments was cited as demonstrating that, should agriculture become oversupplied with labor, manufacturing would open channels to draw away the surplus.[84] From some of the comments made, it is hard to escape the conclusion that many Southerners were interested in manufactures only so long as it appeared possible to conduct them with slave labor; when experience finally demonstrated the superiority of white labor, their interest declined. Other men opposed from the start the employment of slaves in factories. It would weaken slavery; for, as one said, "Whenever a slave is made a mechanic, he is more than half freed...."[85] Moreover, were slaves employed, whites could not be; for whites would not work side by side or in competition with slaves.

The movement to bring the spindles to the cotton was almost synchronous with the period of acrimonious sectional controversy over the extension of slavery which began with the annexation of Texas and continued until the general acceptance of the Compromise of 1850 gave a temporary respite. Southern men were becoming dismayed at the growing strength and vigor of the attacks upon slavery. The growing disparity of the sections in numbers and power was too striking and too ominous not to excite most serious concern. The old political alliance of South and West could no longer be depended upon, and especially not in the case of the slavery issue, to thwart the antagonistic policies of the North. Leaders, from the great Calhoun down, cast about for means of maintaining Southern rights and preserving Southern equality in the Union. A large minority of the people in the South,

[83]Richmond *Whig*, Sept. 19, 1851; *DeBow's Review*, XII, 182-5.
[84]Richmond *Enquirer*, Aug. 30, 1850; Charleston *Mercury*, May 24, 1849; *Hunt's Merchants' Magazine*, XXIII, 575; *DeBow's Review*, IX, 432; XI, 319.
[85]*Ibid.*, VIII, 518.

in one state a majority, were convinced by 1850 that the Southern
states should withdraw from the Union. Widespread discussion of
secession caused consideration to be given to the preparedness of
the South for separate nationality. The intemperateness of the
sectional quarrel and, especially, the necessity for augmenting the
political power of the South, whether to maintain her rights in the
Union or her independence out of it, gave a powerful impetus to
all movements for promoting the economic development of the
South, including the encouragement of manufacturing.

The arguments in favor of encouraging home manufactures
which were suggested by political necessities or purposes took
several forms. One frequently employed was well illustrated by
an editorial in the Richmond *Dispatch*. After one of the instances
of interference with the execution of the Fugitive Slave law by the
people of Boston, the *Dispatch* estimated the value of the Boston-
made shoes used in Virginia, and suggested that Virginia people
should manufacture the shoes used in the state. "That it is time
for Virginia to think of doing some such thing the high-handed
measures lately adopted in Boston sufficiently prove. As long as
we are dependent upon these people, they will insult us at pleasure. Let us cut loose from them thus far at least."[86] The reasoning was weak: If Boston people insulted the Virginians while yet
the latter were good customers, would they not more readily do
so should the Virginians cease to patronize Boston shoe factories?

More logical was the reasoning of J. D. B. DeBow and others
who, while recognizing that Southern enterprise might not convince the enemies of slavery, said it would prepare the South for
the crisis which they professed to believe was inevitable. "We
have long ago thought," wrote DeBow, "that the duty of the people consisted more in the vigorous prosecution of their industry,
resources and enterprise, than in bandying constitutional arguments with their opponents, or in rhetorical, flourishes about the
sanctity of the federal compact. This is the course of action,
which, though it may not convince, will at least prepare us for this
crisis which, it needs no seer's eye to see, will, in the event, be
precipitated upon us by the reckless fanaticism or ignorant zeal
of the 'cordon of free States' surrounding us on every hand. 'Light
up the torches of industry,' was the advice of old Dr. Franklin to his
countrymen, on discovering that all hope from the British cab-

[86] Quoted in *DeBow's Review*, XI, 82.

inet had fled forever. Light up the torches, say we, on every hill-top, by the side of every stream, from the shores of the Delaware to the furthest extremes of the Rio Grande—from the Ohio to the capes of Florida."[87]
Another and more frequently used argument was that diversi-fied industries would be favorable to a more rapid growth of population in the South, and population was necessary to political power. The North had been growing more rapidly in population and political influence, it was said, because immigration from abroad had gone almost exclusively to that section. This was not because slavery had repelled immigration, but because the South had offered no inducements. Southern agriculture was ill adapted to European labor. And what other industry had the South? The construction of railroads had attracted a few Irish and German laborers; but the demand was insufficient to bring a great number. Let industry be diversified, however, and the South would get a share of the influx from abroad. Northern people might come South. Emigration from the Southern states would be checked. The population of the North would then increase less rapidly, that of the South more rapidly; the relative political strength of the South would thus be preserved.[88]
Not all, however, considered immigration desirable. Many feared that immigrants would be hostile to slavery. The diversi-ficationists attempted to overcome these fears. The immigrants could be assimilated and converted into defenders of Southern institutions, they said. In proof of this view they pointed to many men who had come from the North, and were among the staunch-est defenders of the South. They further contended that a large foreign element in the North was a greater menace to slavery than such an element in the South would be; for in the latter it would become convinced of the necessity of the institution.[89] Just as does the fear among the slaveholders of the development of a class

[87]*DeBow's Review*, IX, 120. Cf. *ibid.*, IV, 211; XI, 680; William Gregg to Seabrook, May 10, 1850, *Whitemarsh B. Seabrook Papers;* Richmond *Whig,* Feb. 12, 1851.
[88]Barnard, *Oration Delivered before the Citizens of Tuscaloosa, Alamaba, July 4th, 1851,* 29; *DeBow's Review,* VIII, 558-60; XI, 319; *Hunt's Merchants' Magazine,* XXI, 498.
[89]Barnard, *loc. cit.;* A. H. Brisbane to J. H. Hammond, Oct. 8, 1849, *J. H. Hammond Papers.*

consciousness among the native white labor, this fear of immigration illustrates the difficulties in the way of creating a public sentiment in the South favorable to progress along other lines than agriculture.

During the secession movement of 1849-1852, which has been alluded to, many Unionists supported the efforts to develop Southern manufactures, promote direct trade, construct internal improvements, and otherwise build up the South in an economic way, as a substitute for disunion. Their position was based upon two chains of reasoning: (1) Economic regeneration of the South would tend to preserve the political equilibrium of the sections and thus enable the Southern states to maintain their rights without forsaking the Union. (2) The basic causes for the war being waged against the Union were economic discontent and the belief that the Union had been unequal in its material benefits. The Unionists, in so far as they admitted Southern "decline," attributed it to causes· not connected with the operation of the government or the Union. Successful programs of economic improvement would allay discontent and prove their contentions in regard to the advantages of the Union. This aspect of the political basis for the agitation in behalf of manufactures will be discussed in somewhat greater detail elsewhere.

Although the discussion of the desirability of diversifying Southern industry by no means ceased about 1852, as we shall see, the active agitation in behalf of "bringing the spindles to the cotton" may be said to have come to an end about that date. The explanation of this lies partly in the fact that the comparative prosperity of cotton culture during the fifties weakened the force of the economic arguments for diversification,[90] but chiefly in the fact that the agitation no longer was encouraged by reports of large profits and the erection of new factories.

Accounts of new enterprises continued to appear throughout 1851, and then ceased almost abruptly. In their stead there began to appear reports of reduced profits, failures, and, later, explanations for the sudden collapse of a movement so auspiciously begun. It was not until the later years of the decade that the press again spoke optimistically of the progress of cotton manufactures in the South. William Gregg, who knew more about this sub-

[90]See ch. VIII.

ject than any other man, writing on the very eve of the war, stated
that all the progress made in cotton manufacturing in the South
during fifteen years was made in "about five years—from 1845
to 1850." The meager statistics available tend to sustain this
judgment. According to the estimates of contemporary reviewers
of the cotton trade, the Southern states consumed a quantity of
raw cotton in the year 1849-1850 which was not materially exceeded until 1859-1860.[91] During the years 1850 and 1851 the cotton
manufacturing industry was suffering a depression. It is probable
that, could factories newly built or building in 1850 have operated
at full capacity, the total consumption for the year would have
equalled that of the years immediately preceding the Civil War.
The United States censuses for 1840, 1850, and 1860 may be considered sufficiently reliable to show general tendencies. The value
of the product of cotton factories in states south of Maryland was
$1,912,215 in 1840, $5,665,362 in 1850, and $8,145,067 in 1860.
Thus, while the value of the product nearly trebled between 1840
and 1850, it increased only about 43 per cent during the following
decade. The value of the output of cotton manufactures in the
United States as a whole was $46,350,453 in 1840, $65,501,687 in
1850, and $115,681,774 in 1860, an increase of 41 per cent during
the first decade and 76.6 per cent during the second.[92]

The progress made in cotton manufacturing in the South during
the 1840s must be attributed chiefly to the unprofitableness of
cotton culture during the same period and to the conviction of men
with capital that manufacturing would yield a higher rate of interest upon money invested. In some cases, it is true, subscription to
the stock of cotton manufacturing companies seems to have been
made by public spirited citizens prompted more by a desire to
benefit their communities or states or to advance the cause of
the South than by the desire for profit. To some degree, too, the
agitation was instrumental in securing the liberalization of laws
affecting joint stock companies, and may have contributed indirectly to the development of manufactures. The cessation of
progress about 1851 cannot be attributed to any abatement of

[91]See Appendix, Table IV, for estimates of the cotton consumed in the North,
South, and West, 1839-1861.
[92]Compendium of the Sixth Census, 361; Compendium of the Seventh Census, 180; Eighth Census, Manufactures, Introduction, p. xii.

interest on the part of the public. Some of the causes for depression and failure in the South affected New England factories
as well. Others were peculiar to the South, and serve to illustrate
the difficulties which had to be overcome there, perhaps among
any agricultural people, before new industries could become firmly
established.

One cause of the depression in the cotton manufacturing industry was the sharp rise in the price of raw cotton from 7 cents in
June to 11 cents in October, 1849, double the price of October,
1848. With the exception of the year 1851-1852, the price of cotton remained comparatively high until the Civil War. With the
rise in price, the quantity of cotton taken for Northern mills fell
from 503,429 bales in 1848-1849 to 465,702 in 1849-1850 and 386,-
429 the following year, while the estimates of consumption of the
South and West for the same three years were 130,000, 137,000,
and 99,000 bales, respectively.[93] To add to the hardships occasioned by high priced raw material, there had been a general
fall in the prices of cotton goods, caused partly by the recent rapid
extensions of cotton manufactures in the United States and partly,
it was said, by the increased quantities of English goods put upon
the American market after the Walker tariff of 1846 had become
effective.[94]

Strangely, the factories of the cotton states seem to have weath-
ered the first year or two of hard times better than factories
farther north, and Southern men submitted the fact as evidence
of the superior advantages of those states for cotton manufacturing.[95] In the autumn of 1850, Joseph H. Lumpkin, of Georgia,
said that he knew of no bankruptcy in any cotton company in the
South; while seventy-one mills were reported idle within thirty

[93]See Appendix, Table IV.
[94]*Hunt's Merchants' Magazine*, XXIII, 595 ff., Dec. 1850; XXV, 465.
[95]*DeBow's Review*, X, 93, 143. Virginia and Maryland factories did not
escape the hard times. A convention of manufacturing interests meeting in Richmond, late in 1850, reported that of the 54,000 spindles in that state, 7,000 were
running at three-fourths time, 8,000 at one-third time, 22,000 at full time but
three-fourths wages, while the remainder were either idle or practically so; the
whole averaged about one-half time. In Maryland the conditions were worse.
Of 28 factories, 8 were idle, and only 2 were running full time. *Hunt's Merchants'
Magazine*, XXIV, 262. The iron industry as well as the cotton manufacturing
industry was complaining of depression. The reason assigned was English and
Scotch competition.

miles of Providence, Rhode Island, and numerous others in the North were either idle or upon short time, some Southern companies were declaring a dividend of 10 per cent.[96] The Savannah *News* reported that Southern factories were prosperous, while some Northern mills were closing; and added, "These facts prove what we have often asserted, that we have a decided advantage over the North in the business of manufacturing yarns and coarse cotton goods."[97] Thomas Prentice Kettell, of New York, wrote: "It is the transition of the seat of manufactures from the North and East to the South and West, under which northern manufacturing capital is laboring."[98] But factories in the cotton belt did fail during the years 1850, 1851, and 1852, establishments changed hands at much less than the original cost, and the profits of all were greatly reduced. Moreover, Southern factories revived much more slowly than those of New England. Many of them dragged out a sickly existence until a year or two before the war, when they again became prosperous. The example of these factories discouraged further investments of capital.[99]

[96]*DeBow's Review*, XII, 46. (From an address delivered before the South Carolina Institute at its Second Annual Fair, Nov. 19, 1850.) As late as 1855, William Gregg wrote: "With the exception of the Saluda company and the Charleston factory, there have been no positive failures and very few embarrassed concerns [in South Carolina], and they labored under most of the defects that I have named as elements of embarrassment. There was no failure among the Georgia factories during the terrible pressure of 1850 and '51; they are now, with one or two exceptions, doing well. Those in the vicinity of Augusta, ten miles off, are paying 20 to 30 per cent. The DeKalb factory, near Camden, in our state, is making 15 per cent.; Vaucluse, just above us, is making money. . . ." The net earnings of the Graniteville Company were reported at 8 per cent in 1850, 11½ per cent in 1853, and 18 per cent in 1854. *Report of William Gregg, President of the Graniteville Manufacturing Co.*, 1855, quoted in *DeBow's Review*, XVIII, 788.

[97]Quoted in *ibid.*, XI, 322 (Sept., 1851).

[98]*Ibid.*, XI, 641. It is not probable that Southern mills suffered less than New England mills making the same class of goods.

[99]This was notably true of the failures at Augusta, Ga. There canals had been dug, and, it was supposed, enough water power secured to drive the spindles of a second Lowell. Factories sprang up on a large scale. A long chain of changes and reverses followed. *Ibid.*, XXVIII, 483. William Gregg wrote, in 1860: "The failure of the Augusta Mills has done more to put back the progress of manufacturing at the South than any other failure that has taken place." *Ibid.*, XXIX, 229.

Cotton factories in the South experienced difficulties other than the high price of raw material and the low prices of goods. [100] The factories were often cheaply constructed, and the best machinery was not always provided. Several of them employed steam power, which proved too costly and put them under a big handicap from the start. Local pride in many cases had much to do with raising capital and, consequently, in selecting sites. As a result the mills were often injudiciously located with respect to health, steady motive power, and marketing of goods. The labor problem was a difficult one. Negro labor required too much capital, if bought, and proved unsatisfactory in any case.[101] The whites, though they worked for lower wages than the mill operatives of the North, from ignorance and long habits of indolence, were difficult to train and control.[102] Because of the unskilled labor, Southern factories required more efficient superintendents than Northern factories, but did not pay sufficiently high salaries to command them. (The superintendents were in most cases from the North.) There was the difficulty, also, of forcing the products of infant industries upon a market already supplied with Northern and English goods;[103] and there is evidence that New England manufacturers resorted to quite modern methods in meeting threatened competition from the South. The story was told of a Georgia factory that put upon the market an article known as "Georgia Stripes," which proved very popular. New England mills imitated it with a cheaper article, and drove it from the market. The fact-

[100]For discussions of the causes for failure of Southern factories see: (1) *Report of William Gregg, President of the Graniteville Manufacturing Co.*, 1855 (pamphlet), also in *DeBow's*, XVIII, 777-91. (2) Extract from a letter of James Montgomery, an English manufacturer. *Ibid.*, XXVI, 95 ff. (3) Letter from James Martin, a successful cotton manufacturer of Florence, Alabama. *Ibid.*, XXIV, 382-6. (4) *Hunt's Merchant's Magazine*, XLII, 376 f. (5) William Gregg, "Southern Patronage to Southern Imports and Domestic Industry," in *DeBow's*, XXIX, 77-83, 225-32, 494-500, 623-31, 771-8; XXX, 102-4, 216-23.

[101]Russell, Robert, *North America*, 295.

[102]See Ingle, Edward, *Southern Sidelights*, 74 ff., for a discussion of wages paid in the South. The best success was had where provision was made for housing the employees, enforcing temperance, and providing schools and religious instruction, as at Graniteville, S. C., and Prattsville, Ala. *DeBow's Review*, XVIII, 777-90.

[103]Colwell, Stephen, *The Five Cotton States and New York* (pamphlet, 1860).

ory then turned to "Georgia Plains." Samples were sent North; and soon the market was flooded with Yankee Georgia Plains.[104] Southern manufacturers selected sound raw material and made goods of high quality; but their Southern customers apparently preferred low prices to quality, which was more difficult to recognize. And, despite statements of Southern writers to the contrary, the probabilities are that the Yankee goods were better in proportion to price.[105] Again, the idea was too prevalent that an effort should be made to supply the local demand, and that a little of everything should be made; it would have been better to specialize. The consumer seemed to prefer goods from a distance to those of home manufacture. "Yankee made," "made in the North," or "just from New York," were advertisements which appealed to the purchaser. Manufacturers frequently complained of the want of home patronage; but, except in times of unusual sectional bitterness, appeals to local pride or patriotism were rather ineffective.

One of the chief obstacles to the success of Southern establishments was the lack of sufficient capital. The factories were too often begun with insufficient capital, were in debt from the start, and maintained no reserve of cash to enable them to buy raw material when the price was low and hold back the product from a depressed market. Frequent items are met in Southern papers telling of consignments of goods to Northern cities. The papers of the South were inclined to boast of such incidents without stopping to inquire the reasons for their occurrence.[106] Because of insufficient capital, the cotton manufacturers of the cotton states, as were the tobacco manufacturers of Virginia, were constantly in need of advances. The advances could most readily be secured by drawing upon agents in New York or other Northern cities, who sold the goods. This system meant that the goods sometimes had

[104]*DeBow's Review*, XXIX, 627.

[105]Daniel Lord said the Southern people "found the Yankee-made a better article, and deaf to all appeals to their Southern pride and patriotism, would have it." *The Effect of Secession upon the Commercial Relations between the North and the South and upon each Section*, 17. Edwin Heriot, of Charleston, said the established opinion in the South was that Northern articles were better, although the facts were just the reverse. *DeBow's Review*, XXIX, 218.

[106]*Hunt's Merchants' Magazine*, XXXI, 384. Cf. *DeBow's Review*, XI, 322; F. L. Olmsted, *Journey in the Seaboard Slave States*, II, 184 (Putnam's, 1904).

to be sold in a depressed market to meet the drafts. Southern manufacturers could not sell directly to Southern merchants or jobbers, because the latter bought on long credit, which the manufacturers were unable to extend. Both mill owners and merchants experienced difficulty in procuring loans from home banks— whether because of inadequacy of banking facilities, or, as some believed, because of banking policy, we will not pause here to inquire.[107]

[107]On system of advances and long credits and the question of banking facilities, in the South, see below, pp. 100-107.

CHAPTER III

ECONOMIC ASPECTS OF THE SOUTHERN MOVEMENT, 1844-1852

Discontent with the economic conditions of the South, absolute and as compared with those of other sections, found expression in the direct trade conventions of 1837-1839. It also was expressed in the agitation in behalf of the diversification of industry. While it cannot be said to have been the sole or even primary cause for the Southern movement which culminated in secession, its influence upon that movement was by no means negligible, especially in its earlier stages.

The story of South Carolina nullification, to begin no farther back, can receive only a brief summary here. About 1825 and following years, strong opposition developed in the older planting states of the South, especially South Carolina, to the policy of a high and protective tariff and heavy expenditures for internal improvements. The basis of this opposition lay not only in the fact that the protected industries and the internal improvements at government expense were in other sections, but also in the apparently, or really, impoverished condition of the old planting section compared with other sections of the Union. In no state were conditions more favorable to the growth of discontent than in South Carolina. Industry was not at all diversified. The price of cotton had fallen. Land values were declining. Population was increasing slowly, if at all. Charleston was making comparatively little progress. These conditions were attributed in great measure to the protective tariff and the extravagant expenditures of the Federal government. Failing to secure a reversal of the objectionable policies, opponents of the tariff hit upon nullification as a remedy. Upon nullification as the issue two parties developed. The State Rights party, or Nullifiers, held nullification to be a constitutional mode of resisting palpably unconstitutional laws, which they considered the tariff laws to be, and thought it justified by the oppression suffered under the tariff. They professed to believe that nullification would result in a repeal of the tariff, but were prepared to resort to the remedy even should war and disunion be the consequences. The Union party, on the other hand, opposed nullification as unconstitutional and certain to lead to war, which could result only in the crushing of South Carolina. Furthermore, many of the Unionists either denied that South Carolina was not prosperous, or, admitting it, attributed the lack of prosperity to other causes than the tariff. After a violent struggle of four years duration a convention was called, which adopted an ordinance nullifying the tariff laws of 1828 and 1832. While Andrew Jackson prepared to employ force, Congress enacted the Compromise Tariff of 1833. Thereupon the South Carolina Convention repealed the nullification ordinance. In other Southern states there was much sympathy with South Carolina's opposition to the tariff; many citizens accepted in whole or in part the doctrines of the Nullifiers. This sympathy was especially strong in Georgia and eastern Virginia, and quite strong in North Carolina and Alabama.[1]

After 1833 the division of the people of South Carolina into Nullifiers and Unionists was largely perpetuated, the former being in a growing majority. The Nullifiers first affiliated with the Whig party, which took form about 1834; about 1838-1840 the great majority of them were led back into the Democratic fold by Calhoun, and continued thereafter to call themselves Democrats. After this latter date the Unionists of South Carolina were to be found in the dwindling Whig party and in what may be termed the Jackson wing of the Democratic party. It was the policy of the leaders of the dominant faction to conciliate and assimilate the Unionist faction; this policy was successful in the main. In other Southern states, particularly the cotton states and Virginia, the large majority of those who had sympathized with the South Carolina Nullifiers in 1832 continued in their devotion to the principles of the nullificationist leaders. Perhaps the majority of this class (Georgia and North Carolina may be exceptions) were aligned with the Whig party during the early years of its history. Most of those so aligned, however, shifted to the Democratic party, either with Calhoun during Van Buren's administration, or later, in Tyler's time. Of those who remained with the Whigs, some were ostensibly converted to Whig principles; others retained

---

[1] The above statements are based upon standard special works and monographs covering this period, and upon *Correspondence of John C. Calhoun; Correspondence of Robert Toombs, A. H. Stephens, and Howell Cobb; Correspondence of R. M. T. Hunter;* and other of the more accessible sources.

both their state rights, free trade, and reform principles and their Whig affiliation until almost the end of the Whig party. In the Democratic party the line of cleavage between the Calhoun wing and the Jackson-Benton-Van Buren wing remained fairly distinct until the Civil War. It was the former element which rallied to the support of John C. Calhoun when he came forward in 1843 as the free trade and reform candidate for the Democratic nomination for the presidency.[2]

The Calhoun wing of the Democratic party held extreme state rights principles. Furthermore, it had been and continued to be the conviction of this following that (1) the government of the United States was too extravagantly administered; (2) the Southern people paid more than their proportionate share of the revenues and received back much less than their proportionate share in the form of disbursements; (3) they were compelled by government to pay tribute to Northern manufacturers, shipowners, and merchants, by virtue of the tariff, fishing bounties, exclusion of foreign vessels from the coasting trade, and heavy government expenditures in the North; (4) and these continual and uncompensated drains upon the resources of the Southern states were enriching the North and impoverishing the South. No Nullifier would admit that the Southern states had the prosperity or were making the material progress to which their resources, population, and the industry of their people entitled them. "Abolish Custom Houses," wrote Calhoun, in 1845, "and let the money collected in the South be spent in the South and we would be among the most flourishing people in the world. The North could not stand the annual draft, which they have been making on us 50 years, without being reduced to the extreme of poverty in half the time. All we want to be rich is to let us have what we make."[3] Such views as

[2]It would be impossible in a study of this scope to develop the statements made in the above summary analysis of the party alignment in the South. They are based upon a wide variety of sources quoted elsewhere in other connections; special mention might be made of the *Correspondence of John C. Calhoun* and the *J. H. Hammond Papers*. It is believed the conclusions here presented accord in the main with the evidence and conclusions of Cole, *Whig Party in the South;* Phillips, *Georgia and State Rights;* and Ambler, *Sectionalism in Virginia,* and *Thomas Ritchie.* It is believed, also, that evidence presented elsewhere in this study tends to substantiate the conclusions given here.

[3]Calhoun to J. H. Hammond, Aug. 30, 1845, *Calhoun Correspondence,* 670.

these were expressed in every tariff debate, in the discussion of almost every rivers and harbors bill, fortifications bill, pensions bill—in fact, whenever a proposal was introduced in Congress which involved the raising or appropriation of money. They were presented, as we have seen, in the direct trade conventions of 1837-1839. They came out in almost every comparison of the progress of the North and South and in every defense of slavery; for it was necessary to trace "Southern decline" to other causes than slavery.

It was the constant purpose of Calhoun and other leaders to reform the "fiscal action of the General Government." But it had early become the conviction of some of his followers that the government was beyond redemption, and that the proper policy for the Southern states to pursue was separation from the North. The bitter feelings engendered and the fears for slavery aroused by the several quarrels over governmental policies affecting that institution had led many to calculate the value of the Union from an economic viewpoint who otherwise might not have done so. A consideration of the benefits and disadvantages of the Union led a number to form the conclusion that disunion was not a consummation to be dreaded and avoided but a measure which would' promote the prosperity, power, and happiness of the South.

An example of their reasoning may be found in a great speech against the Tariff of 1842, which George McDuffie, of South Carolina, made in the Senate, 1844. He warned the advocates of protection that there was a point beyond which oppression would not be endured, "even by the most enslaved community in the world." He pictured the Union divided into three confederations—the North and Northeast as one, the West as another, and the Southern states as a third. He showed that

The manufacturing States could not adhere to the protective system one year. They would have no revenue, and would be driven to direct taxation; whereas the Southern confederation would become the importing States, receiving in exchange foreign manufactures for their rice, cotton, tobacco, and sugar; that the Southwestern confederation would be exchangers with the Southern confederation of their products for the products of Europe; for they would never be so foolish as to buy of the New England Confederation at forty per cent higher in price than need be paid for the same goods in the southern confederation. . . . In ten years there would be such a difference that a person absent so long returning, would be struck with the change in the condition of these sections of the country. The West he would see grown up into a great and flourishing empire; the South the seat of commerce and the arts; the great cities of Boston and New York rebuilt in Charleston and New Orleans, and more flourishing than in their original, uncongenial climates. But in New England he would find the prosperity, comforts, wealth, etc., resulting from partial legislation all gone: houses falling to ruin, cities deserted, furniture selling by auction, and all the indications of indigence prevailing...[4]

McDuffie was arguing for a repeal of the tariff; but others in his state used similar arguments in favor of disunion. During the short-lived Bluffton movement, to which reference has already been made, disunion sentiments were openly expressed. Judge Langdon Cheves in a long letter to the Charleston *Mercury* made a thinly veiled argument for disunion;[5] as such it was taken both South and North.[6] A few months later another correspondent of the *Mercury* in an article headed,"Reflections on Re-perusing Judge Cheve's Letter," put the case for secession without any indirection whatsoever. "The institutions and municipal policy, and geographical position, and popular feelings and pursuits of the north and south can never harmonize as one people. Speak it out—for it is spoken *sub rosa* in every group of domestic and political coterie—that the sections divided by interest can never assimilate in sentiment and national amity."[7] Both Cheves and his reviewer described how separation would promote the prosperity of agriculture and commerce in the South.

The saner leaders in South Carolina, at the time of the Bluffton movement, were insistent that any measure taken, whether secession or nullification, must be taken by a united South, and they labored under no delusions in regard to the attitude of the South as a whole. In the spring of 1844 the cry, "Texas or Disunion," had awakened response in several Southern states;[8] but as soon

[4] *Cong. Globe*, 28 Cong. 1 Sess., 206 (Jan. 29).

[5] *Niles' Register*, LXVII, 49 ff.

[6] *A Reply to the Letter of the Honorable Langdon Cheves, by "A Southerner"* (pamphlet); Adams, J. Q., *Memoirs*, XII, 91.

[7] April 4, 1845; *Niles' Register*, LXVIII, 88 ff.

[8] *Ibid.*, LXVI, 313, meetings in South Carolina; *ibid.*, LXVI, 123, quoting the New Orleans *Tropic; ibid.*, 229, 312, accounts of meetings in Barnwell District, South Carolina, and Russell County, Alabama; *ibid.*, 31, quoting the Richmond *Enquirer*, and other Southern papers; *ibid.*, LXVI, 405, disunion meetings in Lawrence county, Alabama, and in several districts in South Carolina; Benton, *Thirty Years' View*, II, 613-619.

as it had achieved its purpose of securing the Democratic nomination for the' presidency for a Southern man who was sound on the Texas issue, the Democratic leaders proved most anxious to clear themselves of any taint of disunion which the Whigs tried to fix upon them.[9] The Charleston *Mercury* admitted that other states would not join South Carolina in resistance.[10] General James Hamilton wrote in a public letter: "I cannot but express my belief that South Carolina is not *now* ready for separate action, nor the southern states for a southern convention." He expressed the same view privately.[11] Langdon Cheves suggested that, instead of South Carolina undertaking separate resistance, an active propaganda be conducted throughout the South to develop among the people a feeling of unity and a sense of their oppression. He would have had a course followed similar to that pursued in the Thirteen Colonies prior to the American Revolution: "Let associations be formed in every southern, and, if possible, in every southwestern state, and let them confer together and interchange views and information; let leading men through committees and private correspondence collect, compare, and concentrate the views of men in their respective states, and when ripe for it, and not before, let representatives from those states meet in convention, and if circumstances promise success, let them *then* deliberate on the mode of resistance and the measure of redress."[12] It became the settled policy of certain South Carolina leaders to bring the Southern states together in convention, to break down party distinctions throughout the South, as they had largely been broken down in their own state, and to "fire the Southern heart."

There was little in the course of events during the next several years to modify the views of men of the South Carolina school or to deplete the ranks of the disunionists. The Walker tariff, the Independent Treasury, and the veto of rivers and harbors bills

[9]*Niles' Register*, LXVI, 313, 347, 369, 391, 406, 411, quoting the Richmond *Enquirer* as denying connection with the "Texas or Disunion" cry and proposed Southern convention at Nashville; *ibid.*, LXVI, 313, 346, and the *National Intelligencer*, July 23, on the meeting in Nashville to protest against the proposed "Texas or Disunion" convention; *National Intelligencer*, July 27, Aug. 10, 11.

[10]Aug. 9, 1844, "Our Position and our Pledges," in *Niles' Register*, LXVI, 406 ff.

[11]*Ibid.*, LXVI, 420; Hamilton to Hammond, Oct. 4, 1844, *J. H. Hammond Papers*.

[12]*Niles' Register*, LXVII, 49.

pleased but did not satisfy the free trade and reform element. Then with the introduction of the Wilmot Proviso, 1846, there began an acrimonious struggle over slavery which continued almost without interruption until about 1852, when the general acceptance of the Compromise of 1850, and the defeat of efforts to resist it, ushered in a short period of relative calm. The disposition evinced by the majority in the North to exclude slavery from the territory acquired from Mexico and other manifestations of hostility to the institution, together with the growing political preponderance and unity of the free states, caused the majority in the South to fear for the security of slavery and other substantial Southern interests. Southern leaders were put to it to know how to meet the issue. Under these circumstances disunion was fully canvassed as a remedy, immediate or ultimate.

The long debates in Congress, the accompanying discussion in the press and from the platform, the Southern conventions at Nashville and their preliminaries, and, finally, the contests waged in several states between those who favored acquiescence in the compromise measures and those who counselled resistance, afforded ample opportunity for a thorough discussion of the advantages and disadvantages of the Union and the expediency and propriety of secession. The discussion revealed how extensively the ideas were held that the Union was a detriment to the prosperity and economic progress of the South, and, the corollary, the South would be more prosperous and develop more rapidly were the Union dissolved. The discussion also, no doubt, contributed to the spread of these ideas. It also revealed, and no doubt increased, the number of those who, while they did not look for disunion to bring positive economic advantages, expected it to bring no serious disadvantages—in short, those who could look to disunion with complacency, for whom it "had no terrors."

Very early in the struggle over slavery in the territory to be acquired from Mexico declarations were given in the South of a determination to resist the adoption and enforcement of the Wilmot Proviso "at all hazards and to the last extremity."[13] As the

[13]Virginia resolutions, Mar. 8, 1847, in Ames, *State Documents on Federal Relations*, 245-7, were the first official declaration. Other state legislatures, as well as party conventions, and numerous meetings of citizens adopted similar resolutions. See Hamer, *Secession Movement in S. C., 1847-1852*, pp. 5, 6, 11, 16 f., 29, 30 f.

struggle progressed these declarations were renewed, and extended, as the issues were presented, to include other threatened acts of Northern aggression. To prove that these were not merely idle threats, Southern men talked long and angrily of Southern rights and Southern honor and pictured the ruin that would be brought to the South by abolition—which they professed to believe would be the ultimate consequence of restriction of slave territory and loss of the sectional equilibrium. Many also endeavored to demonstrate that the South could safely stake the Union upon the issue of the struggle, because the South would suffer very little, if not actually gain, from a dissolution, while the North stood to lose so much in the event that she would yield rather than permit the Union to be destroyed—"calculating the value of the Union," this was termed.

After the election of 1848 and after the Taylor administration had seemed to show anti-slavery leanings, the task of calculating the value of the Union was undertaken in earnest. In the press, in numerous pamphlets, in Congress, during the debates on the compromise measures, threats of a dissolution in case the South should be denied justice were reenforced by more or less elaborate comparisons of the economic advantages or disadvantages of the Union to the various sections. Many of those who thus calculated the value of the Union were conditional disunionists. They professed to be ready to stake the Union upon the satisfaction of their demands. In all probability their demands would not have been so great or so firmly made, had they attached greater value to the Union; nevertheless, they intended to preserve the Union if it could be done without too great sacrifice. But another class was in evidence during the crisis, the disunionists *per se,* who favored disunion irrespective of the character of the settlement of the pending questions of conflict. They would have seized the opportunity to demand guarantees of the North which they would have had no expectation of securing. In their opinion the interests of the two sections had become so diverse that they could no longer live amicably under one government. The Union had become a disadvantage to the South: she would be more peaceful, happy, and prosperous out of it.

As might be expected, the first manifestations of this ultra sentiment were in South Carolina. As early as November 2, 1848, H. W. Connor, of Charleston, wrote Calhoun that he believed "there has been and probably still is a design to revive the old Bluffton move with the same motive and end."[14] The following February, J. H. Hammond expressed to Calhoun his belief that the crisis was at hand.[15] In the summer of 1849 the *South Carolina Telegraph* began openly to agitate for a dissolution of the Union; and by early in 1850 nearly every newspaper in the state was advocating disunion.[16] The Charleston *Mercury* expected it.[17] Meanwhile Governor Seabrook was in correspondence with the governors of other Southern states relative to what action they might be expected to take if the Wilmot Proviso or other objectionable measure should be adopted by Congress.[18] Georgia newspaper editors, in the summer of 1850, boldly inserted communications in their columns, without any marks of disapprobation, openly advocating disunion. Prominent leaders like Joseph H. Lumpkin, William L. Mitchell, W. F. Colquitt, A. G. McDonald, and Joseph E. Brown were known as disunionists, *per se*.[19] John B. Lamar wrote Howell Cobb that if it were not for Cobb's influence Georgia would be more rampant for disunion than South Carolina ever was.[20] There were disunionists *per se* also in Alabama, Mississippi, North Carolina, Virginia, and Tennessee.

It was this disunion element chiefly which was responsible for the meeting of the Nashville Convention of June 1850. The idea of getting the South together in a Southern convention was an old one in South Carolina at least.[21] After the conflict over the Wil-

[14]*Calhoun Correspondence.* Cf. Hamer, *op. cit.*, 26.
[15]Letter of Feb. 19, 1849, *Calhoun Correspondence.*
[16]*National Intelligencer*, Feb. 15, 1850.
[17]*Ibid., loc. cit.*
[18]Gov. W. D. Mosely, of Fla., to Whitemarsh B. Seabrook, May 18, 1849, *Seabrook MSS.* "I do not now see any other executive to whom to address yourself besides those you have already approached." Franklin H. Elmore to Seabrook, May 30, *ibid.*
[19]John H. Lumpkin to Howell Cobb, July 21, *Toombs, Stephens, Cobb Correspondence.*
[20]Letter of Feb. 7, 1850, *ibid.*
[21]Unionists had proposed a Southern convention in 1832 as a substitute for nullification. Boucher, *Nullification Controversy in South Carolina*, 197-203. It was discussed in 1835-1838, when the questions of abolition literature in the mails, abolition petitions in Congress, and kindred questions were causing angry controversy. Calhoun to Hayne, Nov. 17, 1838, *Calhoun Correspondence;* Ambler, *Thomas Ritchie, A Study in Virginia Politics*, 173; Benton, *Thirty Years' View,*

mot Proviso had been fairly joined, Calhoun sounded the views of leading men of his following throughout the South upon the subject.[22] A call could have been secured at any time from South Carolina; but in view of the well known disunion tendencies of that state, it was deemed advisable that it should originate elsewhere. Finally the call was issued by a delegate convention in Jackson, Mississippi, October, 1849. If the report of Daniel Wallace, secret agent of Governor Seabrook, of South Carolina, may be credited, men who were former residents of that state and disunionists, were very influential in the proceedings.[23]

In South Carolina opposition to the Nashville Convention was almost negligible. The character of the delegates elected, their correspondence, and the comments of the press leave little doubt that it was intended to use the Nashville Convention to promote disunion.[24] In most of the other slaveholding states the call of the convention at first met with hearty response. But opposition soon developed. Thomas H. Benton denounced it as a disunion plot.[25] The Whigs generally condemned it; they distrusted the disorganizing proclivities of some of those active in promoting it. The compromising spirit shown in Congress in the early months of 1850 strengthened the opposition to the Southern Convention by making it appear unnecessary as well as dangerous.[26] Six slave states, Louisiana, North Carolina, Missouri, Kentucky, Maryland,

II, 700. It was again mooted in 1844, particularly during the "Texas or Disunion" agitation. James Hamilton to J. H. Hammond, Oct. 4, 1844, *J. H. Hammond Papers; Niles' Register*, LXVI, 229, 312, 369 (accounts of meetings in S. C and Ala.); Benton, *Thirty Years' View*, II, 613-619.

[22]Calhoun to a member of the Alabama Legislature, 1847, Benton, *Thirty Years' View*, II, 698-700; Joseph W. Lesesne to Calhoun, Sept. 12, 1847, *Calhoun Correspondence;* Wilson Lumpkin to Calhoun, Nov. 18, 1847; H. W. Connor to Calhoun, Nov. 2, 1848; John Cunningham to Calhoun, Nov. 12; Calhoun to J. H. Means, Apr. 13, 1849.

[23]D. W. Wallace to Gov. Seabrook, June 8, Oct. 20, Nov. 7, 1849, *Seabrook MSS.*

[24]A. H. Brisbane to Hammond, Jan. 28, 1850, *J. H. Hammond Papers; National Intelligencer*, Apr. 20, May 18, June 5, 1850. Cf. Hamer, *op. cit.*, 46-48. Wm. Gilmore Simms wrote Hammond: "I regard the Southern convention as in fact a Southern confederacy. To become the one it seems to me very certain is to become the other." Quoted in Trent, *William Gilmore Simms*, 179.

[25]*National Intelligencer*, Mar. 20, 1850, account of a meeting in St Louis, Mar. 7.

[26]Cf. Cole, *Whig Party in the South*, 157-62, 168-72.

and Delaware, failed to send delegates. In Georgia a very small percentage of the voters participated in the election of delegates.[27] Western Virginia and several populous counties in the east took no part in the election of delegates,[28] and only six delegates from the state attended the convention. Only South Carolina, Tennessee, Alabama, and Mississippi were represented by full delegations, and in the two last the delegates were appointed by the legislatures.

When the Nashville Convention met the disunionists soon saw that any action looking to immediate resistance was impossible, and, therefore, worked for a second meeting.[29] Several disunion *per se* speeches were made, the most notable being that of Beverly Tucker, of Virginia.[30] The resolutions and the address to the people of the slaveholding states which were adopted declared, in effect, that the compromise measures then pending in Congress were unacceptable and called for the extension of the Missouri Compromise line to the Pacific as a *sine qua non*.[31] The adjourned session of the convention met in Nashville, November 11, 1850, with seven states represented, by delegations reduced in size.[32] Most of the Union men of the first session refused to attend the second, and the disunionists easily dominated it.[33] The resolutions denounced the compromise measures which Congress had adopted, and recommended a congress or convention of the slaveholding states "intrusted with full power and authority to deliberate and act with a view and intention of arresting further aggression, and, if possible, of restoring the constitutional rights of the South, and, if not, to provide for their future safety and inde-

[27]*National Intelligencer*, Apr. 11, 1850.
[28]Ambler, *Sectionalism in Virginia*, 249; letters of Wm. O. Goode to R. M. T. Hunter, Mar. 29, Apr. 20, May 11, 1850, *Correspondence of R. M. T. Hunter.*
[29]Hammond to Wm. G. Simms, June 16, 1850, *J. H. Hammond Papers.*
[30]*DeBow's Review*, XXXI, 59-69; reviewed in *So. Quar. Rev.*, XVIII, 218-23. See also Hammond to Simms, June 16, 1850, *J. H. Hammond Papers.*
[31]The resolutions and the address are in Ames, *State Documents on Federal Relations*, 263-9. Proceedings in *National Intelligencer*, June 4-16, 1850.
[32]Proceedings in *ibid.*, Nov. 16.
[33]Perhaps the most noteworthy incident of the meeting was the three hours speech of Langdon Cheves, of South Carolina, advocating secession. This speech was published as a pamphlet and widely used in the state contests over the acceptance of the compromise measures.

pendence." This action was intended to influence the contests then being waged in four states over the Compromise of 1850.

After the passage of the compromise measures spirited contests ensued in South Carolina, Georgia, Alabama, and Mississippi between those who would acquiesce and those who would resist. In South Carolina the submissionists or Unionists were in a small minority. The real contest lay between the cooperationists and the separate-actionists. The former believed that South Carolina should secede, but only in case other cotton states should take similar action at the same time. The separate-actionists wanted a convention called to take the state out of the Union, in company with others, if possible, if not, alone. They professed to believe that if South Carolina should secede and the Federal government should undertake coercion, the other Southern states would come to her support; if, as was possible, the Federal government should not adopt coercive measures, South Carolina would be prosperous and happy as an independent nation. The issue was not fairly joined until after the failure of the secession movements in Georgia, Mississippi, and Alabama was certain; then the contest became very spirited. At an election held October 13 and 14, 1851, to choose delegates to a Southern congress, which the Legislature had called, the cooperationists cast 25,045 votes to their opponents' 17,710 and carried all of the congressional districts but one.[34] This result was interpreted as instructing the delegates to the State Convention, who had been elected in February. The Convention accordingly adopted a preamble and a resolution which declared the right of secession and resolved that secession was justified by the course of the Federal government but that South Carolina "forbears the exercise of this manifest right of self-government from considerations of expediency only."[35]

In Georgia, Governor Towns, acting upon instructions from the Legislature, called a convention to meet December 10 to consider the compromise measures. During the campaign for the election of delegates, the Union party, which favored acquiescence in the compromise, was opposed by a Southern Rights party, which counselled resistance. The great majority of the Whigs and a respectable minority of the Democrats supported the Union candi-

---

[34]*National Intelligencer*, Oct. 18, 20, 21, 1851; Hamer, *op. cit.*, 123.
[35]*Journal of the State Convention of South Carolina...1852*, p. 18.

dates; while the majority of the Democrats entered the Southern Rights party. Under the leadership of Howell Cobb, A. H. Stephens, and Robert Toombs the Union party won with a large majority of the popular vote and an overwhelming majority in the convention. After this victory the Union party perfected an organization and entered the state campaign of 1851 with Howell Cobb, Democrat, as its candidate for governor. The Southern Rights party nominated as its candidate ex-Governor A. G. McDonald, who had presided over the second meeting of the Nashville Convention. Again the Unionists won a substantial victory. Similar events occurred in Mississippi. Upon the passage of the compromise measures, Governor John A. Quitman called an extra session of the Legislature which, in turn, called a state convention to meet November 10, 1851. A Union party was formed to contest the election of delegates to the convention and the regular state elections of November, 1851. It was composed of the great majority of the Whigs and a minority of the Democrats. H. S. Foote, Union Democrat, was the nominee for governor. The Union party was opposed by a Southern Rights party, officially designated the Democratic State Rights party, led by Quitman and Jefferson Davis and composed chiefly of Democrats. The Unionists won a sweeping victory in the September elections for delegates to the convention, and elected Foote governor over Jefferson Davis by a small majority in November. The Convention adopted resolutions accepting the compromise measures and declaring secession not to be a constitutional right.[36] In Alabama, Governor Collier refused to call a special session of the Legislature, which might have called a state convention. Sentiment was clearly in favor of acquiescence in the compromise. However, Southern Rights associations were formed, as in other states, and the right of secession was made an issue in the campaign for the election of members of Congress in 1851.

The contest in South Carolina evoked the publication of numerous long pamphlets, several long and laborious articles in the *Southern Quarterly Review,* and the proceedings of meetings of Southern Rights associations, as well as voluminous discussion in the press and innumerable stump speeches. Both separate-actionists and cooperationists again and again represented secession

[36]*Journal of the Convention of the State of Mississippi...1851,* p. 47.

not only as a remedy for Northern aggression against slavery (although that was the chief consideration) but also as a measure desirable irrespective of the slavery question. The opponents of separate action demonstrated conclusively that separate secession would adversely affect the prosperity of South Carolina and, especially, the commercial interests of Charleston, even should it be permitted to be peaceful; but it was a rare voice that spoke of the advantages of the Union.[37] The cooperationists were charged with going beyond the separate-actionists in depicting the evils of the Union.[38] J. D. B. DeBow, then of New Orleans, a strong Southern Rights man, objected to most of the papers and documents issued by the South Carolina press because "they go far beyond the necessities of the case, and frame an argument for disunion at all hazards, even were the slavery question closed up and amicably settled."[39]

Early in the contests in Georgia, Mississippi, and Alabama the leaders of the Southern Rights parties saw that the people would not go for secession, and sought to shift the issue from the expediency to the constitutional right of secession;[40] thereafter arguments for disunion *per se,* such as were used so freely in South Carolina, were used rather charily. But the people had opportunity to become acquainted with all the disunionist doctrines.

Outside the four states named the compromise measures were

[37]The best arguments against separate secession are in: *Speech of Mr. Memminger at a public meeting of the friends of cooperation . . . Charleston, Sept. 23, 1851, . . .;* "Letter from W. W. Boyce to J. P. Richardson, President of a convention of the Southern Rights Association of South Carolina held at Charleston, May, 1851," republished in *National Intelligencer,* Nov. 13, 1860; *The Letters of Aricola,* by Hon. Wm. Elliott; Letter of Gen. James Hamilton "To the People of South Carolina," Nov. 11, 1850, *National Intelligencer,* Dec. 2, 1850.

[38]*National Intelligencer,* Oct. 14, 1851, quoting the Greenville, S. C., *Southern Patriot.*

[39]*DeBow's Review,* X, 231.

[40]This was not a mere abstract question: There was still a probability that South Carolina would secede alone, and the other Southern states would then be compelled to determine their course with reference to the coercion of a seceded state. Furthermore, a general recognition of the right of secession would prepare the way for future contests over its expediency.

acquiesced in without noteworthy contests.[41] Disunionists, especially disunionists *per se*, were in a small minority. There were such, however, and they presented the disunion arguments. There was considerable discussion of the proper policy to be pursued in case the cotton states should secede, and considerable speculation in regard to the probable effects of separation from the North upon the economic systems of the respective states. Furthermore, disunionists in states most likely to secede indulged in much speculation as to what other states would be included within the boundaries of the proposed Southern confederacy, and advanced arguments to prove that it would be to the interest of Virginia, Maryland, or other particular state to go with the South in the event of a dissolution. Men in the states which were the subjects of such speculation had to take cognizance.

In analyzing the arguments of an economic nature which were used in behalf of secession or in behalf of taking advanced ground in the sectional struggle, it is not necessary to specify whether they were used by conditional disunionists or unconditional disunionists. The arguments used by the one class differed little from those used by the other; furthermore, it is not always easy to classify any given individual on this basis.

The most elaborate calculation of the value of the Union made during the crisis may be found in a long and well-written pamphlet, published early in 1850, entitled, "The Union, Past and Future, How It Works and How to Save It,"[42] by Muscoe R. H.

[41] In North Carolina the minority was rather strong. In the Legislature of 1850-1851, resolutions affirming the constitutional right of secession were defeated with difficulty. In the congressional campaign of 1851 the right of secession was an issue; the opposition gained two seats in Congress as a result. Cole, *Whig Party in the South*, 192; Wm. K. Boyd, "North Carolina on the Eve of Secession," in Amer. Hist. Assoc., *Rept.*, 1910, p. 171. Cave Johnson, of Tennessee, heard secession *per se* arguments in his state. Letter to James Buchanan, Jan. 20, 1850, in St. G. L. Sioussat, "Tennessee, the Compromise of 1850, and the Nashville Convention," *Miss. Val. Hist. Rev.*, II, 313-47.

[42] Published anonymously in Charleston, 1850; republished, several years later, in *DeBow's Review*, XVIII and XIX, *passim*. The pamphlet was reviewed by E. Haskett Derby, Boston lawyer, in *Hunt's Merchants' Magazine*, XXIII, 371-83, and in a pamphlet *Reality versus Fiction*, Boston, 1850. Garnett answered Derby in an article in *Hunt's*, XXIV, 403-431, "The Union, Past and Future: 'A Brief Review' Reviewed." Derby closed the argument, *Hunt's*, XXIV, 659-681. For other reviews of Garnett's pamphlet see *So. Quar. Rev.*, XIX, 189-226; *DeBow's Review*, X, 132-146, article, "The Future of the South," by Thomas Prentice Kettell.

Garnett, of Virginia, a relative of R. M. T. Hunter and Henry A. Wise, and an able and influential politician of the state rights school. Garnett reviewed the slavery struggle, and found that the South had reached a point where she must insist upon "sufficient guarantees for the observance of her rights and her future political equality, or she must dissolve a Union which no longer possesses its original character." He proposed to put before the North what she would lose if the South should be forced to take the latter alternative. He calculated the value which the laws discriminating against foreign shipping had been to the North—an enormous sum according to his method of calculation. The operation of the tariff, he analyzed in the usual anti-protectionist manner, and calculated that between 1791 and 1845 "the slaveholding States paid $316,492,083 more than their just share, and the free States as much less . . . "; and this when, according to his statement, the whole amount of duties collected in the same period was only $927,050,097. In the only other branch of public revenue of any consequence, the proceeds of the sales of public lands, the disproportion of Northern and Southern contributions had been still greater. From the subject of taxation Garnett passed to disbursements. The free states had received much larger donations of the public lands. Of expenditures for collection of customs, for "bounties on pickled fish, and the allowances to fishing vessels," for coast fortifications, for light houses, for the coast survey, for internal improvements, for Revolutionary pensions, and even for the post office system, the South had received much less and the North much more than her proportionate share. The public debt, held mostly in the North, had been the source of yet more enormous benefits to that section. In summary, he said: "The heads of the federal expenditures which we have examined give a fair notion of the rest; and it may be safely assumed, that while the South has paid seven-ninths of the taxes, the North has had seven-ninths of their disbursements."

According to Garnett this inequality in the operation of the Federal government as respects the sections would account for the growth of cities and the prosperity of the North. The effect upon the North of a dissolution of the Union would be ruinous. She would have to rely on direct taxation to support her government. The South on the other hand would pay less taxes and disburse them among her own people. She would conduct her own commerce and that of the great Northwest. "Norfolk and

Charleston and Savannah, so long pointed at by the North as a proof of the pretended evils of slavery, will be crowded with shipping, and their warehouses crammed with merchandise." The future of Southern agriculture would be equally brilliant. By virtue of her command of the great staple of cotton, her great natural advantages, and her strategic location "midway in the new hemisphere, holding the outlets of Northern commerce, and the approaches to South America and the Pacific, through the Gulf," the Southern confederacy would occupy a powerful position in the world. The pamphlet was concluded with a glorification of slavery and agriculture and a depiction of the demoralizing influences of factories; for Garnett would not encourage manufactures in his free trade republic.

More frequently quoted, perhaps, than Garnett's pamphlet was an article in the *Democratic Review*, January, 1850, written by the editor, Thomas Prentice Kettell, and entitled, "Stability of the Union."[43] It was a plea to the people of the North not to attack an institution upon which their prosperity so largely depended; it was similar in strain to the pleas frequently advanced by organs of the manufacturing and commercial interests of the North.[44] Kettell said nothing about unequal operation of the Federal government, but emphasized the profits realized by the North from manufacturing for the South, carrying her commerce, and acting as her banker. The annual pecuniary value to the North of a union with the South, he estimated in a table[45] containing the following items:

[43]Also in *DeBow's Review*, VIII, 348-363; DeBow, *Industrial Resources*, III, 357-366.

[44]See, for example, *DeBow's Review*, IX, 93-100, quoting the New York *Courier and Enquirer*; *Hunt's Merchants' Magazine*, XX, 292 ff., letter of Colonel Alexander Hamilton, of New York.

[45]*Democratic Review*, XXVI, 13. Quoted in Congress by Thomas L. Clingman, *Cong. Globe*, 31 Cong. 1 Sess., 203 ff.; by Downs, of Louisiana, *ibid.*, Appx., 172; by Averett, of Virginia, *ibid.*, Appx., 396; Thomas L. Harris, of Illinois, *ibid.*, Appx., 411. Mr. Harris said: "But, Mr. Chairman, several gentlemen, both here and in the other end of the Capitol [Senate], have relied upon an article in a late number of the *Democratic Review* to show that the North is reaping upward of $88,000,000 from its connection with the South, while it is careful not to show that the South derives any benefit from the North." See also Aaron V. Brown, *Speeches, Congressional and Political, and Other Writings*, 302 (Governor of Tennessee); Charleston *Mercury*, Feb. 15, 1850, quoted in *National Intelligencer*, Feb. 20.

Freights of Northern shipping on Southern produce...$40,186,178
Profits derived on imports at the North for Southern
   account................................... 9,000,000
Profits on exchange operations..................... 1,000,000
Profits on Northern·manufactures sold at the South.. 22,250,000
Profits on Western produce descending the Mississippi 10,000,000
Profits on Northern capital employed at the south... 6,000,000

    Total earnings of the North per annum..........$88,436,178

There was nothing in Kettell's article to indicate that the Southern people received any pecuniary advantages from their union with the North. Southern men quoted his table not only to show why the North should grant justice to the South, but also what the South would save annually by a dissolution of the Union.

Of the speeches in Congress in which the value of the Union was calculated, perhaps the most notable was that of Thomas L. Clingman, Whig, of North Carolina.[46] He dwelt upon the inequality of taxation and disbursements, and told what ample revenues a Southern confederacy could command with a tariff of thirty or even twenty per cent. "Subjecting the goods of the North to a duty, with those from other foreign countries, would at once give a powerful stimulus to our own manufactures." He described the advantages the Southern states possessed for cotton manufacturing, and added, "We should thus have that diversity of pursuits which is most conducive to the prosperity and happiness of a people." John C. Calhoun in his last great speech, March 4, 1850, did not calculate the value of the Union; he did, however, reiterate his conviction that unequal taxation and disbursements had caused that loss of equilibrium between the sections which, he said, was the "great and primary cause" of the belief of the Southern people, "that they cannot remain, as things now are, consistently with honor and safety, in the Union." Unequal distribution of the taxes and disbursements had transferred hundreds of millions from the South to the North. This had increased the population of the

---

[46]*Cong. Globe*, 31 Cong., 1 Sess., 200-207, speech in the House, Jan. 22, 1850; Thomas L. Clingman, *Speeches and Writings*, 245 ff. Clingman expressed similar ideas in a speech in the House, February 15, 1851, *Speeches and Writings*, 275 ff. This speech was regarded in the South as the platform of the ultras. See *National Intelligencer*, Feb. 1, 1850.

latter by attracting immigration from all quarters and sections.
Had the South retained her wealth and her equality in the territories, she would have divided, at least, the immigration.[47]

Space will not permit an account of the contents of the numerous pamphlets and speeches occasioned by the contests in South
Carolina and elsewhere over the acceptance of the compromise
measures. One example will suffice to illustrate their tone and
temper. John Townsend, a prominent cooperationist of South
Carolina, in a vigorous pamphlet entitled, *The Southern States,
Their Present Peril and Their Certain Remedy,* named aboli-
tionism as the peril and secession as the remedy; but it was a
remedy for more than the dangers threatening slavery. In the
usual strain he told of the unequal operation of the Federal government and its effects. He described the vast resources of the
South, and said:

How different will be the aspect of things in the whole South,
when this tide of wealth is dammed up within our own borders,
and made to roll back among our own people; and when our immense capital is employed by our own merchants in establishing
a direct trade between our own Southern ports and our customers all over the world . . . The arts will revive, manufactures will
spring up around us; our agriculture will rear its drooping head,
our commerce will expand, mechanic labor, meeting with ample
rewards will pour in upon us, and emigration [*sic*], no longer discouraged by the uninviting aspect of our country will flock to our
shores.[48]

In the United States Senate, R. B. Rhett, who had been elected
to fill the vacancy caused by the death of Calhoun, was led by an
attack made upon him by Henry S. Foote, of Mississippi,[49] to
make a long speech explaining why he was a secessionist—he was
the leader of the separate-actionists in his state. He reviewed the

[47]*Works,* IV, 542-73.
[48]P. 17. Other secessionist pamphlets or articles were: Wm. H. Trescott,
The Position and Course of the South; E. B. Bryan, *The Rightful Remedy. Addressed to the Slaveholders of the South;* [A. G. Magrath], *A Letter on Southern Wrongs and Southern Remedies: Addressed to the Hon. W. J. Grayson in
reply to his Letter to the Governor of South Carolina on the Dissolution of
the Union.*
[49]Foote charged Rhett with having said that he expected, through the
agency of the Nashville Convention, by making demands to which he knew
Congress would not accede, to break up the Union. *Cong. Globe,* 32 Cong., 1
Sess., 96.

history of the struggles over slavery, and charged that the Northern people were animated by a desire for its final extinction. But the action of Congress with respect to slavery in the territories, he said, was only a sequence in a course of policy inimical to the South which had been pursued many years. "If I mistake not, from the very foundation of this Government to this day, the operation of it in its financial and pecuniary relations, has had but one uniform tendency; and that has been, to aggrandize the North at the expense of the South." He traced the history of the tariff from the beginning, and reviewed the whole subject of taxation and disbursements in a manner very similar to that of Garnett's pamphlet. "Is it wonderful," he asked, "that under such a course of policy, the poorest section of the Union should be the richest, and the South should, with all her vast resources, linger in her prosperity?" He traced the decline of Southern commerce, and estimated the value to the North of the monopoly of the coasting trade. "The South," he said, "is nothing else now, but the very best colony of the North any people ever possessed."[50] Rhett's colleagues understood his speech to be an argument for secession *per se*. Senator Cass so took it, and condemned it.[51] Senator Mason, of Virginia, declared that his state had no sympathy with those who "preferred disunion."[52] Senator Downs, of Louisiana, asked why discuss further the compromise measures when Rhett had himself admitted that he did not find in them sufficient reason to justify the disunion movement which he had set on foot in South Carolina.[53] In the House, E. K. Smart, of Maine, replied in detail, with a yet more imposing array of statistics than Rhett had used, to the latter's speech and to one of somewhat similar tone which had been made in the House by A. G. Brown, of Mississippi.[54] He did so, he explained, because "I have often thought that a fair and candid investigation of the benefits and advantages of this Government, enjoyed by the South, would disarm the spirit of disunion; that our southern friends, by an examination of the facts, would be induced to demand less of the North."

---

[50]*Cong. Globe*, 32 Cong., 1 Sess., Appx., 42-8.
[51]*Ibid.*, 32 Cong., 1 Sess., 146.
[52]*Ibid.*, 32 Cong., 1 Sess., Appx., 49.
[53]*Ibid.*, 32 Cong., 1 Sess., Appx., 98.
[54]*Ibid.*, 32 Cong., 1 Sess., Appx., 464-71.

Unionists did not fail to seek other causes than the quarrel over slavery and the fears for the security of that institution for the existence of disunion sentiment in the South. F. A. P. Barnard, in an address to the citizens of Tuscaloosa, Alabama, said he believed there were causes much deeper than the slavery agitation for the war which had been waged to the knife against the Union. The agitators had seized upon the soreness produced in the Southern mind by the infringement of undeniable rights as the most available means of accomplishing their ulterior designs. He retold the story of South Carolina nullification; the people of that state were still bitter from the old feud, he said. A conviction prevailed that the Union had been unequal in its benefits: "Such a conviction has been, is probably at this moment, partaken by very many who feel no disposition to rush into disunion as a remedy. Indeed the impression seems extensively to exist, that, by the operation of the Federal Constitution, through Federal Legislation, the South has been made in some sort, tributary to the North." He told of Southern dependence upon the North for manufactures, of the sensitiveness of the Southern people about the matter, and their analysis of the causes of their dependence. "From this condition of things our people have become impatient to be free; and this it is . . . more truly than any other existing evil, which has caused the word disunion to be of late so often and so lightly spoken among us, and the thought of what it signifies to be contemplated with so little horror."[55] The Richmond *Whig* thought much of the dissatisfaction in South Carolina had originated in having attributed to the Federal government consequences which were rather attributable to the competition of fresher and more fertile states of the South, engaged in the culture of the same staple as herself.[56]

The Unionists in the cotton states in their contests with the Southern Rights parties found their best tactics to be to defend the compromise measures, appeal to the patriotism of the

[55]*Oration Delivered before the Citizens of Tuscaloosa, Alabama, July 4, 1851*, 12.

[56]March 5, 1851. A similar statement is in an editorial of March 22.

masses,[57] impeach the motives of Southern Rights leaders, and picture secession as a measure that would bathe the nation in blood. They showed that secession meant division of the South; for the border states could not be expected to secede.[58] In particular localities they pointed out how separation would injure established commercial and agricultural interests. In general they did not find it necessary to refute at length the doctrine that the prosperity of the South suffered from an unequal operation of the Federal government. No doubt many shared this view to some extent. Yet there was a fundamental divergence in the views of the two groups as to the Union's economic effects upon the sections. Unionists were inclined to depict the unexampled peace and progress in wealth and strength of the great republic and to consider the South a partaker therein.[59] The Mobile *Daily Advertiser* said Alabama was never more prosperous. "Why cannot secession orators be serious?"[60] Said H. S. Foote of Mississippi: "It is sufficient for us to know that the Union is of inappreciable value to every portion of this widespread Republic; . . . That the general action of the government has been more or less unequal and oppressive to our local interests of the South, cannot be denied."[61] Particularly in Georgia, the most prosperous of the cotton states, was the plea effective that the state owed its prosperity to the Union. The Richmond *Whig* ascribed the Union victory in Georgia to prosperity—the refusal of the people to be convinced that the Union had inflicted any injury upon them.[62] General James Hamilton, who traveled through the cotton states in the

[57]Henry W. Hilliard said: "The value of the Union which binds these States together is incalculable; its priceless value defies all the ordinary methods of computation; it is consecrated by battles, and triumphs, and glories, which belong to the past; . . . . it secures to us innumerable blessings; it looks forward to a future still more prosperous and more glorious than the past." *Cong. Globe*, 31 Cong., 1 Sess., Appx., 34.

[58]Speech of Senator Jere Clemens, in Huntsville, Alabama, Nov. 4, 1850, in *National Intelligencer*, Nov. 10; letter from Joel R. Poinsett to the people of S. C., Charleston *Mercury*, Dec. 5.

[59]Grayson, W. J., *Letter to the Governor of South Carolina on the Dissolution of the Union*, p. 8. This is one of the best of the Union pamphlets.

[60]Quoted in the *National Intelligencer*, Dec. 6, 1850.

[61]*Cong., Globe*, 32 Cong., 1 Sess., Appx., 59, reply to Rhett.

[62]Mar. 5, 1851.

compromise year, made a similar diagnosis; in Georgia and Alabama the high price of cotton had neutralized the disunion sentiment, while Louisiana had "an average sugar crop and would
acquiesce."[63]

Unionists, in so far as they admitted "Southern decline," were
disposed to emphasize explanations for it other than the fiscal
action of the Federal government. The majority of them were
Whigs, who had, in general, supported those protective and fiscal
measures to which disunionists ascribed the woes of the South.
The Unionists dwelt upon such causes for lagging prosperity as
overproduction of cotton, lack of diversity in agriculture, and the
failure to encourage home manufactures. They showed how the
older states had suffered from the emigration of their citizens to
the richer and fresher lands of the Southwest. Up to this time at
least, the Whigs had given more earnest support than the Democrats to those movements for the diversification of industry which
have been described in previous chapters, and at this juncture
they advocated it as a better method than secession for securing
the rights and prosperity of the South.[64]

The position of New Orleans as an exporting and importing
center for the Mississippi valley plainly operated against the
growth of disunion sentiment in Louisiana; men of that state insisted that the valley could not be divided.[65] Few from Kentucky
and Missouri calculated the value of the Union. Humphrey
Marshall, of Kentucky, offered an explanation for the strong attachment of those states for the Union. There was a region, he
said, where cotton and sugar did not grow, and where manufactures and navigation were not the only employments. "The interests of that people are identical, no matter whether they live in a
free State or a slave State, and they cannot be induced to sacrifice
their welfare or their friendship for the triumph of any extreme
doctrine about slavery."[36] Governor Crittenden expressed the
same idea: "To Kentucky and the other Western States in the

---

[63]"To·the People of South Carolina," in *National Intelligencer*, Dec. 2, 1850.
[64]See Barnard, F. A. P., *Oration Delivered before the Citizens of Tuscaloosa,
Alabama, July 4, 1851.* Cf. Cole, *Whig Party in the South*, 206-211.
[65]Speech of Downs in the Senate, *Cong. Globe*, 31, Cong., 1 Sess., Appx., 171.
[66]*Ibid.*, 31 Cong., 1 Sess., 409.

Valley of the Mississippi, the Union is indispensable to their commercial interests."[67]

In North Carolina the disunion *per se* arguments were well refuted. The absence of identity of interests between the two Carolinas was occasionally emphasized. Said Congressman Stanley, Whig: " . . . . we are invited to contemplate the glories of a Southern Confederacy, in which Virginia and *South* Carolina are to have great cities, to be supported by the colony or plantation of *North* Carolina!"[68] Perhaps in no state other than the older cotton states was a greater disposition shown to listen to the unconditional disunion arguments than in eastern Virginia. But there were strong deterrant influences: trade both with the North and South; prospects of valuable commercial relations with the West when the great internal improvement system already projected should make Virginia the "thoroughfare and rendezvous of our great and united sisterhood of states;"[69] and, more important, the devotion to the Union of the western part of the state, whose economic interests were similar to those of other parts of the Ohio valley rather than to those of the South.[70]

It will have been observed that disunion sentiment and a disposition to put a low estimate upon the value of the Union were not uniformly distributed throughout the slaveholding states. It is true that the states in which the strongest secession movements developed were those in which the ratios of black to white population were highest. (However, it is difficult to demonstrate that within such states secession sentiment was especially strong in the black belts.) But the states in which the disunion movements were strongest were also the states most dependent commercially and industrially—or, to use Calhoun's phrase, they were the "exporting states." They were the states, too, in which the doctrine that the Federal government operated to make one section tributary to the other in an economic way had early found widespread acceptance.

---

[67]Coleman, *The Life of John J. Crittenden*, I, 350-52. Cf. Speech of Henry Clay in the Senate, *Cong. Globe*, 31 Cong., 1 Sess., Appx., 127.

[68]*Ibid.*, 31 Cong., 1 Sess., Appx., 409.

[69]Letter from William C. Rives, U. S. Minister to France, in *National Intelligencer*, May 1, 1850.

[70]Cf. Ambler, *Sectionalism in Virginia*, 248 f.

The evidence in regard to party affiliations is, perhaps, more conclusive as to motives. In the South as a whole the overwhelming majority of the Whig party, as we have seen, was Unionist and accepted the compromise measures without much dissatisfaction. It would seem that the disunionists of 1850, and those who contemplated disunion with complacency, were chiefly of the Calhoun wing of the Democratic party; many of them had been Nullificationists. The Union Democrats of 1850, on the other hand, were chiefly of Jackson, Benton, and Van Buren antecedents.

In South Carolina the alignment is not diffiicult to see. The Unionists were, in the main, the remnants of the Whig party. Of the leaders of the Union group, J. J. Pettigru, B. F. Perry, Judge John Benton O'Neall, Richard Yeadon, and W. J. Grayson were Whigs, Joel R. Poinsett was a Jackson Democrat; all had been Union men in 1832. Waddy Thompson, Whig, was the one conspicuous example of a former Nullifier turned Unionist. Of the separate-actionists, all the prominent leaders who had figured in Nullification days had been Nullifiers; in this category fell R. B. Rhett, B. F. Duncan, F. W. Pickens, I. E. Holmes, W. F. Colcock, A. Burt, and Maxcy Gregg. With one exception these men had been leaders also of the Bluffton movement of 1844. Of the co-operationists of 1851, the majority of the prominent leaders had been Nullifiers; of this class were A. P. Butler, J. H. Hammond, James Hamilton, William S. Preston, F. L. Wardlaw, and W. W. Boyce. Other prominent cooperationists had been Unionists in 1832; in this class were ex-Governor J. P. Richardson, Daniel E. Huger, Richard I. Manning, C. G. Memminger, and James Chesnut. Langdon Cheves had been a cooperationist in 1832. All of the secessionists named were Democrats except William S. Preston, cooperationist, who was a state rights Whig.

In July, 1850, John H. Lumpkin, of Georgia, wrote Howell Cobb: "All who are for resistance and for disunion will be found in the ranks of the democratic party; and if their history should be known, they will be found out to be old Nullifiers in 1832."[71] Other Union Democrats of Georgia complained of those "*secession views*" which have long been entertained by a school of Southern politicians which have always injured and weakened, never bene-

[71]July 21. *Toombs, Stephens, Cobb Correspondence.*

fited or strengthened the Democratic party."[72] The Union Democrats were almost exclusively from the northern counties, which
had never accepted the teachings of the Carolina school. Such
prominent leaders of the Southern Rights party as C. J. Mc-
Donald, George M. Troup, Joseph H. Lumpkin, W. F. Colquitt,
H. L. Benning, William H. Stiles, J. N. Bethune, and John A.
Jones had long been leaders of the state rights wing of the Democratic party. However, in Georgia perhaps to a greater extent than
any other Southern state, the Whig party had retained its state
rights element; this element, with exceptions such as J. M. Berrien, cooperated with their fellows in the Union movement of 1850.
The latter fact probably explains why the Union Convention of
1850 did not deny the constitutional right of secession as did the
Unionists in Alabama and Mississippi.[73]

In Alabama the nullifying state rights faction went into the
Democratic party with Calhoun about 1840; after that time the
state rights element of the Whig party was comparatively small.
But the cleavage between the Calhoun wing of the Democrats, led
by such men as Dixon H. Lewis, J. M. Calhoun, W. L. Yancey,
the Elmores, and David Hubbard, and the Jackson wing whose
leaders were Wm. R. King, Benjamin Fitzpatrick, Jere Clemens,
W. R. W. Cobb, etc., remained clear for years.[74] In 1845
Dixon H. Lewis wrote of the "Calhoun wing of the Party." It
was this wing of the party which formed the Southern Rights
party in 1851, and sought to prepare the state for secession. The
other wing not only allied with the Whigs to form the Union party
but denied the constitutional right of secession.[75]

In Mississippi the situation was very similar to that in Alabama. J. A. Wilcox, a Union Democrat elected in 1851, identified
the Southern Rights men of his state, whom he denounced as

[72]John E. Ward and Henry R. Jackson to Howell Cobb, Feb. 28, 1852, in
Toombs, Stephens, Cobb Correspondence.
[73]Cf. Hodgson, *The Cradle of the Confederacy,* 283.
[74]*Ibid.,* ch. XI; Garrett, *Reminiscences of Public Men in Alabama,* 297.
The author, in telling why David Hubbard, of Lawrence, a Calhoun man, never
attained the senatorship, says: "The same reasons which influenced the Jackson
Democracy in withholding their support in former days from the men who came
over with Mr. Calhoun, operated against him in these aspirations; ...." Garrett
constantly recognizes the division in the Democratic party.
[75]Hodgson, *op. cit.,* 294-296.

disunionists, as "old-line Democrats." This term he defined as designating those whom Jackson had driven from the party in 1832-1833. After that year, he said, they had acted with the Whigs until 1840, when they followed Calhoun back into the Democratic ranks.[76] This description is accurate with the exception that it takes no account of a small element in the Whig party which had not followed Calhoun in 1840, but which nevertheless cooperated with the Southern Rights party in 1851. The leader of this party was John A. Quitman, a native of South Carolina, a Nullifier, and a supporter of Calhoun against Van Buren in 1844.[77]

In no state can the division in the Democratic ranks be more clearly seen than in Virginia. There the Calhoun men constituted a well defined group. For a number of years they acted almost as a third party holding the balance of power between the Whigs and the Democrats. In 1843-1844 they tried to secure the Democratic nomination for the presidency for Calhoun. In 1847 they were able, by taking advantage of factional fights in the general assembly, to elect R. M. T. Hunter and J. M. Mason to the Senate. Thereafter they gradually tightened their grip upon the Democratic party.[78] But in 1850, and later, leaders still spoke of the "Calhoun wing" or the "States Rights party" almost as if it were a distinct organization.[79] Their strength lay chiefly in east-

---

[76]*Cong. Globe*, 32 Cong., 1 Sess., Appx., 282-285.

[77]Claiborne, *Life and Correspondence of John A. Quitman*, I, 211-15—a circular written by Quitman for his political friends, 1845. The factional differences in Mississippi may be traced quite readily in the correspondence of Quitman. In 1835, he wrote: ".... the people of this state are one-third for Van Buren, one-third Nullifiers, and one-third Whigs." P. 139. In December, 1838, he wrote: "I shall cooperate freely and boldly with all genuine Republicans, be they Democrats or Nullifiers, in asserting the principles to which I have alluded." P. 167. In 1845: "In politics I hold much the same position as Calhoun and Troup..... In 1844 I preferred, as I had before and do now, Mr. Calhoun to any other man for the presidency, but I acquiesced in the nomination of Van Buren, and, until the appearance of his anti-Texas letter, gave him my zealous support." P. 214.

[78]These statements are based upon numerous letters in the *Correspondence of John C. Calhoun, Correspondence of R. M. T. Hunter*, and *J. H. Hammond Papers*, as well as newspaper material, etc., and agree, I believe, with Ambler, *Thomas Ritchie and Sectionalism in Virginia*.

[79]*Correspondence of R. M. T. Hunter*, especially letters: James A. Seddon to Hunter, June 16, 1848; L. W. Tazewell to Hunter, Aug. 18, 1850; Seddon to Hunter, Feb. 7, 1852.

ern Virginia. Their leaders were very able; among them were R.
M. T. Hunter, J. M. Mason, James A. Seddon, Henry A. Wise,
Lewis E. Harvie, Beverly Tucker, William O. Goode, Wm. F.
Gordon, Willoughby Newton, Richard K. Crallé, M. R. H. Gar-
nett, and Edmund Ruffin. It was this wing that supported the
Nashville Convention and furnished most of the delegates;[80] in
this wing virtually all of the Virginia disunionists and those of
disunionist leanings were to be found in 1850.

Now, to be sure, the State Rights party claimed to be cham-
pions and defenders of slavery *par excellence*, as well as of other
Southern interests. But this claim was not admitted by their opponents, and had no basis in actual property interest in slaves.
The Whig party contained at least its proportionate share of the
slaveholders. Whig leaders claimed, with justification it seems,
that most of the large slaveholders belonged to their party. Whigs
had, of course, reasons for supporting the compromise measures
originating in the party considerations; for the administration
under whose auspices the measures were enacted was Whig. But
after all qualifications are made, no explanation of the alignment
of the parties and factions in the South upon the question of
Union or disunion is complete which does not take in account the
previous history and the origin of the parties.

[80]Tucker, Goode, Gordon, and Newton were delegates to the first session of
the Nashville Convention, and Gordon was the only representative of Virginia
in the second.

CHAPTER IV
PLANS FOR ESTABLISHING DIRECT TRADE WITH EUROPE, 1847-1860.

Although for a number of years after the direct trade conventions of the 1830s no attempts were made to revive Southern foreign commerce comparable to the efforts of those conventions, at no time did the people of the South become reconciled to commercial dependence upon the North. The suspension of the discussion of direct trade was due to the general stagnation of business and the distrust of all enterprise which characterized a period of several years following the commercial crisis of 1837.

In 1845 and 1846 there was discussion in Congress and the country at large of the policy of adopting the warehousing system. The system permitted goods imported from abroad to be placed in bonded warehouses with payments of duties when the goods were withdrawn, unless withdrawn for re-export, in which case no duties were to be collected. The warehousing system met with general favor in the South, and overenthusiastic individuals hailed it as the panacea which would restore Southern foreign commerce.[1] The cash duties system, they said, prevented Southern merchants, who generally had limited capital and credit, from importing for re-exportation, and gave the advantage to Northern importers of larger means. The warehousing system would enable New Orleans to become the half-way house between Europe and Mexico, and Charleston to conduct the commerce between Europe and the West Indies. According to the memorial to Congress from the New Orleans Chamber of Commerce, the want of a warehousing system had driven the Mexican trade to Havana.[2] J. D. B. DeBow thought that, if there was ever to be any foreign commerce in the South, such a system must have a great influence in bringing it about.[3] Congress enacted a warehousing law, effective August 6, 1846.[4] Being a step in the direction of

[1] *Southern Literary Messenger*, XI, 508, 567, 577, 584, articles by Lieut. M. F. Maury.
[2] *DeBow's Review*, II, 408.
[3] *Ibid.*, II, 193.
[4] *Acts and Resolutions*, 29 Cong., 1 Sess., p. 83.

free trade, it undoubtedly benefited commerce;[5] but more than a warehousing law was necessary to effect a revolution in the course of Southern trade.

With the reawakened spirit of progress in the South during the latter half of the fifth decade, came a general renewal of discussion of direct trade with Europe. This period witnessed a revival of prosperity in all parts of the Union. Numerous railroad projects took form, and construction upon a large scale was undertaken. With the extension of our national boundaries to the Pacific and the discovery of gold in California, grandiose schemes were conceived for establishing communication with the Pacific coast by rail or water. In the South one manifestation of the new spirit was a revival of the direct trade movement. In 1847 DeBow said the subject of direct trade was once again receiving attention;[6] and numerous long articles in his newly founded *DeBow's Review* attest to the revival of interest. He republished the proceedings of the Augusta and Charleston conventions and the reports of McDuffie, Hayne, Elmore, and Longstreet. "We would recall those scenes and times," he said.[7] But whereas in those times the direct trade movement was pretty much confined to the Atlantic seaboard, now it spread to the Gulf ports and the entire South. Until 1861 nothing was recognized with more steadfastness and unanimity as a proper element in the policy not only of seaports but of the South as a section than the encouragement of direct trade. It was a subject of constant discussion in the press. Conventions were held to consider plans for promoting it. It held a prominent place in all the sessions of the Southern Commercial Convention, which met regularly from 1852 to 1859, and was given consideration in the less regular Cotton Planters' Convention. Plans for achieving it demanded consideration from chambers of commerce, city councils, and state legislatures, as well as from individuals.

In the fifties, as in the thirties, commercial dependence was believed to be responsible for the transfer of much Southern wealth

---

[5] Lieutenant Maury wrote a few years later: "These importers [direct] and the warehousing system are recovering back for the South a portion of the direct trade." DeBow, *Industrial Resources*, III, 14.

[6] *DeBow's Review*, III, 557.

[7] *Ibid.*, III, 558.

to the North in the form of profits; as in the thirties, it was said that the Northern merchants and ship owners reaped large profits from importing for the Southern states and conducting their foreign and coastwise commerce. The estimated total of the sums abstracted from the yearly product of Southern industry in the form of importers' profits, interest upon advances, freight charges, insurance, commissions, port and wharf charges, and the expenses of Southern merchants who went North to purchase their stocks, had grown with the nation's commerce and shipping, and, by the processes of Southern arithmetic, had become enormous indeed. Said William Gregg: "It is a hopeless task to undertake to even approximate the vast sums of wealth which have been transferred from the South to the North by allowing the Northern cities to import and export for us."[8] Joseph Segar, of Virginia, cited the report of the Secretary of the Treasury showing the imports and exports of the United States for 1856 to have been $314,000,000 and $326,000,000 respectively. "Now the commercial profit of this vast amount of business inures almost exclusively to the north. The South has scarcely a say in the matter. She not only surrenders nearly all the profit on the import trade, but our productions—the basis of our exports—are mostly shipped to Northern cities, and thence reshipped in Northern bottoms to the foreign market, so that she actually loses the factorage on her own productions. Such a state of things is an annual loss to her of numerous millions, and her bitter reproach."[9] Another Virginian calculated, in 1853, that Virginia lost $9,539,037.76 annually by "allowing" New York to carry her trade.[10]

To such statements as these, and there were hundreds of them, it was not sufficient to reply, as Northern men frequently did, that what the North got was only a fair commercial remuneration.[11] True, people in the South considered the remuneration too great because the indirect course of trade, by reason of the greater mileage, the extra transhipments necessary, and the mediation of a greater number of middlemen, each of whom must exact a profit, made foreign goods more costly to the ultimate purchasers than

[8]*DeBow's Review*, XXIX, 82.
[9]*Ibid.*, XXII, 515.
[10]*Ibid.*, XIV, 501.
[11]Olmsted, *The Cotton Kingdom*, II, 301.

would the direct course. Many believed they were being exploited by Northern merchants and financiers, made the prey of manipulators, and made to pay extortionate prices. But the rather characteristic reply quoted above portrays inability or unwillingness to grasp the chief reasons for dissatisfaction in the South with the manner in which Southern commerce was conducted.

As in an earlier period discussed, so in this it was believed that Northern seaports owed their phenomenal growth and prosperity very largely to their control of Southern foreign commerce. It was a logical conclusion that, could this commerce be conducted by Southern seaports, they would enjoy like prosperity. And in the 1850s the people of every Southern seaport of any pretensions whatever had the natural and laudable ambition to make it a great commercial center. William S. Forrest in his *Sketches of Norfolk* rather naively related that upon September 26, 1850, the Honorable Henry A. Wise, of Accomac, "spoke with startling eloquence, and most convincing power of argument, of the reason that Norfolk is not already a great city, and of the means by which she may become a great Southern emporium."[12] There was much of this type of eloquence.

The public had no reason to be uninformed in regard to the relative advantages and disadvantages of every Southern port. The jealousy of rivals displayed in some of the cities is rather amusing, considering the inconsequence of the majority of them; although it had rather important influence upon the location of railroads in the South, and possibly some small influence detrimental to the success of projects for direct trade with Europe.

The citizens of Norfolk hoped much from her splendid harbor and strategic location at the entrance of the Chesapeake. Richmond, upon the James river, was a larger town, more centrally located with reference to Virginia, possessed of the advantage of being the capital of the state, and her people were determined to make her the commercial capital of Virginia, if not of a much larger territory. The people of North Carolina regretted the

---

[12]P. 260. The same thought recurs frequently, for example: "There are many thinking, practical, and intelligent men, who believe that Norfolk, at some not very distant period in the history of the world, will be a great city. Every person, who thinks upon the subject at all, knows well enough that the place is not what it ought long since to have been. P. 281. Forrest quoted Jefferson and Madison upon the future of Norfolk. P. 296, 297.

necessity of resorting to Charleston and Norfolk because of the want of a good port in their own state, and there was discussion of the possibility of making Wilmington a great Southern emporium. Charleston and Savannah were the only ports of any consequence upon a long stretch of coast line, and were rivals for the trade of several states. In the fifties Charleston was in many respects the most progressive city in the South.[13] With the exception of New Orleans, she had more citizens of wealth and better banking facilities than any other city south of Baltimore. Many of her merchants were natives or residents of long standing, and were imbued with a high degree of public spirit. Her chamber of commerce was aggressive and resourceful. On the other hand, Savannah, while she had all the drawbacks of Southern cities in general, possessed certain advantages of location from which much was hoped. She was more advantageously located for securing railroad connection with the West.

Until the vast possibilities of the railroad for changing the established course of trade were realized, the citizens of New Orleans never doubted that their city was destined to become the metropolis of America, situated as she was at the mouth of a river which drains half a continent, and strategically located with reference to the West Indies, Mexico, South America, and the Pacific.[14] Not until after about 1850 did the people of New Orleans awaken to a realization that the greatness of the city could not be insured merely by permitting time and nature to take their courses, but that they must resort to the methods less favored cities employed. Then the city government was reformed; radiating railroads were projected, and their construction was pushed vigorously. One, the New Orleans, Jackson, and Great Northern aimed at the Ohio; the other, the Opelousas and Western, pointed toward the west and was intended to be the first span of a road to the Pacific. Great interest was taken in projects to establish communication with the Pacific by way of the Isthmus of Tehuantepec. The rivals of New Orleans were not neighboring cities on

[13]Cf. Cordoza, J. N., *Reminiscences of Charleston*, 1866; Trenholm, W. L., *The Centennial Address before the Charleston Chamber of Commerce, 11th Feb., 1884.*

[14]Cf. Cable, Geo. W., *History and Present Condition of New Orleans, Tenth Census*, XIX, Pt. II, 213-95.

the Gulf, although citizens of Mobile regarded her as one, but cities of the Atlantic seaboard which were being connected with the Mississippi valley by railroads and inland waterways.

Mobile was the only other Gulf port of any consequence; her ambitions far exceeded her legitimate expectations. John Forsyth told of the aspirations and the sad deficiencies of Mobile in the same breath: "Mobile is but a chrysalis of commerce . . . . She stands trembling at the portals of a grand destiny which she has not the courage to enter, and paralyzed by the coward fear that the splendid columns and gilded domes, the sapphire pavements and rubied windows of the temple of commercial grandeur, are not for her enjoyment and realization."[15] This, of a town of about 25,000 inhabitants.

It was, then, from chambers of commerce, boards of trade, merchants, editors, and public spirited citizens and officials of Southern seaports that projects for establishing direct trade received much, if not most, of their support. But the achievement of commercial independence was represented not merely as a measure which would promote the prosperity of individual seaports, but also as one which would greatly benefit the South as a whole; the interest in it was not confined to the seaports but was general throughout the South.

The more general reasons why the loyal and progressive Southerners were very desirous of promoting the material development of the section have been given in connection with the account of the movement to bring the spindles to the cotton.[16] It was galling to their pride that their section should be languishing and dependent. They wanted a denser population, cities, towns, railroads, development of natural resources, and the social benefits which they believed would follow material development. They wished to prove by the actual accomplishment that, contrary to the contentions of its Northern and British antagonists, cities, commerce, manufactures, and the "arts of living" could flourish in a slave society. And, more important, they felt that the security of slavery could no longer be safely entrusted to constitutional guarantees and adroit political combinations, but that these must be supported by the power of wealth, numbers, and economic independ-

---

[15]Lecture on "The North and the South," *DeBow's Review*, XVII, 377.
[16]See ch. II.

ence. If, as was possible, the Union should be dissolved, these things would be essential to national existence.

Now direct trade and the retention at home of the "tribute" the South paid New York were expected to supply the capital which would build cities, give a stimulus to manufactures, mining, and agriculture, make possible stronger financial institutions, help finance railroads and other internal improvements, and, by consequence, invite immigration and, thus, redress the political preponderance of the non-slaveholding states. According to the report of the Committee of Ways and Means of the Alabama Legislature, "As the proper adjustment of our foreign and domestic trade, on the principle of economy laid down, involves the value of city, town, and county property, agricultural and manufacturing prosperity, the profits on bank, railroad, and canal stocks, as well as population and political power, it becomes one of the highest considerations to all classes."[17]

Furthermore, there were several evils in the Southern economic and social system for which it was believed the establishment of direct trade with Europe would be a specific remedy. One of these was the absence of a permanent mercantile class whose interests were identified with those of the South at large both financially and politically. The merchants of most Southern towns, interior as well as seaport, were largely Northern men or foreigners who looked upon their abode in the South as temporary. James Stirling said two-thirds or three-fourths of the commercial business was carried on by Northern men or foreigners.[18] Most of the cotton buyers and commission merchants were non-residents; the South was literally overrun by agents and collectors of Northern mercantile houses. "The merchants of the South, like the nobility of Ireland," wrote Lieutenant Maury, "are, for the most part, non-residents. At the season when the Southern staples are coming to market, these flock there from all quarters. When the crop is disposed of, they return whence they came, with their gains in their pockets, and, thus, a continued drain is kept upon that country."[19]

No city suffered more in this respect than New Orleans. The wealthy Creoles owned the real estate and lived upon its rental.

[17] *DeBow's Review*, XIV, 441.
[18] *Letters from the Slave States*, 320.
[19] *So. Lit. Mess.*, XI, 588.

They were extremely conservative, desired to keep down taxes, and opposed new enterprises. The men who directed commerce were strangers, who had no permanent stake in the city but preferred temporary gains to the future growth of the port. Their earnings were expended or invested chiefly in the North.[20] The busy season of New Orleans extended from October or November to the following spring. During this period thousands of laborers, attracted by high wages,' flocked to the city from the Northern states to return thence when the busy season closed. An English observer estimated that of the population from November to May fully a fourth part was migratory.[21]

Practically the whole business of Mobile, Alabama—commerce, banking, the few manufactures—was in the hands of Northern men. Savannah, Georgia, had a large Northern and foreign element; Augusta was known as a Yankee' town—the Yankee element was not transient in this case. Charleston suffered less from transients and temporary residents than any other Southern city or town. Virginia towns, in general, had a more permanent and more Southern population than those of the cotton states.

The want in so many Southern towns of a permanent mercantile class thoroughly identified with the interests of the section deprived the South of a class which, in every community, has much to do with the undertaking of new enterprises. It was largely responsible, too, for the small part cities played in determining state legislative policies. Then, thorough Southerners desired to be rid of the swarms of Northern agents, temporary residents, and migratory population, because they were felt to be unfriendly to slavery. Their presence, it was felt, would divide and distract Southern counsels. Their influence upon native non-slaveholding whites was feared.

Another feature of the economic system of the South which was greatly deplored, and which it was believed direct trade with Europe would go far toward remedying, was financial dependence upon the East, particularly New York City. This was coming to be considered a great evil at the time of the early direct trade

[20]*DeBow's Review*, XI, 77 ff., quoting a speech of James Robb in a Louisiana railroad convention, 1851.
[21]James Robertson, *A Few Months in America*, 66. Cf. Robert Russell, *North America*, 253. During the last decade before the war, however, conditions in New Orleans were considerably improved in this respect.

conventions; it was a matter of greater concern in the 1850s. The immense commerce of New York was believed responsible for the centralization there of so much of the financial power and operations of the country. If direct trade could be established, the importers' profits saved, and commercial centers built up, the banking institutions of the South would be strengthened, and thus enabled to meet the financial requirements of the section.[22]

The Southern people were largely dependent upon New York City for the financing of the marketing of their crops. Every fall when Southern staples began to move, planters and shippers made great demands for cash and credit. Southern banks made such loans as their facilities would permit, and in the case of New Orleans and Charleston they were by no means small; but the chief burden fell upon New York.

To make this clear it is necessary to review briefly the manner in which Southern crops, particularly cotton, were marketed. Virginia products (chiefly tobacco and grain) consumed outside the state were sold mostly in New York, even when destined to be exported to Europe. Of direct exports a large portion was bought and shipped by New York men.[23] Part of the cotton was sold in the ports to speculators and others, many of whom were New Yorkers. The remainder, and perhaps the larger part, was sold in the North or in England through factors and commission merchants representing New York or Liverpool houses. The planters or merchants received advances upon, or payment for, their cotton chiefly in the form of sixty-day sterling bills or four-months New York drafts. These bills and drafts were discounted by Southern banks and forwarded to New York, where they went to pay the debts of Southern merchants and others or to secure cash with which to purchase the other bills which came flooding in as the staples went forward. Sterling bills were bought in New York, of course, because there came the larger proportion of the imports and there normally was the demand for bills. Exchange was fre-

[22]*DeBow's Review*, XIV, 441; remarks of Mr. Wheeler in the Virginia House of Delegates, Richmond *Enquirer*, Dec. 10, 1852; D. M. Barringer, of N. C., in the Old Point direct trade convention, *ibid.*, Aug. 3; H. C. Cabell, of Virginia, *Hunt's Merchants' Magazine*, XLII, 323.

[23]"Letter of a Southern man to Governor Wise of Virginia," Richmond *Enquirer*, Jan. 9, 1856; editorial, *ibid.*, Dec. 17, 1852.

quently in favor of the South (especially was this true in the case of New Orleans), and at such times great sums of specie flowed South to find their way back to the North during the dull seasons of the year.[24]

It is evident that the moving of the cotton crop and, in a large measure, the price the planter received, depended upon the ability and willingness of New York to buy New York drafts and sterling bills. This was strikingly proven at the time of the financial crisis of 1857. The effect of the crash can best be studied at New Orleans, the greatest cotton exporting port in America. The crop of 1857 was short, and the price was expected to be high. Factors, finding money easy, "put out their acceptances" with a liberal hand, expecting the crop coming in to meet all engagements. Cotton went on the market at 16½ cents, with sterling selling at 109¼ to 109½. On September 25 word came from New York that exchange was almost unsaleable. Money became tighter and tighter; sterling fell to 92½-97; and presently banks refused to take it at any price. Cotton buyers withdrew from the market. A large portion of the cotton crop sold for several cents less than the promised price.[25]

The crash brought the evils of financial dependence home to the South as they had never been brought before. Southern journals and writers pointed out that the South had not been responsible for the panic. There had been no speculation in the South, they said. True, she had embarked largely upon railroad building, but because of the scarcity of capital the building had been sanely and economically done. The South was in a position to enter upon a flood-tide of prosperity, "And yet—and yet—almost in the twinkling of an eye, with the suddenness of an earthquake, and unexpectedly as a stroke of lightning from a cloudless sky, cotton was struck down, and became almost unsalable in the

[24]Kettell, *Southern Wealth and Northern Profits*, ch. VII; *Hunt's Merchants' Magazine*, XXIX, 60; XLII, 318; report of a committee of the Cotton Planters' Convention, Macon, 1858, in *DeBow's Review*, XXV, 713 f.; Stone, A. H., "The Cotton Factorage System of the Southern States," *Amer. Hist. Rev.*, XX, 557-65.

[25]New Orleans *Daily Picayune*, June 1, 1858; *Hunt's Merchants' Magazine*, XLII, 315, from "Banking at the South with Reference to New York City," by H. C. Cabell, of Virginia.

[26]*Hunt's Merchants' Magazine*, XLII, 315.

Southern market."[26] The South lost millions of dollars ($35,000,-
000, said Senator J. H. Hammond in his "Mud Sill" speech)[27]
upon the crop of the year 1857-1858.

The New Orleans *Picayune* pointed out the anomaly of the
greatest exporting port in America being "stranded because of a
money panic in Wall Street"— cotton selling at 10 cents a pound
while it was 18 or 19 in London.[28] The moral was drawn that,
had the South direct trade, there would have been a demand at
home for sterling bills, and cotton could have gone forward without waiting for the recovery of New York. The *Picayune* dared
hope that the disturbance caused by the panic might result in direct trade for the South: "The power on which we have been dependent so long has at length given way, and almost without
knowing it, we have come or are about to come, actually to realize
in practice what has hitherto been considered by many an idle
dream—direct trade with Europe. And should this step . . . .
result in our permanent emancipation from a system whose advantages are far outnumbered by their disadvantages—a system
which wrings from us annually, without any return except the loss
of influence and of power, millions of hard earned dollars—we
should think the financial crisis, with all its manifold evils, cheap
to us."[29]

The immense loss occasioned the South by the crash of September, 1857, was but a striking example of the evils of the centralization of commerce and finance in New York. The cotton states, as
did the West for that matter, experienced to a less degree the evils
of centralization every fall when the crops were moved. During
the idle months funds found their way to New York, there to be
used in business or speculation. When the crops of the South and
West began to move, there was a tightness in the money market,
which operated to depress prices.[30] And this did not signify, as
some planters asserted, that New York financial interests were

[27]*Cong. Globe*, 35 Cong., 1 Sess., 961.
[28]Quoted in *DeBow's Review*, XXIII, 656 f.
[29]This is a very moderate statement. For a less temperate one see *ibid.*,
XXIII, 657-9, quoting the Vicksburg *True Southron*.
[30]Kettell, *Southern Wealth and Northern Profits*, 93, 94.

interested in forcing down the price of cotton.[31] It was far preferable to be dependent upon the money power of New York than upon the money power of London; for normally New York was interested in keeping the prices up. Since the Southern staple constituted the chief export of the country, and there was a quite steady demand for it in the world's markets, it became the basis for securing credit in Europe. The cotton crop was at once an index to Northern manufacturers and merchants of the South's ability to buy in the home markets and of the nation's ability to purchase abroad. The solicitude with which the business interests of New York, especially in time of depression, looked forward to the moving of cotton and speculated as to the crop and the price it would bring, abundantly testifies to the role cotton played in keeping the wheels of credit in motion. At the time of the crisis of 1857, New York financial circles considered it essential to revival that cotton continue to move, whatever the price, and hoped the planters would be willing to let it go forward at the low prices shippers could afford to offer.[32]

The cotton planters were not the cnly ones who suffered from the financial dependence of the South upon the North. All who sought to embark in business, to start manufactures, to develop the mineral resources of the country, found themselves handicapped by their inability to secure proper financial support at home. Most of the railroad bonds, for example, had to be sold either in New York or other Northern cities or abroad. No won-

---

[31]Mr. Wheeler of Portsmouth said in the Virginia House of Delegates, Dec. 2, 1852: "...the price, the worth, the market value of all we and the people we represent own of every kind of property, is dependent upon the speculative pleasure of the Merchants, the Bankers, and Brokers of New York. And why? Because Wall Street can depress the money market when it pleases." Richmond *Enquirer*, Dec. 7, 1852. See also A. Dudley Mann, *DeBow's Review*, XXIV, 373.

[32]*Hunt's Merchants' Magazine*, XXXVII, 583. Some of the cotton had not been advanced upon, and the planters were able to hold it; but much of the cotton did go forward. The importance of its movement to Northern business was not overlooked in the South. "What saved you?" asked Senator Hammond. "Fortunately for you it was the commencement of the cotton season, and we have poured in upon you one million six hundred thousand bales of cotton just at the crisis to save you from sinking. That cotton, but for the bursting of your speculative bubbles in the North . . . would have brought us $100,000,000. We have sold it for $65,000,000, and saved you." *Cong. Globe*, 35 Cong., 1 Sess., 961.

der the people of the Southern states, at a time when there was almost a mania for railroad building, when they were becoming aware of the existence of considerable mineral resources and the possession of great advantages for certain lines of manufactures, should chafe at, and try to be free from, the necessity of waiting for the favor of distant money markets before entering upon a career of expansion. Said a correspondent of the Charleston *Courier,* 1854: "At present our principal sources for obtaining funds are through the capitalists of the North and Europe. So long as we are thus dependent, so long may we expect to be used for their benefit, and be made subservient to their interests. When they cannot find better investment they will advance to us freely, and leave us when they can find others more profitable."[33]

A good illustration of the way in which attempts to inaugurate new enterprises in the South were handicapped by the financial deficiencies of the section is found in the efforts which were made to establish direct trade with Europe; for commercial vassalage was effect as well as cause of financial vassalage. Just as they had done in the thirties, retail merchants in the South bought of Northern jobbers on long credit—often twelve months. To compete with the Northern jobbers, Southern importers and jobbers would also have to extend the long credits. But while the Northern jobbers could procure funds upon their long time paper, the Southern importers found it difficult or impossible to discount long time paper in Southern banks.

The reference to long credits raises the question whether after all, had it not been for this pernicious system, the credit facilities of the South might not have been sufficient to permit the launching of many more new enterprises than were actually launched. The New Orleans *Commercial Bulletin* enumerated the greater facilities of the merchants of Northern cities for the extension of long credits as one of the reasons why New Orleans had lost much trade in the South and West: "The twelve months credit system did the business, and attracted an immense amount of Western and Southwestern trade to those cities, which would have otherwise sought this port."[34] In the opinion of the Mobile *Tribune* the South was bound to the North by long credits: destroy that sys-

[33]April 7, 1854.
[34]*Hunt's Merchants' Magazine,* XXXIII, 263.

tem and there might be some chance for direct trade.[35] In fact, just as in the period of the early direct trade conventions, the long credits system was frequently denounced and deplored, and the people were frequently urged to free themselves from it. Yet, it must be said, the people of the Southern states took long credits too much as a matter of course, and did not adequately realize their viciousness. There was almost no other factor that operated so effectively to retard the accumulation of capital in the South. The Southern people paid for these long advances and paid dearly. They paid in interest. They paid in increased prices of articles consumed; for, because of the precarious nature of much of the Southern trade, risks were great, and Northern merchants insured themselves well against such risks. They paid, often, in the sacrifice in the prices of their staples incurred because of forced sales necessary to procure money to meet their obligations at maturity. J. L. Crocheran, of Alabama, said the South put herself at the mercy of speculators by forcing one-third of her cotton into the market in two months in order to pay advances received during twelve.[36]

The financial dependence of the Southern states was not credited only to the absence of foreign commerce, cities, accumulated capital, and varied industries; there was considerable dissatisfaction with the banking system. It was thought by some that the banking laws were too conservative in several of the states. The policies of the banks were criticized on the score that they contributed to the centralization at New York.[37] Representatives of the mercantile interests complained that banks were partial to the agricultural interests. It would take us too far from the subject of this chapter to enter into a discussion of the bank laws and banking operations in the several states. It would seem that in

[35]*Hunt's Merchants' Magazine*, XXXIII, 264. The dissatisfaction with the long credits system was not entirely confined to the South. Some New York men felt that the Southern trade was hardly worth the risks involved. *Ibid.*, XXXIV, 522, article, "Some Suggestions on Southern Trade."

[36]*DeBow's Review*, XXV, 40.

[37]Cabell, H. C., "Banking in the South with Reference to New York City," *Hunt's Merchants' Magazine*, XLII, 311-323; letters of "A Southern Man" to Gov. Wise of Virginia, Richmond *Enquirer*, Jan. 9, 11, Feb. 11, 1856; Gregg, William, *DeBow's Review*, XXIX, 495; Kettell, *Southern Wealth and Northern Profits*, ch. VII; Fitzhugh, *Sociology for the South*, chs. IX, X.

three states, Louisiana, South Carolina, and Georgia, banking
facilities were as adequate as the volume of business done would
justify; there, too, the bankers pursued enlightened policies.[38]
There was undoubtedly great improvement in banking conditions
during the fifties.

There were difficulties to be overcome before direct importations could be established other than deficiency of capital and
credit, the long credit system, or the absence of a thoroughly
Southern mercantile class. One lay in the comparatively small
amounts of foreign goods consumed in the South. There is no
way of calculating accurately the value of the foreign imports
consumed in territory naturally tributary to Southern seaports;
but the probabilities are that it did not so greatly exceed the
direct importations as Southerners generally supposed. Some
Southern writers made the palpably untenable assumption that
the Southern population consumed foreign goods equal in value to
their exports to foreign countries, that is about two-thirds or
three-fourths of the nation's exports, or imports.[39] More reasonable was the assumption that the *per capita* consumption of imported goods in the South was equal to that of the North;[40] but
even that would seem to have been too liberal. A much higher
percentage of the Northern population was urban; and the *per
capita* consumption of articles of commerce by an urban population is greater than the *per capita* consumption by a rural population. Southern writers made much of the number of rich families
in the South who bought articles of luxury imported from abroad;
but there is no doubt that the number of families who lived in
luxury was exaggerated. That the slaves consumed comparatively small quantities of foreign goods requires no demonstration.
Their clothing and rough shoes were manufactured either in the
North or at home. Their chief articles of food (corn and bacon)
were produced at home or in the West. The large poor white
element in the population consumed few articles of commerce,

[38]Cordoza, J. N., *Reminiscences of Charleston*, 44 ff.; Trenholm, W. L., *The
Centennial Address before the Charleston Chamber of Commerce*, 31 ff.; Gregg,
William, *Speech...on a Bill to Amend an Act entitled 'An Act to authorize
aid to the Blue Ridge Railroad Company'* .... *Dec. 8, 1856*, p. 29.
[39]For example, M. R. H. Garnett, *The Union, Past and Present, How It
Works and How to Save It.* Cf. *DeBow's Review*, XVIII, 294 ff.
[40]Richmond *Enquirer*, April 23, 1852, letter signed "Self Dependence."

either domestic or foreign. The same is true of the rather large mountaineer element, because, if for no other reason, they lived beyond the routes of trade. Olmsted had these classes in mind when he wrote: "I have never seen reason to believe that with absolute free trade the cotton States would take a tenth part of the value of our present importations."[41] One of the fairest of the many English travelers wrote: "But the truth is, there are few imports required, for every Southern town tells the same tale."[42]

That portion of the proceeds of Southern exports to foreign countries which was not expended for foreign imports was expended for the products of the North and West. The sales from the South into other sections of the Union were sufficient to pay for only a fraction of the commodities purchased there for Southern consumption. The value of the cotton exported was greater by far than the value of all other Southern exports combined; yet in a normal year less than one-fourth of the cotton went to the North.[43] The exports to the North and West of sugar and molasses, tobacco, rice, grain and flour, timber, turpentine, and naval stores were considerably larger in proportion to the exports of the same commodities to foreign markets; but hardly large enough in the aggregate to pay for the imports from those sections.[44] J. H. Hammond estimated that in 1857 the South sold products abroad to the value of $185,000,000, and to the North and West to the value of $35,000,000.[45] The latter sum is undoubtedly too small; but a liberal estimate could not place the value of the exports to

[41] *Cotton Kingdom*, I, 27.
[42] Robert Russell, *North America*, 290.
[43] Donnell, *History of Cotton, passim*. In the year 1854, for example, 737,000 bales of cotton were shipped North as against 2,528,000 exported to Europe.
[44] According to the estimate of the New Orleans *Price Current*, in the year 1858-1859 four-fifths of the sugar and three-fourths of the molasses exported coastwise from New Orleans went to Baltimore and points north. *DeBow's Review*, XXVII, 477. Sugar and molasses were also sent up the Mississippi in large quantities. The exports of these commodities to foreign countries were not large. Of the tobacco exported from New Orleans about three-fourths went to foreign countries. *Ibid.*, X, 448. No other Southern products were exported from New Orleans in large quantities.
[45] *Cong. Globe*, 35 Cong., 1 Sess., 961. The value of the cotton alone shipped North in 1857-1858 was about $32,000,000. Hammond, *Cotton Industry*, table opposite p. 358. Because of the panic of 1857, the consumption of cotton was less than normal.

the North and West at much more than 50 per cent of the value of the exports to foreign countries. On the other hand, there was almost universal testimony that Southern purchases of Northern and Western commodities greatly exceeded in value the direct and indirect imports from abroad. Most of the big items of Southern consumption were furnished almost entirely by the North or West. Practically all of the boots and shoes came from Massachusetts; coarse cottons came from New England; the agricultural implements not manufactured at home came from the North and West, as did harness and saddles, carriages and coaches, wagons, locomotives, and railroad cars, engines, furniture, and numerous other articles. Great quantities of bacon, pork, lard, and corn were shipped from the Northwest down the Mississippi to be consumed in the cotton states. The cotton states also bought large numbers of mules, horses, and cattle in Kentucky and Missouri, states which in the fifties received practically none of their imports, Northern or foreign, by way of Southern ports.[46] In 1839 a committee of the Charleston Direct Trade Convention had found that one-third of the goods consumed in the South were of Northern production;[47] fifteen or twenty years later no one estimated the value of the foreign goods at more than one-half that of the goods of Northern and Western production. Daniel Lord, a Northern writer, said the South imported from the North ten dollars in domestic productions for every one imported directly or indirectly from Europe.[48]

The ability of the Southern people to purchase their proportionate share of the nation's imports was further diminished, of course, by the payment of those freights, profits, interests, commissions, charges, and expenses which went to Northern men, and which the advocates of a direct course of trade were so anxious to save. Thus the very commercial dependence under which the South

[46]St. Louis was the distributing center for Missouri and parts of Kentucky and Tennessee. Cincinnati and Louisville were distributing centers for Kentucky and parts of Tennessee. In the fifties these cities received practically all of their foreign and Northern goods from the East by interior routes. Western Virginia traded with Cincinnati and Baltimore. Baltimore was rarely classified as a Southern city by men from farther south.

[47]*DeBow's Review*, IV, 495.

[48]Lord, Daniel, *The Effect of Secession upon the North and the South* (pamphlet, 1860), p. 15.

chafed was one of the causes for the want of demand which made the establishment of a more rational system difficult. There was logic in the contention of the advocates of direct trade that, could it once be inaugurated, the saving effected would increase the South's ability to buy, and the increased demand would in turn help to firmly esablish the system.

The meagre demand for imported goods rendered it necessary for Southern importers to keep assorted stocks and for long periods. In the North, on the contrary, the demand was large enough to permit importers to specialize, and sure enough to enable them to replenish their stocks at frequent intervals. The commerce of a port like New York was so great that it offered a certain market for any cargo and certain freights for any part of the world.[49] Frequently cargoes were sold at auction in New York and Philadelphia, sometimes at ruinous prices, against which the importers of smaller cities could not compete. But whatever the demand for imported goods in the South, the demand for Northern goods was much greater. A large number of vessels was engaged in the coastwise trade. The same vessels which carried Northern goods to the South also carried the indirect imports of foreign goods. Often Southern merchants went to Baltimore, Philadelphia, or New York to lay in their stocks of Northern goods, and while there could buy merchandise of foreign origin as well.[50] "Almost every country merchant who visits Charleston has a through ticket for New York in his pocket," wrote William Gregg.[51]

The question may occur, Why did not Southern seaports thrive as distributing centers for the coastwise commerce? The explanation lies in part in the fact just alluded to: Many interior merchants purchased of Northern rather than Southern jobbers. Gregg attributed this to a preference of the people for goods from New York and to the hostility of banks to the mercantile interests— shown by their refusal to extend the support necessary to enable the Southern jobbers to extend the long credits which customers demanded. Charleston jobbers could sell cheaper than New York jobbers, he said, and there was no adequate reason why Charles-

[49]Cf. Richmond *Whig*, Mar. 11, 1851, editorial.
[50]*DeBow's Review*, XXIX, 500, 556.
[51]*Ibid.*, XXIX, 776.

ton should not become a distributing center even without direct trade.[52] Whether the banks did not support the mercantile interests because they would not-or because they could not, it is evident that the Southern jobber and the importer suffered alike in this respect. Another writer said the country merchant bought from the Northern jobber because he knew that the Southern jobber bought his stocks in New York, and he did not wish to pay two sets of jobbers' profits.[53] But there was a deeper reason why the seaports did not grow and prosper as distributing centers: the quantity of goods to be distributed was too small. The commerce of the Southern states was practically limited to transporting a few staples from the interior to the coast and exporting them, and to receiving foreign and Northern goods at the seaports and transporting them into the interior. There was little internal commerce. There was no home market for Southern products. When the first railroads were put in operation, there was general disappointment at the lightness of the traffic upon them. There was little to carry but cotton, which is not a bulky article. It is noteworthy that before the Civil War there was hardly an interior town in the South worthy of mention as a distributing center. In general, Southerners attached too much importance to exporting and importing as factors in the growth of cities. They overestimated the part foreign commerce was playing in the progress of Northern cities, not excepting New York, and underestimated the roles of domestic commerce and manufactures, including shipbuilding.[54] Today, of the eleven cities in the South having over 100,000 inhabitants each, only three are seaports, and the total population of these three is but 35 per cent of the total population of the entire number.

Mercantile business in the South labored under serious disadvantages also from the great variations, from year to year, in the

---

[52]*DeBow's Review*, loc. cit.

[53]*Ibid.*, XII, 300.

[54]There were exceptions; see, for example, a speech of James Robb, of New Orleans, in a railroad convention, 1851. "No city ever grew great by commerce alone. Go back as far as they might, select the most favorably located cities in the world, and they would find their prosperity was transient, evanescent, compared with that of towns situated in the interior, where industry and labor were cultivated and flourished...." *DeBow's Review*, XI, 78. See also *Hunt's Merchants' Magazine*, XXXIV, 137, quoting the New Orleans *Commercial Bulletin*; *DeBow's Review*, XXIX, 630, William Gregg.

ability of the planters to buy, resulting, in turn, from the wide fluctuations in the cotton crop and cotton prices.[55] In the seaports it was rendered precarious by the frequent visitations of yellow fever.[56] The unhealthiness of the ports was partly responsible for absenteeism and the general stagnation of business during the summer months, when many merchants went North or to the interior. Another reason for cessation of business activity in the summer was the fact that the cotton went to market in the fall and winter. This idleness during a large part of the year, together with the lack of variety and stability in the export trade, goes far to explain why the South did not support a larger merchant marine. During the cotton season ships from all quarters were impressed into service, and at its close returned to other employment.[57]

The bars in Southern harbors with the notable exception of Norfolk were shallow; and the fast clipper ships, which carried so much of the world's commerce, could not enter. Large vessels were anchored some thirty miles below Mobile, and were loaded and unloaded by means of lighters.[58] A special type of vessel was constructed to carry cotton from New Orleans.[59] New Orleans citizens were most persistent in appealing to Congress for appropriations for improving the navigation of the Mississippi; but the sums granted were not a tithe of the amount necessary. Elsewhere in the South, the constitutional scruples of congressmen prevented them from demanding the inclusion in rivers and har-

[55]New Orleans *Daily Picayune*, Jan. 14, 1858.
[56]Norfolk was scourged by yellow fever in 1853. Two out of three of the whites died. Burton, H. W., *The History of Norfolk* (1877), p. 23. Enterprise in Norfolk received a blow from which it took several years to recover. *Third Annual Report of the Merchants' and Mechanics' Exchange of Norfolk, Virginia, Jan., 1860.* The same year the plague raged in other Southern towns. In New Orleans it was long remembered as the year of the great plague. There 8215 people died between May 21 and October 31. A vivid description is in *DeBow's Review*, XV, 595-635.
[57]Kennedy, Joseph P., *The Border States, Their Power and Duty*, etc. (1860), p. 25.
[58]Olmsted, *Cotton Kingdom*, I, 283; Hamilton, Peter J., *Mobile under Five Flags*, 270.
[59]DeBow, *Industrial Resources*, III, 16

bors bills of items for the improvement of Southern harbors.[60] The bill of 1852 appropriated $50,000 for the improvement of Charleston harbor. The appropriation was accepted, but proved entirely inadequate.[61] President Pierce vetoed the first general rivers and harbors bill presented to him, 1854, and after that no others were passed before the Civil War, largely because of the constitutional objections raised by Southern Democrats. In 1854 a convention at Wilmington, North Carolina, said to be the largest convention which had been assembled in the state, memorialized Congress in favor of an appropriation for improving the bar at Wilmington. The appropriation was secured by the North Carolina delegation in Congress, William S. Ashe, a staunch Democrat, having charge of the bill in the House.[62] In 1857 the City of Charleston undertook to dredge out the channel in the harbor at her own expense, but the enterprise was soon abandoned.[63] A year later Senator Hammond wrote: "Time, I think, will show that vessels of 1000 tons are as profitable as larger ones, to carry our trade, and these can enter our ports."[64]

The discussion of direct trade included consideration of ways and means to promote it. There were innumerable eloquent appeals to the Southern states and to Southern cities to "shake off their lethargy," to "rouse themselves from their slumbers," and to emulate the example of their Northern "sisters." Individuals were advised to devote their time and their capital to an enterprise so well calculated to promote the prosperity of their section. Commercial education was declared desirable, and a few professorships of commerce were established. Retail merchants and the people in general were urged to patronize those merchants of Southern seaports who imported goods of foreign production directly from

[60]Senator Benjamin, of Louisiana, stated, 1854, that Virginia had not accepted a dollar of the money voted to her for this purpose during the twenty years preceding. Senator Mason, of Virginia, confirmed the statement. *Cong., Globe*, 33 Cong., 1 Sess., Appx., 1201.

[61]*Report of the Commissioners Appointed at the Last Session of the General Assembly to Inquire into the Feasibility of Improving the Channels of the Bar and Other Approaches of Charleston Harbor. Nov. 20, 1852*, p. 5.

[62]*Cong. Globe*, 33 Cong., 1 Sess., 1654, ff. Ashe said the last Legislature had unanimously instructed the North Carolina representatives in Congress to work for the appropriation.

[63]Charleston *Mercury*, July 12, 1859.

[64]*Ibid.*, April 12, 1859.

abroad in preference to those who bought such goods in the North. A rather strong sentiment developed in favor of the imposition by the state legislatures of discriminatory taxes upon goods of foreign production imported into the respective states by way of Northern ports.[65] As in the thirties, much was hoped from the construction of railroads, particularly those which opened new territory or were calculated to attract the trade of the Ohio valley to Southern ports. More specific were the many projects for establishing steamship lines between Southern and European or South American ports and the attempts to induce European interests to establish steamship lines to the South.

Before 1839 only a few steamships had crossed the Atlantic. By 1850 the steamship was rapidly supplanting the sailing vessel in carrying mails, passengers, and the lighter sorts of freight. Great Britain had embarked upon a policy of encouraging the development of a steam marine by granting liberal subsidies, and the United States had followed suit by making liberal contracts with steamship companies for carrying the mails to Europe and elsewhere.[66] The ports selected as terminii for steamship lines evidently had great advantages in foreign commerce over those which had to depend upon sailing vessels alone. There were, for example, the advantages of greater regularity and saving of time; and as the mails and passengers sought the steamlines, it was natural that the importing business should follow the same routes.[67] Needless to say New York captured the lion's share of the steamship lines, and thereby increased her hold upon the nation's commerce. These facts explain why so many of the plans formed in the South for achieving commercial independence involved the establishment of lines of regular steamers between Southern and foreign ports.

In no state were more schemes for rehabilitation discussed than in Virginia. For several years prior to 1850 internal improvements had been an absorbing topic in that state. Among the improvements projected or under construction none figured more prominently than the Virginia and Tennessee railroad, which was to run

[65]The subjects of patronage of home importing merchants and discriminatory taxation are discussed in ch. VI.

[66]*Cong. Globe*, 31 Cong., 1 Sess., 1860; Bates, *American Navigation: the Political History of Its Rise and Ruin*, 346.

[67]See Richmond *Whig*, March 11, 1851.

from Lynchburg to the Tennessee line in the direction of Knoxville, and was designed to be a link in a chain of railroads from
the Chesapeake to Memphis and New Orleans. Another project
was the connection of the Chesapeake and the Ohio valley either
by canal, as some advocated, or by railroad. Besides increasing
the transportation facilities of the sections through which they
ran, these roads were expected to bring to Virginia ports, Richmond, Petersburg, and Norfolk, trade from the Mississippi and
Ohio valleys, and together with foreign commerce, which they
would help to stimulate, restore to the Old Dominion the commercial position she once possessed. The political crisis of 1850
served to call attention sharply to the dependent position of the
South, and lent a strong impetus to movements for commercial
independence. At this juncture the Portsmouth *Pilot* was led to
suggest a direct trade convention to meet at Old Point Comfort,
July 4, 1850.

The Old Point Comfort Convention, while not well attended,
enrolled among its delegates some very respectable men of Virginia and neighboring states.[68] The reasons which had brought the
delegates together were made very clear by the debates. Thomas
L. Preston described the advantages Virginia possessed for securing Western trade. Senator Morehead, of Kentucky, assured his
auditors that Kentucky was with the South in interests, feelings,
and associations, and preferred railroad communication with Virginia to connection with the North. Congressman Ewing, of
Tennessee, gave the warning that the safety of the South depended
upon preserving the equilibrium of the sections, which could be
done by developing commerce and manufactures in the South.
R. K. Meade, of Virginia, emphasized the profits derived by the
North from conducting Virginia's commerce, and the saving which
would be effected if the South would do her own business. The
resolutions adopted by the convention declared it to be the duty
of the Federal government to extend as much aid to a Southern
mail line to Europe as to Northern lines, recommended state
appropriations in aid of a line of steamers, and provided for a
committee to memorialize Congress and the Virginia Legislature.

In the closing days of the first session of the Thirty-first
Congress an unsuccessful attempt was made to secure favorable

---

[68] Proceedings are in the Richmond *Enquirer*, July 9, 12, 1850.

action upon a bill providing for government aid for lines of steamers from California to China and from Philadelphia to Antwerp. A. W. Thompson, a Philadelphia capitalist, was to be the contractor. Senator James M. Mason, of Virginia, moved an amendment to the bill stipulating that the Atlantic line should alternate trips between Norfolk and Philadelphia. The amendment was accepted by the sponsors of the bill.[69] In the short session of the same Congress (1850-1851) Congressmen Meade and Bocock, of Virginia, tried to secure the passage of a similar bill based upon Thompson's plan and the memorial of the Old Point Comfort Convention; but it was defeated,[70] largely because of the opposition of McLane, of Maryland, who was charged with fearing that aid to a Norfolk line might compromise Baltimore's claims to government subsidy for a line of her own,[71] and because of the opposition of one or two Virginia representatives who could not overcome their constitutional scruples against government subsidies. Meanwhile, Thompson, taking advantage of the state of mind in Virginia, had petitioned the General Assembly for aid in establishing the projected line between Norfolk and Antwerp.[72] He stood ready to advance two-fifths of the capital required, provided the state would loan him the use of Virginia six per cent bonds for ten years for the remaining three-fifths. Another proposal submitted to the General Assembly about the same time was that a joint stock company be chartered, three-fifths of whose stock should be subscribed by the state, and two-fifths by municipal and private corporations and by individuals.[73] A select committee of the House of Delegates reported in favor of Thompson's proposition; but its friends were unable to secure action before the Legislature adjourned, 1851.[74]

In September, 1851, a well attended Mercantile Convention was held in Richmond for the purpose of creating public interest in direct trade and working out a plan in support of which all inter-

---

[69]*Cong. Globe,* 31 Cong., 1 Sess., 2051.

[70]*Ibid.,* 31 Cong., 2 Sess., 600, 613, 754, 768.

[71]*Ibid.,* 31 Cong., 2 Sess., 601, 613; Richmond *Whig,* Feb. 25, 1851. McMullin, of Virginia, spoke against the bill. *Cong. Globe,* 31 Cong., 2 Sess., 758.

[72]*Virginia Documents,* 1850-1851, doc. LXVI.

[73]*Ibid.,* 1850-1851, doc. LXX.

[74]*Ibid.,* 1850-1851, doc. LXX; Richmond *Whig,* March 15, 1851.

ests and factions in the state could unite.[75] It proved impossible to harmonize differences. The convention divided upon the question whether a line of steamers should be recommended or it should be left to future investigation to determine which was preferable, steamers or sailing vessels. The latter alternative was adopted. A resolution calling for Federal aid provoked a cleavage along party lines, and had to be withdrawn. Resolutions offered by D. H. London, Richmond importer and president of the Central Southern Rights Association of Virginia, in favor of discriminatory taxation of indirect imports were tabled by an almost unanimous vote after an acrimonious debate. The net official act of the convention was a blanket resolution in favor of lines of steamers or sailing vessels to Europe and South America.

In May, 1852, the State Senate passed a bill based on A. W. Thompson's plan;[76] but the House of Delegates allowed it to go over to the next session, when, in spite of the support of Governor Johnson, John Y. Mason, and an all but unanimous press, it was defeated.[77] The defeat was due to inability to agree upon the mode and time of lending state aid, and to the rivalry of the little bay ports.[78] It was the same spirit of jealousy which stood in the way of the adoption of a practicable policy of internal improvements. The net result of all the discussion and wire-pulling of three years was practically *nil* as far as foreign commerce was concerned; they did serve in a measure the secondary purpose of securing tidewater support for state aid to railroads to the West. Shortly after the Old Point Comfort Convention New York interests established a line of steamships between New York and the Chesapeake; Virginians thought the action had been influenced by the movements in that state looking to the establishment of direct trade.[79] In 1851 Richmond firms began shipping flour to

[75]Proceedings are in the Richmond *Whig*, Sept. 11, 12, and 17, 1851. The report from the Committee of 13, William Burwell, chairman, is in *Virginia Documents*, 1851-1852, doc. I, p. 41 ff.; also in *DeBow's Review*, XII, 30-41.

[76]Richmond *Enquirer*, Dec. 7, 1852.

[77]Governor Joseph Johnson's message of Dec. 5, 1853. *Virginia Documents*, 1853-1854, doc. I. Letter of J. Y. Mason to D. H. London, Sept. 18, 1852. *So. Lit. Mes.*, XVIII, 591 ff. Cf. Richmond *Enquirer*, Dec. 7, 1852. Mason had once been secretary of the navy.

[78]Forrest, Wm. S., *Sketches of Norfolk*, 296; Richmond *Enquirer*, Apr. 30, 1852.

[79]*Ibid.*, Dec. 10, 1852. Cf. *DeBow's Review*, XIV, 501.

Rio de Janeiro and importing hides, coffee, and other South American products. This trade had attained some importance by 1860.[80] While these plans and projects were being debated in Virginia, projects elsewhere had come to naught. The people of South Carolina late in 1850 were considering secession. The time was considered auspicious for inaugurating communication with Europe by a line of steamers. A number of citizens of Charleston secured from the State Legislature a charter for the South Carolina and European Steamship Company to build two steamers to ply between Charleston and Liverpool. Subscription books were opened and the stock promptly taken. One of the steamers, the South Carolina, was built—at Green Port, Long Island—and proceeded to Charleston. After loading, it was found she could not pass the bar. The vessel was sold, and the project abandoned.[81] The only line of steamships between Charleston and a foreign port before the war was the mail line to Havana, established in 1847 and owned by M. C. Mordecai, of Charleston. The mail steamers between New York and Chagres touched regularly at Charleston and Savannah. The Alabama Legislature, 1852, chartered the Alabama Direct Trade and Exchange Company with power to own ships, buy and sell produce and manufactures at home and abroad, receive deposits, deal in domestic and foreign exchange, and make advances on produce, manufactures, and merchandise.[82] No tangible results followed.

Considerable interest was manifested throughout the South, 1852-1854, in a proposal to establish a line of steamers between some Southern port and the mouth of the Amazon river and in the question of the free navigation of the Amazon. Peru and Bolivia, upon the headwaters of the Amazon, declared the river open to the commerce of the world, but Brazil refused to allow foreign vessels to navigate it. Lieutenant M. F. Maury, Superintendent of the Naval Observatory at Washington, became interested in the subject and memorialized Congress, May, 1852, to establish a line of mail steamers between Norfolk, Charleston, or Savannah and Pará. He further suggested that diplomatic efforts

[80]*DeBow's Review*, XII, 32.
[81]A. Brisbane to Hammond, Feb. 25, 1851, *J. H. Hammond Papers; DeBow's Review*, X, 203, 315; XVIII, 68; *National Intelligencer*, Oct. 18, 1851; Richmond *Enquirer*, June 7, 1853.
[82]*DeBow's Review*, X, 445-47; XIII, 318; XIV, 437-49.

be made to secure the free navigation of the Amazon.[83] He appealed to Secretary of State Webster to take the matter up, but Webster refused to move.[84] A series of long articles by Maury on "Amazonia" was published in *DeBow's Review* and the leading newspapers of the South.[85] Maury presented the subject in the Southern Commercial Convention at Baltimore, December, 1852.[86] The subject was given consideration at the sessions of the Commercial Convention in Memphis and Charleston, 1853 and 1854; both endorsed the project for a line of mail steamers.[87] Maury represented that the Amazon valley would be settled and developed and an immense commerce would grow up between the region and the United States. The South was more advantageously located for such a commerce than was the North. Commerce with South America would effect the commercial regeneration of the South. It was this possibility which awakened so much interest in the Amazon among Southerners.[88] From time to time all through the decade the opinion was expressed that the South should "look to the south" rather than to Europe in her efforts to develop a foreign commerce.[89] The line of mail steamers was not established; but the Amazon was opened to the navigation of all nations, largely as a result of Maury's efforts.

One of the most grandiose schemes for establishing direct trade was that conceived by Col. A. Dudley Mann, of Virginia. He had seen being built in England the Great Eastern, by far the largest ship built to that time. In a letter to the people of the slaveholding states, August, 1856, he proposed the establishment of a line of four of these mammoth steamers to ply between the Chesapeake and Milford Haven, England.[90] So bold a plan captivated the

[83]Memorial, *Western Journal and Civilian*, VIII, 174-80.

[84]Maury to Blackford, Sept. 24, 1852, *M. F. Maury Papers*.

[85]Also in book form. *DeBow's Review*, XVI, 231. Articles are in *ibid.*, XIV, 136-45, 449-60, 556-67; XV, 36-43. See also *ibid.*, XII, 381 ff.; XVI, 231-51.

[86]*Western Journal and Civilian*, IX, 321-28.

[87]*DeBow's Review*, XV, 254-74; XVI, 640; XVII, 201, 402-5.

[88]Maury expected that the Southern states would soon have a redundant slave population, and hoped the Amazon Valley would prove an outlet. *Western Journal and Civilian*, IX, 328; DeBow, *Industrial Resources*, III, 13.

[89]For example, letter of Gov. H. A. Wise, of Virginia, to a citizen of Norfolk, in Barton H. Wise, *Henry A. Wise of Virginia*, 216 f.; *DeBow's Review*, XXVI, 73-6.

[90]*Ibid.*, XXI, 411-25.

imaginations of the Southern people. The Southern Commercial
Convention at Savannah endorsed it.[91] In July, 1857, an en-
thusiastic convention in its support was held at Old Point Comfort,
Virginia.[92] Ex-President Tyler presided; letters from Secretary of
State Cass and other members of the cabinet were read; books
were opened for subscriptions of stock. An appeal was made to
sectional feeling. With a view to secure a wide diffusion of the
stock among the people, subscribers were limited for a period
to one $100 share each. Most of the prominent men of Virginia
subscribed. President Buchanan headed the list in the District of
Columbia.[93] The Virginia Legislature, almost without opposition,
granted a charter to "The Atlantic Steam Ferry Company,"
March, 1858.[94] The thirty-six directors of the company must all
be residents of the slaveholding states or the District of Columbia,
and were to be apportioned on the basis of stock subscribed. But
by this time interest had begun to wane. The Commercial Convention, meeting at Knoxville, August, 1857, had refused to
recommend the "steam ferry."[95] Many pronounced it chimerical.
The project was not completely abandoned, however, until the
war.[96]

Several other direct trade projects were under way or under
consideration in Virginia on the eve of the war. A convention of
merchants and officials of fourteen railroads met at Bristol, Virginia, June, 1857, upon call of officers of the Virginia and Tennessee railroad, then on the point of completion, to consider the
subject of direct trade.[97] William Ballard Preston, a former secretary of the navy, was sent to Europe to disseminate information
in regard to the demand for foreign goods in Virginia and her
hinterland and to confer with capitalists, especially the owners of
the Great Eastern, upon the establishment of a steamship line.
French officials and capitalists were much interested in extending

[91]*DeBow's Review*, XXII, 96. Mann was present and a member of the
general committee.
[92]Proceedings, *ibid.*, XXIII, 321-24; XXIV, 352-74; Richmond *Enquirer*,
Aug. 1, 3, 5, 1857.
[93]*Ibid.*, Aug. 11, 17, 1857.
[94]*Acts of the General Assembly, 1857-1858*, p. 125; *DeBow's Review*, XXIV,
352, 375.
[95]New York *Herald*, Aug. 11, 17, 1857.
[96]*Ibid.*, Mar. 19, 1861.
[97]Richmond *Enquirer*, June 8, 1857; *DeBow's Review*, XXII, 553; XXIII, 86.

the foreign trade of the Empire at the time. Preston was able to make a conditional agreement with officials of the Orleans Railway Company relative to a line of steamers between Norfolk and the mouth of the Loire.[98] The Virginia Legislature ratified the agreement by an act of March 27, 1858, incorporating the Norfolk and St. Nazaire Navigation Company.[99] One-half the stock was to be subscribed in America, one-half in France; the directorate also should be composed of an equal number of Americans and Frenchmen. American interests were to subvent the company to the extent of $12,500 per round trip—this subsidy it was hoped the Federal government would grant for carrying the mails—and the French government was to be asked to lend assistance. A long correspondence between the president of the Merchants' and Mechanics' Exchange of Norfolk and M. Lacoutre and other gentlemen of France and the visit of an agent, John D. Myrick, to France, resulted in the trial trip of the steamer Lone Star, which was said to have been successful and to have proved the feasibility of direct trade.[100] By an act of February 2, 1858, the Virginia Legislature chartered the Southern Virginia Navigation Company to establish a line of steamships or sailing packets between the Chesapeake and Europe.[101] Before November, 1860, the company had built one ship, engaged another, and had two or three others under construction.[102] On the very eve of secession the Virginia Legislature incorporated a Richmond and Liverpool Packet Company, and extended welcome to a proposal of M. Pierre and Brothers, of Paris, to establish a line of steamers between Virginia and France.[103]

Elsewhere projects did not reach the stage of development they did in Virginia. In 1857 W. C. Barney, of Washington, attempted to promote a line of steamers between New Orleans and Bordeaux, France. He memorialized Congress for the usual subsidy for carrying the mails. The House Committee on the Post Office and Post Roads reported favorably upon it. The Bordeaux Chamber of

[98]*DeBow's Review*, XXVI, 584-5.
[99]*Acts of the General Assembly, 1857-1858*, p. 127.
[100]*Third Annual Report of the Merchants' and Mechanics' Exchange of Norfolk, Virginia, June, 1860*, p. 13.
[101]*Acts of the General Assembly, 1857-1858*, p. 187.
[102]New York *Herald*, Nov. 26, 1860.
[103]*Acts of the General Assembly, 1861*, p. 278, 342.

Commerce promised cooperation and a loan. A prospectus was got out and subscription books opened; but the project got no farther.[104] In 1860 British parties proposed to establish a line of six iron steamers between New Orleans and Liverpool. The vessels were to be built in England and fly the British flag, but one-half the stock was to be subscribed by Americans. The project was endorsed by the New Orleans Chamber of Commerce.[105]

Thus virtually all of these projects, and several not described, for establishing lines of ocean steamers came to naught. Had the Federal government not abandoned, 1859, the policy of subsidizing steamship lines, it is very probable that one or more Southern lines would have been in operation before 1861. Trans-Atlantic lines of steamships had not yet proved profitable without government aid. The failure to secure steamship lines does not signify that the direct foreign imports did not increase during the decade. A few lines of sailing packets were established, and the number of irregular vessels entered considerably increased, as did the total value of the direct imports.[106] But there was no revolution in the course of Southern commerce. In fact, the employment of steam vessels in the coasting trade tended to fix Southern commerce in its former channels. Several lines of steamships were engaged in the coasting trade between New York and New Orleans and other Southern ports in 1860. Such lines had been established in response to the demands of actual commerce. The tendency of the times was toward closer commercial relationships between the sections, the efforts of the advocates of direct trade to the contrary notwithstanding.

[104] *DeBow's Review*, XXII, 318-20; 410-14, 554; XXIII, 415-18.
[105] *Ibid.*, XXVIII, 462-4.
[106] See the tables in the Appendix.

CHAPTER V
THE SOUTHERN COMMERCIAL CONVENTION,
1852-1859

During the years 1852-1859 there met annually or oftener, in turn at Baltimore, Memphis, Charleston, New Orleans, Richmond, Savannah, Knoxville, Montgomery, and Vicksburg, sessions of the so-called Southern Commercial Convention. After the first the time and place of meeting and, to some extent, the organization and program of each were determined by its predecessor; so there was a degree of continuity in their endeavors. Several of the gatherings were very respectable in point of numbers; in most of them, all or nearly all of the Southern States were represented; some able and well-known men were among the delegates in every case; their proceedings were watched in the South and even in the North with considerable interest. As their name indicates, they were sectional in character. The term "commercial" does not accurately indicate their purpose, but cannot be considered a misnomer. A study of this series of meetings is conducive to a better understanding of the state of public opinion in the South during the decade before the war upon questions affecting the material progress and prosperity of the section.

The origin of the Southern Commercial Convention is not to be explained by any single event or isolated circumstance. A non-political or semi-political convention was by no means a new thing in the South in 1852. Although none of those assembled prior to that time was quite of the type of the Southern Commercial Convention, several may be considered forerunners of it. The direct trade conventions of the late thirties may be so classed, although they were more restricted in their objects, and not section-wide in their representation.[1] Those held in Virginia were gatherings of Virginians with a few scattering delegates from border North Carolina counties.[2] They were interested primarily in local problems, although there was recognition that the cause of Virginia was in a way the cause of the South, and although the connection between them and the direct trade conventions of South Carolina and Georgia was very close. The Charleston and Augusta conven-

[1] See ch. I.
[2] Savannah *Republican*, April 7, 1838.

tions, likewise, were composed almost entirely of South Carolina and Georgia men. Attempts to win the younger states farther west to the cause failed of the accomplishment; they were urged to send delegates to each of the conventions, but did not do so. Among other reasons for this was the fact that the Southwest was not yet concerned about "Southern decline."

More widely representative than the direct trade conventions, but perhaps with less justification considered a forerunner of the Southern Commercial Convention, was the Southwestern Convention in Memphis, November, 1845.[3] In composition and sentiment it was more Western than Southern. Delegates were present from Ohio, Indiana, Illinois, Missouri, and Iowa Territory as well as from states of the Southwest and South. The primary purpose of the meeting was to present the demands of the West for the improvement by the Federal government of the navigation of Western rivers—demands which were very insistent for several years prior to the building of railroads in the Mississippi valley. An attempt was made to find constitutional justification for the improvement by the Federal government of the Mississippi and its tributaries which would be acceptable to all parties in the West and South. John C. Calhoun, who understood better than any other Southern leader the growing power of the West and the strength of the demand for improvement of Western rivers and harbors, presided over the convention. He had not yet abandoned hopes of attaining the presidency of the United States; he was still firmly convinced of the desirability of maintaining the political alliance of the South and West. In his address before the convention and later in his report to the Senate upon the Memorial of the convention, he went to such lengths in meeting the views of the Western men that it was with difficulty he held his strict constructionist followers in line.[4] The convention dealt with other

---

[3]Proceedings are in *Journal of the Proceedings of the Southwestern Convention, began and held at the city of Memphis on the 12th of November, 1845.* Cf. *DeBow's Review,* I, 7-22; *Niles' Register,* LXIX, 212-14; Memphis *Daily Eagle,* Nov. 18, 1845. There were present 529 delegates from 12 states and one territory.

[4]Calhoun's address to the convention is in the *Journal of the Proceedings of the Southwestern Convention,* p. 7 ff. His report to the Senate on the Memorial of the convention is in *Works,* V, 246-93. For Calhoun's motives, see Calhoun to James Edward Calhoun, July 2, 1846; to Thomas G. Clemson, July 11, 1846; Duff Green to Calhoun, Sept. 24, 1845, *Calhoun Correspondence.* For re-

subjects, it is true. It was employed to stimulate interest in rail-road communication between the Mississippi valley and South Atlantic ports; a system of railroads was outlined which would effectually bind together the South and Southwest.[5] It endorsed in a qualified manner the warehousing system, which some hoped would promote the foreign commerce of Southern ports.[6] It gave some attention to the question of overproduction of cotton, and. to the diversification of agriculture and the introduction of manufacturing as remedies.[7] The sequel of the Memphis convention was not so much the Southern Commercial Convention, however, as it was the large Rivers and Harbors Convention held in Chicago in July, 1847.[8]

The alliance of the South and West had carried the Walker Tariff bill of 1846; but the Rivers and Harbors bill of that year had been carried by logrolling methods, the friends of Eastern harbors, Lake harbors, and Western rivers pooling their interests. President Polk vetoed the bill.[9] He did not follow the constitutional arguments employed by Calhoun in his report to the Senate upon the Memorial of the Memphis convention, but employed reasoning which Calhoun believed would preclude the possibility of uniting the South and West in support of a reasonable program of river improvement.[10] The Chicago convention, which was as strongly dominated by the Whigs as the Memphis convention had been by the Democrats and contained more Eastern men than the Memphis convention had contained Southern, sought to make capital of Polk's veto. There was an attempt to unite the West and East upon broad Whig principles, much broader than Calhoun could accept. It was more than intimated that the way to improve rivers and harbors was to elect a president who would sign a bill

ception of Calhoun's address and report see *Niles' Register*, LXIX, 214, quoting the Charleston *Mercury; So. Quar. Rev.*, X, 377 ff., 441-512, 515; *DeBow's Review*, I, 83 f.; *Cong. Globe*, 33 Cong., 1 Sess., 246; Calhoun to Mrs. Thomas G. Clemson, June 11, 1846, *Calhoun Correspondence.*

[5]*Journal*, 29-40. See also Sioussat, St. G. L., "Memphis as a Gateway to the West," *Tenn. Hist. Mag.*, II. 77-114.

[6]*Journal*, 96-99; Memphis *Daily Eagle*, Dec. 17, 1845.

[7]*Journal*, 41-55.

[8]Proceedings in *Niles' Register*, LXXII, 309-10, 331-33, 344-46, 365-67.

[9]*Messages and Papers of the Presidents*, IV, 460-66.

[10]Calhoun to James Edward Calhoun, Aug. 8, 1846; to J. L. M. Curry, Sept. 14; to Thomas G. Clemson, Sept. 20, *Calhoun Correspondence.*

for that purpose.[11] The Memphis convention had been used to stimulate interest in railroad communication between the Mississippi valley and the South Atlantic seaboard; the Chicago convention was similarly used to promote various projects for railroads between the East and the West.[12]

In October, 1849, a great Pacific Railroad Convention met in Memphis.[13] Its purpose was to crystallize sentiment in favor of a railroad to the Pacific and give a demonstration of the strength of the supporters of a Southern route, whose eastern terminus would presumably be Memphis. Five days earlier a still bigger convention had been held in St. Louis, for the purpose of crystallizing sentiment in favor of a railroad to the Pacific and canvassing the support which a central route could command.[14] Both of these conventions professed to look upon the construction of the Pacific railroad as a great national undertaking, which should receive in some way the aid of the Federal government, and which would redound to the benefit of the whole nation; but each was largely sectional in composition and sentiment, and each saw the special advantages, political and commercial, to accrue to the section and locality fortunate enough to secure the eastern terminus of the proposed railroad. Inasmuch as the Memphis convention was so largely sectional and dealt with a project which occupied much of the time of the later convention and whose accomplishment would do much to promote the progress and prosperity of the South, it may be considered a forerunner of the Southern Commercial Convention.

[11]Calhoun to Duff Green, June 10, 1847, *Calhoun Correspondence; Niles' Register*, LXXII, 266-67, 310; LXIII, 24, Daniel Webster's letter to the convention; 219, Webster's speech at the opening of the Northern New Hampshire Railway; *American Review*, VI, 111-22; *DeBow's Review*, IV, 122-27; 291-96.

[12]*American Review*, VI, 111 ff.; *DeBow's Review*, IV, 258.

[13]*Minutes and Proceedings of the Memphis Convention, assembled October 23, 1849; DeBow's Review*, VII, 36, 188, 550, 551. Cf. *National Plan of an Atlantic and Pacific Railroad and Remarks of Albert Pike, Made Thereon, at Memphis, November, 1849*; Cotterill, "Memphis Railroad Convention, 1849," *Tenn. Hist. Mag.*, IV, 83-94.

[14]*Proceedings of the National Railroad Convention, which assembled in the City of St. Louis, on the fifteenth day of October, 1849*. A third Pacific Railroad Convention was held in Philadelphia, April 1-3, 1850. *Proceedings of the Convention in Favor of a National Railroad to the Pacific Ocean—Held in Philadelphia, April 1, 2, and 3, 1850*. Cf. *Mo. Hist. Rev.*, 203-15.

A local railroad convention which met in New Orleans in the summer of 1851 appointed a committee to address the people of the Southern and Western states in the interest of a general railroad convention of the South and West to meet in New Orleans in January, 1852.[15] The address, while emphasizing the railroad needs of the Mississippi valley and of New Orleans in particular, did not overlook "Southern decline" and the necessity for united action in the South to advance her commercial interests. "They [the Southern states] have an interest in each other's prosperity, founded upon common hopes, and fears, and dangers. . . . The interests of Mobile, New Orleans, Charleston or Savannah in each other's advancement are stronger than their interest in the advancement of Boston and New York. These interests should preclude all jealousies and rivalries and induce a generous co-operation in every instance where the benefit of the whole South is at issue."[16] The convention which met in pursuance of this call,[17] while primarily interested in launching New Orleans and Louisiana upon an internal improvement program, had many of the earmarks of the later Commercial Convention. Delegates were present from eleven states. Frequent references were made to Southern commercial dependence and its remedy. A committee on railroad routes, William Burwell, of Virginia, chairman, reported a list of internal improvements which were regarded as not only indispensable to the development of the agricultural, commercial, and mineral wealth of the Southwestern states, but also as "essential to the equality and unity of the states of this confederacy."[18]

By this time conditions had reached a stage when a Southern Commercial Convention could be assembled. The internal transportation systems of the country were developing along lines which promised to bind the Northwest firmly to the East and the Southwest to the old South. The Pacific railroad question had taken on the form of a sectional struggle over the selection of a route. The entire South had been interested in the discussion of

[15]*DeBow's Review,* XI, 74, 217, 340.

[16]*Ibid.,* XI, 142-78 (quotation from p. 154); *Address to the People of the Southern and Western States, and more particularly to those of Louisiana, Texas, Mississippi, Alabama, Tennessee, Arkansas, Kentucky, and Missouri,* New Orleans, 1851 (pamphlet).

[17]Proceedings, in *DeBow's Review,* XII, 305-332, 543-68.

[18]*Ibid.,* XII, 315.

diversification of industry and the development of cotton manufactures, and had been awakened thereby to a realization of the
disparity of the sections in industrial development. The people
of other Southern cities and states than those of the Atlantic
seaboard had become aware of Southern commercial decline and
its baneful effects, and were talking direct trade. Finally, and
more important, the sectional struggle over slavery had reached a
most bitter stage; the Southern Convention, the long dream of
men of the South Carolina school, had met in Nashville, and the
Union had been in danger of dissolution. True, a compromise had
been effected after a protracted debate; but it had been accepted
in the South with misgivings, and in several states only after
violent political struggles. And the effect of the whole episode was
not to allay sectionalism but to aggravate it. The old alliance of
South and West was breaking up. The number was growing
rapidly of those who felt that the South could trust only herself,
that the Southern people must unite and learn the art of co-
operation, that they must develop their resources and increase
their wealth and population, if the South were to maintain her
equality in the Union or her independence out of it.

It is difficult to state whence came the specific suggestion
which resulted in the call of the first meeting of the Southern
Commercial Convention. James D. B. DeBow, a true son of
South Carolina, had been a persistent proponent of the idea of
bringing the South together in convention, and had used *DeBow's
Review* to effect with that end in view. When the interest in
cotton manufactures was at its height, DeBow suggested a manufacturers' convention.[19] He tried to arrange the meeting of an industrial convention in New Orleans in the spring of 1851.[20] He
claimed to have been one of the original Southern Convention men
and was disappointed that "action" could not be taken at Nashville. After the compromise measures had been enacted he felt
that the danger to the South was only postponed. He, therefore,
favored a Southern convention to agree upon what would constitute grounds for resistance, a Southern mercantile convention as a
proper means of strengthening the South by promoting shipbuilding and direct trade, thus making possible the retention at home of

[19]*DeBow's Review*, IX, 256; X, 107.
[20]*Ibid.*, IX, 256, 460.

millions of wealth contributed annually to the North, and a Southern manufacturers' convention to agree to pay no more tribute to Northern looms.[21] In the New Orleans Railroad Convention of January, 1852, he proposed that the convention resolve itself into an association for the promotion of the industrial interests of the Southern and Western states and provide for annual meetings, but his proposal was not acted upon.[22] DeBow was always considered one of the founders of the Southern Commercial Convention. C. G. Baylor, editor of the *Cotton Plant*, a Baltimore publication, also advocated a convention, and later claimed to have been instrumental in arranging for the meeting in Baltimore in December, 1852.[23] Finally, a number of Southern leaders, chief of whom was Senator William C. Dawson, of Georgia, who thought it time for the South to make a concerted effort to achieve commercial and industrial independence, asked Baltimore business men to inaugurate the movement.[24] Baltimore was chosen because she was the largest city in slaveholding territory, and it was believed her name would lend prestige.[25] A call was issued by the Baltimore Board of Trade for a convention to meet in that city December 18, 1852; the object as stated in the call was to promote foreign and interstate trade.[26] The delegates of the Baltimore convention were carefully selected with the idea of avoiding anything like a mass meeting.[27] A number of congressmen from the South and the Ohio valley came up from Washington. The other delegates were mostly business men. Senator Dawson was made president. Brantz Mayer read in behalf of the Board of Trade a carefully prepared address of welcome.[28] He described the advantages of Baltimore, her merchants, her manufacturers, her banks, and her facilities for direct trade with

[21]*DeBow's Review*, X, 107.

[22]*Ibid.*, XII, 554, 561.

[23]Richmond *Enquirer*, Dec. 24, 1852; Memphis *Daily Appeal*, Jan. 23, 1853.

[24]*DeBow's Review*, XV, 257; New York *Herald*, April 15, 1854; New Orleans *Commercial Bulletin*, Jan. 17, 1855.

[25]Memphis *Daily Appeal*, June 23, 1853.

[26]Baltimore *Sun*, Dec. 17, 1852; *DeBow's Review*, XIII, 427.

[27]Baltimore *Sun*, Dec. 17, 1852; Richmond *Enquirer*, Dec. 24, 1852, C. G. Baylor's remarks in the convention.

[28]Proceedings, in Baltimore *Sun*, Dec. 20, 1852; Richmond *Enquirer*, Dec. 24, 1852. The resolutions and Brantz Mayer's address are also in *DeBow's Review*, XIV, 373-79.

Europe. The Baltimore and Ohio railroad was about completed to the Ohio river, and Baltimore would soon compete with New York and Philadelphia for Western trade. The delegates were assured that Baltimore was a Southern city, devoted to the Southern cause, and disposed to join the South in achieving commercial independence of New York, Boston, and Philadelphia; the way to achieve commercial independence was to make Baltimore the commercial and financial center of the South. The convention endorsed all of Baltimore's aspirations. The only incident which occurred to mar the harmony of the proceedings was a remark of William Burwell, of Virginia, that he considered Norfolk a better port than Baltimore. Some consideration was given to the Pacific railroad, for whose construction it was expected Congress would provide in the session just beginning, and to other important internal improvements in the Southern states. A line of steamships to Liverpool was recommended, and also steam communication with the Amazon valley. The convention sought to justify itself against the charge of sectionalism by the following resolution:—

Resolved, That while we disdain the slightest prejudice or hostility to the welfare and prosperity of any particular section or city, North or South, we would promote, as we think we reasonably might, consistent with the laws of trade, its great central position, the commercial interests and prosperity of Baltimore, as being well calculated to excite a wholesome and beneficial competition with more northern Atlantic cities, which could not fail to be particularly advantageous to the whole South, Southwest, and West, and, in fact, to the nation at large.

The convention sat but one day; it adjourned to meet in Memphis in June, 1853. The proceedings present a striking contrast with those of later conventions, which sat from four to six days, with their wranglings, fiery declamation, numerous committees, and innumerable resolutions.

The Baltimore convention did not give universal satisfaction. The Richmond *Enquirer* thought the address of welcome made too many allusions to Baltimore.[29] Only Lieutenant Maury, it remarked, remembered that there was such a place as Virginia. The press of New Orleans thought that the movement had been got up by Baltimore to catch trade. New Orleans, they said, was

---

[29]Dec. 21, 1852. Cf. *ibid.*, April 14, 1854.

a better Southern city than Baltimore; and it was wrong for Baltimore to try to injure New Orleans by diverting her commerce.[30] The feeling was pretty general that the Baltimore Board of Trade had attempted to turn what was intended for a Southern movement to her own account.[31] However, a beginning had been made.

The Memphis convention was a somewhat larger body.[32] Delegates were present from fourteen states, including Missouri, Kentucky, Illinois, and Indiana. Thus, like the Baltimore gathering, it was not strictly Southern; in fact, each was officially designated the "Southern and Western Commercial Convention." Like the Baltimore convention, also, it was not marked by bitter sectionalism. Senator Dawson again presided, and several other prominent leaders of the South were among the delegates, notably General John A. Quitman and H. S. Foote, of Mississippi, and John Bell, of Tennessee.

The objects of the convention had not yet been clearly defined. Upon taking the chair, Senator Dawson stated them as he understood them. His statements may be taken as the expression of a moderate leader who had had a considerable part in the inauguration of the convention. The members of the convention were not, he said, actuated by feelings of hostility to any section of the Union; but it had been seen for years that the people of the Southern and Western states were suffering from a want of the proper development of the natural resources of their section. Immediate action was necessary. The important interests of agriculture, commerce, and manufactures were all proper subjects for discussion. Better transportation facilities, development of seaports, direct trade, lines of steamers to Europe and South America, improvement of rivers and harbors, encouragement of manufactures,

[30]*DeBow's Review*, XVIII, 354; Charleston *Courier*, Mar. 3, 1854, quoting the New Orleans *Delta*; Memphis *Eagle and Enquirer*, June 16, 1853, letter from C. G. Baylor, editor of the *Cotton Plant* (Baltimore); Memphis *Daily Appeal*, June 23, 1853; New Orleans *Commercial Bulletin*, Jan. 4, 1855.

[31]The Baltimore *Sun* of Dec. 27, 1852, quoted a number of Southern papers as expressing friendliness to Baltimore.

[32]Four hundred ninety-six delegates were present. Proceedings, in *Proceedings of the Southern and Western Commercial Convention at Memphis, Tennessee, in June, 1853* (pamphlet, 64 pp.). See also the Memphis *Daily Appeal*, June 7, 10, 20, 1853; *DeBow's Review*, XV, 254-274; *Western Journal and Civilian*, X, 191-197.

and, finally, the Pacific railroad, "the great work of the age and the world," were all specified as subjects which deserved the consideration of the convention.[33]

This statement suggested a wide range of discussion; the convention went even beyond it. After considerable debate resolutions were adopted asking Congress to appropriate money to improve the channels of the mouths of the Mississippi river, the Des Moines and Rock river rapids, and the harbors of Charleston, Savannah, Wilmington, Norfolk, Mobile, and Galveston. Other resolutions looked to aid from the Federal government in protecting the lands along the Mississippi from inundation. Resolutions were adopted relative to direct trade and steamship communication with Europe. Provision was made for a committee to prepare for publication and distribution, particularly in the manufacturing districts of Europe, a full report on the peculiar facilities offered by the South and West for the manufacture of cotton. The convention resolved that Southern youth should be educated at home rather than in Northern schools. Native teachers should be employed, and textbooks written by Southern men should be used. The state governments were requested to consider the establishment of normal schools. There were long speeches on the free navigation of the Amazon river—a subject which Lieutenant M. F. Maury had been agitating for a year or two. The projected railroad across the Isthmus of Tehuantepec was endorsed, and the government was requested to hasten the negotiations with Mexico relative to the right of way. The New Orleans delegation was especially interested in the Tehuantepec project. A St. Louis project for a Mississippi valley railroad from New Orleans to St. Paul via St. Louis was likewise endorsed, and Congress was requested to grant unsold lands along the route in aid thereof.

But the subject that occupied the largest share of the time and interest of the convention was the Pacific railroad. "This," said the New Orleans *Delta*, "was the Aaron's rod that swallowed up all others. This is the great panacea, which is to release the South from its bondage to the North, which is to pour untold wealth into our lap; which is to build up cities, steamships, manufactories, educate our children, and draw into our control what Mr. Bell

[33] *DeBow's Review*, XV, 256 ff.

calls 'the untold wealth of the gorgeous East.' "[34] The convention unanimously adopted resolutions which declared the road a national necessity, and requested Congress, as soon as the surveys of routes which were then being prosecuted should be completed, to adopt such measures as would insure the construction of the main trunk at the earliest possible period. It refused to suggest that the Federal government construct the main trunk; but it did declare it right, expedient, and proper for the government to make large donations of the public lands to the different states bordering on either side of the Mississippi to enable all sections to connect themselves with the main line by branches. No specific route was recommended.

The third session of the Southern Commercial Convention was held in Charleston in April, 1854. It was a much larger gathering than either of its predecessors.[35] Senator Dawson again presided. The convention sat six days. The debates were longer and covered an even wider range of subjects than those at Memphis. The Pacific railroad again occupied the center of the stage; but such subjects as direct trade, the encouragement of manufacturing and mining, the remission of duties on railroad iron, and the improvement of rivers and harbors were discussed at some length. Among the other topics which received consideration were opening the Amazon river to the navigation of the world; the repeal of the United States tonnage duties and fishing bounties; the admission of foreign vessels to the American coasting trade; direct shipments of cotton to the ports of Continental Europe—European manufacturers purchased their stocks in Liverpool usually—; uniform coinage among the nations of the earth; improved mail service in the South; milling and lumbering; agricultural exhibits and institute fairs; and education in the South. The tone and temper of the gathering were unmistakable; it was a Southern convention determined to find some means of advancing the interests of the South as distinguished from the North. The multiplicity of sub-

---

[34]Quoted with approval in the Richmond *Enquirer*, June 24, 1853.

[35]It was in fact the largest of the whole series. There were present 857 delegates from 13 states. The proceedings are in the Charleston *Courier*, April 11-14, 17, 18, 1854; New York *Herald*, April 14-19 (taken in part from the *Courier*); *DeBow's Review*, XVI, 632-41; XVII, 91-99, 200-213, 250-61, 398-410, 491-510 (taken from Charleston papers, chiefly from the *Courier*).

jects pressed upon it for attention indicates the earnestness, at least, of many of the men who composed it.

Several essays were made to define the objects of the Southern Commercial Convention. C. K. Marshall, of Mississippi, offered a resolution to the effect that, while commerce was the subject for special consideration by the convention, other matters tending to the accomplishment of the general design of the development 'of the rights and resources of the Southern and Southwestern states were legitimate subjects.[36] DeBow, who was unable to be present, wrote to the committee in charge of arrangements stating his understanding of the objects of the convention. He emphasized the point that these conventions were successors of the direct trade conventions of the late thirties, the Memphis conventions of 1845 and 1849, and the New Orleans Railroad Convention of 1852. He believed these conventions had contributed largely to the great development which had been exhibited everywhere throughout the South during the several years preceding. Furthermore, they had taught the South to see and feel with humiliation her dependence upon the North, not only in industry and commerce but in matters not of a material character. As he saw it, the task which lay before them was no less than the regeneration of the South.[37] This seems to have been the view also of gentlemen who addressed the convention; and this must be set down as the purpose of the Southern Commercial Convention when at its best.

The lengthiest debates of the session were upon a scheme proposed by Albert Pike, of Arkansas, for building the Pacific railroad along a Southern route without aid from the Federal government. The Legislature of Virginia was called upon to charter a Southern Pacific Railroad company with sufficient capital to build the road. The stock was to be subscribed by the Southern states and California to the sum of $2,000,000 each, by cities, by private corporations, and by individuals. Texas was expected to make a liberal grant of public land. The Cherokee, Choctaw, and Creek nations were to be invited to join the enterprise. The board of directors was to consist of an equal number from each state. The corporation was to be granted power by its charter to negotiate

[36] *DeBow's Review*, XVII, 92 f.
[37] *Ibid.*, XVII, 95 ff.; Charleston *Courier*, April 10, 1854.

with Mexico for, and to purchase if necessary, a right of way through her territory to the Pacific or the Gulf of California; and to agree that the company would maintain military posts along the portion of the road which should lie in Mexico.[38]

This extraordinary plan was opposed upon the floor by some of the ablest and most practical men of the convention, including Senator Dawson, Lieutenant Maury, Judge Nesbit, of Georgia, Governor J. A. Jones, of Tennessee, and N. D. Coleman, of Mississippi—the last two being railroad men. According to these men, the plan was chimerical; it would be impracticable to unite the Southern states upon it; it would disrupt the South; it was too sectional; it savored too much of politics; definitely broke with the Western states; was of doubtful constitutionality; and the constitutions of several states forbade them entering any such corporation. Yet the convention, voting by states, unanimously endorsed Pike's scheme: Pike was a brilliant orator and presented his plan in a most convincing manner;[39] some support may have been attracted among strict constructionists by the omission of any demand for Federal aid; but the chief recommendation of the plan was its sectional nature.

Sectionalism was running high at this time. The Kansas-Nebraska bill was before Congress. A Pacific railroad bill had been defeated in the short session of the Thirty-second Congress, 1853, largely because partisans of a Southern route feared that it gave some advantage to the North.[40] Since that time partisans of the several proposed routes had been exerting themselves to the utmost to gain some advantage in the struggle. Surveys made in 1853 under the direction of Jefferson Davis, Secretary of War, had shown that the best Southern route ran south of the Gila River in Mexican territory.[41] Very late in the same year the Gadsden treaty had been negotiated with Mexico securing, among other things, the desired route. While the Charleston convention was sitting, the treaty was being considered by the Senate in secret

[38]Resolutions embodying the plan, *DeBow's Review*, XVI, 636-37.

[39]For debate see *ibid.*, XVII, 205-13, 408-10, 492-506.

[40]This statement is based upon an unpublished study, made by the author, of the struggles in Congress over the Pacific railroad.

[41]*Reports of the Explorations and Surveys, to Ascertain the Most Practical and Economical Route for a Railroad from the Mississippi River to the Pacific Ocean*, I, 4, 29.

session; and, rumor had it, was meeting opposition, which was attributed to the unwillingness of Northern men to purchase a Southern route to the Pacific.[42] General Gadsden himself addressed the convention in favor of a resolution in support of ratification of the treaty and in favor of Pike's plan.[43] Albert Pike took strong sectional grounds in his speech in support of the resolutions embodying his plan. He invited the attention of the convention to the great Northwest, which, he said, never seemed to be taken into consideration by Southern men. This region was bidding for immigration: laws granting foreign immigrants the suffrage before they had declared their intention of becoming United States citizens were one inducement; the proposed homestead legislation was another; the Kansas-Nebraska bill another. The North was increasing her political power at the South's expense. "And with this continued increase in foreign and Northern influence was it not obvious that the prospect of the South ever getting a Pacific Railroad was put further and further off every year?" The North was looking out for her own interests; "the North knew full well that wherever the Pacific Railroad went, there too, would go the power and wealth of the country." The South should look to her interests. He wanted his plan to be a "sort of declaration of independence on the part of the South."[44]

After the great meeting at Charleston, the Southern Commercial Convention languished for a couple of years. The session in New Orleans in January, 1855, was very poorly attended and attracted little attention from the South at large.[45] There were several reasons for the poor showing. The Western rivers were low, making travel difficult. Congress and the state legislatures were in session. The country was suffering somewhat from a tem-

---

[42]*DeBow's Review*, XVII, 210, 408; New York *Herald*, April 19, 1854.

[43]*DeBow's Review*, XVII, 408-9; letter from John R. Bartlett, one of the Mexican boundary commissioners, taking umbrage at Gadsden's remarks in the convention, Charleston *Courier*, April 28, 1854.

[44]I have followed the synopses of his speeches as given in *DeBow's Review*, XVII, 208-12, 499-506. The same arguments are set forth in a very striking and able manner in a memorial to the state legislatures which Pike prepared. *Ibid.*, XVII, 593-99.

[45]Two hundred twelve delegates from twelve states. The proceedings are in *ibid.*, XVIII, 353-60, 520-28, 623-35, 749-60; New Orleans *Commercial Bulletin*, Jan. 10-16, 1855.

porary financial stringency.[46] The presence of so many radicals in the Charleston convention had discredited the movement in the eyes of many of more conservative opinions.[47] But the chief reason for the poor showing made was the attitude of the people of New Orleans and vicinity. The city council took tardy action, and the committee on arrangements did little. The Governor of Louisiana neglected to appoint delegates. Several of the New Orleans newspapers were antagonistic, expressing the opinion that the convention had been decidedly hostile to New Orleans from the beginning.[48] A specific grievance was the refusal of the Charleston convention to adopt resolutions requesting Congress to make appropriations for the improvement of the navigation of the Mississippi.[49] On the other hand there was a feeling throughout the South that the people of New Orleans were only lukewarm for the Southern cause. This feeling of hostility on the one hand and distrust on the other found expression upon the floor of the convention, and visiting delegates left with the feeling that they had not been cordially received.[50] The session at Richmond, Virginia, early the following year, 1856, made no better showing, only seven states being represented;[51] but in this case the want of success seems to have been largely due to severe weather and to the fact that, the meeting having once been postponed indefinitely because of an epidemic of small-pox in Richmond, too

[46]Charleston *Courier*, Jan. 13, 1855.
[47]Savannah *Daily Republican*, Nov. 17, 1856; *DeBow's Review*, XVIII, 523. Senator Benton, of Missouri, had denounced the Charleston convention as a disunion convention and Pike's plan for building the Pacific railroad as a plan for dissolving the Union. *Ibid., loc. cit.*
[48]*DeBow's Review*, XVIII, 353; New Orleans *Commercial Bulletin*, Jan. 4, 1855. "This feeling of indifference and apathy is not at all to be wondered at. All disclaimers to the contrary notwithstanding, the series of Southern Commercial Conventions, commencing at Baltimore, and continued at Memphis and Charleston, were decidedly antagonistic to the interests of New Orleans; and this inimical tendency was more than once exhibited in a manner invidiously offensive and calculated to disturb and wound our *amour propre.*" *Ibid.*, Jan. 17, 1855.
[49]*DeBow's Review*, XVIII, 628.
[50]*Ibid.*, XVIII, 354, 624, 632, 634.
[51]Proceedings, in *ibid.*, XX, 340-354; Richmond *Enquirer*, Jan. 31, Feb. 1, 2, 4, 5, 1856. The resolutions are in *Hunt's Merchants' Magazine*, XXXIV, 392. There were 213 delegates present, of whom 183 were from Virginia.

short notice was given of the time of the meeting.[52] The chief topic
of discussion at New Orleans was the Pacific railroad; at Richmond, direct trade. Most of the other topics discussed at previous
sessions were considered in a more or less perfunctory manner.
The Richmond convention determined that a greater effort than
theretofore should be made to insure a large attendance at the
next meeting; a committee was appointed to address the Southern
people in its behalf.[53] The Savannah committee on preparations
worked hard. But it was the political situation which was chiefly
responsible for the large attendance at Savannah: the convention
met in December, 1856, a month after the exciting presidential
campaign had resulted in the narrow defeat of the "Black Republican" party.[54]

The fire eating element in the Southern Commercial Convention had been gradually growing. Several members of the committee which issued the call for the Savannah convention were
known to be disunionists.[55] Many friends of the Union had come
to look upon the convention with distrust, and branded the
Savannah session in advance a disunion scheme.[56] The city council
of Nashville, Tennessee, for example, refused to appoint delegates
to the convention, because it feared its disunion proclivities.[57] On
the other hand, the New Orleans *Delta,* a journal which had been
antagonistic when the dominant purpose was the economic regeneration of the South, gave cordial support now that the objects
were becoming political.[58] The convention at Savannah was composed largely of politicians, and a large minority, if not an actual
majority, were disunionists.[59] James Lyon, of Virginia, upon tak-

[52]*DeBow's Review,* XX, 340.
[53]*Ibid.,* XX, 351; XXI, 550-552 (the call).
[54]Savannah *Republican,* Oct. 17, 21, 29, 1856. There were 564 delegates from
ten states.
[55]The Savannah *Republican* thought that "aside from the known character
and sentiment of the men who compose that committee," there was nothing in
the call that could be tortured into a disunion sentiment. Nov. 17, 1856. The
Republican was a Union paper.
[56]The Savannah *Republican,* Dec. 1, 1856.
[57]*Ibid.,* Nov. 25.
[58]Quoted in the Charleston *Courier,* Nov. 6, 1856.
[59]The Savannah *Republican,* Dec. 16, 1856, thought the convention was by
large odds a "conservative body," but admitted the presence of a considerable
number of disunionists. A list of the delegates is in *DeBow's Review,* XXII, 82 ff.

ing the chair, stated the objects of the convention as they had
already been stated several times. He defended the convention
against the charge of disunionism. It was commercial and not
political independence the South sought. But, in a strain quite
common in that day, he "looked to the future," and expressed
the fear that the time might come when the South would have to
defend her rights. For such a time it behooved her to be strong
and ready.[60]

The convention considered rather perfunctorily the subjects
discussed at previous sessions.[61] Albert Pike was again able to
secure endorsement of his plan for building a railroad to the
Pacific. A. Dudley Mann's scheme for establishing a "steam ferry"
between the Chesapeake and England was endorsed; as was also
Thomas Rainey's project for a line of steamships from New York
to the La Plata, via Savannah. But the chief interest was in
questions more political in character. Robert Toombs addressed a
letter to the convention proposing that the state legislatures encourage direct trade by levying an ad valorem tax upon the sale
of all goods imported into their respective states except goods imported directly from foreign countries. Such a tax, Toombs believed, would not only enable the states to dispense with direct
taxation, but would also provide ample revenue to carry out works
of internal improvement.[62] The letter was referred to the general
committee, which reported not Toombs' plan but resolutions in
favor of free trade and direct taxation as measures best calculated
to promote direct trade. The report was tabled (by a vote of
57-24); but the subject was kept alive by the appointment of a
committee to report upon it at the next session.[63]

Resolutions in favor of reopening the African slave trade, an
issue raised shortly before,[64] were introduced and debated at

[60]Savannah *Republican*, Dec. 9, 1856; *DeBow's Review*, XXII, 86-7.

[61]Proceedings, in *Official Report of the Debates and Proceedings of the Southern Commercial Convention, assembled at Knoxville, Tennessee, August 10, 1857*,
Appendix: *Proceedings of the Southern Convention at Savannah*. Also in *De-
Bow's Review*, XXII, 81-105, 216-24, 307-18; Savannah *Republican*, Dec. 9-13,
1856; Charleston *Courier*, Dec. 11-13.

[62]*DeBow's Review*, XXII, 102-104; Charleston *Courier*, Dec. 15, 1856. The
plan was not original with Toombs. For fuller discussion see below, p. 167 f.

[63]Proceedings and debate, in *DeBow's Review*, XXII, 92 ff., 307-18.

[64]The question was fairly launched by Governor Adams, of South Carolina,
in his message to the Legislature, Nov. 24, 1856. Charleston *Courier*, Nov. 26.

length, the debate turning not so much upon the propriety of considering such a question in a commercial convention as upon the expediency of reopening the foreign slave trade. This question, too, was carried over by the appointment of a committee to report at the next meeting of the convention.[65] Resolutions were also adopted recommending organized Southern emigration to Kansas; requesting Southern representatives in Congress to inquire whether their respective states had received their full quota of the public arms, and to insist that Southern posts be properly fortified; recommending the establishment of state armories; and expressing sympathy with the "efforts being made to introduce civilization in the States of Central America, and to develop these rich and productive regions by the introduction of slave labor," that is, with the Walker filibusters.[66]

The Southern Commercial Convention had now reached a stage where nothing could be expected from it in the way of advancing commerce and industry in the South. The committee which issued the call for the succeeding session at Knoxville styled it, rather suggestively, the "Southern Convention," and declared its purpose to be to unite the South upon a sectional policy. "Every other purpose," said the committee, "is of trifling importance in comparison with the high moral and social objects of the Convention. They are intended to spread far and wide, correct, enlarged, and faithful views of our rights and obligations, and to unite us together by the most sacred bonds to maintain them inviolate for ourselves and our posterity."[67] At Knoxville in August, 1857,[68] J. D. B. DeBow, already an avowed disunionist, was made president, and opened the convention with a ringing disunion speech. He admitted that the convention had built no railroads and established no steamship lines; but it had caused the people of the South to understand the importance of all those things; and they would come in the fullness of time. It had taught the people that the South had rights a thousand times more valu-

[65]DeBow's Review, XXII, 216-224 (summary of the debate).
[66]Ibid., XXII, 96-102 (resolutions of the convention in full).
[67]Ibid., XXIII, 193.
[68]Proceedings, in Official Report of the Debates and Proceedings of the Southern Commercial Convention, assembled at Knoxville, Tennessee, August 10th, 1857; DeBow's Review, XXIII, 298-320; New York Herald, 17, 18, 19 (best report). There were 710 delegates from eleven states and Arizona territory.

able than the Union, and that she had resources sufficient to make her important in the Union or to enable her to maintain herself as an independent nation.[69]

Resolutions in regard to reopening the foreign slave trade were introduced and debated at great length. By a scale vote of 66 to 26 a resolution was adopted which put the convention on record in favor of the annullment of that article of the Webster-Ashburton treaty, ratified November 10, 1842, which provided for keeping a squadron of naval vessels off the coast of Africa for the purpose of suppressing the slave trade. An amendment offered by a Tennessee delegate declaring it "inexpedient and contrary to the settled policy of this country to repeal the laws prohibitory of the African slave trade" was defeated by a vote of 40 for, 52 against.[70] The amendment was almost identical in language with a resolution introduced in the House of Representatives, December 15, 1856, by James L. Orr, of South Carolina, and adopted with only eight dissenting votes.[71] One delegate broached the subject of free immigration, but it did not meet with favor among the body of delegates;[72] it was, of course, a much more practical subject. Another long debate occurred upon the resolution, offered by W. W. Boyce, of South Carolina, declaring that the system of duties on imports should be abandoned by the Federal government and direct taxation be resorted to exclusively.[73] Whatever the merits of absolute free trade, its establishment in the Union was about as impossible as was reopening the foreign slave trade.[74]

It is true, the former objects of the convention were not completely lost sight of. A. Dudley Mann's scheme for establishing a steamship line between Chesapeake Bay and Milford Haven was debated and endorsement defeated, probably at the instigation of friends of rival Virginia projects.[75] A resolution was adopted

[69]DeBow's Review, XXIII, 225-38; Richmond Enquirer, Aug. 17, 1857.

[70]DeBow's Review, XXIII, 309-10; New York Herald, Aug. 18.

[71]Ibid., Aug. 19; Cong. Globe, 34 Cong., 3 Sess., 125-126.

[72]New York Herald, Aug. 19; DeBow's Review, XXIII, 319.

[73]Ibid., XXIII, 313 ff.

[74]The convention was not of a practical bent: a good part of two days was spent debating a resolution to exclude reporters of Northern newspapers. New York Herald, Aug. 17, 1857; DeBow's Review, XXIII, 302-305.

[75]New York Herald, Aug. 17; DeBow's Review, XXIII, 306, 308.

recommending the extension of state aid to steamship lines between Southern and foreign ports. The Federal government was requested to grant to Southern steamship lines the same subsidies for carrying the mails that it granted to Northern lines. The meeting recommended patronage of home manufactories and of merchants who imported directly from foreign countries. Resolutions were adopted asking the Federal government to fortify the harbors of Port Royal, South Carolina, Mobile, Alabama, and Beaufort, North Carolina, and make them coaling stations for large government steamers. A resolution recommending taxation by the Southern states upon sales within their respective borders of articles manufactured in the North was rejected. A committee was appointed to memorialize Congress upon the subject of duties imposed by foreign countries upon American tobacco;[76] the duties imposed by some countries were very high, and it was felt that the American government had not made the effort it might have made to secure their reduction. The Pacific railroad was not mentioned. There were the usual resolutions relative to Southern education. The disposition to call for Federal aid for various purposes is noteworthy.

In the earlier sessions of the Commercial Convention there had been a sprinkling of public men of more than local prominence, and, of course, a larger number of local politicians. The majority of the delegates came from towns and cities; but the planters had been well represented. In the earlier meetings, as in the later, there were editors, preachers, physicians, and professors; but there were also a large number of business men, bankers, merchants, a few manufacturers, and men interested in promoting particular railroad projects, steamship lines, or other enterprises, for which they hoped to secure the endorsement of the convention. By the time of the Knoxville convention this latter element had practically ceased to attend. After the Knoxville meeting the dwindling conservative element also disappeared from the convention, and it fell everywhere into disrepute except among the disunionists, who continued to hope that it would serve some useful purpose in making Southern men acquainted with each other, in consolidating

[76] The memorial is in *DeBow's Review*, XXIV, 291-300.

Southern feeling, and in harmonizing differences between different
.quarters of the South.[77]
The Montgomery convention, May, 1858, was well attended.[78]
The debates, as far as oratory was concerned, were more brilliant
than those of any other session of the series. Among the orators
were Henry W. Hilliard and William L. Yancey, of Alabama, rivals
of long standing.[79] But it was not a commercial convention; it was
a gathering of disunionists. The Montgomery *Daily Confederation*
said, "every form and shape of political malcontent was there
present, ready to assent in any project having for its end a dissolution of the Union, immediate, unconditional, final."[80] Edmund
Ruffin, of Virginia, himself an ardent secessionist, found only two
delegates outside the Virginia delegation who were not disunionists.[81] But the proceedings took a turn which all secessionists even,
could not approve. Practically the whole time of the session was
devoted to debating the question of reopening the African slave
trade. The debate proved the delegates to be hopelessly divided,
not only upon the expediency of reopening the foreign slave trade,
but also upon the more practical question, whether or not agitation for the repeal of Federal laws prohibitory of the slave trade
would promote or injure the cause of disunion.[82] Ridiculed both

[77]Address of the committee which called the Montgomery convention.
Charleston *Mercury*, April 8, 1858; *DeBow's Review*, XXIV, 424-28. The *Knox-
ville* (Tenn.) *Citizen* thought the call "an invitation to take counsel whether the
Union can be longer maintained or is worth maintaining." Quoted in Charleston
Mercury, April 20, 1858.

[78]About 400 delegates were present from ten states. Proceedings, in *DeBow's
Review*, XXIV, 574-606; Montgomery *Daily Confederation*, May 11-15, 1858.

[79]Yancey's part in the convention is discussed at length in DuBose, *The Life
and Times of William Lowndes Yancey*, 358 ff. Cf. *Ruffin's Diary*, entry for May
13, 1858; *DeBow's Review*, XXIV, 583-88.

[80]May 18, 1858. "When the South gets ready to dissolve the Union, all she
has to do is to reassemble the Southern Commercial Convention which met at
Montgomery and give the word." Milledgeville (Georgia) *Federal Union*, quoted
in the New Orleans *Picayune*, May 25, 1858. A. P. Calhoun, son of John C.
Calhoun, and a disunionist *per se*, was president.

[81]*Ruffin's Diary*, May 11, 1858.

[82]Charleston *Mercury*, May 15, 1858. The press of South Carolina was almost unanimous in recommending that delegates be sent to Montgomery, thinking the result would be to harmonize and consolidate the South. When, however, the introduction of the slave trade question served only to sow seeds of

in the North and the South,[83] denounced by the Union element in the South, and distrusted by the cooler headed disunionists,[84] the Vicksburg meeting, in May, 1859, was able to summon only a corporal's guard, chiefly of the more radical type of disunionists. For five days the convention indulged in heated debate upon the great questions confronting the South, particularly the reopening of the African slave trade, adopted a string of resolutions as long as those of its predecessors, and adjourned to meet again at the call of the president.[85] That gentleman chose not to issue the call; and, thus, rather ingloriously the Southern Commercial Convention came to an end.

There were reasons for the change in the character of the personnel and the perversion of purpose of the Southern Commercial Convention other than the growing intensity of the sectional struggle and the aggressiveness of the disunion elements. With the exception of the one at Baltimore, these assemblies were practically mass meetings. The task of insuring a large attendance was, in the majority of instances, left to a committee of the city council or board of trade of the city in which the convention was to meet. Delegates were appointed by governors, mayors, city councils, boards of trade, and meetings of citizens. In making their selections they were governed solely by their own judgment; for no qualifications for membership were prescribed. Distinguished individuals were sometimes invited by the local committee; a general invitation was always extended to editors. Not a tenth part of those designated as delegates attended. No one participated in the

dissension, the press of the state very generally condemned it. Camden, (S. C.) *Journal*, quoted in the Montgomery *Daily Confederation*, May 15, 1858. Edmund Ruffin was very much disappointed at the turn the convention took, though he saw redeeming features. *Diary*, May 11-16, 1858.

[83]"Was there ever such another gathering in all this world as the Vicksburg fire eaters' convention? Let Garrison and his motley crew of old women in breeches, and would-be-men in petticoats retire from the field. They are tame, flat and stupid compared with these fiery, fussy, belligerent, and terrible Southern salamanders." New York *Herald*, May 18, 1859.

[84]"When Georgia and Alabama refused to appoint delegates, the Montgomery *Daily Confederation* remarked: "These Southern Commercial Conventions have run their course and we shall hear no more of them forever." May 14, 1859.

[85]Proceedings in New York *Herald*, May 18, 21; *DeBow's Review*, XXVI, 713; XXVII, 94-103, 205-20, 360-65, 468-71 (taken largely from the New York *Herald*).

proceedings who had not been certified as a delegate;[86] but, it is evident, anyone who desired to attend could readily secure the necessary credentials. Thus there was nothing in the organization of the convention to present a change in the character of the personnel.

When the convention failed to produce the results which its founders hoped for it, many of its early patrons confessed it a failure and ceased to attend it. This failure was due in large part to the inherent limitations of a convention as a means of effecting a revolution in commerce and industry. It was unreasonable to expect, as many seem to have expected, a convention to build railroads, establish steamship lines, erect cotton factories, or open mines. Numerous examples can be cited of individual local conventions, particularly railroad conventions, held during the decades preceding the Civil War which aided greatly in crystallizing the sentiment of their respective communities in favor of particular railroad or other projects and in securing subscriptions to the capital stock. A few might be mentioned which powerfully influenced a city or state to embark upon an internal improvements program. But a convention representative of many so widely separated communities and so many conflicting interests as was the Southern Commercial Convention could not be expected to accomplish anything so tangible in character.

The convention failed largely, however, to accomplish what it might legitimately have been expected to accomplish. The meetings were not well managed. No programs were made before convening; and no efforts were made to have subjects presented by those best prepared to discuss them. There was no steering committee. The rules of the House of Representatives were followed; the chair recognized the first to claim the floor, and debate was rarely limited. The most fluent orators were able to monopolize the time of the convention to the exclusion of practical business men, whose counsels might have been more worth while. As the objects of the convention were not strictly defined, anyone with a hobby could secure a hearing. Too large a part of the time was spent in discussing panaceas, magnificent schemes like the Pacific railroad or the navigation of the Amazon. Things of just

[86]However, the conventions sometimes invited distinguished visitors present to participate in the proceedings as delegates.

as great importance but appealing less to the imagination, such as geological surveys, banking facilities, boards of trade, advertising, encouragement of home industry by correction of the irregularities of taxation systems or by bounties, were not taken up in real earnest. Immigration, except of negro slaves, was not discussed. No consideration was given the possibility of utilizing the poor white population in productive industry. No invitations were sent to foreign capitalists.

Great faith was put in the efficacy of resolutions. All resolutions introduced were referred to a general committee composed of a number of delegates from each state, from which they were reported after due consideration to be acted upon by the whole convention. Resolutions deemed important were debated at length, and the voting thereon would not have been watched more jealously had the convention been a legislative body framing the laws of the land.[87] Said the New York *Tribune:* "For a quarter of a century past she has been holding conventions, at which it has been resolved that Norfolk, Charleston, and Savannah *should* become great commercial cities, which obstinately they refuse to be."[88] The convention might have been employed to better advantage had it collected useful information in regard to economic conditions in the Southern states and disseminated it. Such a work would at least have contributed to a better understanding of the causes for the backwardness of the South—a useful preliminary to a prescription of the remedies. The convention left no reports or publications, however, comparable even to the reports and addresses of McDuffie, Hayne, Longstreet, and Mallory, of the direct trade conventions of 1837-1839. This was due to the disinclination of individuals to contribute anything, except speeches and resolutions, to make the convention a success.

[87]Voting was by states. In some of the conventions (Memphis and Charleston) each state was allowed one vote, in others a number equal to the state representation in Congress. This system had some incongruous results; often one or two delegates from a poorly represented state cast the entire vote of the state, and thus had as much to do with determining the official action of the convention as a hundred delegates from another state.

[88]Reprint, *The North and the South*, 1854. Also quoted in Charleston *Courier*, April 24, 1854. "Much time is consumed in talking, and most scrupulous attention is paid to punctilio and the rules of debate . . . . but as soon as the fiat of the convention has gone forth, the members seem to think that their task is complete."

Time and again recess committees were appointed to investigate and report, to memorialize Congress or the state legislatures, and for other purposes. With a few exceptions they failed to do the work assigned them. At Memphis an able committee was named to prepare for publication and distribution, especially in the manufacturing districts of Europe, a full report of the peculiar facilities offered by the Southern and Western states for the manufacture of cotton. This was a very worth-while task. The committee was not supported in its labors,[89] however, and there is no record that it made any report. The Charleston convention appointed a committee of three from each state to gather statistics and other information on mining, manufacturing, lumbering, milling, internal improvements, and capacities for trade and commerce in the South, to address the people, urge the legislatures to action in favor of education, manufacturing, shipbuilding, direct trade, and mining, and report to the next convention. The committee was divided into five sub-committees with able chairmen.[90] This committee, notwithstanding the immensity of the task imposed upon it, might have performed a useful service had it gone intelligently to work. At the succeeding convention the chairmen of the sub-committees had no reports whatever, and the chairman of the committee transmitted certain documents and a letter relative to his duties.[91] Naturally this failure to take seriously the work assigned the committees tended to convince practical men that no good could come from these meetings. "But it cannot be expected," said one delegate, "that a commercial convention can produce any useful result when committees appointed by it pay no attention to subjects committed to them, after adjournment."[92]

In the earlier sessions of the convention an apparently honest attempt was made to keep party politics out of the proceedings. It proved well nigh impossible to do so. Politics played a very large part in the life of the South; from the very first many of the delegates were politicians; and many of the matters which legitimately came before the convention had become party questions. Whig and Democratic members of the convention watched mem-

[89]*DeBow's Review*, XV, 268, 432.
[90]*Ibid.*, XVI, 635; XVII, 325.
[91]*Ibid.*, XVIII, 357.
[92]*Ibid.*, XVIII, 524, remarks of Albert Pike.

bers of the opposite political faith closely to see that they did not
attempt to make political capital from the action of the convention.
The more partisan journals approved or disapproved the convention according as their party or the opposition party could better
capitalize its proceedings.[93] At Memphis a political debate over
resolutions calling upon the Federal government to appropriate
money for the improvement of rivers and harbors was avoided
with difficulty.[94] The opponents of Federal aid to internal improvements, led by General John A. Quitman, forced the omission
from the resolutions on a Pacific railroad, of a clause calling upon
the government to build the main trunk.[95] At Charleston the same
questions were fought over. It was evident that a large majority
was willing to ask the government to improve rivers and harbors.[96]
A Louisiana delegate threatened to speak all week before he would
see the convention turned into a Whig meeting. Governor Chapman, of Alabama, served notice that the next convention would
see few delegates from Democratic Alabama if the resolution was
passed. A Georgia Whig appealed to the convention to keep out
party questions, and the resolution was withdrawn.[97] The introduction of party politics discredited the convention in the eyes of
many who had hoped that some real good would flow from it in
the way of promoting the material prosperity of the South.

Defenders of the Southern Commercial Convention admitted
the justice of many of the criticisms made of it both at home and
in the North. They sometimes countered, however, with the complaint that the fault lay in the failure of Congress and the state
legislatures to act upon the convention's recommendations. And,
with a very few exceptions, it would be impossible to name any
concrete suggestions which were acted upon. This defense over-

[93]Before the Charleston convention met, the Richmond *Enquirer* believed it
would be composed of able and practical men and confidently hoped it
would take action towards securing Southern commercial independence. But
some of the views there expressed were too "federal" to harmonize with the
Enquirer's strict construction principles; and the convention was described as
"an abortion if not something worse." April 4, 14, 21, 1854. Two years later the
Enquirer was again the champion of the convention. Jan. 28, 31, 1856.
[94]*DeBow's Review*, XV, 265.
[95]*Ibid.*, XV, 265 ff., 270 f.
[96]*Ibid.*, XVII, 261.
[97]*Ibid.*, XVII, 400 ff.; New York *Herald*, April 19, 1854.

looks the fact that the convention might have served the cause in other ways than through recommendations to legislative bodies; in fact, it is questionable how far the economic development of the South could have been promoted by legislation. But this aside. It was one of the inherent limitations of the convention that it could not legislate, but only recommend legislation. No doubt action by the state legislatures or by Congress in accordance with many of the recommendations of the convention would have greatly benefited the South. On the other hand, the recommendations were not always well advised, were often indefinite, and, in general, were not pressed upon the state legislatures and Congress with vigor.

Defenders of the convention claimed for it important results in the way of creating public sentiment and educating the public in regard to its objects. It had aroused the public mind, they said, to the need of diversifying industry, fostering commerce, and developing the South's natural resources. It had been the means of disseminating useful information, teaching the South the extent of her resources, and pointing the way to their utilization. These claims are true to a degree. Perhaps the judgment of the New Orleans *Picayune* was as fair and as near the mark as could be made. When the movement was initiated, it said, practical men had hoped that at last the public would be aroused. To some extent this hope had been realized. The importance of commercial enterprise had been impressed upon the public mind. The necessity of manufacturing industry to local independence was generally acknowledged. The certainty of the ultimate growth and importance of Southern seaports, aided by the completion of projected internal improvements, was perceived. These results were due in part to the Southern Commercial Convention.[98]

Men of the disunionist faction, which had dominated the later sessions of the Southern Commercial Convention, claimed that the convention has been a potent means of uniting the South, consolidating public opinion, and preparing the people for the crisis. It had made Southern men more extensively acquainted with each other, and had shown that, while they might disagree as to measures, they were one in purpose. The convention had also taught the people that the South had resources sufficient to maintain herself

[98] May 20, 1858.

as an independent nation. According to the Charleston *Mercury,* one result of the convention was a knowledge that nothing could be done in the Union to change the course of Southern commerce; and "To know our condition, is the first great requisite for altering it."[99] These claims may be admitted with qualifications. The meetings of the Southern Commercial Convention no doubt contributed to the spread of disunion sentiment; but it was through declamation rather than argument. They were conducive to passion and resentment rather than clear thinking and sound judgment. While they brought men from widely separated states together in a common cause, they also exposed to view the divisions in Southern opinion, the discordant elements, the local jealousies, and the inability of too many Southern men to rise above petty politics. Finally, they countenanced the agitation of a question, the reopening of the foreign slave trade, which bade fair to wreck the disunion cause altogether. The Southern Commercial Convention did not tend to put the disunion cause upon a high plane.

Perhaps the chief significance of the Southern Commercial Convention for the student of the period lies in the fact that a convention professing the purposes which it did, met year after year, attracted a considerable degree of interest, and, as long as it retained its original purpose of regenerating the South, commanded the good will of a great majority of the Southern people.

[99]May 16, 1858.

CHAPTER VI

ATTITUDE TOWARD PROTECTIVE LEGISLATION, FEDERAL, STATE, AND LOCAL, 1840-1860

The attitude of the South upon the tariff was determined in the main by the dominant economic interests of the section. The South was practically unanimous in opposition to the Tariff of 1828. One state went to the extreme of declaring it and the amendments of 1832 null and void. There was much sympathy with this action in other Southern states, particularly Georgia. The Southern delegation in Congress was all but unanimous in voting for the Compromise Tariff of 1833. At this period the demand for protection came only from the hemp growers of Kentucky and Missouri, the sugar planters of Louisiana, and mining interests in Virginia and Maryland.

In the early years of its existence the Whig party in the South was more strongly anti-tariff than the Democratic. As late as 1840 the party, because of divisions in its ranks, went before the country without committing itself upon the subject. In 1842, however, Southern Whigs in Congress, with a few exceptions, were whipped into line in support of the protective tariff measure of that year.[1] Again in 1844, during a presidential campaign in which Henry Clay, the champion of the "American System," was the Whig candidate, every Southern Whig member of the House of Representatives but one voted against the McKay bill, which was supported by every Southern Democrat but one.[2] The action of the Whigs may be attributed chiefly to political considerations; Southern Whig leaders felt the need of a broadly national conservative party, and recognized that it could be built only upon the basis of compromise.[3] In 1842 the state of the public treasury imperatively demanded an increase in the revenues, so that the tariff of that year could be plausibly defended as a revenue measure offering incidental protection by discriminatory schedules.[4] In 1844

[1]Cole, *Whig Party in the South*, 98, 99.
[2]*Cong. Globe*, 28 Cong., 1 Sess., 622; *Niles' Register*, LXVI, 177.
[3]Cole, *op. cit.*, 100; *National Intelligencer*, Jan. 4, 1844, letter of Wm. A. Graham accepting the Whig nomination for governor of North Carolina; *ibid.*, Jan. 13, letter from Wm. C. Rives; *ibid.*, Jan. 20, Feb. 15, Mar. 7.
[4]*National Intelligencer*, Mar. 19, 1844, address to the people of Virginia on the Tariff of 1842 by the Whig State Convention.

repeal could be opposed upon the grounds that the revenues were
still required, and that the tariff was working well.[5] Whigs pointed
to the signs of reviving prosperity after the panic of 1837 as evidence that the tariff was not injuring the South. Furthermore,
they welcomed the cotton factories which were springing up here
and there throughout the Southern states as a justification of the
protective policy, and prophesied that soon the divergence of interests between the sections, upon which the division on the tariff
issue was based, would cease to exist.[6] They charged the slow
progress of manufactures in the South to the hostility of the
Democratic party, and declared the absence of diversified industry to be the cause of the declining prosperity which all deplored.[7]

Southern Democrats in Congress were unanimous in opposing
the Tariff of 1842; but the majority at that time did not hold
extreme views. In 1843 Calhoun came forward as the free trade
and reform candidate for the Democratic nomination for the
presidency. Finding his chances poor, he wrote, early in 1844, a
letter announcing his withdrawal.[8] The section devoted to the
tariff was too extreme for his friends outside of South Carolina,
and at their request was modified before the letter was published.[9]
The McKay bill, upon which an attempt was made to unite the
Democratic party in the summer of 1844, was a moderately protective measure.[10] Although there was considerable dissatisfaction
with it among Southern Democrats, every Southern Democrat in
the House but one voted for it.[11] When a faction in South Carolina proposed to take the defeat of the McKay bill by the defec-
tion of twenty-seven Northern Democrats and the subsequent
publication of Polk's "Kane Letter," designed to hold Northern
tariff Democrats in line, as proof positive that no relief from the

[5]*Cong. Globe*, 28 Cong., 1 Sess., 511, 612; *National Intelligencer*, Aug. 6,
1844, quoting the Charleston *Courier*.

[6]*Niles' Register*, LXII, 71; LXVII, 132, quoting the Vicksburg *Whig*; *Cong.
Globe*, 28 Cong., 1 Sess., 512, Berrien, of Georgia, in the Senate.

[7]See ante, pp. 37-41.

[8]*Works*, VI, 239-54; *National Intelligencer*, Feb. 3, 1844.

[9]"But I soon found, it was altogether too high to be sustained by a large
portion;—much the majority; and among them many of the most intelligent and
devoted." Calhoun to Jas. Edw. Calhoun, Feb. 14, 1844, *Calhoun Correspondence*; Calhoun to Duff Green, Jan. 15, 1844.

[10]*Cong. Globe*, 28 Cong., 1 Sess., 369, text of the bill.

[11]*Ibid.*, 28 Cong., 1 Sess., 622; *Niles' Register*, LXVI, 177.

burdens of protection could be expected from the Democratic party, and sought to put the state again "upon its sovereignty," they received remarkably little sympathy outside their own state. A correspondent of the Charleston *Mercury* wrote, "It is not to be disguised that, out of South Carolina, the whole tariff battle has to be fought over."[12] The Walker tariff, enacted in 1846 after a sharp struggle, was by no means a free trade measure.[13] Tea and coffee were put on the free list; raw materials used in manufactures were taxed only five per cent; duties on most manufactured articles were high enough to afford considerable incidental protection to those engaged in their manufacture; whereas the Compromise tariff of 1833 had recognized the principle of a horizontal rate, the Walker tariff contained nine schedules. Upon the whole, the bill was satisfactory to Southern Democrats. Senator Haywood, of North Carolina, however, resigned his seat rather than vote for it.[14] He opposed it because it abandoned the principles of the McKay bill, upon which the party had appealed to the country; it broke faith with Northern Democrats; it would not meet the demands for revenue created by the Mexican War; it did not give sufficient notice to interests formerly protected; and together with the independent treasury constituted too great a revolution in the government's financial policy. On the other hand, the bill was not revolutionary enough to satisfy some of the free trade members from South Carolina and other cotton states, and they voted for it only because they considered it a decided improvement over the Tariff of 1842, and because nothing better could be secured.[15]

The election of 1844 had cut down materially the number of Southern Whigs in Congress. With two exceptions in the House and one in the Senate, they voted with their colleagues of the North against the bill.[16] After a few years Southern Whigs manifested a disposition to acquiesce in the continuance of the Walker tariff, and for several years the tariff was not an issue in Southern politics. Whigs contended that in yielding opposition to the exist-

[12]Quoted in *Niles' Register*, LXVI, 435.
[13]Cf. Dewey, *Financial History of the United States*, 249-52.
[14]"Address of Honorable Wm. H. Haywood, Jr., to the people of North Carolina," etc., in *National Intelligencer*, Aug. 19, 1846; *Niles' Register*, LXX, 410-15.
[15]*Cong. Globe*, 29 Cong., 1 Sess., 1043, W. L. Yancey's speech in the House.
[16]*Ibid.*, 1053, 1157.

ing tariff they abandoned none of their principles; for, they said, the duties were high enough to afford a fair degree of protection, and protective principles were recognized. From time to time, particularly from the border states, there came restatements of the arguments for a protective tariff and reaffirmations of the faith. In 1849, when the Southern people were interested in the possibility of developing cotton manufactures, a suggestion from Hamilton Smith, of Kentucky, that the Constitution should be amended to permit the imposition of an export duty upon raw cotton was received in some quarters with favorable comment.[17]

As long as the tariff was a party issue the opponents of protection were inclined to oppose the introduction of manufacturing. Men too often confused manufactures and protection, and in opposing the latter were led into hostility to the former. Calhoun, indeed, always protested that he was not opposed to manufactures as such,[18] and the same may be said of other leaders. But, in general, there was a feeling that the establishment of diversified industry would take the edge from the anti-tariff sentiment.[19] The advocates of diversified industry had to be very chary in asking for fostering legislation, especially in Democratic states. They frequently gave the assurance that the only thing needed in the way of encouragement was liberal incorporation laws and freedom from discriminatory taxation. It was difficult to secure even the passage of general corporation laws. Corporations were unpopular in the forties as a result of the experience of the previous decade with banking institutions, in particular. In 1847-1848 the question of granting liberal charters to corporations for manufacturing purposes became a political issue in Georgia. Governor Crawford, Whig, recommended such legislation. He was supported by the Whig press and a portion of the Democratic press. Other Demo-

---

[17]"I enclose you a letter of Ex. Pres. Tyler. The only objection he makes to my first proposition is that it would act as a bounty to foreign cotton growers." Smith to Hammond, Mar. 4, 1849, *J. H. Hammond Papers*. Cf. Smith to Hammond, Aug. 14, 1849; *DeBow's Review*, VII, 48 ff. Smith's suggestion was first made in two letters to the Louisville *Journal*. The idea was amplified by S. R. Cockrill, a planter, of Tennessee. *DeBow's Review*, VII, 484-90; *Western Journal and Civilian*, III, 95-106.

[18]Calhoun to Abbott Lawrence, May 13, 1845, *Calhoun Correspondence; Works*, IV, 183-84.

[19]*Niles' Register*, LXVIII, 374 (Aug. 16, 1845), quoting Charleston *Mercury*.

cratic organs, however, were persuaded that Crawford's suggestions were parcel of a design to "quench the growing spirit of
Democracy everywhere," and *"ride us down by the Massachusetts
policy of incorporated wealth,* under the false plea of 'developing
our resources.' "[20] The general incorporation laws were enacted.[21]
In 1850, Governor Seabrook, of South Carolina, wrote William
Gregg asking what measures he considered necessary for the encouragement of manufactures. Gregg replied that he considered
unnecessary and unwise any pecuniary aid from the state either
in the form of loans or otherwise. The only thing needed was the
"privileges and advantages granted in other states in the use of
associated capital." He told how cheaply goods were being made
in the Graniteville factory; this fact, he said, should "disarm all
opposition from those who fear that we may ultimately join the
Northern people in a clamor for protection...."[22]

After the Walker tariff had been in effect a few years, and the
tariff controversy had abated, opposition to diversified industry
on anti-protectionist grounds gave way to a considerable extent,
and many anti-tariff men and journals strongly supported the
movement to bring the spindles to the cotton and to diversify industry generally. Typical of their reasoning was the reply of the
Richmond *Enquirer* to a Whig contemporary's charge of inconsistency. Said the *Enquirer:* "We have never denounced home
industry. We have, however, steadily denounced that hot-bed
system of legislation, whose effect is to pamper one class at the
expense of all others, and especially, to foster the monopolies of
the North, which have flourished and grown fat upon the tribute
of the South. It was to benefit home manufactures and not to
destroy them that we opposed the tariff."[23] There was a common
element in the contention of the free traders that the tariff ben-

---

[20]Hopkins Holsey, editor of the Athens [Georgia] *Southern Banner,* to Howell
Cobb, Dec. 3, 1847, *Toombs, Stephens, Cobb Correspondence.*

[21]*DeBow's Review,* XVII, 257.

[22]Gregg to Seabrook, May 10, 1850, *Whitemarsh B. Seabrook Papers.* The
absence of general incorporation laws was not an insurmountable obstacle. Little
difficulty was experienced in getting special characters through the legislatures.
The session laws of the various states are full of such special legislation.

[23]July 23, 1850. James H. Hammond, who certainly could not be charged
with protective principles, carefully distinguished between manufactures and the
protective system. *DeBow's Review,* VIII, 508.

efited New England and Pennsylvania manufactures at the expense of Southern agriculture, and the contention of those who labored for Southern industrial independence that it was the manufacture of Southern staples and the sale to the Southern people of numerous articles which should be produced at home which strengthened and enriched the North while weakening and impoverishing the South. Both arguments represented one section as paying tribute to the other. This common element made it easy for anti-tariff men to support efforts being made to diversify Southern industry.

When the desirability from both the economic and political viewpoints of making the South commercially and industrially independent of the North was understood, it was inevitable that a demand should arise for the protection of home enterprises against Northern competitors. A tariff might protect American industries from European competition; but more dangerous to the infant industries of the South than foreign competition were the firmly established industries of the North.

In fact, in the forties several Southern states intermittently discriminated in their tax laws in favor of home manufactures. The laws of Virginia in 1840 and a number of years thereafter exempted articles made within the state from the tax on sales.[24] By act of 1843 South Carolina exempted from this tax "the products of this State, and the unmanufactured products of any of the United States or Territories thereof."[25] Alabama also, by an act of January 15, 1844, exempted articles manufactured within the state from the tax on sales.[26] Taxation during the period was very light, and these exemptions amounted to little. There were also as many cases of exemptions of other classes of property from taxation, for example, farm implements and mechanics' tools.

In the tariff debates of 1844 and 1846 anti-tariff men from the South referred to the possibility of adopting a policy of state protection. "If the protective policy," said R. B. Rhett, "is wise and just with foreign nations, it must be equally so between the States, for there is far more intercourse and affinity of interest between portions of the United States and foreign nations, than between

[24] Acts of the General Assembly of Virginia, 1839-1840, act of Mar. 3, 1840.
[25] National Intelligencer, Aug. 10, 1844, "Precept and Practice of South Carolina."
[26] Acts of the General Assembly of Alabama, 1843-1844, p. 65.

different portions of the Union."[27] George McDuffie threatened, in 1844, to resign his seat in the United States Senate, secure a seat in the South Carolina legislature, and bring forward a proposition to tax all manufactured goods brought into the state.[28] Seaborn Jones, of Georgia, also suggested that Southern states had a remedy at hand for unjust taxation in "countervailing legislation, putting excise duties upon manufactured articles which have not paid revenue duty to the Government."[29]

During the political crisis of 1850 and thereabouts many proposals were made in the South for non-intercourse with the North, discriminatory taxation of Northern manufactures, exclusion of Northern ships from Southern harbors, cessation of business and pleasure trips to the North, withdrawal of subscriptions to Northern newspapers, and a number of other measures of the same general character. They can be attributed chiefly to a desire to retaliate against the anti-slavery party, to arouse the business interests of the North to the necessity of curbing the abolition agitation, and to teach the North the "money value of the Union"; but it was an added recommendation that these measures would tend to promote commercial and industrial independence. J. C. Calhoun wrote to public men throughout the South requesting their views upon two lines of procedure for bringing the North to a sense of justice. One was the assembling of a Southern convention, the other, retaliation against Northern states for unconstitutional acts.[30] In one of these letters he suggested that closing Southern ports to Northern seagoing vessels would promote direct trade with Europe.[31]

In the Nashville Convention of 1850, retaliation was supported by a minority as a proper measure to employ in case the North did not grant justice to the South.[32] At the adjourned session, November, 1850, the Tennessee delegation supported resolutions

[27]*Cong. Globe*, 28 Cong., 1 Sess., Appx., 658.
[28]*Niles' Register*, LXVI, 230.
[29]*Cong. Globe*, 29 Cong., 1 Sess., 991.
[30]Wilson Lumpkin to Calhoun, Nov. 18, 1847; Joseph W. Lesesne to Calhoun, Sept. 12, 1847; H. W. Conner to Calhoun, Nov. 2, 1848; Calhoun to John H. Means, Apr. 13, 1849, *Calhoun Correspondence*.
[31]Benton, *Thirty Years' View*, II, 698-700, quotation from a letter from Calhoun to a member of the Alabama Legislature, 1847.
[32]See above, pp. 73-76, for a discussion of the Nashville Convention.

which accepted the recently adopted compromise, outlined the line of conduct Northern states would be expected to pursue in the future, and recommended that, in case this line should be transgressed, the people of the South resort to the "most rigid system of commercial non-intercourse" with all offending states, cities, and communities. The legislatures of the several states were invited to join in the recommendation. Counties, towns, and neighborhoods were asked to adopt resolutions against purchasing or using articles from offending Northern states or communities. To make it possible to follow these recommendations, it was further recommended that the states encourage their own mechanics and manufactures, and push forward their internal improvements to the seaboard.[33]

In Virginia such a remedy met with considerable favor. When, after the passage of the Compromise of 1850, a disposition was shown in the North, particularly in Boston, not to acquiesce in the execution of the Fugitive Slave law, Virginians took fire, and a strong sentiment for retaliation developed. The citizens of Prince George County met for the purpose of forming a Southern rights association.[34] Resolutions were adopted pledging those present to buy in the North no coarse cottons or woolens, ready made clothing, carriages, buggies, plows, axes, harness—in general, nothing which could be produced in the South or obtained from Europe. The resolution furthermore pledged them to employ no Northern teachers; to withdraw patronage from Northern schools, newspapers, and books; to take no pleasure trips to the North; to buy of no merchant or employ no mechanic not identified with the South; and to employ no vessels owned or commanded by a Northern man or manned by a Northern crew.[35] Similar associations were formed in other counties.[36] The most important and permanent of the Southern rights associations in the state was the Central Southern Rights Association of Virginia, which was organ-

[33]*National Intelligencer,* Nov. 16, 19, 1850; A. V. Brown, *Speeches, Congressional and Political,* etc., 318-21 (text of the resolutions);DuBose, *Life and Times of Yancey,* 248; *Speech of the Hon. Langdon Cheves in the Nashville Convention,* p. 20.

[34]Richmond *Enquirer,* Nov. 15, 1850.

[35]*Ibid.,* Nov. 20, Dec. 10, 1850.

[36]*Ibid.,* Dec. 31, 1850.

ized in Richmond in December, 1850,[37] and continued in existence until the outbreak of the Civil War. Some of the ablest and most prominent men of Richmond and the state at large were members. The members were pledged to "use all lawful and constitutional means in our power to arrest further aggressions of the non-slave-holding states," and to appeal to the legislature of the state to enact such laws as were "prudent and constitutional for effecting, ultimately, commercial independence" of such states as by laws or otherwise sought to prevent the execution of the Fugitive Slave law.[38] The first petition addressed by the association to the State Legislature requested the passage of excise tax laws discriminating in favor of articles of Virginia manufacture or of direct importation from abroad. Such taxation was believed to be the most certain means of securing ultimately Virginia's commercial independence and the safety of her property and institutions.[39]

A year earlier Governor Floyd had suggested discriminatory taxation in a special message to the General Assembly.[40] In November, 1850, he introduced the subject in the state Constitutional Convention.[41] In his last message to the General Assembly, shortly after, he again recommended it.[42] As a member of the Legislature he championed a bill to impose a tax of five per cent on all goods brought into the state for sale except direct imports.[43] The Democratic press of the state generally supported the plan of discriminatory taxation.[44] In the opinion of the Richmond *Enquirer*, it would check the abolition movement in the North, "give tone and strength to Southern manufactures, commerce and all the interests of the South," and ward off disunion.[45] The *Enquirer* charged the Whigs with inconsistency in opposing Floyd's proposal while advocating a higher tariff.[46] The conservative press generally op-

[37] Richmond *Enquirer*, Dec. 10, 13, 17, 24, 31, 1850.
[38] *Virginia Documents*, 1850-1851, doc. LX, "Petition of the Central Southern Rights Association of Virginia, and Accompanying Documents," p. 5.
[39] *Ibid.*, doc. LX; *DeBow's Review*, XII, 109.
[40] Richmond *Enquirer*, Nov. 15, 1850.
[41] *Ibid.*, Nov. 19, 1850.
[42] *Ibid.*, Dec. 3, 1850; *Virginia Documents*, 1850-1851, doc. I.
[43] Richmond *Enquirer*, Jan. 31, 1851.
[44] *Ibid.*, Nov. 15, 22, 1850, quoting a number of Virginia newspapers.
[45] Dec. 13, 1850.
[46] Dec. 17, 1850.

posed the plan.[47] They denounced it as calculated to lead to a dismemberment of the Union and as "subversive of the true interests of the Southern states." In the North it would not injure the abolitionists but rather the friends of the South; for the former were not engaged in commerce. It was said to be unconstitutional; the *National Intelligencer* called it "another form of nullification."[48] In opposing Floyd's proposal the Whigs resorted to good free trade arguments: Virginia must depend upon the North for materials with which to construct her internal improvements; she could not rely upon her own resources. Were discriminatory taxation imposed, the North would lose a market, and both sections would be sacrificed to the cupidity of England. The tax would be paid by the consumer.[49] The Whigs were not, of course, animated by any feeling of hostility to the cause of Southern commercial and industrial independence.

Senator Berrien, of Georgia, a Whig, in public speeches expressed views similar to those of Governor Floyd. At Macon he was reported to have said that he did not wish the Georgia Convention to propose non-intercourse nor an import tax, as both would be unconstitutional; but he thought it best to recommend a measure by which Northern goods, after they had arrived in Georgia and had been delivered into the hands of the merchants, should be charged with a high and discriminatory tax. Such a measure would encourage Georgia manufactures, greatly abridge importations of Northern goods, and arouse the North to a sense of the power of the South to protect herself.[50] In Alabama, Southern rights associations were formed, and resolutions adopted similar to those adopted by the associations in Virginia.[51] In Mississippi, members of the Southern rights party expressed themselves in favor of excluding by legislative enactment goods manufactured north of Mason and Dixon's line.[52]

In South Carolina, after the passage of the Compromise of 1850, public opinion was, as we have seen, widely divided in regard to

[47]Richmond *Whig*, Jan. 2, 22, Feb. 12, 1851; *National Intelligencer*, Dec. 9, 12, 17, 28, 1850.

[48]Dec. 17, 1850, editorial.

[49]Richmond *Whig*, Jan. 2, 22, 1851.

[50]Richmond *Enquirer*, Nov. 15, 1850.

[51]*Ibid.*, Nov. 22, 1850; DeBow's *Industrial Resources*, III, 122.

[52]*Cong. Globe*, 32 Cong., 1 Sess., Appx. 284.

the proper policy to be pursued. In the hope of unifying the state, J. H. Hammond brought forward a "Plan of State Action," which, although not adopted, met with considerable favor.[53] He proposed that the State Convention declare the right of secession; prohibit citizens from holding Federal offices outside the state; refuse to accept Federal appropriations for any purpose; impose a double tax upon the property of non-residents; "as far as it constitutionally may," impose taxes upon manufactures of non-slaveholding states; encourage manufactures by granting liberal charters to companies; encourage agriculture; and with state funds "aid in the establishment of direct commercial intercourse with foreign nations, by steamships adopted to purposes of war, in case of need." Already Governor Seabrook had recommended the encouragement of manufactures by liberal corporation laws[54] and the Legislature had discussed a proposal to levy discriminatory taxation upon Northern goods.[55]

A bill was introduced in the North Carolina Legislature, November, 1850, to impose a tax of ten per cent upon goods brought into the state from non-slaveholding states after January 1, 1852.[56] The House of Commons adopted resolutions introduced by a Whig member which declared[57] that (1) North Carolina was absolved by the abolition agitation from further obligation to protect Northern manufactures by a tariff; (2) if North Carolina industries required protection, it could be "better effected by State than by Congressional Legislation;" (3) the Walker tariff was high enough; (4) and requested that members of Congress from North Carolina vote against any increase. These resolutions were adopted by votes of 105-2, 62-32, 75-18, and 84-8 respectively, Whigs as well as Democrats composing the majorities.[58] Even before these reso-

[53]J. H. Hammond Papers, No. 22,198, a broadside printed by the Charleston Mercury, accompanied by a note to the editors, dated April 29, 1851; Hammond to Wm. Gilmore Simms, April 29, 1851; A. P. Aldrich to Hammond, May 16, Nov. 10; Hammond to Simms, May 29, July 1; Maxcy Gregg to Hammond, Nov. 14, 1851. Edmund Ruffin to Hammond, Nov. 13, 1851.

[54]Richmond Enquirer, Dec. 3, 1850.
[55]National Intelligencer, Dec. 9, 12, 1850.
[56]Richmond Enquirer, Nov. 29, 1850.
[57]Richmond Whig, Jan. 17, 1851.
[58]Cong. Globe, 31 Cong., 2 Sess., Appx. 206, Thomas L. Clingman, in the House, Feb. 15, 1851.

lutions had been adopted, Southern Whig members of Congress, particularly from North Carolina, had defeated attempts made in the first session of the Thirty-first Congress to revise the tariff upward in the interest, chiefly, of the Pennsylvania iron industry.[59]

The action of the North Carolina Whigs was indicative of a marked falling off in tariff sentiment in the South. So staunch a protectionist organ as the Richmond *Whig* wavered in its faith, and warned manufacturers that they need not expect further protection.[60] For several years after the attempt of the iron interest in 1850 to secure higher duties, the tariff question was not before Congress or the country except for occasional attempts of Southern and Western congressmen to secure the remittance or repeal of the duty on railroad iron. North as well as South came to acquiesce in the Walker tariff, with the exception, in the South, of men of the South Carolina school, who professed to find the Tariff of 1846 oppressive, just as they had found that of 1842 to be.[61]

The Walker tariff, however, proved an excellent revenue producing measure, receipts exceeded expenditures, and an accumulating surplus in the treasury finally forced Congress to undertake revision. A late attempt in the second session of the Thirty-third Congress, March, 1855, failed;[62] but it was generally understood that the next Congress must act. Contemporaneously, agitation was started by extreme anti-tariff men in the South for the abandonment of the tariff system altogether and the substitution of direct taxation. In the Southern Commercial Convention, Savannah, December, 1856, resolutions were reported which pronounced the tariff to be the cause of the decline of Southern commerce and declared for absolute free trade and direct taxation.[63] The resolutions were not adopted, but were referred to a committee instructed to report at the next convention.

[59]*Cong. Globe*, 31 Cong., 1 Sess., 1728, 1812, 1951; *ibid.*, 31 Cong., 2 Sess., Appx. 206, Clingman's explanation of the action of North Carolina men.

[60]Jan. 17, Feb. 12, Mar. 19, 21, and 31, 1851.

[61]*Cong. Globe*, 32 Cong., 2 Sess., 35, Woodward, of South Carolina, in the House, Dec. 10, 1852.

[62]The House attached sections reducing the tariff as a rider to the Civil and Diplomatic bill, the Senate struck them out. *Ibid.*, 33 Cong., 2 Sess., 914, 1088, 1178.

[63]*DeBow's Review*, XXII, 92.

The Tariff of 1857 was passed after short and rather desultory debates in the House and Senate. The debates contained remarkably little of a sectional nature, and the only interests greatly dissatisfied were the iron manufacturers and the wool growers. The bill as finally passed was written by Senator Hunter, of Virginia. As did Secretary of the Treasury Guthrie, Hunter took a fairly liberal attitude toward the manufacturing interests.[64] The rates were somewhat lower than those of the Walker tariff. In one respect, however, the bill was more in accord with protective principles than the former act; it provided for free raw materials where the demand was for manufactures. Cotton manufactures were favored by leaving the duties nearly as high as those of the Tariff of 1846. Some objection was raised by Southern members to the enlarged free list. The only out-and-out free trade views expressed came from South Carolina men. Senator A. P. Butler said, "Cotton would rise to twenty cents tomorrow...if we had no tariff."[65] Representative W. W. Boyce, of Charleston, declared for free trade and direct taxation.[66] Only two Southern congressmen voted against the bill.[67] Outside Congress there was little dissatisfaction except among the ultras. DeBow, for example, was at first inclined to approve the measure as a step in the right direction, but later found that "the manufacturers have again had a victory in the adroit combinations made."[68]

The free trade faction in the South followed up this partial victory over protection by a general attack against every form of protection and privilege granted by the Federal government. In the Southern Commercial Convention, at Knoxville, August, 1857, W. W. Boyce again brought forward the proposal for free trade and direct taxation. A committee reported it adversely, while the debate showed sharp divisions of opinion.[69] A Virginia delegate offered resolutions declaring that the merchant vessels of foreign nations should be admitted to the United States coasting trade

[64]*Cong. Globe*, 34 Cong., 3 Sess., Appx. 328 ff., speech in the Senate, Feb. 26, 1857; *ibid.*, 36 Cong., 1 Sess., 3188.
[65]*Ibid.*, 34 Cong., 3 Sess., Appx. 350.
[66]*Ibid.*, 34 Cong., 3 Sess., Appx. 215 ff.
[67]*Ibid.*, 34 Cong., 3 Sess., 971; Appx. 358 (votes in the House and Senate).
[68]*DeBow's Review*, XXII, 381, 554.
[69]*Ibid.*, XXIII, 305, 309, 310-15.

upon the same footing as our own.[70] Roger A. Pryor, of Virginia, secured the appointment of a committee to memorialize Congress for the repeal of the fishing bounties, which benefited New England particularly.[71] In the next session of Congress W. W. Boyce secured the appointment of a select committee of the House to inquire into and report upon a reduction of the expenditures of the government, the navigation laws, the existing duties on imports, and a resort exclusively to internal taxation.[72] As chairman of the committee, Boyce brought in an able and elaborate report, presenting all the free trade arguments.[73] Senator C. C. Clay, of Alabama, attacked the fishing bounties, and secured the passage through the Senate, 1858, of a bill repealing them.[74] He regarded this action as but the initial step to the repeal of the "ship-building, coast-wise trade, and other monopolies now enjoyed by the North to the wrong of the South."[75] The policy entered upon during the preceding decade of subsidizing steamship lines by making liberal contracts for carrying the mails was repeatedly attacked by Southern Democrats led by Senator Hunter, of Virginia.[76] After June 14, 1858, no new contracts were made; finally, on October 1, 1859, notice was given of complete abrogation of existing contracts.[77]

The Tariff of 1857 had been in operation but a few months when the financial crash of that year occurred. Imports fell off greatly, and shortly the treasury was confronted by a deficit. It soon be-

[70]*DeBow's Review*, XXIII, 306, Fuqua, of Virginia.

[71]*Ibid.*, XXIII, 307. The subject was not a new one. It had been brought up in previous commercial conventions, and time and again in Congress. See, e. g., *ibid.*, XVII, 204, Ruffin in the Southern Commercial Convention in Charleston, 1854.

[72]*Cong. Globe*, 35 Cong., 1 Sess., 509.

[73]*DeBow's Review*, XXV, 1-27; Charleston *Mercury*, June 1, 4, 1858.

[74]*Cong. Globe*, 35 Cong., 1 Sess., 1930 ff., Clay's speech, May 4, 1858; *ibid.*, 35 Cong., 1 Sess., 2239, vote upon passage of the bill.

[75]C. C. Clay to Wm. Burwell, May 7, 1858, *Wm. M. Burwell Letters*. Cf. DuBose, *Life and Times of W. L. Yancey*, 368 ff., quoting letter from Yancey to Thomas J. Orme, May 22, 1858.

[76]Hunter's most famous speech on the subject is in *Cong. Globe*, 32 Cong., 1 Sess., 1147 ff. (April 21, 1852). He termed the policy the adoption of the "protective system in one of its very worst forms."

[77]Bates, *American Navigation: the Political History of Its Rise and Ruin*, 346 (a table of mail subsidy legislation); *U. S. Statutes at Large*, Act of June 14, 1858.

came apparent that another revision of the tariff would have to
be undertaken. The discussion then provoked revealed that in
certain quarters of the South the same feeling against the tariff
existed as had been displayed in 1832 and 1844. After the Kansas
question had been temporarily put at rest in the spring of 1858
by the passage of the English Bill, Senator Hammond told his
constituents that the state could now remain in the Union "with
honor." He gave warning, however, that an attempt would be
made in the next session of Congress to increase the tariff, and
declared that the "plantation states should discard any government" which adopted protection. "Unequal taxation is, after
all, what we have most to fear in this Union."[78] A. P. Calhoun, in
an address in which he advocated secession, also put the tariff
foremost among the grievances of the South.[79] In Georgia there
was a group of free traders, led by John A. Jones, who were as
violent in their opposition to the tariff as were those of South
Carolina. The Montgomery *Daily Confederation* thought free
trade had already "culminated into universal sanction and adoption" in the Southern states, and pronounced "woe to the statesman that should attempt to lend himself to any move to restore"
the protective system.[80]

President Buchanan in his annual message, 1858, and Secretary
of the Treasury Cobb in his annual report, both recommended a
revision of the tariff; but the Democratic caucus considered it
inexpedient to make any changes in the tariff during the session.[81]
In the next Congress, the Thirty-sixth, the Republicans controlled
the House. Justin S. Morrill, of Vermont, reported a bill whose
level of rates was about equal to that of the Tariff of 1846, although it was constructed more in accord with protective principles.[82] The bill was passed over the opposition of the
Democrats.[83] There was little sectionalism in the debates; few
Southern men spoke upon the bill. Several Southern Democrats

[78]Charleston *Mercury*, July 22, 1858, Feb. 3, 1859.
[79]*DeBow's Review*, XXVI, 476.
[80]Feb. 1, 1859.
[81]Montgomery *Daily Confederation*, Feb. 3, 1859.
[82]*Cong. Globe*, 36 Cong., 1 Sess., 1830 ff.
[83]*Ibid.*, 2056.

declared their willingness to restore the Tariff of 1846.[84] The Democratic Senate postponed action upon the bill until the short session, 1860-1861, when, after the secession of several Southern states had withdrawn a number of senators from the opposition, it was passed.

On the very eve of the Civil War, however, there still lingered in some quarters of the South a sentiment for a protective tariff. The Louisiana sugar planters persistently demanded protection.[85] In Virginia, Tennessee, and North Carolina there were interests which asked for governmental encouragement. Even in South Carolina such men as Richard Yeadon, of the Charleston *Courier*, and William Gregg retained their tariff views to the end.[86] And in general, it is safe to say, the South as a whole was not committed to free trade, but rather to a tariff for revenue with incidental protection. Many Democratic leaders admitted the propriety of discrimination in duties within the revenue limit. Only in South Carolina, if, indeed, in any state, would a majority have been willing to substitute internal taxation for duties upon imports.

Nor can the general opposition to a high tariff, the agitation for free trade, and the concerted attack upon monopolies, bounties, and special privileges of all kinds be taken as proof that the doctrine of *laissez faire* had come to prevail in the South more than elsewhere. A protective tariff was opposed not only because it fostered manufactures at the expense of the planting interests, but also because the manufactures were in the North. Likewise, the fishing bounties were opposed not only because they were bounties, but also because they directly benefited only New England. The navigation laws were objectionable to Southern men not only because they enhanced freight rates in coastwise trade, but also because the shipping industry which profited thereby was almost a monopoly of the North. If we turn our attention to local policies, we find about as much disposition in the South as elsewhere to attempt by legislative enactments to modify the courses capital and labor might take.

[84]*Cong. Globe*, 36 Cong., 1 Sess., 3187, Jefferson Davis in the Senate. Cf. Charleston *Mercury*, Feb. 26, 1859, quoting Rep. Taylor of Louisiana.

[85]*DeBow's Review*, XXII, 320-25, 433-36; XXVI, 481.

[86]*Ibid.*, XXX, 102 f., for an expression of Gregg's views.

The policy of encouraging manufactures and direct trade by levying discriminatory taxes upon goods manufactured in the non-slaveholding states and upon articles imported from foreign countries through Northern ports, or by offering bounties or granting exemption from taxation to home industries, was kept under advisement in the South until secession. In the Southern Commercial Convention in Charleston, 1854, General Tilghman offered in behalf of the Maryland delegation a resolution that the legislatures of the Southern states should encourage manufactures and commerce "by the granting of bounties and all such other benefits and privileges as the powers reserved and possessed by the States may permit."[87] His arguments were strikingly similar to those which might be employed in the advocacy of a protective tariff. The convention appointed a committee upon the subject of promoting "Southern and Western manufactures and mining operations," and recommended the encouragement of direct trade either by exempting the goods imported from taxation or by allowing direct importers an equivalent drawback or bounty.[88] D. H. London, president of the Central Southern Rights Association of Virginia thought: "If there were absolute free trade, Southern ports would soon surpass the North, not only in commerce but in industry and arts." Since, however, it was impossible to secure free trade, he thought the state legislatures should place an excise tax upon indirect imports.[89]

In Georgia, in 1854, a proposal was being discussed to exempt from taxation property of corporations engaged in manufacturing.[90] At the same time, Nelson Tift, of the Albany *Patriot*, and others were advocating as a purely retaliatory measure the imposition of a tax of one hundred per cent upon the sale of goods from states which did not observe their constitutional obligations.[91] A Democratic party convention, 1855, unanimously adopted resolutions requesting the Legislature to enact effective retaliatory measures.[92] Somewhat different was the proposal submitted by

[87]*DeBow's Review*, XVII, 255.
[88]*Ibid.*, XVII, 254, 258.
[89]Charleston *Courier*, Mar. 16, 1854, D. H. London to F. W. Connor.
[90]*DeBow's Review*, XVII, 257.
[91]*Ibid.*, XVII, 399; Savannah *Republican*, Dec. 25, 1856.
[92]Phillips, *Georgia and State Rights*, 183.

Robert Toombs to the Southern Commercial Convention in Savannah the following year.[93] He proposed to secure direct trade "by imposing a State tax of—per cent. *ad valorem* upon all goods, wares, and merchandise offered for sale within the State, other than those which shall be imported from foreign countries." The rate should be high enough to prevent all indirect importations of foreign merchandise and "to raise sufficient revenue for all the wants of the State, without imposing upon the people any capitation or other direct tax whatever." "Levy our taxes on consumption," he said; "it can be more easily paid; we shall then fill our treasury to the extent of our wants, protect ourselves against the unjust legislation of our sister States, bring direct trade to our ports, give profitable employment to our capital and labor, educate our people, develop all our resources, and build up great, powerful, and prosperous commonwealths, able to protect the people from all dangers from within and from without." Such a tax, with the exemption of direct imports, would be constitutional, he said, and could be easily collected. This plan, it will be observed, did not call for discriminatory taxation upon sales of Northern made goods; it would have operated as hardly upon Georgia manufactures as upon those of New England. Toomb's proposal was not widely endorsed.[94]

The Southern Commercial Convention which met at Richmond, January, 1856, adopted by acclamation a resolution recommending the release of direct importations from license fees.[95] About the same time ex-Governor Floyd introduced a bill in the Virginia House of Delegates providing for an excise tax upon goods brought into the state for sale except goods directly imported from abroad.[96] Attacks were made upon the merchants' license tax and the tax on sales, which were imposed both by the state and municipal governments.[97] These taxes were said to act as bounties to induce retail merchants to go outside the state to purchase their stocks; for if they bought of home jobbers who, in turn, bought

[93]*DeBow's Review*, XXII, 102 ff. The latter was headed, Washington, Ga., Dec. 6, 1856.

[94]Savannah *Republican*, Dec. 22, 25, 1856, quoting other journals.

[95]*DeBow's Review*, XX, 351.

[96]Richmond *Enquirer*, Feb. 16, 20, Mar. 14, 1856.

[97]*Ibid.*, March 2, 5, 1856, letters signed "Junius."

of Virginia importers, the consumers paid the taxes three times, whereas if the retailers bought in states where no such taxes were levied, the consumers paid the taxes only once.[98] The Finance Committee of the House of Delegates was dominated by the planting interests of the tidewater region, and proposals for tax reform met little favor.[99] However, a provision was included in the tax bill of 1856 allowing the importing merchant a deduction from the amount of sales on which he paid license tax equal to the value of the goods imported by him plus the duties paid upon them.[100] This was not a very considerable concession; for a sales tax upon imported goods sold in the original packages was unconstitutional.[101]

After the John Brown Raid at Harper's Ferry, October, 1859, the Central Southern Rights Association of Virginia became active again.[102] In a memorial to the General Assembly it presented commercial independence as the "means of remedy and redress" for the grievances of the South. The memorialists asked that the pilot fees be decreased upon vessels owned in Virginia and upon vessels from foreign nations and increased upon Northern vessels engaged in the coasting trade. They would give bounties for direct importations of goods most needed within the state. They recommended that importing merchants be reimbursed for duties paid and exempted altogether from the license tax.[103] In response to the memorial the House of Delegates passed a bill exempting direct importations from all sales taxes. It was defeated in the Senate, largely by the votes of members from districts having the largest slave populations.[104] An act of February 29, 1860, exempted

[98]*DeBow's Review*, XX, 623; *ibid.*, XXVIII, 316, argument of D. H. London, president of the Central Southern Rights Association of Virginia, before the General Assembly.
[99]Richmond *Enquirer*, Feb. 20, 21, 1856, Report of the Finance Committee, Muscoe R. H. Garnett, Chairman.
[100]*Acts of the General Assembly of Virginia*, 1855-1856, act of Jan. 5, 1856. A similar provision was in the tax act of Mar. 30, 1860.
[101]Brown *vs.* Maryland, 12 *Wheaton*, 419; *DeBow's Review*, XXVIII, 178.
[102]*Ibid.*, XXVIII, 356-7.
[103]*Ibid.*, XXVIII, 173-182. Cf. *ibid.*, XXVIII, 314-324, "Argument of D. H. London before the General Assembly of Virginia"; *ibid.*, XXIX, 466-88, "Commercial, Agricultural, and Intellectual Independence of the South," by D. H. London.
[104]*Ibid.*, XXIX, 471, 472.

vessels four-fifths owned in Virginia from the payment of pilot fees.[105] But so difficult was it to secure fostering legislation that an enactment ambitiously entitled an "Act to Encourage Direct Foreign Trade" provided only for the exemption of Virginia flour from the small inspection fees if exported in ships four-fifths owned in Virginia.[106]

In other Southern states, legislation similar to that proposed in Georgia and Virginia was advocated. Louisiana, by act of the Legislature, March 18, 1852, offered a bonus of five dollars per ton for every ship of over one hundred tons built in the state.[107] There was sentiment in the state for the extension of aid in a similar manner to other industries.[108] The Alabama Legislature exempted the sale of all foreign goods directly imported into the Southern states from any description of state, county, or city taxation.[109] South Carolina exempted goods imported in vessels owned in the state from taxation while in the hands of the importers.[110] In Mississippi discriminatory taxation was advocated both as a means of retaliation against Northern aggression and of promoting direct trade and developing manufactures.[111] In Tennessee there was discussion of the desirability of liberalizing the tax laws.[112] Tennessee and South Carolina appropriated money in aid of mechanics' institutes whose purpose was to encourage manufactures and the mechanic arts.[113] The legislatures of North Carolina, Alabama, Mississippi, and Arkansas took a first step toward developing the mineral resources of those states by providing for geological surveys.[114]

---

[105]*Acts of the General Assembly of Virginia*, 1859-1860, p. 145.

[106]*Ibid.*, 167; act of Mar. 31, 1860.

[107]*Acts of the Legislature of the State of Louisiana*, etc. 129. The act was somewhat modified three years later. Act of Mar. 15, 1855.

[108]New Orleans *Picayune*, Jan. 17, 1858; Kettell, *Southern Wealth and Northern Profits*, 66.

[109]*DeBow's Review*, XXVIII, 492.

[110]Richmond *Enquirer*, Mar. 24, 1854, Mar. 5, 1856.

[111]*DeBow's Review*, XXIX, 233-6, 545-61; Charleston *Mercury*, Nov. 24, 1859, message of Governor McWillie, of Mississippi, Nov. 8.

[112]*Republican Banner and Nashville Whig*, Oct. 6, 1856, message of Governor Andrew Johnson.

[113]*DeBow's Review*, XXIX, 499.

[114]*Ibid.*, XXIV, 403 ff.; XVII, 677 ff.; XXVII, 350.

The sum total of protective legislation enacted in the South, either in the form of discriminatory taxation upon Northern goods, exemption of home manufactures and direct imports from state taxation, or in the form of bounties, was small. The fact cannot, however, be taken without qualification as due to the prevalence of free trade opinions. Discriminatory taxation was advocated as a mode of retaliation for the aggressions of the North as well as a measure of political economy. It was a remedy decidedly unfriendly to the North, subversive of one of the primary purposes of the Constitution, and likely to disturb the peace between the sections and lead to disunion. It was extremely doubtful that laws could be so framed as not to be held in violation of the Federal Constitution and, for that matter, the constitutions of some of the Southern states. Such measures were opposed by moderate men who were trying to allay sectional feeling rather than aggravate it, as well as by bona fide free traders who might have been content with their political significance. Furthermore, measures of discriminatory taxation or of non-intercourse would have been unsuccessful unless taken in concert by a number of states. Charleston and Savannah, for example, were rivals for much the same territory; discriminatory taxation in one's state and not in the other's might have put the cities upon unequal terms.[115]

State and local encouragement of desired industries by loans, bounties, and tax exemptions were not objectionable from the political standpoint, though their efficacy may be doubted. That they were not employed to a greater extent was partly due to the fact that the Southern people put the building of internal improvements first in their programs for developing the South. Taxes had to be increased to meet the growing expenditures on their account, and the people of the South were not accustomed to heavy taxation. In the case of manufactures and mining, there was no considerable class directly and primarily interested in securing protective legislation. The influence of directly interested parties was further lessened because they were generally Northern men or foreigners. State legislatures were too frequently controlled

[115]C. G. Memminger, Commissioner to Virginia, in an address to the Virginia Legislature, 1860. DeBow's Review, XXIX, 770. Also in Capers, Life and Times of Memminger, 247 ff.

by professional politicians, and their time monopolized by consideration of national issues and policies to the sacrifice of state interests.

As far as principles and theories are concerned, it was not a very far cry from the advocacy of fostering commerce and industry by discriminatory taxation or by granting bounties and drawbacks to the advocacy of the extension of public credit or of capital in aid of steamship lines to Europe or other enterprises. It should not be forgotten that Southern commercial conventions, even those in which most was said about free trade, were constantly calling upon the state and Federal governments to grant financial aid to projects for promoting the objects of the conventions. And, in relation to *laissez faire* and free trade doctrines, what shall be said of state and municipal aid to railroads and other internal improvements? Every Southern state lent aid to internal improvements.[116] Virginia was almost bankrupt by her loans. After 1852 Tennessee extended aid to the extent of $8,000 per mile to every mile of railroad built within her limits.[117] Georgia, in addition to aiding the construction of other roads, built, owned, and operated a railroad from Atlanta to the Tennessee line, near Chattanooga. North Carolina followed a very liberal policy.[118] So also, did Louisiana and Mississippi. Texas offered liberal grants of public lands. By no means least in the extent of financial aid to internal improvements was that free trade state, South Carolina. No city in the South voted more money to further the construction of railroads than did Charleston.

It is true, state aid to internal improvements met with opposition in the South; but the alignment upon the question by no means coincided with the alignment upon the tariff, Federal aid to internal improvements, or Federal subsidies and bounties, although there was a tendency in that direction. In Virginia the Democratic party was in power when the immense debt was contracted

---

[116]It is impossible to develop this subject here. For brief accounts, see Million, J. W., *State Aid to Railroads in Missouri*, ch. VI; *DeBow's Review*, XX, 386-389.

[117]The Commissioner of Railroads reported in October, 1857, that the state's obligations to railroads were about $16,000,000. *Hunt's Merchants' Magazine*, XXXVIII, 243.

[118]The railroad debt of North Carolina in 1860 was $8,833,305. *DeBow's Review*, XXIX, 245.

for aiding railroads, turnpikes, and other internal improvements. In North Carolina the Democrats were in power when aid to railroads was voted upon the largest scale; in fact, after 1848 the Democratic party was recognized as being more favorable to the policy of state aid than the Whig. Texas, Mississippi, and Arkansas were overwhelmingly Democratic during the fifties; yet all had internal improvement programmes. Alabama, partly because of her peculiar geographical divisions, lent no aid to railroads, and not a great deal to any form of improvements; but there was a strong sentiment for state aid. In 1855 a nearly defunct Whig party almost won the state election by raising the issue.[119] Mobile lent heavily to the construction of the Mobile and Ohio railroad.

Only one degree removed from the proposals to encourage industry and commerce by legislation were the innumerable pleas addressed to the people to patronize home industries and enterprises, to buy Southern-made in preference to Northern-made goods, to purchase from Southern jobbers and importers rather than from Northern, to hire Southern teachers and mechanics wherever possible, to use school books published in the South, to patronize home literature, to cease sending their youth to Northern colleges, and to visit Southern rather than Northern pleasure resorts. Every one of these pleas asked the individual, either directly or by implication, to sacrifice his own immediate profit or preference to the supposed public good. And all admitted the propriety of appeals for patronage of home industry. Every Southern commercial convention, when the members could not agree upon more effective plans for promoting its objects, fell back upon resolutions appealing to the people to patronize home enterprises; for upon such resolutions all could agree.

There were many, indeed, in the South who believed patronage of home industry to be the most efficacious means for achieving economic independence. An associate justice of the Supreme Court of Alabama said the efforts made to promote direct trade and manufactures had begun at the wrong end; the demands for the goods should be created first, and the steamship lines and factories would follow. Let the people resolve to buy nothing made or grown in the North if they could buy a substitute made or grown elsewhere; let them resolve to buy nothing imported into

[119]DuBose, *Life and Times of Yancey*, 311.

a Northern port if they could buy a substitute imported into a Southern port.[120] A letter of a Charleston mercantile house expressed the opinion that little could be effected by legislative enactments "as long as we are in the Union; a non-intercourse law will be a dead letter, and bounties of goods of direct importation will not result in any large increase in importations." What was necessary was a determination on the part of the people to patronize Southern merchants.[121] There was much impatience with the magnificent schemes which some men, particularly in the Southern Commercial Convention, were bringing forward for achieving the regeneration of the South, and the advice was given to pay more attention to little things. "Great steamships, and grand expansions, and magnificent speeches will do well enough, but there are little things, and a thousand of them, too, which might have a little attention, and perhaps lead to some small advantages. Could there not be some purpose, some real resolution to encourage not only by precept, but by example, a little home industry?"[122]

William Gregg, protectionist though he was, put Southern patronage of Southern imports and domestic industry foremost as a measure for promoting direct trade and manufactures.[123] He suggested the formation of societies and clubs for practising and preaching patronage of home industries.[124] He charged that the people preferred Northern-made articles because they were Northern-made.[125] Women did not consider themselves in fashion unless their clothing came from New York. There was "a rage for cheap Yankee goods." Merchants who handled Southern-made goods had to conceal their origin. The failure of so many Southern cotton factories during the hard years following 1849, he attributed largely to the want of home patronage.[126]

Gregg was not alone in his complaints. Fifty-eight Charleston importing and jobbing houses ran an advertisement in the papers in the form of an address to the merchants of the South and South-

---

[120]*DeBow's Review*, XXIX, 104-107.

[121]*Ibid.*, XXVIII, 589.

[122]*Ibid.*, XXIV, 573 (taken from a Virginia paper).

[123]Gregg, "Southern Patronage to Southern Imports and Domestic Industry," in *ibid.*, July, 1860, to Feb., 1861.

[124]*Ibid.*, XXX, 222.

[125]See especially *ibid.*, XXIX, 629, 776.

[126]*Ibid.*, XXX, 102.

west. They urged their claims for the patronage and custom of merchants of the interior, and begged them to "lay aside the prejudice (for it is only a prejudice) that your customers prefer goods from New York to those from Charleston . . ."[127] Norfolk merchants advertised goods as "just from the North."[128] The plaint was made that "The very men who most vehemently abuse the Yankees and their humbugs, are generally the first to contradict their own doctrines . . . ." The city council of Charleston sent to Troy, New York, for a fire alarm bell, although one could be procured at home. Charleston mechanics were greatly aroused over the incident.[129] Individuals protested against the continual harping upon Southern dependence; instead of advertising weaknesses they proposed to tell of possessions and possibilities. Occasionally journals of the Southern Rights persuasion declared their desire to publish only Southern advertising matter. The results were disappointing; their columns continued to be filled with Northern advertising. DeBow rather bitterly remarked that he was convinced the South had nothing to sell.[130]

These constant appeals to individuals to patronize home industries and home importing merchants were unobjectionable, but could not be otherwise than ineffectual except, possibly, during short periods of great excitement of the public mind.

After the John Brown Raid at Harper's Ferry a determination was expressed on all sides to practise stern and uncompromising non-intercourse with the North as the best means of silencing the abolitionists and teaching the North the money value of the Union. The governors of several states recommended throwing Southern ports open to the world and levying high excise taxes upon Northern made goods. The legislatures of Virginia and Tennessee adopted resolutions pledging the enactment of effective measures of retaliation.[131] Southern travel in the North fell off. Many Northern teachers and agents were driven from the South. Occasional business firms cancelled orders for Northern goods. Northern firms reported a falling off in their Southern business,

[127]Charleston *Mercury*, Dec. 17, 1859.
[128]W. S. Forest, *Sketches of Norfolk*, 410.
[129]Charleston *Mercury*, June 1, 1858.
[130]*DeBow's Review*, XXII, 555, 556; XXVIII, 124, 493.
[131]*Ibid.*, XXIX, 559.

and the business interests of the Northern states became alarmed.[132] Citizens of Baltimore hastened to declare Baltimore ready to take the place of more northern cities as a commercial center for the South.[133] Southern men did not fail to note that the ill feeling between the sections operated as a form of protection to home industries. "Let non-intercourse be established, and how easy it will be for Georgia to supply half of the Southern States with plantation goods such as she now manufactures."[134] Merchants were advised to take advantage of the excited state of the public mind to establish direct trade.[135]

The South produced no Horace Greeleys or Henry C. Careys; but a discussion of free trade versus protection in the South would be incomplete without mention of George Fitzhugh, of Virginia. A lawyer by profession, he took up his pen, about 1850, to defend the South and slavery. He proved himself a bold, ingenious, learned, and prolific, though quite eccentric and erratic, writer. The South conceded him a place alongside Dew, Harper, Hammond, and Stringfellow as a Southern apologist. With his defense of slavery and his attack upon free society, with its exploitation of labor by capital, we are not here directly concerned. Although not consistently, he was generally aligned with those who believed the South should diversify industry, build up cities and towns, construct internal improvements, and conduct her own commerce. He was particularly interested in improving Southern education, both secondary and primary, and in developing Southern literature and "Southern thought."

Fitzhugh repudiated *laissez faire*, and declared the world "too little governed." Fitzhugh believed in small nations. He repeatedly depicted the evils of centralization, not only of government but also of commerce, industry, finances, and literature. He dedicated his *Cannibals All* to the Honorable Henry A. Wise, because "I am acquainted with no one . . . who has seen so clearly the evils of centralization from without, and worked so earnestly to cure or

---

[132]Charleston *Mercury*, Dec. 29, 1859, quoting the Boston *Commercial Bulletin;* Wolfe, *Helper's Impending Crisis Dissected*, 128 ff., 164-6, quoting Northern papers.

[133]*DeBow's Review*, XXVIII, 331, quoting the Baltimore *Prices Current*.

[134]Wolfe, *Helper's Impending Crisis Dissected*, 129.

[135]*DeBow's Review*, XXX, 223.

avert those evils by building up centralization within."[136] And centralization without, he declared to be the "daughter of that Southern goddess, Free Trade." The free traders were "old fogies, sitting like an incubus on the South."[137] The disease under which the South suffered was free trade—free trade with the North. The protection Fitzhugh demanded was against the North, not against Europe. He agreed with Southern free traders that a protective tariff imposed by the Federal government would be unconstitutional. He thought a revenue tariff afforded ample incidental protection against foreign nations; it was sufficient to enable the North to almost monopolize the Southern market. When the results of the elections of 1858 threatened the enactment of a protective tariff, he suggested that state protection could neutralize and "peaceably and lawfully nullify federal protection." Fitzhugh would not wait for the South to unite upon measures of protection, but have each state take such individual action as it saw fit.[138] When non-intercourse was suggested, he espoused it. "Disunion within the Union," as he termed it, would "lead at once to direct trade—encourage, promote, and build up, Southern commerce, manufactures, agriculture, education, etc.," and make the South independent at the same time it was bringing the abolitionists to terms.[139] He considered disunion to be a measure that would put an end to free trade with the North; but as late as the middle of 1859, at least, was inclined to prefer the "State protective or taxing system" because it was "safer than disunion, equally efficient, and," so he said, "involves no breach of the constitution."[140]

It did not escape Fitzhugh's notice that the South had largely abandoned, if she had ever practised, a let-alone policy. "For twenty years past," he said, "the South has been busy in *protect-*

[136]*Cannibals All, or Slaves Without Masters*, Richmond, 1857. In addition to this work Fitzhugh wrote, *Sociology for the South, or the Failure of Free Societies; Slavery Justified* (pamphlet, 1849); and numerous articles for *DeBow's Review* and other periodicals.
[137]*DeBow's Review*, XXVI, 659, 662. See *Sociology for the South*, especially chs. I, XIV.
[138]Fitzhugh's views upon state protection are concisely set forth in an article, "State Rights and State Remedies," *DeBow's Review*, XXV, 697-703.
[139]*Ibid.*, XXVIII, 7, article entitled "Disunion Within the Union."
[140]*Ibid.*, XXVI, 661.

ing, encouraging, and diversifying Southern industrial pursuits, Southern skill, commerce, education, etc." Fitzhugh was not far from the truth when he said: "The South has not only adopted the protective policy, but, strange to say, the editors, legislators, and statesmen, who are loudest in professing free trade doctrines, are, invariably, the warmest advocates of exclusive and protective state legislation." And there was also a measure of truth in the statement: "Southern commercial conventions are composed of this class of men, who are actively at work in endeavoring to encourage, direct, and control Southern pursuits, by legislation and all other feasible means, while they profess to be *par excellence* free trade men. . . ."[141]

From this survey of their attitude toward protective tariffs and state and local measures to encourage industry and commerce, 1840-1860, we may conclude that just prior to secession the Southern people were by no means thoroughly committed to *laissez faire*. With regard to duties upon foreign imports, while a respectable minority wanted absolute free trade, the great majority favored a tariff for revenue with incidental protection. The sentiment for protection would have been stronger had it not been for the conviction that, while North and South were bound together in the Union, tariffs would redound almost wholly to the advantage of the former. In case the South should become independent, a considerable protectionist party might be expected to develop.

[141] *DeBow's Review*, XXV, 699-701.

CHAPTER VII
ECONOMIC ASPECTS OF THE DISUNION
MOVEMENT, 1852-1860

After the defeat of the disunion movement of 1850-1851 the disunionists were comparatively quiet for a few years. The struggles over slavery were temporarily abated. All parties seemed to turn with more or less earnestness to efforts to see whether something could not be done in an organized way to hasten the economic and social progress of the South—a policy which Unionists had earlier supported as a substitute for disunion. It was during this short period that the Southern Commercial Convention was instituted, and went about its work with a hope of accomplishing results. Meanwhile, however, the Southern Rights wing strengthened its control of the reunited Democratic party. In doing this it was aided materially by the Pierce administration. In his distribution of the patronage Pierce tried to conciliate the Southern Rights faction, and failed to recognize the more conservative element. He submitted himself largely to the guidance of the radical Southern leaders in the formulation of policies. Meanwhile, too, the Whig party began to dissolve.

In 1854 the lull in the quarrel over slavery was rudely interrupted by the repeal of the Missouri Compromise—the motives of which we shall not pause to discuss. The repeal served as the occasion for the organization of a sectional party in the North, which in turn reacted to strengthen the hands of the extremists in the South. The Kansas troubles and the presidential campaign of 1856, with its threat of the election of the candidate of a sectional party, called forth again threats of disunion, and once more the subject was canvassed in all its aspects. From this time on little reserve was shown in expressing disunion sentiments.

The session of the Southern Commercial Convention held in Savannah a month after the election showed unmistakably the growth of disunion sentiment, and proved to be the last controlled by the conservative element; its successors were little more than gatherings of disunionists. A large proportion of the representative newspapers of the South, especially of the cotton states, openly and almost constantly advocated disunion. The Richmond *Enquirer*, in the summer of 1857, complained that the Charleston

Mercury "does nothing from year's end to year's end but to announce the speedy dissolution of the Union."[1] Among others scarcely less open in their advocacy of disunion were, not to mention South Carolina journals, the Richmond *Examiner*, Roger A. Pryor's Richmond *South*, the Columbus (Georgia) *Corner Stone*, the Mobile *Register*, the Mobile *Mercury*, the Montgomery *Advertiser and Gazette*, the New Orleans *Crescent*, the New Orleans *Delta*, the Vicksburg *True Southron*, and the Memphis *Appeal*. J. D. B. DeBow had by this time become an avowed disunionist, and *DeBow's Review* was disunionist in the whole tendency of its teaching. The *Review* had some quite able writers among its contributors, had won for itself a considerable circulation and much prestige, and exercised great influence in the South. The avowed secessionists in Congress had come to be a considerable group, which included Miles, Keitt, and Bonham, of South Carolina, Iverson, of Georgia, Roger A. Pryor, of Virginia, John A. Quitman, J. D. McRae, Reuben Davis, and Barksdale, of Mississippi, C. C. Clay and J. L. Pugh, of Alabama, and Wigfall, of Texas. Many who did not publicly avow themselves secessionists were known to lean strongly in that direction. Outside of Congress were dozens of men of reputation and influence, most conspicuous of whom was William Lowndes Yancey, of Alabama, who devoted their best energies to advancing the cause of disunion. Through public agitation and discussion and the later meetings of the Southern Commercial Convention,[2] through private conferences and the wide correspondence carried on by various individuals— some unsuccessful attempts were made at organization[3]—the disunionist leaders in the several states became acquainted with each other, came to have a good understanding of the state of public

---

[1] August 13.

[2] *Edmund Ruffin's Diary* gives a good understanding of the way in which the Southern Commercial Convention, aside from the formal meetings, was used to promote the cause. See entries covering the session at Montgomery, which Ruffin attended.

[3] League of United Southerners. Hodgson, *Cradle of the Confederacy*, 393-396; DuBose, *Life and Times of Yancey*, 377; Charleston *Mercury*, Aug. 3, 1858; Montgomery *Daily Confederation*, May 21, 1859, quoting an editorial in the Mobile *Mercury; DeBow's Review*, XXV, 250.

sentiment in all quarters of the South, and strove to approach an agreement in regard to the proper policies to be pursued.[4]

Disunionists frankly expressed their hope that a pretext could be found which would precipitate the cotton states into a revolution.[5] Their desire to make an issue in part explains the agitation for repealing the laws against the foreign slave trade. When the Southern members in Congress compromised the Kansas question, in April, 1858, by accepting the English bill, several prominent disunionists expressed their disappointment that an issue had not been made.[6] Finally, the issue was presented when, largely through the agency of the disunionists, the Democratic party was split in twain at Charleston and Baltimore, and the triumph of a sectional party made inevitable.

The discussion of disunion during the several years preceding the actual launching of the experiment left no phase of the subject untouched. Every possible angle of the question was explored— the ability of the Southern states to support a separate government; the probability of their being permitted to secede without war; the attitude the border states would take in case the cotton states should secede; the most desirable boundary line; the division of the territories; the policies the new confederacy should pursue with respect to commerce with the North and Europe, the tariff, the navigation of the Mississippi, the Pacific railroad, immigration, the slave trade, expansion of the confederacy to the southward, and the military establishment; the effect of dissolution

[4]In a letter to Roger A. Pryor, Yancey said he did not expect Virginia to take the initiative. "Her position as a border state, and a well considered Southern policy—(a policy which has been digested and understood and approved by some of the ablest men in Virginia, as you yourself must be aware)—would seem to demand that, when such movement takes place by any considerable number of Southern states, Virginia . . . . should remain in the Union." Hodgson, *op. cit.*, 397; *National Intelligencer*, Sept. 4, 1858.

[5]W. L. Yancey to James S. Slaughter, June 15, 1858, in Hodgson, *op. cit.*, 393; DuBose, *Yancey*, 376.

[6]Yancey to Thos. J. Orme, May 22, 1858, in Montgomery *Daily Confederation*, June 5, 1858; DuBose, *Yancey*, 366-75; M. L. Bonham, of South Carolina, in the House of Representatives, June 9, *Cong. Globe*, 35 Cong., 1 Sess., Appx. 509-11. A correspondent of the Charleston *Mercury* wrote of the Southern Commercial Convention at Montgomery: "I have not met a single man except the Virginians who approves the late compromise in Kansas." May 15, 1858.

upon the prosperity and development of the South as a whole and of particular classes, interests, and localities.

The various arguments in favor of disunion did not appeal with equal force to all disunionists. Many emphasized the greater security of slavery in a separate republic and the freedom from the quarrels over slavery, which seemed interminable in the Union; and there can be no doubt that, could the slavery quarrel have been hushed, and the issue amicably settled, disunion sentiment would never have reached alarming proportions or have been translated into action. Others were prone to contemplate the glories of a great republic stretching from the Ohio to Panama and encircling the Gulf of Mexico. Others were influenced by the possibility of reopening the foreign slave trade. Too many politicians, it must be said, felt that their political careers had been blighted in the Union, and hoped for better fortune in the narrower confines of a Southern confederacy. But almost all disunionists believed, or professed to believe, that the South in the Union was being exploited economically for the benefit of the North; that the Southern states had somehow become tributary provinces of the Northern; that Northern wealth largely represented the product of Southern labor; and that, could the Southern states but cut loose from their Northern connections and be permitted to work out their own destiny in their own way, their prosperity would be greater and their development quickened.

The arguments advanced in support of these propositions were similar to those used in 1850 and 1851, but had been modified to some extent by circumstances. Since that time there had been much discussion of diversification of industry and development of varied resources; commercial conventions had been held and public opinion educated; and various plans for regenerating the South had been tried or proposed, and, in general, had failed. Whereas in the earlier period most of those who hoped for a diversification of Southern pursuits had held aloof from or had opposed the disunion movement, in the latter many of that class, despairing of success in the Union, lent it their support.

The doctrine that the South paid more than her share of the taxes and received less than her share of the disbursements had been so frequently repeated that it was becoming generally accepted. One estimated at $50,000,000 the sum the South paid annually, and at $10,000,000 the amount returned in the form of expenditures; $40,000,000 annually would be saved by going out of the Union. Such a sum distributed among the states would give an enormous impetus to manufactures and all other branches of industry which suffered from a deficiency of capital in the South.[7] Southern men did not cease to attribute Southern decline to unequal taxation and disbursements.[8]

Direct trade with Europe would follow, it was said, closely upon the heels of separation; for importers would never pay the duties imposed by the North in addition to the moderate duties imposed by the Southern confederacy. "With a horizontal duty upon all imposts it would be impossible for foreign products to come to us by way of the cities of the North."[9] If necessary, navigation laws could be enacted discriminating against Northern shipping. Foreign ships would flock to Southern ports; Northern ships would be transferred to the South. Northern seaports would decline; Southern would flourish.[10] The South, having control of its own commerce, would control the "exchanges" also, and thus become financially independent. The establishment of direct trade would give an impulse to every other pursuit: "Manufactories would then grow up, commerce would extend, mechanical arts would flourish, and, in short, every industrial and every professional pursuit would receive a vivifying impulse."[11]

Of all those who speculated in regard to the proper policy of a new confederacy, it is worthy of note that very few proposed that the government should be supported without resort to duties on

[7]*DeBow's Review*, XXI, 543. Similar statements are in the Charleston *Mercury*, Feb. 25, 1858, quoting the Mobile *Mercury*; *DeBow's Review*, XXX, 252; *ibid.*, XXI, 532; speech of J. A. Jones, of Georgia, in Vicksburg, New York *Herald*, May 21, 1859.

[8]John Forsyth's lecture on "The North and the South," Mobile, 1854, *DeBow's Review*, XVII, 368-73; *ibid.*, XIX, 383-4; *ibid.*, XXVI, 476 (A. P. Calhoun, 1859); *ibid.*, XXX, 436 (DeBow, 1858); W. P. Miles, of South Carolina, in House of Representatives, Mar. 31, 1858, Charleston *Mercury*, Apr. 17; *Southern Literary Messenger*, XXXI, 238; "Barbarossa" [John Scott], *The Lost Principle, or the Sectional Equilibrium*, Pt. I, ch. V; Claiborne, *Life and Correspondence of John A. Quitman*, II, 186-7.

[9]*DeBow's Review*, XXI, 543.

[10]*Ibid.*, XXI, 519; XXV, 373; XXIII, 604; *Cong. Globe*, 33 Cong., 1 Sess., 375 (Preston S. Brooks).

[11]*DeBow's Review*, XXIX, 462.

imports. It is true many spoke of a free trade republic; but "free trade" was generally equivalent to "tariff for revenue only." Almost all would have had low duties; but while some told how low they would be and emphasized the blessings of free trade, others dwelt upon the incidental protection which would be afforded by a tariff for revenue. Said Willoughby Newton, a Virginia disunionist of long standing, "A tariff for the support of the new government would give such protection to manufacturers that all our waterfalls would bristle with machinery."[12] Men from border states were more inclined to speak of the advantages of protection against Northern competition than were men from the cotton states, though the latter often held out as an inducement to Virginia and North Carolina to go with the Gulf states the probability that they would supplant New England in manufacturing for the South. There were free traders, however, who thought it might be well to leave the Northern slave states out of the confederacy lest they should demand protection for their industries. Disunionists believed that, in case of separation, the North would have to resort to direct taxation to support her government; for she would no longer be able to import on Southern account, and she could not tax imports from the South, since they were chiefly raw materials.[13] The consequences of direct taxation would be the transfer to the South of much capital invested in manufactures.

The disunionists often took a somewhat skeptical attitude toward the efforts which were being made to promote Southern commerce and industry while the Union continued. Each failure confirmed their opinion that such efforts were futile. The Charleston *Mercury* said that in the Union "Direct trade with the customers of the South in Europe is an impossibility....Norfolk, Charleston, Savannah, Mobile, are only suburbs of New York."[14] According to a contributor to *DeBow's Review*, the process of development went on much more slowly than in the North, and ·must as long as the South remained in the Union with the North to lean upon. Disunion would call for and foster a variety of home products. Pride would demand protection for home indus-

[12]*DeBow's Review*, XXV, 373 (Sept., 1858).
[13]*Ibid.*, XXI, 541-44.
[14]May 20, 1858.

tries. Diversification would develop and unfold the wealth of the South. "True, we *might*, in the course of time, unfold this wealth *in the Union*, but not till the teeming North has 'embellished all her slopes,' and of her superabundance and for lack of other lands to conquer, empties her surplus on us, . . . With all these aids and stimulants we must advance with equal or faster steps than they."[15] A. J. Roane, of Virginia, wrote: "Experience has demonstrated that direct trade to Southern ports cannot be established to any considerable extent in the Union. It can only be accomplished by the stress of the necessity which separation would create."[16] In Virginia the opinion was held that in case of disunion the very necessity of her condition of estrangement from the manufacturing North would impel her to add a manufacturing phase to her already innumerable sources of wealth.[17]

As we have seen, certain south Atlantic ports, particularly of Virginia, which was slowly building the Chesapeake and Ohio railroad, aspired to export and import for the Ohio and the upper Mississippi valleys, and had high expectations of the beneficial effects of such a commerce upon the prosperity of the seaboard regions. A considerable part of the exports and some of the imports of the Northwest still followed the Mississippi river with New Orleans as their port of entry and departure. The people of New Orleans, furthermore, hoped to retain or increase her share of the Western commerce by the building of north and south railroads. There continued to be considerable exchange of products between the South and the West. It was to be presumed that the people who profited or expected to profit by this Western trade would be loath to have a measure taken which might injure that trade and destroy the prospects of future benefits from it. Disunionists sought to overcome the objections of those who yet expected much of Western trade in the way of promoting Southern prosperity. To meet the demands of New Orleans and preserve peace with the West, they generally agreed that, in case of separation, it would be necessary to guarantee free navigation of the Mississippi; it was frequently suggested that Western products be admitted free of duty.[18] Some Southerners professed

<hr>

[15]*DeBow's Review*, XXIII, 471-474 (Nov., 1857). Cf. *ibid.*, XXI, 177-186.
[16]*Ibid.*, XXIX, 463.
[17]New York *Herald*, October 23, 1860.
[18]*DeBow's Review*, XXX, 93 (Maj. W. H. Chase, of Florida).

to believe that, in case of a dissolution of the Union, the close commercial relations of the two sections and the absolute necessity to the West of the Mississippi river as an outlet for her commerce would induce the West to cast her lot with the South rather than with the East;[19] they were not averse to admitting free states into their slaveholding republic.

It is rather strange how tenaciously Southern men on the eve of secession clung to the belief that the old alliance of the South and West, based upon commercial relations and common opposition to the tariff and financial policies of the East, still continued. For example, Governor Wickliffe, of Louisiana, in his message of January, 1859, said: "The position of the Northwestern States of the Mississippi Valley, on this question [slavery] is of especial interest to us. These States are, by geographical position, commercially our allies, whether slave or free, while many of the States on the Atlantic side of the Alleghanies are necessarily hostile in commercial interest. . . . It is cheering to find our commercial allies of the Northwest sustaining our Southern policy."[20] This statement is accurate in no particular. The value of the trade between the West and East was several times greater than the value of the trade between the West and South. Not only did most of the foreign imports of the West come by way of the East; but by far the larger part of Western exports went that way. The travel between East and West was much greater than between South and West. Much Eastern capital was invested in the West. In politics, too, the West and East had been drawing closer together. The tariff no longer divided them as it did in the days of Calhoun. Both stood for a liberal policy in regard to improvement of rivers and harbors. The South had abandoned her old liberal attitude on the public lands question, and steadily opposed homestead bills and land grants to railroads; while in some quarters the old demand for distribution of the proceeds from the sale of public lands was revived. The East, on the other hand, was inclined to support the public lands policies of the West. On the immigration question, the West agreed with the East rather

[19]Senator Hammond, of South Carolina, Mar. 4, 1858, *Cong. Globe*, 35 Cong., 1 Sess., 961; "Barbarossa," *The Lost Principle*, 225; *DeBow's Review*, XXIII, 603, (Edmund Ruffin).

[20]New Orleans *Daily True Delta*, Jan. 19, 1859.

than with the South; the same was true of the Pacific railroad question. On the paramount issue of slavery, the people of the free states of the Northwest were rapidly losing their old indifferent attitude, and becoming more hostile to the institution.

Along with their pictures of the prosperity and progress which would follow the formation of an independent Southern confederacy, disunionists frequently advanced arguments to prove that it would be accompanied by no countervaling disadvantages. Secession would be peaceful, they said, because the interruption of Southern trade, in case the North should undertake coercion, would bring such prostration to Northern industry and commerce that she would not have the means to go to war. Furthermore, England and France would not permit a blockade, because a cutting off of the supply of cotton would bring ruin to important industries.[21] Thus the disunionists had an argument at every turn.

About the time of Lincoln's election there was published a volume by Edmund Ruffin entitled, *Anticipations of the Future to Serve as Lessons for the Present Time, in the Form of Extracts of Letters from an English Resident in the United States, to the London Times, from 1864 to 1870*, etc.[22] Ruffin was a man of considerable ability. He was known throughout the South, and his name carried great weight because of his long record of valuable services to Virginia and the South at large, chief of which were his contributions to improved methods of agriculture. He was a secessionist of long standing, and one of the leaders of the movement.[23] His book gives such a complete statement of the disunion arguments, colored perhaps by his Virginia viewpoint, that a summary of it is desirable.

Ruffin allowed Lincoln to serve one term and his more radical successor, Seward, to serve part of one without a dissolution of the Union. When, however, Seward proposed to stand for a

[21]*DeBow's Review*, XXIII, 596-601; XXIX, 457-463; XXX, 95 ff.

[22]The earliest notice I have seen of the book was in the *National Intelligencer*, Nov. 15, 1860, which said the work belonged to the "disunion literature of the current day." It was published anonymously, but the authorship was evident from the appendage of a series of essays on "The Causes of the Independence of the South" which had appeared in 1856 and of which Ruffin was known to be the author. Essays were in Richmond *Enquirer*, Dec. and Jan., 1856-1857; *DeBow's Review*, XXII, 583-93; XXIII, 266-72, 546-52, 596-607.

[23]For a brief biographical sketch, see *ibid.*, XI, 431-436.

second term, six cotton states seceded. Whereupon, after some attempts at settlement, the Federal government established a blockade of Southern ports, and war ensued, the northern slave states remaining neutral. By May, 1868, because of the loss of Southern trade and cotton, there were great suffering, threatening mobs, and sanguinary riots in the North. Northern merchants and manufacturers felt very severely the loss of $40,000,000 due them from the South and sequestered by the government of the new confederacy. The South suffered also from the blockade; but there were compensations in that it taught the Southern people to be independent of the North. Soon Virginia, North Carolina, and Maryland found it no longer possible to remain neutral, and entered the war on the side of the South. Another $50,000,000 of debts were sequestered. The North did not attempt to carry the war into the border states. In July, 1868, it was reported that the imports and revenues of the North had fallen off tremendously; for the "greater part of the former importations to Northern ports and in Northern ships, was for transhipment to and consumption in the Southern states."[24] In August outbreaks and violence were reported in the impoverished Northern cities; New York was sacked and burned—a rather bitter commentary on the supposed friendship of the South and New York City. Soon the North was unable to continue the war; and a truce was made.

By February, 1869, renewal of commercial intercourse and peaceful relations had given a wonderful impulse to trade and business in the South. But Southern merchants had entirely ceased going to the North to purchase goods of any kind: "For all Northern fabrics being now subject to high duties, would thereby be so much enhanced in price, that but few kinds can be sold in Southern markets, in competition with European articles subject to the same rates of duties only—or of Southern manufactures, now protected by the same tariff law which had formerly been enacted by the superior political power of the North, and to operate exclusively for the profit of Northern capital and industry."[25] Northern ship owners were transferring their ships to the South; Northern manufacturers were coming; and much Northern capital was seeking investment there. A month later it was reported that the "commercial prosperity of the South is growing with a force

[24]P. 283.
[25]P. 318.

189]   THE DISUNION MOVEMENT, 1852-1860   189

and rapidity exceeding any previous anticipations of the most sanguine early advocates for the independence of the Southern states."[26]

The Western states had taken but little part in the war. The South had granted them free trade and free navigation of the Mississippi. Because of this indulgent and conciliatory treatment the people of the Northwest had not tried to open direct trade with Europe, but were content to trade principally with New Orleans. On April 7, 1869, it was reported that New England and the West were at loggerheads over the tariff.[27] The volume closes with a prediction that the North would soon split, the Western states, upon their own offer, going with the South. "And should New England be left alone, thenceforward its influence for evil on the Southern states will be of as little effect, and its political and economical position scarcely superior, to those conditions of the present republic of Hayti."[28]

By April 14, 1869, it was reported, commercial treaties had been made by the South with European powers. No duties were to be over 20 per cent. The treaties might be terminated after ten years. The tobacco growers, who had so often in the old Union requested the government to attempt to secure a relaxation of the heavy duties imposed upon their product by France and England, now had their wishes gratified.[29]

Ruffin's book was written during a political campaign when it was well understood that, in case of Lincoln's election, the cotton states would in all probability secede; but its content was only an amplification of a series of letters published in the Richmond *Enquirer* in December, 1856, and January, 1857. And the arguments for secession which he used were typical of the secessionist *per se* propaganda to which the people of the South had been accustomed for at least a decade.

Southern people were strengthened in their expectations of beneficial economic effects to follow secession by a class of politicians, writers, and newspaper editors representing those Northern commercial and mercantile interests whose business was largely with the South, and those Northern manufacturing inter-

[26]P. 323.
[27]P. 328.
[28]P. 338.
[29]P. 329. Cf. "Barbarossa," *The Lost Principle*, 176 ff.

ests who either sold their products in the South or purchased their raw material there, or both. The best known and most trustworthy individual of this class was Thomas Prentice Kettell, mentioned before in connection with the secession movement of 1850. He was, in 1860, the editor of *Hunt's Merchants' Magazine.* His views carried considerable weight, especially in the South, where his free trade principles, his sympathetic attitude on the slavery question, and his interest in Southern economic development had long been known. Early in the presidential campaign of 1860 there was published a book by him entitled, *Southern Wealth and Northern Profits, As Exhibited in Statistical Facts and Official Figures; Showing the Necessity of Union to the Future Prosperity and Welfare of the Republic.* The book showed an excellent understanding of the commercial and financial relations of the North and South; the conclusions were supported by tables of statistics, largely drawn from official sources. The burden of the book was, as the title indicates, that the South produced wealth, but that this wealth accumulated in the North: Capital, said Kettell, accumulates slowly in all agricultural countries and rapidly in commercial and manufacturing countries.[30] He described the resources of the South, her enormous production of cotton and numerous other products, and her immense exports to the North as well as to Europe. He further showed the extent of Southern purchases in the North, the value of the commerce carried for the South by the North, the Northern tonnage so employed—in short he discussed every form of profit derived by the North from her relations with the South. The total profits the North derived annually from Southern wealth he summarized in the following table:[31]

[30] P. 126.

[31] P. 127. There is no way to check these items with any accuracy, were it worth while to do so. The fishing bounties were paid from the general revenues, and, therefore, by both North and South in proportions of their respective contributions. The second is undoubtedly greatly exaggerated. The average yearly receipts from customs, 1856-1860 inclusive, was $54,487,600. Assuming that the people of the South paid as much *per capita* as the people of the North, which they probably did not (See ante p. 103.), the South paid about $21,440,000 annually. A part of this at least was disbursed in the South. The sixth item is probably much too large. So, also, is the last. Northern investments in the South and loans and extensions of credit greatly exceeded in amount Southern invest-

Bounties to fisheries, per annum	$ 1,500,000
Customs, per annum, disbursed at the North	40,000,000
Profits to Manufacturers	30,000,000
Profits to Importers	16,000,000
Profits to Shipping, imports and exports	40,000,000
Profits on Travelers	60,000,000
Profits of Teachers, and others, at the South, sent North	5,000,000
Profits of Agents, brokers, commissions, etc.	10,000,000
Profits of Capital drawn from the South	30,000,000
Total from these sources	$232,500,000

In sixty years, according to Kettell's estimate, $2,770,000,000 had been transferred from the South to the North in these ways. Such heavy drains had prevented the accumulation of capital in the South.[32]

Kettell's arguments were addressed to the Northern people; he urged them not to endanger their prosperity by the unnecessary agitation of the slavery question. The South and West were portrayed as having great natural resources, whereas the East had few; the prosperity of the latter depended upon manufacturing and shipping for others.[33] He described the efforts which had been made in the South to make the section independent of the North, and the progress already made toward that goal; these he attributed to the anti-slavery agitation. He considered the possibility of a dissolution of the Union. In that case, "it is quite apparent that the North, as distinguished from the South and West, would be alone permanently injured." As for the South, "in the long run it would lose—after recovering from first disasters—nothing by separation."[34]

Disunionists saw in Kettell's book an argument for secession. John Townsend, of South Carolina, cut Kettell's estimate of Northern profits from Southern industry to less than half—$105,000,000 annually or $2,100,000,000 in twenty years. What would not this sum have accomplished for the South in twenty years? he asked. Direct trade and flourishing cities. *"Domestic*

ments in the North and deposits of Southern funds in Northern banks. The item should read, "interest on Southern debts to Northern citizens;" at any rate such an item, and it would not be a small one, should be included in the table.

[32]P. 127.
[33]P. 75.
[34]P. 75.

manufactures would have occupied every water power, and the whole South,—wealthy and equipped, and armed at every point, —would have been able to defend herself against the world."[35] DeBow, another disunionist, in his review of *Southern Wealth and Northern Profits,* said: "The author deserves, by his labors, not only on this occasion, but during a long and active career, the most substantial recognition, as one of the noblest and truest patriots, the most profound economists, and ablest statistical philosophers of the age."[36]

Of Northern newspapers which encouraged the Southern people to believe that disunion would be followed by unprecedented prosperity, none was more widely read and quoted or wielded greater influence in the South than the New York *Herald.* It kept close watch of events and the state of public opinion in the South, and should have known, perhaps did know, the temper of the people. It constantly advocated a policy of meeting Southern demands and avoidance of wounding Southern sensibilities in order that the South might not be compelled to resort to measures which would work injury to the navigating, mercantile, and financial interests of New York, which the *Herald* represented. In case of disunion, according to the *Herald,* the imports of the Northern confederation would so fall off that it would have to resort to direct taxation, while the South would have ample revenue. Manufactures would be established in the South with Northern capital. Northern shipping would rot at its docks. Part of the Northern population would migrate to the South, so the disproportion in numbers would cease to exist. The value of real estate in the North would be greatly reduced.[37]

The views which disunionists, and others both South and North, held in regard to the economic benefits to follow the formation of a Southern confederacy did not go uncontroverted in the South. Conservative journals, such as the New Orleans *Picayune,* perhaps the best newspaper in the South, the Montgomery *Daily Confederation,* the *Republican Banner and Nashville Whig,* and the Savannah *Daily Republican,* did not consider that the Union

[35]*The South Alone Should Govern the South. And African Slavery Should Be Controlled by Those Only Who Are Friendly to It* (pamphlet), 3rd edition, p. 51.

[36]*DeBow's Review,* XXIX, 213.

[37]October 30, 1860, editorial, for example.

injuriously affected the economic interests of the Southern states.
Said the *Picayune*, 1858: "One of the most erroneous ideas,
strangely obtaining considerable currency at the South, is that
which attributes apparent decay of the older, and comparative slow
growth of the younger Southern States, to a fixed policy of the
General Government, assumed to be partial to sections in which
slavery does not exist."[38] The Montgomery *Daily Confederation*
said, 1859: "Nor are we wanting in a proper appreciation of the
value of the Union. . . . We sing no anthems to its glories, at
the same time we cannot forget that under it, we have grown to be
a great, prosperous, and after all, a happy people."[39] Occasionally
DeBow's Review contained an article which refuted the views
presented by the majority of its contributors.[40] Conservative
statesmen often described the South as prosperous, and attributed
that prosperity to the Union. Such a one was Alexander H.
Stephens.[41] Senator Bell, of Tennessee, in his speech on the
Lecompton bill, 1858, described the disunionists *per se* of the South,
and expressed his dissent from their doctrines.[42]

Disunionists were forced to admit on the eve of the war that
the South was enjoying a comparative degree of prosperity; and
they expressed concern lest a feeling of content with their economic condition would make the Southern people incapable of
maintaining their rights.[43] The Charleston *Mercury* found it
necessary to protest against an editorial of the New Orleans *Bee*,
"an inveterate old Whig paper," for intimating "that the Southern
people are so cankered by prosperity as to be incapable of resisting the sectional domination of the North, and that the Union will

[38]May 22, 1858.

[39]May 19, 1859. A year earlier it had said: "We scout the position so often
assumed that we are inferior—that we are degraded in this Union . . . That the
North does our trading and manufacturing mostly is true, and we are willing that
they should. If we thought as some seem to think on the subject, we should
boldly raise the standard of secession, and never cease the strife until the Union
were dissolved." May 19, 1858.

[40]XXIV, 431-39, e.g.

[41]Letter to J. J. Crittenden, Jan. 2, 1860; address to his constituents, Aug.
14, 1857, *Toombs, Stephens, Cobb Correspondence*, 415 ff.

[42]*Cong. Globe*, 35 Cong., 1 Sess., Appx., 139-40.

[43]Speech of R. B. Rhett, July 4, 1859, in Charleston *Mercury*, July 7; address of Col. A. P. Aldrich at the fair of the South Carolina Institute, Nov. 17,
1859, *ibid.*, Nov. 19.

be continued because of this prosperity."[44] Disunionists found it
necessary, also, to allay the fears of those engaged in industry and
commerce who, while desirous of Southern industrial and commercial independence, believed that the sudden disruption of
established relationships which disunion might cause would prostrate their business.[45] Much of the disunion argument seems to
have been designed to win over this class of men.

Some of the leaders in the various efforts made to effect an
industrial and commercial revolution in the South were not convinced by the arguments of the unconditional disunionists. James
Robb, to whom more than to any other individual belongs the
credit for the successful building of the New Orleans, Jackson,
and Great Northern railroad, undertook to expose the fallacies of
the secession arguments. It would be suicide for the South to
abandon the Union. The pursuits of the people of the South were
incompatible with any considerable progress in manufacturing
and commerce. The remedy for dependence upon the North was
not secession but a change of habits. The South had better be
dependent upon the North than upon Europe. "The Southern
mind is deluded in the belief that England and France will give
to a separate Southern Confederacy, founded on Slavery, Free
Trade, and Cotton, their entire sympathies." If self-interest did
not appeal to New England, would it appeal to England and
France? The belief that the withdrawal of Southern trade would
ruin the East was too absurd to merit notice. "Where," he asked,
"is the evidence of the prosperity of the Southern States being
seriously endangered by a continued fellowship with New England? Our material progress for the last fifteen years is without
example, . . . "[46]

William Gregg, one of the ablest and sanest thinkers in the
South upon questions affecting the economic interests of the section, was not a secessionist *per se*.[47] The South was not ready

[44]April 30, 1859.
[45]See, for example, A. J. Roane in *DeBow's Review*, XXIX, 462.
[46]Letter to Alexander H. Stephens, Nov. 25, 1860, in a pamphlet, *A Southern Confederacy. Letters by James Robb, late a citizen of New Orleans, to an
American in Paris and Hon. Alexander H. Stephens, of Georgia*, pp. 11-24.
[47]The statements relative to Gregg's position are based upon a series of
essays on "Southern Patronage to Southern Imports and Domestic Industry"
which appeared in *DeBow's Review*, July, 1860, to February, 1861, but all of

for independence, he said. The Southern people should make themselves commercially and industrially independent of the North before going out of the Union. There would be no advantage in turning from the Yankees and relying upon Europe.[48] Free trade among the states he considered the greatest bond of Union; and at the time he wrote, 1860, still thought it, "if properly poised and equalized throughout our common country, will dispel the dark cloud which hangs over truth and justice . . ."[49] Yet Gregg was not oblivious to some of the possible advantages of disunion. If a line were drawn which would be a barrier to the importation of Northern locomotives, for example, two years would not elapse before the South would manufacture them herself. Disunion would stop the practice followed by Southern banks and money lenders of employing their money in New York rather than at home, which was a "monstrous barrier to Southern enterprise."[50]

Yet, after giving due weight to such Union arguments as we have just analyzed, it remains that the disunionist arguments in regard to the material benefits of their project were not adequately refuted in the South. Unionists more frequently took the course of appealing to the common history of the American people, their common republican institutions, the greatness of the Union, its prestige among the nations of the earth, its vast military strength, the weakness and insignificance the South would have as an independent nation, her inability to protect an institution condemned by the opinion of the world, and the danger of plunging the country into fratricidal war. They also found it effective to cast aspersions upon the motives of the secessionist leaders, to represent them as restless spirits, broken down politicians, disappointed in their political ambitions.

Northern men contributed but little to a true understanding of the causes of the disparity of the sections in prosperity and progress, and of the effect which a division of the Union might have upon the great material interests of the country; such an

which were written before Lincoln's election. But see Victor S. Clark in *The South in the Building of the Nation*, V, 323.

[48]*DeBow's Review*, XXIX, 78, 79, 773, 778.
[49]*Ibid.*, XXX, 217.
[50]*Ibid.*, XXIX, 79, 495.

understanding, it is believed, would have tended to allay disunion sentiment. Northern men were not as well informed as they should have been of the number of disunionists *per se* in the South, nor of the arguments they advanced. Practically all of the discussions dealing with disunion were colored by partisan bias. As we have seen, representatives of those business interests of the East which were closely allied with the cotton power exaggerated the value of the Southern connection and the injurious effects of disunion upon the North. They sought to fix the guilt for endangering the Union upon the Northern "fanatics" who were agitating the slavery question. Republican and anti-slavery writers and orators, who, it must be remembered, were not trying to win converts in the South but to build up a great party in the North, dealt with disunionism in a variety of ways. They denounced as mercenary those who would calculate the value of the Union in dollars. They commonly charged that threats of disunion were mere gasconade for the purpose of frightening Northern men into voting for Southern measures. They often, also, as did William H. Seward in his great speeches during the campaign of 1860, protrayed the magnitude of Northern productions and Northern internal commerce as compared with the products exchanged between the sections, and minimized the value of the Southern trade and Southern raw materials to the North and the injury which would be inflicted upon Northern interests by disunion.[51] Senator Wilson, of Massachusetts, said cotton was not king; cotton made but one-seventeenth part of the manufactures of the North.[52] The Republicans, and anti-slavery men generally, attributed the "decline" of the South and its dependence upon the North chiefly to the blighting effects of slavery; they saw no hope of remedy so long as slavery continued to exist.[53]

---

[51]In a speech at Palace Garden, New York City, Nov. 2, 1860, he said: "New York is not a province of Virginia or Carolina, any more than it is a province of New York or Connecticut. New York must be the metropolis of the Continent." New York *Herald*, Nov. 3.

[52]*Cong. Globe*, 35 Cong., 1 Sess., Appx., 169, speech of Mar. 20, 1858, in reply to J. H. Hammond's "Mud-sill" speech of Mar. 4.

[53]The speech of Senator Wilson just quoted is a good example. Another is Hannibal Hamlin's reply to Hammond, Mar. 8, 11, 1858, *Cong. Globe*, 35 Cong., 1 Sess., 1002-1006, 1025-1029.

Perhaps the ablest and most philosophical exposition of moderate Republicanism made between 1854 and 1861 is George M. Weston's *Progress of Slavery*,[54] a work which it would have been well worth the while of Southern thinkers to study. We are here concerned only with those of the propositions he sought to establish which relate to disunion. He told of nullification in South Carolina and of its partisans and sympathizers in other slave states. "The real cause of this Southern predisposition to listen to the appeals of the Palmetto nullifiers, was Southern discontent at the prosperity of the North. . . . Refusing to see the true cause of their own misfortunes, and eager to attribute them to every cause but the right one, they insisted that they alone were the real producers of wealth, and that the North was thriving at their expense." This doctrine of the nullifiers had been steadily insisted upon during the following quarter of a century. "It has, without doubt, become the settled conviction of large numbers of persons in the slave States, that in some way or other, either through the fiscal regulations of the Government, or through the legerdemain of trade, the North has been built up at the expense of the South."[55] These were the views which prompted disunion. He illustrated the reasons for wanting to dissolve the Union by an extract from a public address of John Forsyth, of Mobile:

I have no more doubt that the effect of separation would be to transfer the energies of industry, population, commerce, and wealth, from the North to the South, than I have that it is to the Union with us, the wealth-producing States, that the North owes its great progress in material prosperity. . . . The Union broken, we should have what has been so long the dream of the South—direct trade and commercial independence. Then, our Southern cities, that have so long languished in the shade, while the grand emporia of the North have fattened upon favoring navigation laws, partial legislation by Congress, and the monopoly of the public expenditure, will spring into life and energy, and become the entrepots of a great commerce.[56]

The slavery agitation was not the cause of disunion feeling but the pretext, according to Weston. The disunionists had been chiefly instrumental in getting it up: "It is quite notorious that it

[54]Published in 1858.
[55]P. 68.
[56]P. 69.

is not the slaveholding class at the South which particularly
favors nullification."

The impoverished condition of the South, which Weston considered the source of the disunion feeling, he thought attributable in
part to slavery and in part to, "that unnatural diffusion of their
population over new territories," which the Republican party was
opposing.[57] There were no internal elements of change in slave
society. The slaves were held to their condition by force. The
masters were confined to planting by the want of flexibility and
adaptibility in the character of the labor which they controlled
and upon the proceeds of which they subsisted. The non-slaveholding whites were degraded by slavery with no hope of escape
from their abject poverty.[58] There was no hope from any
elements of such a population of the growth of towns, of the
mechanic arts, or of manufacturing and commercial interests.
"Throughout the South, towns are built up only by Northern and
European immigration, and without it there would be scarcely any
manifestation of civilization. Mills, railroads, cotton presses, sugar
boilers, and steamboats, are mainly indebted for their existence in
the Southern States to intelligence and muscle trained in free
communities."[59] The redemption of the South would come only
with the gradual encroachment of the free-labor system of the
North and Europe and the non-slaveholding regions of the South
upon the slave belts. That encroachment had begun, or soon
would begin. As the slave area should be contracted, the discon-
tented area would also be diminished, and the Union would be
strengthened. "If the course of events in the immediate future
be such as may reasonably be anticipated, no separate Southern
Confederacy could possibly embrace more than a few States in
the southeast corner of the existing Union; and the scheme of such
a Confederacy would be put down by the good sense of the people
in that quarter, if, indeed, their patriotism would allow it to be
even entertained."[60]

[57]P. 58.
[58]P. 13.
[59]P. 15.
[60]P. 70.

CHAPTER VIII
FACTORS WHICH TENDED TO ALLAY DISCONTENT WITH THE SOUTH'S ECONOMIC SYSTEM,
1850-1860

During the decade 1850-1860 there were factors and conditions whose tendency was to make the people of the South better content with their economic system and position. These factors were in part economic, in part political and social. The economic factors tended also, in part—not altogether, to allay Southern sectionalism. That on the whole sectional feeling increased during the period was due, in the main, to other and stronger factors.

Southern agriculture was comparatively prosperous during the decade. This was especially true of the cotton planting industry. During the decade of 1840-1850 the average price of cotton at Southern seaports was 8 cents;[1] during the following decade it was 10.6 cents.[2] The price was steadier also during the later period. The higher price level was maintained in spite of a rather remarkable succession of large crops from 1851 to 1861. The average yearly production during the first decade was 2,155,400 bales, and during the second, 3,374,100 bales,[3] an increase of over 56 per cent, while the total value of the cotton produced during the latter period was about double that of the former. The crop of 1852-1853, the largest to that time, brought cotton planters nearly $150,000,000. This crop was exceeded both in amount and aggregate value by that of 1855-1856. A considerably smaller crop the following year brought in an even greater aggregate, which was exceeded the next year, although the financial crash of 1857 cost the planters many millions. The high-water mark of the antebellum cotton industry was reached in 1859-1860, when a crop of 4,861,000 bales was sold for nearly $250,000,000.

The tobacco and sugar industries were almost as prosperous. As a result of the development of improved varieties and better methods of curing, the demand for tobacco increased, and production in the United States grew from 200,000,000 pounds in 1849

[1] C. F. M'Cay, of Georgia, in *Hunt's Merchants' Magazine*, XXIII, 602.
[2] *DeBow's Review*, XXVII, 106. The increase was due in part to an expanding money supply.
[3] Donnell, *History of Cotton, passim.*

to 434,000,000 in 1859, about 124 per cent. In Virginia and Kentucky, the leading tobacco-producing states, the production was doubled, while in North Carolina it was tripled.[4] Although the tobacco growers continued to complain of the heavy duties imposed by foreign countries upon American tobacco,[5] there can be no doubt that the industry was more prosperous during the decade before the Civil War than in any other period since colonial times. The sugar industry was a somewhat uncertain one. The crop fluctuated widely from year to year because of occasional early frosts and other unfavorable weather conditions. The price fluctuated even more widely, being dependent not only upon the crop in the United States and the tariff, but also upon the crop in Cuba and Hayti, whence sugar was imported.[6] In 1856 the crop in Louisiana, which produced virtually all of the United States sugar, was only 73,976 hogsheads, and sold for $110 per hogshead. In 1858 the crop was 362,296 hogsheads, and the price $69. However, the industry seems to have been more prosperous from 1850 to 1860 than during the previous decade. The average price was $63, and the average crop 273,450 hogsheads from 1850-1860; the same items for 1840-1850 were $49.75 and 165,150 hogsheads respectively.[7]

It was an axiom in the South that when the planting sections were prosperous, the grain-growing and stock-raising regions were also prosperous. In the decade before the war their prosperity was enhanced by the readier access to market which improved roads and newly built railroads afforded. At the same time competition with the agricultural states of the Northwest was rendered less injurious because prices were kept up by the growing demand of the East and Europe for foodstuffs.[8]

[4]Meyer Jacobstein, *The Tobacco Industry in the United States*, 38-39; Eighth Census, *Agriculture*, Introduction, pp. xcvi-xcvii.

[5]"Barbarossa," *The Lost Principle*, 176 ff.; memorial to Congress, by a committee of the Southern Commercial Convention, Knoxville, in *DeBow's Review*, XXIV, 291-300, Apr. 1858; *ibid.*, XXVI, 315.

[6]*Ibid.*, XIX, 353, XXII, 320-25, 433-36; Robertson, *A Few Months in America*, 88; Stirling, *Letters from the Slave States*, 182.

[7]*DeBow's Review*, XXIX, 524; Eighth Census, *Agriculture*, Introduction, xcix.

[8]*Ibid.*, cxli, cxlvi-cxlix (tables illustrating growth of trade between the West and the East and Europe).

The growing degree of content with the rewards of the cotton industry was reflected in the increased frequency of expressions of fear for the security of America's monopoly of the production of raw cotton. Livingston was said to have reported that cotton grew in the interior of Africa.[9] Attention was given to the possibility that India might be stimulated to increased production. Much interest was taken in the Cotton Supply Association, which was organized in 1857 by English spinners for the purpose of stimulating cotton production in India and elsewhere.[10]

It has always been true in the South that when cotton prices have risen pleas for the diversification of agriculture have fallen upon deaf ears; so it was during the decade before the War. The agricultural reformers in the cotton belt pleaded with the planters not to make more cotton, but to raise their own hogs, cattle, horses, and mules, and to grow their own corn and wheat—thus they would cut down expenses and conserve the fertility of the soil. The reformers told the planters that the high prices were only temporary, and were caused in part by the increased gold supply resulting from the opening of the California mines.[11] The rise in the price of cotton was no greater than the rise in the prices of other things.[12] A small cotton crop, they said, and truly, often brought a greater aggregate than a large one. But planters could not resist the temptation to take advantage of prevailing high prices by increasing their acreage.[13] Somewhat better transportation facilities between the planting and the farming regions promoted the tendency to specialization. The agriculture of the planting belts was no more diversified, if as much, in 1860 than in 1850.

The sugar and cotton planters seem to have resorted, to no diminishing extent, to Tennessee, Kentucky, Missouri, and states

[9]*DeBow's Review*, XXIV, 580; Donnell, *History of Cotton*, 466.

[10]Donnell, *op. cit.*, 454, 466, 478; *Hunt's Merchants' Magazine*, XLIII, 640.

[11]*DeBow's Review*, XIV, 280.

[12]Address of A. P. Aldrich at the fair of the South Carolina Institute, 1859, Charleston *Mercury*, Nov. 19, 1858.

[13]"The price of cotton has raised the price of land, so there is no chance of buying you a cleared plantation now. And during such prices it would be folly to take hands from making cotton in Baldwin to clear the place in Dooly, so we shall have to let planting affairs remain in 'statu quo.'" John B. Lamar to Howell Cobb, Feb. 7, 1850, *Toombs, Stephens, Cobb Correspondence*.

even farther north for horses and mules, hay, bacon, pork, and beef, and even corn and flour. "There is no reason," wrote a planter, "why Tennessee, Arkansas, Mississippi, Alabama, Georgia, and Texas should not raise all of their own horses and mules. There is no earthly reason why these states should not also raise all their own corn, hogs, cows, etc."[14] James L. Orr described the planter of South Carolina as buying his bacon and pork, much of his beef, and not infrequently his corn and flour.[15] Robert Russell, an English traveler, writing of the planters of Mississippi, said, "The bacon is almost entirely imported from the Northern States, as well as a considerable quantity of Indian corn."[16]

Exports of Western produce from New Orleans to the North and to Europe fell off very rapidly after the building of railroads from the North Atlantic ports to the West; but there was no falling off in the total receipts of Western products at New Orleans.[17] This was due in part to the increased demands of New Orleans herself, in part to the increased demands of the South generally. Of 1,084,978 barrels of flour received at New Orleans in 1858-1859, 306,090 were exported to Northern ports, 133,193 to foreign countries, and 165,397 to other Southern ports.[18] The following year 965,860 barrels of flour were received at New Orleans, of which 58,739 went to the North, 80,541 abroad, and 247,231 to other Southern ports.[19] The statistics for corn, bacon, pork, and other articles produced north of the planting belt show similar proportions. Moreover, only a portion of the Western provisions shipped down the Mississippi reached New Orleans. For example, of 92,919 barrels of flour shipped from Cincinnati in

[14]*DeBow's Review*, XIX, 229.

[15]*Ibid.*, XIX, 21 (July, 1855).

[16]*North America*, 265, 290.

[17]Eighth Census, *Agriculture*, Intro., clvi, clvii, Tables N and O; *DeBow's Review*, IV, 391; VI, 434; X, 448; XII, 83; XVII, 530; XXIII, 365; XXV, 469; XXVII, 471-479. "As an outlet to the ocean for the grain trade of the west, the Mississippi river has almost ceased to be depended upon by merchants." "And even, at no distant date, all the western grain and flour which found a market in New York or New England was shipped to New Orleans in steamboats, and thence around the coast in ocean ships." Eighth Census, *Agriculture*, Intro., clvii, clv.

[18]*Ibid.*, Intro., clvii; *DeBow's Review*, XXVII, 479.

[19]*Ibid.*, XXIX, 784; Eighth Census, *Agriculture*, Intro., clvii.

1860 to points below Cairo, only 35,146 went to New Orleans.[20]
By 1860 the railroads were carrying no inconsiderable amounts of
provisions from the West and the farming sections of the South
into the planting sections.[21]

A comparison of the census reports for 1850 and 1860 indicates
that the agriculture of the South as a whole was less diversified
in the latter than in the former year. It is sufficient to compare
such large items as cotton, tobacco, corn, wheat, oats, potatoes,
hogs, sheep, cattle, and draught animals.[22] The *per capita* production of Indian corn in the South was 33 bushels in 1840, 32.75
bushels in 1850, and 31 bushels in 1860. The population of the
South increased 23.9 per cent between 1850 and 1860; during
the same time the annual production of cotton had been doubled
and of tobacco more than doubled. In the leading cotton state,
Mississippi, the cotton crop was increased 150 per cent, and the
corn crop, 32 per cent. The percentages for Alabama were 73
and 18, for Louisiana 336 and 65, and for Georgia 41 and 0.
South Carolina produced less corn but 17 per cent more cotton in
1860 than in 1850. Tennessee, the leading corn state of the
South, grew no more corn in 1860 than in 1850, but had increased
her cotton crop by one-half. Virginia and North Carolina gained
but little in corn produced; but tobacco production had been
doubled in the one and tripled in the other. During the decade
the annual oats crop had declined in every Southern state except
Virginia and Texas; for the South as a whole the falling off was
over 40 per cent. In 1850 the Southern states produced 4.87
bushels of sweet potatoes *per capita;* in 1860, 4.16 bushels. There
were fewer hogs in the South in 1860 than in 1850; the leading
hog-raising states, Tennessee and Georgia, showed decreases,
while Virginia, Texas, and Arkansas showed increases. Outside
Texas there were fewer neat cattle in the South in 1860 than in
1850. The number of milch cows, however, increased 20 per cent;
and the production of butter increased from 6.12 to 6.55 pounds
per capita. The number of sheep had increased less than 10 per
cent, and the wool clip but 18. The statistics for hogs, neat cattle,
and sheep may be contrasted with those for draught animals,

[20]Eighth Census, *Agriculture*, Intro., clviii.
[21]*DeBow's Review*, XXIV, 214.
[22]Eighth Census, *Agriculture*, Intro., *passim*.

which were employed in the culture of the staples. The number of mules, oxen, and horses increased between 1850 and 1860 by 103, 42, and 22 per cent respectively. The only important food stuff of which there was a remarkable increase of production was wheat. The crop was 17,795,761 bushels in 1850 and 31,441,826 bushels in 1860, a gain of 77 per cent and an increase from 2.5 to 3.5 bushels *per capita*. The largest gains were made in Tennessee, North Carolina, and Georgia; they were attributable very largely to the building of railroads which gave access to market to the farmers of eastern Tennessee, western North Carolina, upper Georgia, and north Alabama.

As the great staple industries became more profitable, a tendency was manifested to boast of the prosperity of the South, to proclaim her strength rather than her dependence, and to glorify agriculture and assert its superiority to other industries in every respect—in productivity, in the development of individual character and strength, as the conservator of the moral and social order, as a guarantee of the permanence of republican institutions, and as a basis for the political power of a nation.

Planters had long complained that they were at the mercy of the "money power," the Bank of England or combinations of speculators and spinners, who took advantage of the necessity of cotton planters to realize quickly upon their cotton in order to pay advances they had received while their crop was growing. As late as October, 1851, a cotton planters' convention at Macon, Georgia, published a scheme for organizing the planters to keep up the price of cotton.[23] Later in the decade, with demand outrunning production, the "law of supply and demand" seemed sufficient guarantee against exploitation. "Cotton has outlived and outgrown the influence of the money power of the Bank of England," wrote a contributor to *DeBow's*. "Many years since, Mr. Van Buren . . . said that a combination of the Bank of England 'diminished the value of every man's property in America.' This was particularly true at the South, . . . That plan was tried to check the rising values in 1856 and 1857; but for the first time without success. . . . The combinations of spinners are of no avail; the manufacturing wants exceed the

[23]*DeBow's Review*, XII, 110, 121-6, 275-80.

power of the South."[24] There were even signs of a breaking away from the deplorable system of advances to planters; and certain it is that the advances came more frequently from home banks and less frequently from foreign factors than formerly.[25] The South was beginning to accumulate the capital with which to market her staples.

There was reason for self-congratulation also in the way the South came through the financial crash of 1857. The South was not as hard hit as the West and North, and, because of large crops at good prices, recovered more rapidly.[26] Southern merchants paid their debts in Eastern cities as usual in 1858;[27] and Eastern merchants were induced to seek purchasers in the South rather than in the West.[28] Never before had Southern banks held so large a proportion of the nation's specie as in 1858, 1859, and 1860.[29] This favorable balance may have been due in some degree to smaller purchases of Northern and foreign goods after the panic, and, possibly, to a partial carrying out of threats of non-intercourse in retaliation for Northern "aggressions"; but the chief explanation lies in the unusual sums realized from the crops of those years.

Formerly when comparisons had been made between the slaveholding and the free states, Southern men had generally been content to trace " 'Southern decay' to other causes than Slavery which in fact is all that saves us."[30] In 1849 Ellwood Fisher, of Cincinnati, in a lecture there, maintained, "in opposition to the existing opinion on the subject," that the "South is greatly the superior of the North in wealth in proportion to the number of their

---

[24]*DeBow's Review*, XXVII, 107. "Cotton is king. The Bank of England was until lately, but the last time she tried to put on the screws she failed." J. H. Hammond in the Senate, Mar. 4, 1858, *Cong. Globe*, 35 Cong., 1 Sess., 961.

[25]*DeBow's Review*, XXVII, 107; *Hunt's Merchants' Magazine*, XLII, 157; Charleston *Courier*, Nov. 5, 1860.

[26]*DeBow's Review*, XXVI, 92, 582, quoting the *United States Economist*.

[27]Charleston *Mercury*, Mar. 11, 1858, quoting the New York *Herald*; *Hunt's Merchants' Magazine*, XXXVIII, 583.

[28]*Ibid.*, XLII, 70; *DeBow's Review*, XXVI, 583.

[29]*Hunt's Merchants' Magazine*, XXXIX, 459; XLII, 157; XLIII, 455.

[30]J. H. Hammond to Calhoun, Aug. 18, 1845, *Calhoun Correspondence*.

citizens respectively."[31] This proposition he sought to demonstrate by a formidable array of miscellaneous statistics ingeniously arranged. Both the thesis and the method of demonstration were comparatively new to the South. J. H. Hammond, reviewing the lecture for the *Southern Quarterly Review*, said: "It will be perceived . . . . that Mr. Fisher strikes out into a bold and to most persons we doubt not an entirely new train of facts and arguments in his discussion of this subject."[32] He refuted some of Fisher's arguments. Fisher's lecture, however, was well received in the South.[33] Both his conclusions and method were followed with increasing frequency in succeeding years, chiefly, no doubt, because slavery must be defended, but partly because the economic position of the South seemed to justify doing so. Alexander H. Stephens defended slavery by demonstrating the superiority of the slave state of Georgia over the free state of Ohio in prosperity and all other respects in which abolitionists were wont to make invidious comparisons.[34] B. F. Stringfellow used Fisher's method in his pamphlet, *Negro Slavery No Evil*, as did many other less able defenders of the institution.

The arguments of those who would diversify Southern industry were more frequently refuted during the few years preceding the war than before. This was due in part to improved economic conditions in the South, in part to growing fears on the part of the dominant social class that diversification would tend to undermine the existing social order, and in part to the political situation. "For fifty years," wrote George Fitzhugh, "she [the South] has been more usefully, more industriously, more energetically, and more profitably employed than any people under the sun. Yet all the while she has been envying and wishing to imitate the little *truck patches*,' the filthy, crowded, licentious factories, the mercenary shopkeeping, and the slavish commerce of the North."[35]

[31]*Lecture on the North and the South, delivered before the Young Men's Mercantile Library Association, of Cincinnati, 1849* (pamphlet), p. 7. The lecture is in *DeBow's Review*, VII, 134 ff., 262 ff.
[32]*Southern Quarterly Review*, XV, 276.
[33]*DeBow's Review*, VII, 134. Fisher was made editor of the *Southern Press*, a short-lived organ established in Washington, 1849, by Southern members of Congress.
[34]Cleveland, *Alexander H. Stephens in Public and Private*, 429-32; 432-59.
[35]*DeBow's Review*, XXIII, 587.

The Montgomery *Daily Confederation,* a conservative organ, protested against the doctrines which found favor in the Southern
Commercial Convention: "That the North does our trading and
manufacturing mostly is true, and we are willing that they
should. Ours is an agricultural people, and God grant that we
may continue so. We never want to see it otherwise. It is the
freest, happiest, most independent, and, with us, the most powerful condition on earth."[36] Those who attended the Southern
Commercial Convention and interested themselves in schemes for
the regeneration of the South made much of the argument that
commercial and industrial independence would augment the
political power of the South and enable the Southern people to
better defend their rights and interests. But the majority seem to
have preferred to stake the security of Southern rights and interests upon the efficacy of the "cotton is king" argument, and the
"cotton is king" argument arose from the fact that the people of
the South were chiefly engaged in producing a few great staples
for export.

Frequent reference has been made in former chapters to the
use of this argument in some form or other. It may be briefly
recapitulated: The South produced an immense surplus for export
of great staples, particularly cotton, which had become necessities
for millions of people the world over, supported a large part of the
commerce and trade of the world, constituted the raw material for
factories in England and America employing millions of capital
and hundreds of thousands of hands, and furnished the basis for
American credit in Europe. With the return from their staples the
Southern people purchased manufactured goods from the North
and from Europe and provisions from the West, whose production,
sale, and transportation gave employment to factories, farmers,
shippers, and merchants. When one computes the capital and
labor dependent either directly or indirectly upon the production
and export of Southern staples, he has a stupendous total, and
the Southerner was only too prone to exaggerate the part his cotton played in keeping the wheels of the world's industry in motion.
And cotton and negro slavery were said to be synonymous: the
South had a monopoly of the world's cotton supply; only negroes
held in slavery could make the great crops of cotton; therefore,

[36]May 19, 1858. See also above, pp. 50-58, and below, pp. 222-23.

destroy slavery and the mighty structure reared upon it would come down with a crash.[37] Also, as long as the sections were dependent upon each other, the South had at hand a powerful political weapon in the form of threats to limit the cotton supply, to manufacture it herself, to conduct her own commerce, to adopt a policy of non-intercourse, to secede, to do anything, in short, which would injure interests elsewhere, the prosperity and permanence of which depended upon the continuance of existing commercial relationships between the sections. Furthermore, those who desired disunion or believed it inevitable could plausibly argue that secession would be peaceful: the interruption of Southern trade and the cutting off of the cotton supply, which war would cause, would so prostrate Northern industry that the section would be incapable of waging war; England and France would not tolerate a war which might involve the interruption of their supply of cotton. A Southern confederacy once established, they could further argue, cotton would be the power which would preserve the peace and secure favorable commercial treaties.

It is apparent that the continued potency of the "cotton is king" argument depended upon the South's remaining exclusively agricultural; to the extent the Southern people should become industrially and commercially independent the argument would lose force. George Fitzhugh wrote: "Indeed, the South will commit a fatal blunder, if, in its haste to become nominally independent, it loses its present engines of power, and thereby ceases to be really independent . . . . It is our great agricultural surplus that gives us power, commands respect, and secures independence. . . ."[38] It is apparent also that for the "cotton is king" argument to be an entirely satisfactory one from the Southern

---

[37] "It seems, indeed, when the whole of the facts brought together are considered, that American slavery, though of little force unaided, yet properly sustained, is the great central power, or energizing influence, not only of nearly all the industrial interests of our own country, but also all of those of Great Britain and much of the continent; and that, if stricken from existence, the whole of those interests, with the advancing civilization of the age, would receive a shock that must retard their progress for years to come." Christy, *Cotton is King* (second edition) 163.

[38] *DeBow's Review*, XXIII, 341 (Dec., 1857). Fitzhugh found reason soon to change his opinions somewhat.

point of view, the agricultural system upon which it was based must be satisfactory to the Southern people.

Southern statesmen and politicians had long used the "cotton is king" argument in one form or another without reserve and with considerable effect. During the crisis of 1850, for example, it appeared in the frequent calculations of the value of the Union. But at no time did cotton seem more powerful, and the Southern people more inclined to exult in it and wield it as an instrument of political power, than during the several years immediately preceding the Civil War. After the passage of the Kansas-Nebraska bill, Professor Christy, of Ohio, published a very ingenious volume entitled, *Cotton is King*, one of whose theses was that an alliance had been struck between the planters of the South and the producers of provisions in the Northwest.[39] But it was chiefly to the industrial and commercial centers of the North that the appeal was made. Jefferson Davis, speaking to a Boston audience in Faneuil Hall, said: "Your interest is to remain a manufacturing, and ours to remain an agricultural people. Your prosperity, then, is to receive our staple and to manufacture it, and ours to sell it to you and buy the manufactured goods."[40] John B. Floyd said in New York: "I rejoice that the great staples of the South are the chief means by which your commerce is fostered, and your mechanics and artisans kept constantly at work."[41] During the campaigns of 1856 and 1860 Southern orators were sent to Northern cities. R. M. T. Hunter, Robert J. Walker, Henry W. Hilliard, Herschel V. Johnson, and even William L. Yancey were all adept in appealing to the business interests.[42]

Nor did these appeals to interest fail to raise up powerful allies for the South in the North—the "Northern men with Southern principles." Leading journals closely identified with the business interests, such as the New York *Herald*, the New York *Express*, the Boston *Post*, the Boston *Courier*, and the Philadelphia *Atlas*, defended the South and slavery and described the dire effects upon the North of goading the Southern states into non-intercourse or

[39]Pp. 144 ff., especially.
[40]Mrs. Varina Davis, *Jefferson Davis*, I, 630.
[41]*DeBow's Review*, XXI, 604.
[42]*Ibid.*, XXI, 530-38; 589-602; Hilliard, *Politics and Pen Pictures*, 294-302; New York *Herald*, Sept. 22, Oct. 11, 1860, speeches of Yancey in Washington and New York.

secession. Slavery had its defenders in the pulpit and in the schools. Northern politicians friendly to the South were not courting Southern popularity only. So effective was cotton as an argument for slavery that optimistic men from time to time detected a "returning sense of justice" in the North and a change in the attitude of the people of England and France toward slavery.[43]

The improved condition of Southern agriculture in the fifties was reflected in, and gave rise to, a somewhat different aspect of the labor problem. Between 1840 and 1850 when prices of cotton and slaves were low, the feeling was pretty strong throughout the South that there was a redundancy of labor engaged in the culture of cotton. Planters welcomed suggestions that slaves be diverted from cultivating cotton to other labor. The possibility of employing them in factories and in the construction of internal improvements was canvassed. The experiment was tried in both fields, and in the latter, at least, proved successful.[44] In the next decade the prosperity of Southern agriculture, especially cotton growing, and to some extent the employment of slaves upon works of internal improvement, created a strong demand for labor. Prices of slaves rose to unprecedented figures. A contributor to *DeBow's*, 1856, said the price of field hands had nearly doubled in five years.[45] A Georgia delegate to the Southern Commercial Convention, the same year, said negroes were worth from $1000 to $1500 each, and there were ten purchasers to every seller.[46] Frequent accounts of the sales of slaves affirm the truth of these assertions.[47] The prices continued to rise until secession.

This remarkable rise in prices occurred notwithstanding the fact that the labor force engaged in the production of cotton and sugar was receiving large increments in addition to the natural increase of slaves. Partly because of the high prices offered for

[43]Cleveland, *Alexander H. Stephens*, 647 ff.; *DeBow's Review*, XXIV, 423; New Orleans *Picayune*, Jan. 5, 1858; J. H. Hammond, speech at Beech Island, S. C., July 22, 1858, in Charleston *Mercury*, July 27.

[44]*DeBow's Review*, XXIX, 254; XVII, 76-82; Phillips, *American Negro Slavery*, 375-378.

[46]*DeBow's Review*, XXI, 158.

[46]*Ibid.*, XXII, 222.

[47]This subject is thoroughly discussed in Phillips, *American Negro Slavery*, 373-375, and chart, p. 370.

slaves by planters, and partly because of the influx of foreigners and the increasing difficulty of controlling slaves in cities, the slave population of such large cities as Baltimore, New Orleans, St. Louis, and Charleston declined between 1850 and 1860. The slave population of Charleston fell from 19,532 in 1850 to 13,909 in 1860; that of New Orleans declined from 16,845 to 13,385, notwithstanding there was a remarkable increase in the total population of the city.[48] In Richmond, Savannah, Augusta, Columbus, Memphis, Nashville, Mobile, Natchez, and other towns there was a considerable decline in the proportion which the slave population bore to the white population.[49] Thousands of slaves were transferred each year from the border states and the older cotton states to Arkansas, Mississippi, Louisiana, and Texas; and there can be no doubt that they went to the cotton and sugar plantations of those states. Olmsted estimated the number of slaves annually sold south from the northern slave states at more than 20,000.[50] Winfield Collins estimated from the reports of the U. S. Census that during the period 1850-1860, 207,000 slaves were transferred from the selling states, which included North and South Carolina, to the buying states.[51] In Delaware and Maryland the slave population declined during the decade.[52] In Virginia it increased only 3.88 per cent; in South Carolina, 4.53 per cent; in Kentucky, 6.87 per cent; in North Carolina, 14.73 per cent; and in Tennessee but little more. The increase in the total slave population of the United States during the decade was 23.39 per cent, of which at least 20 per cent represented natural increase. A by no means inconsiderable increment to the labor force of the planting belts of the cotton states consisted of slaves imported from outside the United States in violation of Federal and state laws. Collins considers 70,000 a "moderate and even low" estimate of the number of slaves imported between 1850 and 1860.[53] DuBois, in his *Suppression of the African Slave Trade*, asserts that the laws against the foreign slave trade were

[48]*Compendium of the Seventh Census, passim;* Eighth Census, *Population, passim.* The slave populations of St. Louis, Baltimore, and Louisville were small.

[49]*Ibid.; DeBow's Review,* XXX, 70.

[50]*Cotton Kingdom,* I, 58 n.

[51]*Domestic Slave Trade,* 66.

[52]Eighth Census, *Population,* 599.

[53]*Op. cit.,* 20.

"nearly nullified," and that the increase of illicit traffic and actual importations in the decade 1850-1860 may almost be termed a reopening of the slave trade.[54]

But these additions to the labor force of the cotton and sugar plantations were incommensurate with the demand, and could not be made indefinitely. Considerable speculation was indulged in as to whence would come the labor which would enable the cotton planters to extend their operations in the future, and the South to maintain her position as the chief source of the world's cotton supply. John M. Cordoza, an old and reliable commercial editor of Charleston, said the yearly increase in the cotton crop of the United States was regulated by a fixed law, namely, the increase in slave population, which was three per cent per annum. True, production had been increasing at a more rapid rate because of the transfer of slaves from the non-cotton states to the cotton belt and from poorer to more fertile lands within the belt; but this process could not go on indefinitely. Improved methods and labor saving machinery could be considered negligible factors in increasing production. He had no fear of foreign competition.[55] Other observers thought the tobacco and grain growing states had no redundancy of labor, and were unlikely to have "so long as their present prosperity continues."[56] J. B. Gribble, a New Orleans cotton factor who reviewed the trade for *Hunt's Merchants' Magazine*, believed that the poor whites would be induced by the high prices to labor; in fact a change was already perceptible, and soon many "small crops" would tell with some effect upon the aggregate yield.[57] The *United States Economist*, 1859, pictured the cotton states as prosperous and the prospects for the future of the cotton industry as brilliant. With the advancing prices of slaves it would be "impossible to limit the increase of supply to the rule which now governs it, *viz.*, the natural increase of hands." Cultivation would be undertaken by whites.[58]

About 1856 there was begun a lively agitation in the cotton states in favor of the repeal of the laws prohibiting the foreign

[54]Pp. 178, 183.
[55]*DeBow's Review*, XXII, 337-49 (Apr., 1857).
[56]Charleston *Mercury*, May 4, 1858, article by P. A. Morse, of Louisiana. The same is in *DeBow's Review*, XXIII, 480.
[57]XXXVII, 554-61.
[58]Quoted in *DeBow's Review*, XXVI, 582.

slave trade; this agitation continued until after secession. The movement for the renewal of the slave trade may be attributed in part to the demand of the planting interest for a larger and cheaper labor supply; to the extent this may be done, the movement testifies to the prosperous condition of Southern agriculture. The movement and the accompanying discussion also brought out clearly two divergent conceptions of a proper Southern policy. One looked to the diversification of industry, the encouragement of white immigration, and the development of free rather than slave labor. In this view, the future lay with the white race; and the South had other interests than slavery. The other conception of policy looked to the preservation of a slave society and the plantation system, and was antagonistic to any changes which might endanger the existing social and economic order. A study of the movement for reopening the slave trade should contribute to an understanding of this deep seated division in Southern public opinion. The movement illustrates also the growth of sectional feeling and disunion sentiment and the existence of sectional divisions in the South, with their basis in conflicting interests.

As early as 1852, L. W. Spratt, the editor of the Charleston *Standard*, advocated the reopening of the African slave trade. For a few years he was almost alone. In 'the Southern Commercial Convention, New Orleans, 1855, a Louisiana delegate introduced a resolution recommending that Southern congressmen work for the repeal of the Federal laws against the slave trade; but the resolution elicited no discussion.[59] The first responsible leader to publicly espouse the cause was Governor Adams, of South Carolina. In his message to the Legislature, November, 1856, he argued at length for revival of the trade, examining the subject in all of its aspects, economic, political, social, and moral.[60] The lower house of the Legislature after a short but animated debate referred the governor's recommendation to a special committee, which was permitted to defer its report until the next session. Apparently only a small minority wished to agitate the subject.[61] In South Carolina, as elsewhere, Adams's recommendation was considered

[59]*DeBow's Review*, XVIII, 628.
[60]Charleston *Daily Courier*, Nov. 26, 1856.
[61]*DeBow's Review*, XXVII, 364. Savannah *Republican*, Dec. 15, 19, 1856.

a move to advance the cause of disunion.[62] The Savannah *Republican* had no idea that it was made in good faith, but only as the "handmaid and twin · sister of Disunion."[63] Southern leaders in Congress hastened to correct the impression which the discussion in South Carolina was creating elsewhere, and resolutions were introduced and adopted declaring against reopening the foreign slave trade.[64]

But these resolutions failed to check agitation. The subject was injected into the proceedings of the Southern Commercial Convention at Savannah, December, 1856, and the revival of the trade was favored by a very aggressive minority.[65] At Knoxville, the following year, the subject occupied the larger part of the time of the convention.[66] A resolution declaring that the joint patrol article of the Treaty of Washington, 1842, should be abrogated, was adopted. At the sessions of the Commercial Convention held in Montgomery, 1858, and Vicksburg, 1859, the foreign slave trade was virtually the only subject discussed.[67] At Vicksburg the convention adopted a resolution declaring that "all laws, state or Federal, prohibiting the African slave trade, ought to be repealed." The delegates from Louisiana, Mississippi, and Arkansas formed an "African Labor Supply Association," of which J. D. B. DeBow was made president.[68] The avowed purpose of the organization was not, as the name may suggest, to encourage the importation of slaves notwithstanding the laws against it, but to conduct an agitation for their repeal.[69]

Meanwhile the question had come before the state legislatures. The Mississippi Legislature, 1857, had before it a plan to charter the "African Labor Immigration Company" authorized to bring in

[62]Savannah *Republican*, Dec. 5, 1856; *Daily National Intelligencer*, Dec. 2, 1856.

[63]Dec. 6, 1856.

[64]*Cong. Globe*, 34 Cong., 3 Sess., 123-26.

[65]Proceedings, in Savannah *Republican*, Dec. 9-15, 1856; *DeBow's Review*, XXII, 81-105, 216-24.

[66]Proceedings, in *ibid.*, XXIII, 298-320.

[67]Proceedings of the Montgomery session are in *ibid.*, XXIV, 473-491, 574-606. Debate upon the slave trade is in Hodgson, *Cradle of the Confederacy*, 371-392. Proceedings of the Vicksburg session are in *DeBow's Review*, XXVII, 94-103, 205-220, 468-471; New York *Herald*, May 18, 21, 1859.

[68]*DeBow's Review*, XXVII, 120.

[69]Letters, Yancey to DeBow, DeBow to Yancey, in *ibid.*, XXVII, 231-35.

negroes as "apprentices."[70] No action was taken upon it. The Louisiana House of Representatives, by a large majority, passed a bill providing for the importation of 2,500 African negroes to be indentured for a term of not less than fifteen years. A select committee of the Senate reported the bill favorably. The Senate, by a majority of only two votes, postponed the bill indefinitely.[71] Both the Mississippi and the Louisiana measures were said to be compatible with the Federal Laws prohibiting the slave trade.[72] In the South Carolina Legislature of 1857-1859 the subject was again considered. In January, 1859, DeBow wrote: "Certainly no cause has ever grown with greater rapidity than has that of the advocates of the slave trade, if we may judge from the attitude it is assuming in most of our Southern Legislatures."[73] In the press also the subject received its full share of attention.

The great increase in the illicit foreign slave trade during the 1850s can be attributed largely to the enormous profits made possible by the high prices slaves were commanding; but the state of public opinion in the South was also favorable to it. It was notorious that the laws were being violated. The newspapers commented upon the slave smuggling and sometimes with approval. Federal officials were remarkably inefficient and apathetic in the enforcement of the laws against it. It seemed impossible to get a jury in the South to convict a slave trader.[74] In the Southern Commercial Convention at Vicksburg, L. W. Spratt and others openly advocated violation of the laws. When opponents declared the agitation useless because Congress would never legalize the trade, Spratt replied that if the trade were approved by Southern sentiment, it would matter little what might be the

[70]New Orleans *Delta*, Feb. 9, 1858; *DeBow's Review*, XXV, 627.

[71]New Orleans *Picayune*, Mar. 5, 21, 27, 1858; *DeBow's Review*, XXV, 491 ff., 627. The report of the select committee of the Senate is in *ibid.*, XXIV, 421-24.

[72]Henry Hughes, "State Liberties, or the Right to African Contract Labor," in *ibid.*, XXV, 626-53; report of the select committee of the Louisiana Senate, just cited. But see opinion of Secretary of the Treasury Cobb, *House Exec. Docs.*, 36 Cong., 2 Sess., IV, No. 7, pp. 632-36.

[73]*DeBow's Review*, XXVI, 51. See also *ibid.*, XXVII, 493, quoting the Richmond *Whig*.

[74]New Orleans *True Delta*, May 5, 1859. Also Charleston *Mercury*, Mar. 4, 11, 1858, quoting the New Orleans *Delta*; *Mercury*, May 22, Aug. 5, 1858; DuBois, *Suppression of the African Slave Trade*, 183-87.

course of Congress.[75] More honorable was the suggestion frequently made that the laws against the foreign slave trade were unconstitutional and should be nullified. The Committee on Federal Relations of the Senate of Louisiana argued that the Federal laws against the foreign slave trade were unconstitutional, and the state was in duty bound to interpose; the legislature had an unquestionable right to enact a law permitting the importation of slaves from Cuba, Brazil, etc., and any attempt on the part of the Federal authorities to interfere with its operation would be tyranny.[76]

We cannot be too critical of the motives either of those who favored or of those who opposed reopening the African slave trade. The prominent leaders of the movement were disunionists, and were known as such before the agitation had well begun. They saw in the foreign slave trade another issue which would divide the sections, and in the certain refusal of the North to permit the revival of the trade another pretext for dissolving the Union. The debate turned almost as much upon the advisability of debating the question as it did upon the advisability of reopening the trade. The Charleston *Mercury* deplored the agitation of the question because it divided and distracted the South.[77] Others answered that if disunionists waited for a united South they would never get out of the Union.[78] The great majority of the Unionist leaders and newspapers were opposed to raising the question. They charged that the agitation had been got up to promote disunion.[79] Advocates of reopening the slave trade made the counter charge that its opponents were afraid to debate the question on its merits. They were willing to sacrifice the interests

[75]*DeBow's Review*, XXVII, 212; New York *Herald*, May 18, 1859. H. S. Foote branded such utterances as "high treason."

[76]*DeBow's Review*, XXVI, 485 (extract from the report). Such prominent men as W L. Yancey and ex-Governor J. D. McRae argued that the Federal laws prohibiting the foreign slave were unconstitutional. Hodgson, *Cradle of the Confederacy*, 379; *DeBow's Review*, XXVII, 362-64.

[77]Mar. 10, 1859. Also speech of R. B. Rhett, July 4, 1859, in *Mercury*, July 7.

[78]E. g., John A. Jones, of Georgia, in the Montgomery Commercial Convention, Hodgson, *op. cit.*, 377.

[79]New Orleans *Picayune*, Mar. 21, 1858.

of the South to avoid raising an issue which might endanger the stability of the Union.[80]

The agitation for the revival of the slave trade may be regarded as, in a measure, merely a reaction to the excesses of the Garrisonian abolitionists in the North. J. J. Pettigru, in his report to the South Carolina Legislature, said: "It is not intended to impute directly or indirectly a want of sincerity to the supporters of the measure; . . . . but a great many worthy persons are honestly disposed to make issue with the North from a spirit of pure combativeness, without regard to ostensible causes."[81]

It could very plausibly be argued that the reopening of the African slave trade was necessary if the South were to maintain the sectional equilibrium upon which the maintenance of her rights and interests in the Union was said to depend. The North was said to be gaining three congressmen a year and rapidly settling new free states and territories by virtue of foreign immigration.[82] How could the South maintain her political equality when the only class of immigration she could attract and use was barred? A bitter contest was being waged over Kansas. Kansas, it was painfully evident, was being lost to the South because there was no excess of slave population to go into it. Plans for acquiring Cuba and territory in northern Mexico or Central America with a view to making slaveholding states of them were said to be futile without the reopening of the foreign slave trade; for either there would be no slaves to populate them, and they would become free states; or the older slave states would be drained of their slave population, and become free states. Alexander H. Stephens and Jefferson Davis both said the South could not hope for any great extension of slave territory unless the slave trade were reopened.[83] Indeed, without population to take advantage of them, the Kansas-Nebraska bill and the Dred Scott decision were empty victories. Even without further extension of territory, it

[80]E. g., W. H. McCardle, of Mississippi, in the Vicksburg convention, New York *Herald*, May 18, 1859.

[81]*DeBow's Review*, XXV, 306.

[82]Temple, of Tennessee, in Southern Commercial Convention, Knoxville, 1857, *ibid.*, XXIII, 319.

[83]Stephens's farewell address to his constituents, Augusta, Georgia, July 2, 1859, in Cleveland, *Alexander H. Stephens*, 647; Davis, quoted in Cairnes, *The Slave Power*, 243 n.

was said, there was a possibility of the loss of Maryland, Kentucky, and Missouri to slavery through the transfer South of the slave population and the influx of elements hostile to it. "There is no denying," said Yancey, "that there is a large emancipation interest in Virginia and Kentucky and Maryland and Missouri, the fruits of which we see in Henry Winter Davis, Cassius M. Clay, and Thomas H. Benton."[84]

Advocates of reviving the slave trade contended that the measure was necessary to secure slavery against the attacks of present or future foes within the cotton states themselves. If there should arise a serious shortage of labor, Northern and European labor, unfriendly to slavery, would come in to supply the deficiency. Governor Adams, of South Carolina, said, that, if the South could not supply the demand for slave labor, "we must expect to be supplied with a species of labor we do not want, and which is from the very nature of things antagonistic to our institutions."[85] Fears were expressed that the "labor base" was already becoming too narrow. "We need to strengthen this institution," said Yancey, "and how better can we do that than by showing the non-slaveholding class of our citizens that they can buy a negro for $200, which, in a few years, by his care and instruction, will become worth a thousand dollars?"[86] Some of these agitators accepted the "irrepressible conflict" doctrine. " . . . . in Tennessee, and even Georgia, Alabama, Mississippi, and Louisiana," said L. W. Spratt, "there is a large class of persons who have to make their own bread with their own hands, and these are distinctly conscious that there is a difference between 'labor' and 'slave labor.' "[87] Opponents of reopening the slave trade denied that it would make slavery more secure: slavery was most secure when the prices of slaves were highest.[88] They also denied the presence in the South of a large class inimical to slavery. Roger A. Pryor characterized it a "foul libel upon the citizens of the

[84]In Southern Commercial Convention, Montgomery, *DeBow's Review*, XXIV, 587.

[85]Charleston *Daily Courier*, Nov. 26, 1856.

[86]*DeBow's Review*, XXIV, 587.

[87]"Report on the Slave Trade—Made to the Southern Convention at Montgomery," etc., in *ibid.*, XXIV, 473-91. (Quotation on page 489.)

[88]E.g., H. S. Foote, in the Vicksburg convention, *ibid.*, XXVII, 219; Pettigru, Minority Report in S. C. Legislature, *ibid.*, XXV, 176.

South to thus endorse what Greeley and Seward have been asserting so many years . . ." He admitted that "emigrées" from the
North might be considered hostile to slavery. The facts seem to.
have been against Pryor's contention.[89]

Everywhere in the South where white laborers came into competition with slaves there was hostility on the part of the whites
toward negroes and their masters and a demand, not for the emancipation of slaves to be sure, but for their exclusion from the
employments in which competition was felt. This spirit was
noticeable especially among mechanics and artisans and unskilled
laborers in the cities. In South Carolina the white mechanics
memorialized the Legislature, 1858-1859, for laws prohibiting slaves
from hiring their own time and working at mechanical employments.[90] In the Southern Commercial Convention at Vicksburg, Mr.
Purdon, of Mississippi, offered resolutions, which had been adopted
by a meeting of white mechanics, condemning the practice of making
public mechanics of negroes, and declaring that slave labor should
be confined to the corn, cotton, and sugar plantations.[91] In Alabama and North Carolina also there was opposition to the employment of slaves in mechanical pursuits.[92] In the latter state
workingmen's associations began the agitation for the *ad valorem*
tax upon slave property, which became the leading issue of state
politics during the few years immediately preceding the war.[93]
The author of *The Impending Crisis of the South* claimed to represent the free labor of North Carolina with whose development
slavery interfered. In New Orleans and other cities of the South
the practice of employing slaves as draymen was abandoned because of the objections of whites.[94] Nor were all of those who
favored the restriction of slave labor to the plantations working-

[89]*DeBow's Review*, XXIV, 581.

[90]Extract from the report of the committee on negro population, J. Harlston
Read, Jr., chairman, in *ibid.*, XXVI, 600 ff.

[91]*Ibid.*, XXVII, 102:

[92]Montgomery *Daily Confederation*, Jan. 19, 1859; Olmsted, *Cotton Kingdom*, II, 137; *Republican Banner and Nashville Whig*, Aug. 18, 1857 (riotous
demonstration of white mechanics of Wilmington, N. C., against negro mechanics).

[93]J. W. Moore, *History of North Carolina*, II, 137, 138; Wm. K. Boyd,
"North Carolina on the Eve of Secession," in Amer. Hist. Assoc., *Rept.*, 1910,
pp. 168, 174.

[94]*DeBow's Review*, XXIV, 602.

men. Others favored it to prevent a "war between free labor and slave labor in our midst," to make white labor "aristocratic" and invite immigration, and to obviate difficulties of controlling slaves in cities and towns.[95] Immigrants from the North and Europe were generally unfriendly to slavery. There were farming communities in the cotton states from which the whites would have been glad to have all negroes expelled.[96] In several of the slaveholding states, notably Alabama, Tennessee, North Carolina, and Virginia, there were political divisions based upon the division of each into a farming, largely non-slaveholding section and a planting section or black belt. The people of the farming sections were not generally hostile to slavery, but they did resent the political dominance of the planters. So the fears of Spratt and others that opposition to slavery might grow up in its very midst were not at all groundless.

All of these classes hostile or potentially hostile to negroes or slavery or both were opposed to reopening the African slave trade. If the South were to have immigration, they preferred that it be white immigration. They were joined by those who, while devoted to slavery, feared it to be a doomed institution: if emancipation should ever occur, they thought, the South would have a quite sufficient race problem with the natural increase of her existing negro population.[97]

On the question whether or not it would be to the economic interest of the cotton planters and the South to increase the labor force engaged in the production of cotton by the importation of slaves from abroad, there was a difference of opinion. In the opinion of the advocates of reopening the slave trade, the demand for cotton was growing so rapidly that production could be materially increased without reducing the price. A failure on the part of the South to produce sufficient cotton to supply the demand might result temporarily in exorbitant prices which would stimulate production in other quarters of the globe, and, consequently, cause the loss of America's monopoly and, finally, a

[95]Charleston *Courier*, Dec. 28, 1856, letter on "Policy of Planters"; *So. Quar. Review*, XXVI, 447.

[96]Olmsted, *A Journey in the Back Country*, II, 236, and *passim* (Putnam's ed., 1907).

[97]*DeBow's Review*, XXVII, 219.

permanent decline of prices. The cotton crop could not be sufficiently increased without fresh supplies of labor. Reopening the African slave trade would supply the deficiency. Further, a revival of the slave trade would lower the prices of slaves, and thus reduce the cost of production.

The possibility of producing cotton by white labor received considerable attention, especially from a class of Northern and English writers who were interested not so much in the future of cotton as in the future of slavery.[98] White labor, they asserted, was cheaper than negro slave labor, and whites could work in the climate of the cotton belt. Robert Russell, the most competent of the British observers, put a high estimate upon the advantages of the plantation system, but saw no bar in the climate to production of cotton by white labor. He remarked the considerable amount of cotton already grown in the pine barrens, whose climate was even warmer than that of the middle zone or uplands, where most of the plantations were located.[99] Of the people of the South some believed white labor for cotton production available, but considered it undesirable; others, waiving the question of desirability, professed to believe it unavailable. Many seem to have believed the assertion so frequently made that, as one put it, "In the cotton, rice, and sugar regions, slave labor is not only more productive, but is the only species of labor which can be depended upon for the cultivation of these great staples."[100] Those who made this assertion knew, of course, that thousands of non-slaveholding whites were engaged in a small way in the production of cotton. DeBow estimated the number so engaged in 1850 at 100,000; the number of slaves employed in the cotton fields he set at 800,000.[101] The great majority of the planter class seem to have taken little interest in the poor whites, and to have had less faith in making them productive members of society. As for European labor, it was not forthcoming, whether for climatic, social, or other reasons. Said DeBow: "It is plain, and time and events have

[98]F. L. Olmsted, *Cotton Kingdom*, II, 254-59, 265-67; *Journey in the Back Country*, 377 ff.; Edward Atkinson, *Cheap Cotton by Free Labor, by a Cotton Manufacturer*; Weston, *Progress of Slavery*, 44; Stirling *Letters from the Slave States*, 234, 302 ff.; Russell, *North America*, 284 ff.

[99]*North America*, 284, 285. Cf. M. B. Hammond, *The Cotton Industry*, 94 ff.

[100]A. J. Roane, of Washington, *DeBow's Review*, XX, 661.

[101]*Industrial Resources of the Southern and Western States*, I, 175.

demonstrated the fact, that *it is not European labor which we want,* since that labor, during so long an experiment has *not* taken foothold in our limits, evidencing thus an incapacity to adopt itself to our conditions and to become amalgamated with us."[102] Naturally the planters themselves, from economic motives alone (although this aspect of the matter was not publicly discussed), would not invite competition from a large number of white farmers, whether native or immigrant.

Opponents of reopening the slave trade denied that it would benefit the agricultural interests. A material increase in the cotton crop would depress prices. Cheap cotton would benefit only the manufacturer. America's position as the chief source of raw cotton was not endangered. Slaves from Africa would constitute a poor grade of labor, and, therefore, would not lessen the cost of production, however much they might depress the price of slaves.[103]

Advocates of the reopening of the African slave trade claimed that it would be beneficial to other industries as well as agriculture. The great obstacle, they said, was lack of labor. As long as cotton culture paid more for labor than other employments could afford, it was idle to attempt to divert labor to them.[104] The use of such an argument was plainly an attempt to meet the opposition to the slave trade of those who were urging diversification of industry as a proper policy for the South. The argument was inconsistent with the contention that renewal of the slave trade would benefit agriculture. And diversificationists were not desirous of diverting labor to less profitable industries; in their opinion, the development of varied industry would benefit all. The suggestion made, that slave labor might be used in manufactures, could not carry great weight. It had been tried with small success. However, the great obstacle to the development of diversified industry in the South was not so much lack of labor as a deficiency of capital. There was much unprofitably employed white labor in the South.

[102]*DeBow's Review,* XXVII, 232.

[103]J. J. Pettigru, minority report of a committee of the S. C. Legislature, in *ibid.,* XXV, 166-185; 289-308; speech of ex-Senator Brooke, of Miss., in the Vicksburg Convention, *ibid.,* XXVII, 360-62; and most of the speeches and papers against reopening the slave trade.

[104]The best statement of this argument is in L. W. Spratt, "Report on the Slave Trade," etc., Montgomery Convention, in *ibid.,* XXIV, 473-91.

On the very eve of the war, William Gregg wrote, "The idea that we lack laborers at the South, and will be under the necessity of importing wild Africans, is preposterous." He told why the immigrant did not come South: When he learns that "one-half of our white people, who are willing to work, can not procure employment —that able-bodied men are roaming about the country glad to get work at seventy-five cents per day and find themselves—while similar labor commands a dollar or more at the North and West, is it at all surprising that he does not come to the South?"[105]

We come again to the fact that many of the slaveholding element in the South, including advocates of the reopening of the slave trade, feared the development of white labor and sought to prevent it by keeping the white laborers in a minority. They neither wished to employ profitably that already in the South or to invite immigration. Gregg and others of his way of thinking, on the contrary, had no fear of white labor. They wanted to put the whites to work as well as the blacks, and they were inclined to welcome immigration from the North and Europe. They professed to believe that a white population, profitably employed, would not be inimical to slavery. They were not hostile to slavery, but they saw no necessity for subordinating every other interest to this single one. Reopening the African slave trade, could it have been accomplished, would have been a measure to perpetuate the old order in the South. The New Orleans *Picayune* took note of this fact. After describing at some length the progress being made in manufactures and internal improvements and the changes which were coming over the South, it said: "It is worse than folly to arrest the present direction of capital and enterprise by plans whose effect, if successfully carried into execution, would restore the former tendency of all Southern enterprise to the channel of agriculture."[106]

It could not be concealed that there was very strong opposition to the foreign slave trade on moral and religious grounds. L. W. Spratt, the arch-agitator, said all the women and all the "pious" were against him.[107] The influx of a horde of barbarians, said opponents, would change Southern slavery from a patriarchal

[105]*DeBow's Review*, XXIX, 623, 630.
[106]May 22, 1858.
[107]*DeBow's Review*, XXVII, 213.

institution to one like that of Cuba, where cruelty and severity were necessary to control the slaves.[108] The people of the South were very sensitive to the opinions of the world. "This proposition, if endorsed, would shock the moral sentiment of Christiandom," said Roger A. Pryor.[109]

The people of the border states were almost unanimously opposed to the agitation of the slave trade proposal. They were charged (by W. L. Yancey and others) with being desirous of maintaining the high prices of slaves because they held the position of sellers of slaves to the buyers in the cotton states.[110] Virginians, against whom the charge was particularly made, repelled the charge with indignation. Virginia was prospering, they said; she had opened a field for slave labor which rendered it profitable at home.[111] No doubt many slave owners in Virginia and other slave selling states were interested in keeping prices up; but we need not emphasize economic motives to explain the opposition in the border states. They were the states with the largest non-slaveholding population, the largest foreign element (excepting Louisiana, of the cotton states), and the largest Northern element. In each of the border states there was considerable emancipation sentiment. Being nearer the North, their people were more sensitive to criticisms of slavery than the people farther south. Their institution was milder and more patriarchal; and their moral repugnance to the slave trade had not been blunted by familarity with it.

It is worthy of note that, although every coast state had either laws or constitutional provisions or both against the foreign slave trade, not one of them was repealed. Not a single state legislature went so far as to pass resolutions demanding the repeal of the Federal laws against it. In Mississippi, where, with the exceptions

---

[108] J. J. Pettigru, Roger A. Pryor, H. W. Hilliard, in *DeBow's Review*, XXV, 289 ff.; XXIV, 582, 592.

[109] *Ibid.*, XXIV, 582. Russell formed a different impression. In Charleston he overheard a conversation on reopening the slave trade. "One made the remark that the South now paid little regard to what England might think of the matter . . . I was somewhat mortified to find how little impression all that has been said and written about slavery has had on those whose pecuniary interests are interwoven with the institution." *North America*, 162.

[110] Yancey in the Montgomery Convention, *DeBow's Review*, XXIV, 585.

[111] Wm. Ballard Preston's reply to Yancey, *ibid.*, XXIV, 595.

of Louisiana and Texas, the movement was strongest, the Democratic party was afraid to take it up as a new political issue.[112] In South Carolina, after two years of agitation, only in the Charleston district was it made an issue in the political campaign of 1858.[113] South Carolina leaders who found the agitation prejudicial to the cause of disunion by dividing the South were able to silence the agitation in all but two of the newspapers of the state. Sectional politics was no doubt largely responsible for the origin of the agitation. Once begun, however, it is questionable whether considerations of sectional politics did not operate more strongly against the movement than for it. A fair conclusion perhaps would be that only in two or three Southwestern slave states was the movement strong enough to have insured legalizing the reopening of the trade had not Federal laws imposed an obstacle. And the strength of the movement there can be attributed chiefly to economic causes; agriculture was expanding rapidly; thousands of slaves were being bought for the plantations at prices so high as to absorb a large share of the profits.

The comparative prosperity of Southern agriculture during the decade before the War was reflected to a degree in other industries. In 1850 there were 2,004.37 miles of railroads in the Southern states, constructed at a cost of $42,181,665. In 1860 the mileage was 8,946.9, representing a cost for construction of $237,376,097.[114] Unlike the railroads of the West they had not been built entirely with capital borrowed in the East or abroad.[115] Southern promoters experienced difficulty in selling their bonds in the North or in England. Public opinion demanded that the roads be built, and every expedient was resorted to to sell the stock at home. Because of the difficulty of raising capital, Southern railroads had been economically built, and, too often, cheaply constructed and poorly equipped. Traffic had proved light and dividends generally small, and the mileage had been extended beyond the immediate requirements, although by 1860 there was promise of better conditions in the industry.

[112]Henry S. Foote, Scylla and Charybdis, 254-56.
[113]DeBow's Review, XXVII, 364, remarks of Mr. Farrow, of S. C.
[114]Ringwalt, Development of Transportation Systems in the U. S., 151.
[115]Hunt's Merchants' Magazine, XLII, 315; Kettell, Southern Wealth and Northern Profits, 50, 88; Powell, Notes on Southern Wealth and Northern Profits; Cong. Globe, 32 Cong., 1 Sess., Appx., 1056.

The rapid extension of agriculture, under the influence of higher prices, naturally absorbed most of the capital accumulated from the profits of the industry. The building of the railroads likewise constituted a heavy drain upon the capital of the South. Notwithstanding, noteworthy extensions were being made in several lines of industry, and plants already established were prospering.

The railroads brought in with them machine shops and repair shops. Several rolling mills had been established before 1860. The value of the bar, sheet, and railroad iron made in the South increased from $1,504,443 in 1850 to $2,458,119 in 1860, or 63 per cent.[116] Railroad cars were made in a few shops; the Tredegar Locomotive works at Richmond made 19 of the 470 locomotives made in the United States in 1860. Stationary engines were being constructed in many places. The production of coal had nearly trebled, although the aggregate was still small, about one-ninth of the total production of the United States. The iron industry had not yet been greatly affected by the coming of the railroads; in the production of pig iron there was a decline between 1850 and 1860.

During the years just before the war the cotton factories, after several years of great difficulty, were again prosperous. In 1855 the Georgia factories were reported in thriving condition. A year or two later similar reports came from northern Alabama and western Tennessee.[117] Occasionally the building of a new factory was reported. The attention of the North was attracted to the revival.[118] General Charles T. James, of Rhode Island, again put his services at the disposal of any company proposing to establish new factories.[119] During the decade 1850–1860 the number of cotton factories in Georgia grew from 29 to 33, the number of hands employed from 2,107 to 2,813, and the value of the product from $1,395,056 to $2,371,207, or 69.97 per cent. These gains made Georgia the leading cotton manufacturing state of the South, and,

[116]All the statistics given in the next few pages are taken from the reports of the Sixth, Seventh, and Eighth censuses unless otherwise specified. The term "the South" is used to include only the eleven states which seceded. The census reports include mining and lumbering with manufacturing; and there would be no point in making a distinction here.

[117]*Hunt's Merchants' Magazine*, XXXVII, 111; XXIX, 755.

[118]Charleston *Mercury*, May 25, 1858.

[119]*DeBow's Review*, XXVIII, 244.

in part, justified her reputation as the "Massachusetts of the South." Considerable gains were made also in Alabama and Tennessee. Virginia and North Carolina made no progress in this industry. South Carolina showed a decline. The revival in the cotton manufacturing industry came too late to greatly improve the showing the South as a whole made in 1860. The progress in the South had been smaller proportionally than in the country at large, and the product of Southern factories was only one-fourteenth of the total for the United States.

The value of the product of Southern woolen manufactures increased 143.55 per cent between 1850 and 1860; the increase for the country at large was 42.14 per cent. During the same period the value of men's clothing produced in the South increased 65.96 per cent; in the United States, 51.55 per cent. For boots and shoes, the percentages of increase were 89.9 and 70.27. The production of paper was increased almost threefold, and of printing over sevenfold. But in the case of each of the items named the Southern states produced only three or four per cent of the total output for the United States, a quantity entirely inadequate to meet the home demand. A respectable beginning had been made in the manufacture of carriages and coaches, wagons and carts, saddlery and harness, nails and spikes, sashes, doors, and blinds, and in cooperage. In the manufacture of agricultural implements progress had been much slower than in the United States as a whole; the South produced less than six per cent of the total. Of the manufacture of one article, however, the South had almost a monopoly; of 57 cotton gin factories in the United States, 54 were in the Southern states, notably Alabama. The value of the ships and boats built in the South in 1860 was $789,870, which sum may be compared with $11,667,661 for the United States. Of the 631 articles listed by the census as manufactures of the United States in 1860, 398 were not made in the South in any quantity whatever, and many others were made only in insignificant quantities. In these two classes fell such common and necessary articles as hats and caps, men's furnishings, women's clothing, millinery, carpets and rugs, furniture and cabinet ware, earthenware, glassware, hardware and cutlery, tools, and stoves and ranges. Packed meats may also be mentioned.

The Southern states made the best showing, both as regards aggregate value of product and percentages of increase, in types of manufacture which were closely related to agriculture, or which were comparatively simple in their processes. Thus the value of the flour and meal ground increased from $16,581,597 to $37,996,470, or 129 per cent, between 1850 and 1860; and in the latter year was equal to nearly one-fourth the total value of all Southern manufactures. The value of lumber, planed and sawed, was $19,696,863 in 1860, an increase of 133 per cent over 1850, and was one-eighth the value of all Southern manufactures. The value of the tobacco manufactured was $14,612,442 in 1860, 125 per cent more than in 1850. A fourth big item was turpentine, crude and distilled, valued at $7,409,745. These four items together accounted for one-half the total value of the product of all Southern manufactures; and the capital invested in their manufacture was nearly one-half the capital invested in all the manufactures of the South.

The capital invested in manufactures in the South was 13.6 per cent of the capital so invested in the entire country in 1840,[120] 10.4 per cent in 1850, and 9.5 per cent in 1860. The increase in capital so invested in the South was 51.5 per cent between 1840 and 1850 and 73.6 per cent the following decade; for the entire United States the percentages were 95.5 and 91.3. Southern manufactures employed 88,390 hands in 1850 and 110,721 in 1860, an increase of 25.3 per cent. In the same period the population of the eleven Southern states had grown 23.9 per cent. The number of hands employed in all the manufactures of the United States in 1850 was 957,059, in 1860 the number was 1,311,246, or 37 per cent more. The population of the United States was 35.4 per cent greater in 1860 than in 1850.

Statistics are not available for a full comparison of the progress of manufactures and agriculture, but comparison in a few respects may suffice. Between 1850 and 1860 the value of Southern manufactures increased 96.5 per cent. During the same period the value of the cotton crop increased 102.7 per cent; the tobacco crop, 119 per cent; the sugar product, 80.3 per cent; and the live stock in the South, 96.4 per cent. As we have seen, the progress in other branches of agriculture was not great.

[120]The statistics for 1840 are meager and can rarely be used for comparisons.

Southern cities had not established direct trade, nor had they become industrial centers. Among the cities of the United States in 1860, New Orleans, Charleston, Richmond, Mobile, Memphis, Savannah, and Petersburg ranked in size 6, 22, 25, 27, 28, 41, and 50 respectively. In value of manufactures they ranked 17, 85, 13, 79, 74, 65, and 49 respectively. Thus Richmond and Petersburg only could be considered industrial towns. However, as commercial centers the towns of the South reflected accurately the prosperity of the section.

The South was not in the throes of an industrial revolution at the outbreak of the Civil War, and there seems to be little evidence that she was upon the verge of such a revolution. However, there were factors in the situation which pointed to a more rapid development of varied industry in the future. Capital which might be so employed was accumulating. Southern banks had never been in a stronger condition. The railroads must soon have justified their construction by giving isolated regions access to market, increasing intercourse, and creating new wants. They were breaking down those frontier conditions which, because of the great extent of the section, the sparse population, and the natural difficulties of forests and rough lands, still lingered in much of the South. The attention of Southern men had been directed to the varied resources of the land. Geographical surveys had revealed the coal and iron fields of Alabama and Tennessee, lying in close proximity. Railroads were ready to penetrate them, and the processes were being developed which would make possible their utilization. Stock had been taken of the water power, and the people were beginning to realize what a wealth lay in the forests. Small industrial towns were springing up here and there. Northern men with experience in various branches of industry were filtering in; Northern capitalists who theretofore had found sufficient fields for investment in the North and West were beginning to show an interest in the possibilities offered by the South, as were also, to some extent, English and French capitalists. It is conceivable that a temporary depression in the price of cotton at the time might have given a decided impetus to the cotton manufacturing industry, just as it had promised to do twelve or fifteen years earlier.

These facts were not unappreciated in the South. The New Orleans *Picáyune*, in the autumn of 1858, said the South had been making progress, slow but positive. "Like a bow in the heavens after the storm clouds have swept by, we may now see, in looking upon the results of the sectional agitations of the immediate past, indications of the commencement of a new era for the South —an era singularly marked with home progress."[121]

So there were factors which operated on the eve of the Civil War to make the people of the South better content with their economic system and position. These may be briefly summarized: (1) The comparative prosperity of Southern agriculture. (2) A measure of prosperity and progress in other lines of industry. (3) Confidence that the possession of and the ability to control a large agricultural surplus for export constituted an element of great political power. (4) A growing consciousness among slaveholders that any considerable diversification of industry was incompatible with the security of slavery. The first two of these would have a tendency to allay sectional feeling. However, the comparative prosperity of agriculture was largely the cause of the movement in behalf of reviving the foreign slave trade, and it had decidely the opposite effect.

[121]Quoted in *DeBow's Review*, XXV, 590.

CHAPTER IX

ECONOMIC ASPECTS OF THE SECESSION OF THE COTTON STATES, 1860-1861

After the election of November, 1860, the cotton states made haste to put into execution their threats of secession in case of the election of a Republican president. In South Carolina the opposition to secession was very weak and ineffectual. The Legislature met in special session, November 5. The members were almost unanimously for immediate, separate secession. A few voices were raised in favor of cooperation with other Southern states.[1] The Legislature called a state convention to meet December 17. With few exceptions only immediate secessionists were elected to it. On the fourth day that body unanimously adopted an ordinance of secession. In taking this speedy action South Carolina was not taking a leap in the dark. Her leaders were confident that other states would soon follow. They had been assured by disunion leaders elsewhere that bold action would strengthen the disunion movements in other states.[2] If a conflict with the Federal government should ensue, there could be no doubt of the decision of the cotton states, at least, upon the issue, as it would then be, of sustaining a sister state against coercion.

Meanwhile vigorous contests were being waged in the other cotton states between those for immediate and separate secession on the one hand and coalitions of unconditional unionists, cooperationists, and temporizers on the other. The governors, with one exception, were secessionists, and the legislatures were controlled by secessionists. Conventions were called in all the states. Brief campaigns ensued to influence the election of delegates and the action of the conventions. These campaigns were conducted amidst great excitement. Governors and legislatures anticipated the action of the conventions by seizing forts, arsenals, and other United States property, and by taking measures to put their respective states on a military footing. Congressmen sent inflammatory messages from Washington, where Senate and House were

[1]Proceedings and debates in the South Carolina Legislature, New York *Herald*, Nov. 9-14, 1860.
[2]Speech of Mr. Elmore, Commissioner from Alabama, before the South Carolina Convention, in *ibid.*, Dec. 22, 1860.

vainly attempting to patch up another compromise to save the Union. Commissioners from one state to another lent their influence to the secession cause.

Considering the tactical advantages of the immediate secessionists, their opponents showed unexpected strength in three states. In Alabama they elected 46 of 100 delegates, and claimed to have cast a clear majority of the votes in the election. In the Convention they united upon a substitute proposal for a convention of all the Southern states at Nashville, and waged a bitter fight in its behalf. The bitterness of the struggle was intensified because the alignment was the old sectional one between northern (Unionist in this case) and southern Alabama. The struggle did not cease when the convention adopted a secession ordinance.[3] In Georgia the opposition cast 42 per cent of the popular vote.[4] In the Convention their substitute proposal for a convention of all the slave holding states was defeated by the narrow margin of 164-133; and this, notwithstanding the fact that Georgia was already assured the cooperation of four states if she should secede. In Louisiana also the contest was hot, and the popular vote close, although in the Convention the immediate secessionists prevailed by a large majority. In Texas the tactical advantages lay with the opponents of secession; for Governor Houston was opposed to it and refused to call the Legislature in special session. However, a self-constituted committee of citizens called an election for delegates to a convention. Their action forced Governor Houston to assemble the Legislature, which approved the action of the committee. The Convention met and passed an ordinance of secession; the people approved its action. After their defeat in the several states the cooperationist and Unionist leaders, with exceptions, expressed a determination to support the course determined upon by the majority. To conciliate them and their following, the secessionist majority admitted them to positions of power and trust in numbers proportionate to, if not in excess of, their strength.

[3]Remarks of W. R. Smith in the Alabama Convention. Smith, *History and Debates of the Convention of the People of Alabama*, 67 f.; Hodgson, *Cradle of the Confederacy*, 502 ff.; letter of T. R. R. Cobb to his wife, Feb. 4, 1861, in So. Hist. Assoc., *Publ.*, IX 274.

[4]Avery, *History of Georgia*, 149.

On February 4, delegates from six states, soon joined by delegates from a seventh, met at Montgomery. A provisional constitution for the Confederate States of America was adopted. A provisional government was organized. Commissioners were sent to Washington and to Europe. Measures were taken to provide revenue and to organize an army and navy. A permanent constitution was drafted by the Provisional Congress and submitted to the states for ratification.

Meanwhile the secession movement in other slaveholding states had received decided checks, although aggressive fights had been waged by the secessionists in several. In North Carolina the Legislature, after much debate, provided for an election for delegates to a convention and the submission to the people, at the same time, (January 28), of the question whether or not a convention should be held. The people elected 82 Unionists and 38 secessionists, and decided against the convention by a small majority.[5] In Tennessee the question of holding a convention was submitted to the electorate and decided adversely by a large majority. In Arkansas the electorate approved the assembling of a convention, but elected delegates a small majority of whom were opposed to immediate secession. The action of Virginia was expected greatly to influence that of the other border slave states. The Legislature met in special session at Governor Letcher's call, and provided for a delegate convention. At the convention election, February 4, the people returned a distinct majority against immediate secession. Although the secessionists waged a hard fight in the Convention, all efforts to pass an ordinance of secession were foiled until after Sumter. In Maryland and Delaware no conventions met, in the former because Governor Hicks refused to call a special session of the Legislature. Governor Magoffin, of Kentucky, recommended the call of a convention, but the Legislature refused. In Missouri a Legislature dominated by State Rights Democrats called a convention, but the electorate returned an overwhelming majority of Union delegates.

As long as any hope remained that Congress or the Peace Conference would agree upon a settlement which would restore the Union, the people of the border states gave unmistakable evidence of their desire to remain in the Union. Even after it became clear that no such settlement was possible, and when the question be-

[5] *Appleton's Annual Cyclopedia*, I, 538.

came one of choosing between the United States and the Confederate States, they seem to have preferred the Union. However, notice was early given (by North Carolina, Virginia, Tennessee, and Arkansas) that continued adherence to the Union was contingent upon no attempt being made by the Federal government to coerce the seceded states. When, after Sumter, President Lincoln issued his call for troops, these states seceded, and united their fortunes with the Confederacy. The other border states were saved for the Union.

With a view to determine whether or not they reveal any evidences of economic motives for Southern sectionalism, it is proposed to analyze (1) the arguments advanced for and against secession after the election of Lincoln; (2) the alignment of the people upon the secession issue; (3) the official statements of causes of secession which were published; (4) contemporary unofficial essays at interpreting events; and (5) the formulation of the early economic policies of the seceded states and of the Confederacy. The considerations determining the action of the border states were manifestly so different from those determining the action of the cotton states that they require a separate treatment. This chapter will deal with the first four points mentioned with special reference to the cotton states. The succeeding chapters will deal with the early economic policies of the seceded states and of the Confederacy and with the peculiar economic considerations affecting the decision of the border slave states.

There can be no doubt that the arguments for and against secession in the cotton states used after Lincoln's election related chiefly to the dangers besetting slavery and how the institution could best be defended. The leading arguments of the secessionists may be summarized: (1) The election had resulted in the triumph of a party which was founded upon and held together by hostility to slavery, which proposed to exclude it from the common territories, in spite of a decision of the Supreme Court, which opposed the acquisition of additional slave territory, which looked to the ultimate extinction of slavery, and whose candidate had declared the Union could not exist half slave and half free. If the South should acquiesce in Black Republican rule, slavery would be doomed, and *the destruction of slavery would ruin the South.* (2) The triumph of a sectional party established a sectional des-

potism of the stronger section over the weaker. Just now slavery
was the interest in gravest danger; but sectional power might be
wielded to the detriment of all the interests of the South. The
Constitution would not protect the weaker section because in the
North the true view of the Union as a federation of sovereign
states had been lost, and the old Federalist idea of a consolidated
government had prevailed. (3) The Constitution was a compact
between equal sovereign states. The Personal Liberty laws of
Northern states were violations of the compact. A violation of
the compact by some of the parties to it released the others from
their obligations under it. (4) The quarrel between the sections
had become so venomous as to subvert one of the purposes for
which the Constitution had been formed, namely, to insure domestic tranquility. The constant denunciation of the South and
slavery by politicians, press, pulpit, platform, and teachers of the
North was a constant insult to the South, and no longer to be
borne. (5) Secession was a constitutional remedy. (6) It would,
in all probability, be peaceful. One party in the North believed in
the constitutional right of secession. Prominent leaders of the
other had declared against coercion. Northern industry would be
paralyzed by the interruption of commerce with the South which
war would entail, and the North would be unable to fight. The
threat of coercion would unite the South, and the Northern people
would perceive the folly of waging war against a united South. (7)
The Southern states, even the cotton states, together possessed
population and resources sufficient to enable them to take their
place among the nations of the earth.

The opponents of immediate and separate secession agreed with
the secessionists that the crisis must not be allowed to pass without some action being taken. They did not consider separate and
immediate secession the proper action, however, for the following
reasons: (1) The election of Lincoln was not a just cause for
secession. He had been elected in a constitutional manner. The
politicians of the South were partly responsible for his election.
The border states would not sustain the cotton states on such an
issue; it was doubtful if the people of the cotton states could be
united upon it. It would be better to wait for some overt act
against the rights of the South on the part of the Lincoln government; that would unite the South. (2) Lincoln would be a minor-

ity president. Both houses of Congress and the Supreme Court would be controlled by the Democrats. Lincoln could not even choose a cabinet without consent of the Senate; the interests of the South were in no immediate danger. (3) The Personal Liberty laws were unconstitutional and unfriendly; but the South had never made a united effort for their repeal. This should be done. If appeals failed, retaliatory legislation might be tried. (4) While anti-slavery sentiment had become fanatical with many, much of the anti-slavery agitation was due to politicians, North and South, who had used the slavery question to inflame the passions of the people. A revolution in the attitude toward slavery was even then in progress in the North and in England. The South had many friends in the North; they should not be deserted. (5) Peaceful secession was an absurdity—unless, possibly, the entire South could be united. The South was not prepared for war. The masses, who must fight it, were not convinced of the necessity for secession. (6) Delay would unite the South. Let all the slave states get together in convention and deliver an ultimatum. If that were rejected, all would go out together. The cotton states had no right to attempt to dictate to the other slaveholding states. (7) The cotton states alone would make a contemptible, obscure, little republic whose rights no foreign nation would respect. Wars and strife would be its lot. (8) The dissolution of the Union would be hailed in Europe as the failure of free government. It was a duty to mankind to attempt to preserve it.

These, it is believed, were the arguments most frequently used in the cotton states during the few weeks which elapsed between the election of Lincoln and secession.[6] Their use, however, can easily be made to prove too much. The election of 1860 turned ostensibly upon the slavery issue. The election of a Republican president had for several years been discussed and announced as the proper occasion, or a sufficient cause, for the secession of the Southern states. An effort had been made during the campaign to commit as many as possible to secession in case of Lincoln's election. After the event, conditional disunionists, notwithstanding the fact that often they attributed the result to the folly or wicked-

[6]The sources upon which this summary is based are too many to enumerate here. Special mention might be made of Candler, *The Confederate Records of the State of Georgia*, Vol. 1, and Smith, *op. cit.*

ness of Southern leaders, could, now that it was a *fait accompli,*
with justification and good conscience see in it a necessity for
secession. Secession *per se* sentiment in the South had been a
growth of thirty years. It was a known and dependable quantity.
It could not be increased over night. Unconditional secessionists
would naturally adapt their arguments to fit the occasion. The
occasion required that advantage be taken of the excitement of
the public mind as a result of Lincoln's election. Such considerations as these must be kept in mind in any study of secession.

However, the secession *per se* arguments were not altogether
neglected during the canvass. Very few advocates of secession
spoke for it without expressing the view that the Union had been
unequal in its material benefits. Scarcely one advocated secession
who did not express the belief that secession would be followed by prosperity. Said Yancey at the close of an argument
based upon Northern violations of Southern rights: "While
ever loyal to a constitutional Union, I have been satisfied that
if Alabama, even, reassumed her full power and sovereignty
it would be attended by a glorious prosperity."[7] Most of Alexander H. Stephens's famous Union speech before the Georgia
Legislature, November 14, 1860, was devoted to proving that in the
Union the South as well as the North had "grown great, prosperous, and happy," and was in refutation of one by Robert Toombs,
who had presented a contrary view.[8] *DeBow's Review* continued
to give the unconditional disunionist arguments.[9] The New York
papers commented upon the "commercial view" of the Union
which was being taken at the South.[10] The existence of disunionists *per se* was assumed at every point of the contests to control
the conventions which were to decide the question of secession.
Union orators often prefaced their remarks by saying that their
arguments were not addressed to unconditional disunionists but
only to those who preferred a "constitutional Union"—i.e., one in
which the rights of the South would be respected.[11] Secessionists

[7]Letter of Nov. 15, 1860, in New York *Herald,* Nov. 26.
[8]Candler, *Confederate Records of the State of Georgia,* I, 183 ff.; New York
Herald, Nov. 22.
[9]See especially XXX, 93-101. See also, *ibid.,* 42-53, 114-16.
[10]I have used the New York *Herald* and the New York *Times.*
[11]For example, Benj. H. Hill in speech at Milledgeville, Ga., Nov. 15, 1860.
Hill, *Senator Benjamin H. Hill of Georgia, His Life Speeches and Writings,* 238.

frequently denied being of the *per se* type; it may have been considered good tactics to do so.

It is impossible to determine with any degree of accuracy how many in the cotton states had by 1860 arrived at the conclusion that the true interests of the South lay in separate nationality irrespective of the outcome of the pending presidential election. There were no test votes on the question. During the presidential campaign supporters of Bell and of Douglas charged the Breckinridge men with having broken up the Democratic party with the design of making possible the election of a Black Republican president and consequent dissolutions of the Union; they appealed to the voters to "rebuke" the secessionists. The statement has sometimes been made that the vote for Breckinridge and the combined vote for Bell and Douglas indicate fairly accurately the relative strength of the secessionists and Unionists respectively.[12] The statement is inaccurate. An analysis of the result of the election shows that many voted against Breckinridge to rebuke the secessionists, and many were attracted to Breckinridge by the secessionist tendencies of his following, but in the main the people divided according to their old party affiliations. In Georgia, for example, fourteen counties which elected Union delegates to the State Convention in December went for Breckinridge in November; and fifteen counties which gave majorities for Bell and Douglas elected secession delegates.[13] Northern Alabama gave a majority for Breckinridge (although somewhat less than the normal Democratic majority) but was strongly against secession. The secessionists from principle had steadily grown in numbers. Their leaders were able and determined. They had become strong enough to gain control of the Democratic party organization in several states. But there is no reason to believe they were in a majority except in South Carolina. L. Q. C. Lamar, describing the state of public opinion in the South shortly after Lincoln's election, said: "There is a fourth class of energetic, resolute, and high spirited men who consider the Federal Government a failure, the connection of Northern and Southern States as unnatural, and the independence of the latter a supreme good. These are for im-

---

[12]See Avery, *History of Georgia*, 135; Thomas, "Southern Non-slaveholders in the Election of 1860," *Pol. Sci. Quar.*, XXVI, 227.
[13]See Phillips, *Georgia and State Rights*, 205-210.

mediate, unconditional, and even abrupt secession . . . This class is dominant in one State, commands perhaps a majority in another, and is influential in all."[14] The statement was substantially correct.

After Lincoln's election this class was joined by those who had not desired secession but believed it necessary under the circumstances in order to preserve slavery. The classes which came over to secession were chiefly Whigs of the black belts and, it would seem, the propertied, mercantile, and financial elements of the cities and towns. These classes had been conservative. They had long protested against useless agitation, believing that the best policy was one of conciliation and avoidance of contest. Those who persisted in their opposition to secession to the last were chiefly the people of the farming districts and the back country, where the slave population bore a relatively smaller proportion to the whites. They were Democrats of the Jackson type or Whigs of the Clay type. They had never accepted the teachings of the secessionists. They were not hostile to slavery; but they did not have the same interest in its preservation which the planting class had. Party lines largely gave way during the contests for control of the state conventions; but in two states at least, Whigs showed themselves more favorable to the preservation of the Union than Democrats of the same districts. The decision in a few localities was influenced by considerations peculiar to each. These general statements may be illustrated by a brief analysis of the alignment upon the secession issue in each of the more populous of the cotton states.

In South Carolina the Unionists of 1851 were with some diminution of numbers the Unionists of 1860. The only locality in which there was a pronounced Union sentiment was the up-country farming district about Greenville. B. F. Perry was the leader there, as he had been in 1851. Hopes that the commercial interests of Charleston would be adverse to secession proved ill-founded. The cooperationists of 1851 did not insist upon waiting for cooperation in 1860; they were confident it would come.

The secessionists of Georgia in 1861 were the Southern Rights party of 1850 with accretions. About the only prominent leader

[14]Letter to P. F. Liddell, Dec. 10, 1860, in Mayes, *L. Q. C. Lamar: His Life, Times and Speeches*, 633 ff.

who had favored secession in 1850 but opposed it in 1861 was
Herschel V. Johnson. Robert Toombs, Howell Cobb, and E. A.
Nesbit were the most prominent of the large number who counselled acquiescence in 1850 and secession a decade later. Georgia
was not divided into sections as were several other Southern
states. The only large compact group of counties which elected
Union delegates to the State Convention lay along the Northern
border. In these counties the white population greatly outnumbered the black. They had long returned Democratic majorities. They had been Unionist in 1850. It is significant that every
county which had a city or considerable town elected secession
delegates, notwithstanding the white population preponderated
in most of them, and most of them could be classified as Whig
counties. The general tendency of the districts in which the
whites constituted a majority to favor maintenance of the Union
and of the black belts to go for secession is illustrated by the accompanying table. Counties having a population more than 50
per cent slave are classified as black; others, white. Counties are
classified as Whig which gave Whig majorities at a majority of
the presidential elections between 1844 and 1860; others, Democratic. Counties are classified as Union, secession, or divided according as their delegations in the State Convention voted upon
H. V. Johnson's substitute for the ordinance of secession, which
was the test question.[15]

	Secession	Union	Divided	Totals[16]
Black counties	25	13	5	43
White counties	45	39	5	89
Whig counties	25	23	4	52
Democratic counties	45	29	6	80
Whig, black counties	14	12	3	29
Democratic, black counties	11	1	2	14
Whig, white counties	11	11	1	23
Democratic, white counties	34	28	4	66
Totals	70	52	10	132

[15] *Journal of the . . . Convention of . . . Georgia, 1861*, p. 32.

[16] If the counties in which the negroes comprised from 40 per cent to 50 per
cent of the total population be classified as black, the number of such counties
would be increased by 28, of which 20 elected secession, 7, Union delegates, and
one, a divided delegation. Of the 20, 14 were Democratic, 6 Whig. Of the 7, 5
were Whig, 2 Democratic.

Of 29 counties which elected secession delegates to the Convention of Alabama, 28 lay in a compact group in the southern part of the state. Of the 23 Union counties, 22 formed a compact group in the northern part of the state. This division corresponded roughly with the division between the black belt and the white counties; only a few counties in the northern half of the state had large slave populations, and but few more in the southern half could be classed as white. The alignment also coincided with an old sectional alignment which had characterized the state politics of Alabama.[17] The basis of this long standing sectionalism lay in part in the social differences between the planting region and the farming section, in part in geography. The people of southern Alabama found an outlet for their productions through Mobile. The people of a large part of northern Alabama were cut off by mountains from seeking the same outlet; the chief outlets for their productions were the Tennessee river, and, for a few years before 1860, the Memphis and Charleston and other railroads. All of these routes led into or through Tennessee. The people of northern Alabama felt that it would be ruinous to their section of the state to secede unless Tennessee should also secede. Threats were made that, in case Tennessee should not secede, north Alabama would separate from the remainder of the state and ask for union with her.[18] The Whigs of southern Alabama, where they were in the majority, generally went over to the secessionists. Such Whig leaders as H. W. Hilliard, T. H. Watts, and T. J. Judge now took their stand with Yancey, whom they had hitherto opposed. The Democrats of northern Alabama, where they were in a large majority, had always been of the Jackson rather than the Calhoun wing of the party.[19] Mobile and Montgomery, the one in a white county, the other a black, both went for secession. The accompanying table, with items defined as were those of a similar table for Georgia, may serve to illustrate certain tendencies to division in Alabama. It does not illustrate the sectional division, and it does not accurately indicate the position of the Whig party.

[17]Jack, Sectionalism in Alabama.
[18]Smith, History and Debates of the Convention of Alabama, passim, especially remarks of Mr. Clark, of Laurence, pp. 81-90; New York Times, Jan. 18, 1861; Journal of the Convention . . . of South Carolina, 1860, 1861, and 1862, pp. 233-234, report of A. P. Calhoun, Commissioner to Alabama.
[19]Cf. Hodgson, Cradle of the Confederacy, 475.

	Secession	Union	Totals
Black counties	18	2	20
White counties	11	21	32
Whig counties	15	3	18
Democratic counties	14	20	34
Whig, black counties	10	0	10
Democratic, black counties	8	2	10
Whig, white counties	5	3	8
Democratic, white counties	6	18	24
Totals	29	23	52

The opposition to secession in Mississippi centered chiefly in a few Democratic counties situated in the extreme northern part of the state and having relatively small slave populations, and in several Whig counties with large black populations and lying along the Mississippi river. The counties in which Vicksburg, Natchez, and Jackson, the only considerable towns of the state, were located, all gave majorities against immediate and separate secession. It would seem that, except in a few northern counties mentioned, the opponents of secession were chiefly Whigs. In the Convention the opponents of immediate and separate action were led by Yerger, a Whig. The continued Whig opposition to secession counterbalanced in this state the tendency to division between districts having large and districts having small slave populations. This fact is illustrated in the following table:

	Secession	Union	Divided	Totals
Black counties	21	7	2	30
White counties	23	5	2	30
Whig counties	7	7	2	16
Democratic counties	37	5	2	44
Whig, black counties	7	5	2	14
Democratic, black counties	14	2	0	16
Whig, white counties	0	2	0	2
Democratic, white counties	23	3	2	28
Totals	44	12	4	60

The contest in Louisiana presented no remarkable features. Old party divisions were swept away. In general the parishes with the largest slave populations went for secession; there were exceptions. There were few parishes which could not be considered as belonging to the black belt. There were no marked sectional divisions in the state. A group of Democratic parishes in the north-central part of the state and another of Whig parishes near the Mississippi in the southeast corner of the state elected delegates opposed to immediate secession. New Orleans, which had always been considered a Union stronghold because of its large foreign and Northern population and its commerce with states of the upper Mississippi valley, elected 20 secession and 4 Union delegates. The city had given a majority for the Bell electors in November; the population was overwhelmingly white. The result in New Orleans may be attributed in part to the prevalent excitement and the failure of the conservative Creole population to poll its full voting strength in the convention election.

Several of the secession conventions, following the example of the Second Continental Congress, adopted declarations of the causes for secession. These documents were drawn up, no doubt, with less regard to historical accuracy than to the effect they might have upon public opinion at home, in the border states, in the North, and even in Europe. They all rest the cause of the South primarily upon the necessity of protecting slavery against Northern assaults.

The South Carolina Convention published two statements of causes. One, "The Address of the People of South Carolina . . . to the People of the Slaveholding States . . . ,"[20] was presented by a committee of which R. B. Rhett was chairman;[21] the other, "A Declaration of the Immediate Causes which Induce and Justify the Secession of South Carolina from the Federal Union,"[22] was brought in by a committee of which C. G. Memminger was chairman.[23] In all probability the chairmen of the respective committees wrote the reports.[24] Rhett's committee represented secessionists of long standing of the more extreme sort. They were of the faction which had advocated separate action in 1851-1852. Memminger represented the more moderate element which had constituted the cooperationist party in 1851-1852. The Rhett following seems to have wished to play up the establishment of a free

[20]*Journal, of the Convention of South Carolina,* 467-76; McPherson, *History of the Rebellion,* 12-15; *DeBow's* Review, XXX, 352-57.

[21]*Journal,* 21.

[22]*Ibid.,* 461-466; McPherson, *op. cit.* 15 ff.

[23]*Journal,* 31, 39.

[24]Capers, *Life and Times of C. G. Memminger,* 289-95.

trade republic for the purpose of enlisting European support. The group of which Memminger was a member considered it of first importance to unite the South. It would seem that the two committees were appointed in order that both factions might express their views. The Convention showed a disposition to divide along these lines on several questions.

Of the two documents the "Address" was much the abler and more worthy of a great cause. The entire substance of it may be found in Calhoun's last great speech in the Senate, March 4, 1850,[25] the address of the Nashville Convention,[26] and Rhett's speech in the United States Senate in which he avowed himself a disunionist.[27] It justified secession by "the accumulated wrongs of half a century." The great wrong was represented to be the overthrow of the Constitution and the transformation of the federal republic into a consolidated democracy, in which a sectional majority in the North could rule over the minority in the South and carry out its measures of "ambition, encroachment, and aggrandizement." A parallel was drawn between the relation of the Thirteen Colonies to Great Britain and the relation of the South to the North. The South had been taxed for Northern benefit; her cities made "mere suburbs of Northern cities;" her foreign trade "almost annihilated." The much employed economic interpretation of the anti-slavery movement was given: hostility to slavery had been made the criterion of parties in the North in order to consolidate the power of the section to rule the South in the interest of the former. The address further portrayed the dangers to which slavery was exposed in a consolidated republic, argued the constitutional right of secession, and appealed to the slaveholding states to form a *slaveholding* confederacy.

Memminger's "Declaration of Immediate Causes" was a brief constitutional argument. It stated the compact theory of the Constitution, and contended that the Northern states had violated the letter of the compact by their Personal Liberty laws, and the spirit of it by the anti-slavery agitation and the election to the presidency of the candidate of a sectional party. The declaration was attacked by Maxcy Gregg, L. W. Spratt, and others on the ground

[25]*Works*, IV, 542-73.
[26]*National Intelligencer*, July 13, 1850.
[27]*Cong. Globe*, 32 Cong., 1 Sess., Appx., 42-48. See above, p. 83.

of incompleteness. It set forth only some of the causes; it omitted the tariff altogether, and laid emphasis on "an incomparably unimportant point." The reply was made that Southern congressmen voted for the existing tariff; the Whig party had always favored the tariff; the tariff argument would not appeal to Missouri, Kentucky, and Louisiana; the issue should not be raised now. Memminger thought it expedient to put their action before all the world upon the simple matter of wrongs on the question of slavery, and that question turned upon the fugitive slave law.[28]

The declarations of causes adopted by the Georgia, Mississippi, and Texas conventions bore greater resemblance to Memminger's "Declaration of Causes" than to Rhett's "Address." Robert Toombs wrote the Georgia statement of causes.[29] He told how the North had outgrown the South in material prosperity, and attributed the disparity to bounties, tariffs, subsidies, and other protective legislation. He charged that the anti-slavery agitation had been fomented in the East for the purposes of winning over the West from her Southern alliance and uniting East and West to wield the power of the government to promote sectional interests. The chief theme of the document, however, was the rise of the anti-slavery party, the history of aggression upon aggression, and their culmination in the victory of a sectional party, which left no protection for the South but the Constitution. No confidence was placed in Republican promises to respect the Constitution: "They [the Southern people] know the value of parchment rights, in treacherous hands, and therefore, they refuse to commit their own to the rulers whom the North offers us." The Mississippi declaration is fairly epitomized in two sentences: "Our position is thoroughly identified with the institution of slavery—the greatest material interest of the world. . . . Utter subjugation awaits us in the Union, if we should consent longer to remain in it."[30] The Texas declaration added little to this except the assertion that

---

[28]Debate in *National Intelligencer*, Dec. 27, 29; McPherson, *op. cit.*, 16 ff.

[29]*Journal of the Convention of Georgia, 1861*, pp. 104-113. Mr. Nesbit, chairman of the committee to report an ordinance of secession, said the statement was written by Toombs. *Journal*, 104.

[30]*Journal of the State Convention* [of Mississippi], 86-88.

the Federal government had failed to protect life and property upon the frontier.[31]

President Davis devoted a large part of his first message to the Confederate Congress, April 29, 1861, to a discussion of the causes of secession. The Constitution of the United States provided for a *federal* government, he said; but that had not prevented the rise of a "political school which has persistently claimed that the Government thus formed was not a compact between States, but was in effect a National Government, set up above and over the States." This doctrine gained the more ready assent in the North because, as that section gained preponderance in Congress, self-interest tempted her representatives to use their power to promote Northern interests at the expense of the South. "Long and angry controversies grew out of these attempts, often successful, to benefit one section of the country at the expense of the other." In addition there had existed for nearly half a century another subject of discord, *slavery,* which involved interests of such "transcendent magnitude" that the permanence of the Union had long been endangered. With slavery as the issue there had developed in the North a sectional party, which had finally gained control of the government. Meanwhile, great interests had developed in the South. "With interests of such overwhelming magnitude imperilled," the people of the South could not consent to live under a sectional government.[32]

Some people in the North believed that President Davis had emphasized the unequal operation of the government upon the economic interests of the sections and minimized the slavery question for the purpose of influencing opinion abroad. They were disposed to take, as a more accurate interpretation of the causes of secession, a speech of Vice-President Stephens in which he spoke of slavery as the corner stone of the new republic. The speech accorded well with Stephens's earlier utterances. He, it should be said, was one of the more conservative leaders of the South; he had never shown sympathy with the unconditional disunionists; he had taken little interest in those progressive Southern movements which have been described; he opposed secession to the

[31]Texas Library, and Historical Commission, *Journal of the Secession Convention of Texas, 1861,* pp. 61 ff.

[32]*Annual Cyclopedia,* I, 614 ff.

last. Moreover, his "Corner Stone" speech should be read in its entirety. He did not fail to pay his respects to a protective tariff and appropriations for internal improvement. "This old thorn of the tariff, which was the cause of so much irritation in the old body politic, is removed forever from the new. . . . The true principle is to subject the commerce of every locality to whatever burdens may be necessary to facilitate it." The people of the North, he said, wanted to preserve the Union because "they are disinclined to give up the benefits they derive from slave labor." According to the reporter, "Mr. Stephens reviewed at some length the extravagance and profligacy of appropriations by the Congress of the United States for several years past, . . ."[33]

Unofficial Southern essays at interpreting events after their occurrence also fail to show general agreement. Of them, too, it must be said that they were not made to facilitate the task of the student. The Charleston *Mercury,* speaking of the Confederate Constitution, said: "The system of partial legislation in the imposition of taxes which has been the prime cause of all the corruption and sectionalism which have finally overthrown the Union of the United States is repudiated by this constitution."[34] According to J. D. B. DeBow: "At bottom, the quarrel between the North and South is, Shall the North support itself, or, by means of Government action and machinery, be supported by the South? It is the old quarrel of nullification continued under a new name."[35] A report submitted for the consideration of the Merchants' and Planters' Convention, at Macon, Georgia, October, 1861, expressed the thought that the "chief of the causes of our separation must be found in questions affecting our selling the products of the soil and the purchase of our supplies from others."[36] Governor Joseph E. Brown, of Georgia, who was already defending state rights against the encroachments of the Confederate government, in his annual message, November, 1861, followed a chain of reasoning quite like that of President Davis in the message already referred to. The people of the North had become consolidationists because they had found that tariff laws, naviga-

[33]Moore, *Rebellion Record,* I, Doc. pp. 44-49.
[34]Mar. 15, 1861.
[35]*DeBow's Review,* XXXI, 2. See articles in *ibid.,* XXXI, 13-17, 69-77.
[36]*Ibid.,* XXXI, 333.

248 ECONOMIC ASPECTS OF SOUTHERN SECTIONALISM, 1840-1861 [248

tion acts, fishing laws, etc. had fostered their interests. "By the instrumentality of these laws, the government of the United States has poured the wealth of the productive South into the lap of the bleak and sterile North, . . ." The slavery question had been used to excite the masses. The Southern people had tried to maintain state rights. In the same message, with a different bearing (the capacity of the South for self-government), he praised slavery as conducive to the perpetuity of republican institutions.[37]

Others put the emphasis on other causes. L. W. Spratt, the indefatigible advocate of reopening the African slave trade, believed that the South had seceded, or should have seceded, for the purpose of perpetuating slave institutions; by the provision of the Confederate Constitution prohibiting the foreign slave trade, the mission of the South had been betrayed.[38] The Reverend Dr. J. H. Thornwell, some time editor of the *Southern Quarterly Review*, sought to put the Southern cause upon the highest possible plane. The Southern states had seceded because of "the profound conviction that the Constitution, in its relations to slavery, has been virtually repealed." He repudiated the suggestion "that all this ferment is nothing but the result of a mercernary spirit on the part of the cotton-growing states, fed by Utopian dreams of aggrandizement and wealth, to be realized under the auspices of free-trade, in a separate confederacy of their own." Considerations of such character had been advanced in the South not to justify secession, but to reconcile her to the necessity of it. Neither had secession been desired to make possible the reopening of the African slave trade; the agitation of that question had only been the natural reaction of irresponsible Southern hot-heads to Garrisonian abolition in the North.[39]

Numerous incidents and miscellaneous comments illustrate how firmly grounded were the opinions relative to the economic effects of disunion, which had been inculcated by years of disunionist propaganda. Mayor McBeth, of Charleston, notified agents of Northern steamship lines that he would not permit the landing of

---

[37]Candler, *Confederate Records of the State of Georgia*, II, 77-125.

[38]Letter to Hon. John Perkins, of Louisiana, in Moore, *Rebellion Record*, II, 357-65.

[39]*The State of the Country: An Article Republished from the Southern Presbyterian Review* (pamphlet, New York, 1861), pp. 6 ff.

steerage passengers unless it was guaranteed that they would not become public charges. He expected that paupers, fearing destitution in the North as a result of the loss of Southern trade, would flock South.[40]   Eli T. Shorter, of Alabama, wrote to a friend in Missouri saying that the people of the South greatly sympathized with the conservatives of the North and would gladly preserve them, if possible, from the general bankruptcy which awaited New York City.[41] It seems to have been expected that Northern shipping and Northern capital would be transferred to the South, and from time to time during the winter of 1860-1861 reports came of such transfers which had been or were about to be made.[42] Evidence will be given later of the disposition shown at an early date to take advantage of secession to promote schemes for direct trade; it was said to be desirable to get "started right." As late as July, 1861, DeBow wrote: "That magic word, Secession, has transferred thousands of millions of wealth from the North to the South. The North is bankrupt. Her people must migrate to the West or starve. . . . They cannot produce their own food and clothing, and will have nothing wherewith to purchase it. . . . Their local wealth, derived from houses, factories, cities, railroads, etc., ceased to exist the instant secession became an accomplished fact."[43]

In the border slave states, where the majority did not believe that the election of Lincoln justified precipitate abandonment of the Union, frequent expression was given by opponents of secession of a belief that fears for slavery did not constitute the chief cause for the action of the cotton states, but were largely a pretext. A notable example is found in Governor Letcher's message to the

[40]New York *Herald*, Nov. 15, 1860. Also *ibid.*, Nov. 20, quoting the New Orleans *Courier and Bee* on effects of secession upon North and South; *ibid.*, Dec. 11, on a threatened exodus to the South.

[41]Quoted in New York *Times*, Jan. 12, 1861.

[42]*Ibid*, Feb. 25, 1861; New York *Herald*, Nov. 19, Dec. 20, 1861; G. B. Lamar to Howell Cobb, Mar. 25, 1861, *Toombs, Stephens, Cobb Correspondence*.

[43]*DeBow's Review*, XXXI, 5. Many others wrote and spoke in a similar strain, for example, Vice-President Stephens, speech at Augusta, July 11, 1861, in Moore, *Rebellion Record*, II, Doc. p. 276 ff.; Secretary of State Toombs, instructions to Yancey, Rost, and Mann, commissioners to Great Britain, France, etc., Mar. 16, 1861, in Richardson, *Messages and Papers of the Confederacy*, II, 7.

General Assembly of Virginia, January 7, 1861. The cotton states in seceding without attempting to secure cooperation of all the slaveholding states were consulting their own interests, he said. Why should not Virginia consider her own? He criticized the tendency of Virginians to ignore the just complaints of their own state against the North and to unite in the complaints of the cotton states. "The complaints of those states are rather against the financial and commercial policy of the Federal Government, than any action or want of action on the subject of slavery."[44]

John A. Gilmer, of North Carolina, said secession had been an object in South Carolina for thirty or forty years. The secessionists had desired Lincoln's election. They did not want guarantees for slavery.[45] Governor Hicks, of Maryland, took a similar view.[46] The *National Intelligencer* put a desire to reopen the slave trade as the foremost cause of secession.[47] John P. Kennedy, of Maryland, a former secretary of the navy, told the history of disunion sentiment in South Carolina. As causes of secession he mentioned a disposition of Southern leaders to undervalue the strength and beneficence of the Union; the belief that the planting states paid all the taxes; visions of a great Southern confederacy including Cuba, San Domingo, Mexico, and perhaps Central America, with free trade, powerful alliances, and peopled by "swarms of reenforcements from the shores of Africa." He did not overlook the fact, however, that the slavery quarrel had become "venomous."[48] John Bell, of Tennessee, said the disunion movement was led by men of distinguished ability with whom the expediency of secession was a foregone conclusion, and who only waited a plausible pretext—"men whose imaginations have been taken possession of, and their judgments led captive, by the dazzling, but, as I think, delusive vision of a new, great, and glorious republican empire, stretching far into the South."[49]   Andrew Johnson and W. G. Brownlow, of Tennessee, attributed secession to the machinations

[44]Virginia, *Senate Journal and Documents*, Extra Session, 1861, pp. 9-49, especially, 13-21.

[45]*Cong. Globe*, 36 Cong., 2 Sess., 580 ff.

[46]*Annual Cyclopedia*, I, 443.

[47]Editorials of Nov. 29, Dec. 29, 1860.

[48]*The Border States, Their Power and Duty in the Present Disordered Condition of the Country.* (Pamphlet, 46 pp.)

[49]Letter to A. Burwell, Dec. 6, 1860, in New York *Herald*, Dec. 12.

of disappointed politicians, and emphasized the long standing hatred of the Union in South Carolina.[50]

"A Kentuckian," in an able pamphlet, *South Carolina, Disunion, and a Mississippi Valley Confederacy*, seemed to be well acquainted with South Carolina history for thirty years, and ascribed to her the leadership in the disunion movement. "Having made up her mind to disunion for the sake of re-opening the African Slave Trade, or for the sake of some other supposed local advantage of her own, or for the sake of vengeance in her gratification of her hate to the Union and the nation, her policy was to precipitate as many of the other Cotton States as she could into disunion also." Among other objects he mentioned the "cherished policy of free trade, direct taxation, and no tariff," and disappointed political aspirations.[51] Union men in Missouri tried to account for the secession movement by other causes than fears for slavery in a Union with the free states. General John B. Henderson, Democrat of the Benton wing, said: "They never left this confederacy . . . on account of any fear whatever as to their rights in negro property. It is a false idea of commercial greatness. They have, since 1832, inculcated a doctrine that a tariff upon imports is a mere burden upon exports; that their cities have languished under the revenue laws of the Government; that their fields have become barren under the oppressions and actions of an unjust government. The merchant of Charleston today, candidly and sincerely believes, in case his government can be established, that South Carolina can be separated from the Federal Union, Charleston in the course of ten years will become a New York. The merchants of Savannah have the same opinion, the merchants of Mobile and the merchants of New Orleans have the same opinion, and unfortunately I must say that this delusion of the day is entertained by some of the merchants of the West." Another cause for secession was the desire to filibuster for Cuba and Central America.

[50]Speech of Andrew Johnson in the Senate, Feb. 5, 1861, in *Cong. Globe*, 36 Cong., 2 Sess., 744 ff.; W. G. Brownlow, *Sketches of the Rise, Progress, and Decline of Secession*; etc., 110 and *passim*.

[51]Pp. 4, 8.

But the *excuse* which had been given for secession was the one which found sympathy among the people of Missouri.[52]

In the North also there was from the first a large class who professed to believe that the cotton states had seceded chiefly for other reasons than fears for slavery and a belief that constitutional rights had been disregarded. This class reposed no confidence in compromises and concessions as Union savers or restorers; no doubt most of them would have been opposed to compromise or concession upon the slavery issue in any case. They advanced various explanations of secession. William H. Seward, in a speech of which the Union savers had expected much, credited disunion chiefly to the defeat of Southern politicians and their loss of power to govern the country. But he did not overlook the influence of the unconditional disunionists: "More than thirty years there has existed a considerable—though not heretofore a formidable—mass of citizens in certain States situate near or around the delta of the Mississippi, who believe that the Union is less conducive to the welfare and greatness of those States than a smaller confederacy, embracing only slave States, would be."[53] Senators Wade, of Ohio, Wilson, of Massachusetts, Cameron, of Pennsylvania, Chandler, of Michigan, and Trumbull, of Illinois, inclined to take the view that secession was the outcome of a "rule or ruin" policy on the part of Southern leaders.[54] Senator Simmons, of Rhode Island, engaged in a colloquy with Thomas L. Clingman relative to the effect of secession upon revenues North and South and upon the imports of the respective sections. "I know," he said, "part of this scheme has been to make Charleston the great commercial emporium of the South."[55] A select committee of the House of Representatives reported that "the difficulties growing out of the existence of slavery, however viewed by the common people, are so far as the leaders are concerned, but a mere pretense, their real object being to overthrow the Government,

---

[52]*Journal and Proceedings of the Missouri State Convention . . . 1861*, Proceedings, p. 86. See also majority report of the Committee on the Commissioner from Georgia, *ibid.*, Journal, p. 50 ff.

[53]*Cong. Globe*, 36 Cong., 2 Sess., 343, speech in the Senate, Jan. 12, 1861.

[54]*Ibid.*, 102, 1088 ff., 494, 1370, 1380 (in order).

[55]*Ibid.*, 1476.

that a Southern Confederacy, of a military character may arise. . . ."[56]

The New York *Times* consistently sought other motives for secession. An editorial of January 4, 1861, gave the desire to reopen the African slave trade a prominent place among the motives for secession. A week later "the expectations of great advantages" which seaboard cities were to derive from a free trade policy were canvassed.[57] Another editorial of the same issue considered the long taught belief in the South that, "they supported the Union— that they contributed far more than the Northern States to the support of the Government—that the industry of the North was entirely dependent upon their staples—and that if these should be withdrawn universal bankruptcy, beggary, and ruin would instantly overtake the people of the North." Another editorial reviewed a disunion *per se* article by Major W. H. Chase, of Florida, in *DeBow's Review;*[58] another was headed, "Proportion of the Burdens of Government Borne by the South;"[59] another dealt with schemes to form "a grand *Slave* Empire to embrace the islands of the Gulf of Mexico and the territories facing it."[60] A number of articles of this character from the *Times* were published as a pamphlet under the caption, *The Effect of Secession upon the Commercial Relations between the North and the South*, apparently intended to influence opinion in the border states. It asserted that "the leading motive or inducement to Secession has undoubtedly been the anticipated material advantages that were to result."[61]

Another able pamphlet, *The Five Cotton States and New York*, etc., took up and refuted in order the Southern views that (1) "the commercial policy of the United States is injurious to Southern interests;" (2) "the present course of business in the United States is extremely unfavorable, if not unjust, to the South, espec-

---

[56]*Cong. Globe*, 36 Cong., 2 Sess., 1294.
[57]Jan. 12.
[58]Jan. 15, "The Ideas on which Secession is Based."
[59]Jan. 17.
[60]Feb. 5.
[61]P. 3. Daniel Lord was the author.

ially, the five cotton states . . .;" (3) cotton is king.[62] Another pamphleteer, Samuel Powell, in *Notes on "Southern Wealth and Northern Profits," Kettell,* thought Kettell's thesis, namely, that the South had supplied the capital which had accumulated at the North, was the keynote of secession. He refuted Kettell's statements *seriatim.* Even the New York *Herald,* for which no concessions or guarantees to slavery were too great, occasionally ascribed to secessionists other motives (similar to those already mentioned) than a desire to force concessions from the North, or to protect the institution of slavery.[63]

It is believed that such expressions as those quoted above were representative of the professed opinions of a considerable class in the Northern and border states, and that these opinions had some basis in fact. The majority of the people of the North and of the Unionists in the border states, however, seem, clearly, to have been of the opinion that the cotton states had seceded chiefly because of a justifiable or mistaken belief that slavery was endangered, and that constitutional rights had been violated in the Union. In the opinion of many, perhaps most of this class, at least before the organization of the Provisional Confederate government, the Southern states, with the exception of South Carolina, could be saved to the Union by concessions and guarantees relative to slavery. After the organization of the Confederacy the primary object of the compromisers was to save the border states.

[62]Stephen Colwell, *The Five Cotton States and New York, or Remarks upon the Social and Economic Aspects of the Southern Political Crisis,* Jan. 1861, 64 pp. See also J. F. Clarke, *Session, Concession, or Self-Possession. Which?* (Pamphlet, Boston, 1861, 48 pp.) pp. 7-11.

[63]For example, Nov. 19, 1860, Financial and Commercial; Dec. 8, Feb. 19, 1861, editorials.

CHAPTER X

EARLY ECONOMIC POLICIES OF THE CONFEDERATE STATES, 1861-1862

As soon as secession was assured in the cotton states, indications were given of an intention to take advantage of political separation from the North to promote industrial and commercial independence. In studying these indications, however, it must be remembered that from the very first individual seceded states and the Confederate government were not free to formulate economic policies with reference solely to their economic effects. In the brief period before Sumter the policies were determined largely by the necessity of winning over the border slave states, the desire to avoid war with the North, which leaders feared, if they did not expect, and the need for gaining friends in Europe. After Sumter everything else had to be subordinated to the conduct of the war.

An ordinance was adopted by the Georgia Convention, January 29, 1861, declaring it to be "the fixed policy of Georgia to protect all investments already made, or which may be hereafter made by citizens of other states, in mines or manufacturing in this state, and capital invested in any other permanent improvement."[1] A resolution was introduced in the Louisiana Convention to instruct the committee on commerce to report on the expediency of exempting from taxation all capital and property employed in manufacturing within the state for a term of five years.[2] In the Texas Convention a resolution was introduced recommending that the Legislature give adequate protection to the manufacturing interests and enterprises of the state.[3] From South Carolina and elsewhere, before Sumter, came reports of efforts of the people to make themselves independent of the North industrially as well as politically. Arguments in favor of home industry appeared. Southern manufacturers and merchants appealed for patronage on the ground that the South must be independent in all respects.[4] Secession gave an impetus to projects for establishing direct

[1] *Journal . . . of the Convention . . . of Georgia, 1861*, p. 117.
[2] *Official Journal . . . of the Convention . . . of Louisiana*, 34.
[3] *Journal of the Secession Convention of Texas, 1861*, p. 41.
[4] *DeBow's Review*, XXX, 371; New York *Herald*, Mar. 26, 1861, quoting a number of such appeals; editorial commenting thereon, *ibid.*, Mar. 27.

trade with Europe. Governor Gist, of South Carolina, asked the
Legislature to guarantee the interest of 5 per cent per annum upon
the capital invested in a line of steamers to Liverpool, which private parties proposed to establish.[5] In February, following, a
public meeting was held in Charleston to consider a well advanced
project for establishing a line of three screw propellers between
Charleston and England. A committee was appointed to solicit
subscriptions.[6] The Legislature of Alabama chartered a "Direct
Trade and Exchange Company."[7] The Committee on Commerce,
Revenue, and Navigation of the Louisiana Convention was instructed to report upon the propriety of state aid for direct communication by steam between New Orleans and Europe.[8]

Governor Brown, of Georgia, discussed the subject of direct
trade in his message to the Legislature, December 8, 1860. He
asked authority to send a commissioner to Europe to investigate
a company which had offered to establish a line of five steamers
to made weekly trips between Savannah and a European port if
the state of Georgia would guarantee a 5 per cent return upon the
investment.[9] The Legislature chartered the "Belgian American
Company."[10] Thomas Butler King was sent to Europe to promote
direct trade and to represent the state of Georgia in England,
France, and Belgium. He was instructed "to not fail to present a
clear view of the effect which our Federal connection with the
Northern States has had in attracting, or forcing our commercial
exchanges with Europe, coast-wise through the port and City of
New York . . ." He was to show further that the result of secession "must necessarily be to establish direct commercial and diplomatic intercourse with all the world." Northern manufacturers
also, who had been protected by a tariff, must now compete on
equal terms with European manufacturers.[11] When the Legislature met again in November, 1861, it had at least three direct
trade projects to consider. Two had resulted from King's mission;
the third was that of an association of Georgians who would

[5]New York *Herald*, Dec. 1, 1860.
[6]*Hunt's Merchants' Magazine*, XLIV, 524-5; New York *Herald*, Mar. 4, 22.
[7]*DeBow's Review*, XXX, 381.
[8]*Official Journal . . . of the Convention . . . of Louisiana*, 36.
[9]Candler, *Confederate Records of the State of Georgia*, II, 6, 7.
[10]*Ibid.*, II, 116; Avery, *History of Georgia*, 131.
[11]Candler, *op. cit.* II, 20 ff.

establish a line of steamers as soon as the blockade should be raised if the Legislature would subsidize their enterprise.[12] In urging the matter of direct trade, Governor Brown said: "But our deliverance from political bondage will be of little advantage if we remain in a state of commercial dependence."[13]

In March, 1861, a committee of the Provisional Congress of the Confederacy was formed to organize an excursion trip from Savannah to Antwerp via Havre for the purpose of affording Southern merchants an opportunity to make arrangements for direct importations.[14] Up to the time of his departure for England as a commissioner of the Confederate States, Colonel A. Dudley Mann pursued his plans for establishing direct trade.[15] A convention of merchants, bankers, and others met in Macon, in October, 1861, to devise a plan to establish credits between the Confederacy and Europe. *DeBow's Review* commended the purpose of the convention, saying, "It is necessary to start right on the removal of the blockade, in order that our former vassalage to the North may not be renewed."[16]

Immediately South Carolina had seceded from the Union, her Convention and Legislature were confronted by the problem of framing tariff and navigation laws. Each of the other states which seceded before the organization of the Confederacy had to solve the same problem. When the Provisional government was formed the task devolved upon it. The development of the tariff and navigation policies of the Confederacy was watched with considerable interest at home, in the border states, in the North, and in Europe, and throws some light upon the motives of Southern leaders.

When South Carolina seceded, hot heads in the Convention wished to throw the ports open to the commerce of the world at once. The Convention rejected the proposal by a large majority, and provided instead that the revenue and navigation laws of the United States should be continued in effect, but no duties should

[12]Candler, *op. cit.*, II, 115-17, 322-24, messages of Gov. Brown, Nov. 6, 1861, and Nov. 18, 1862; *ibid.*, II, 324, report of a special committee of the Georgia House of Representatives.

[13]*Ibid.*, II, 115.

[14]New York *Herald*, Mar. 19, 1861.

[15]*Ibid.*, Mar. 19, 23, 1861.

[16]*DeBow's Review*, XXXI, 325. Also *ibid.*, XXXI, 333-47.

be collected upon imports from states of the late Federal Union, and no tonnage duties should be collected upon vessels from the said states. Vessels owned to one-third part by citizens of South Carolina or of other slaveholding states might be registered as South Carolina vessels.[17] The action upon the tariff was determined by a number of considerations. Revenue was needed. The members of the Convention were divided upon the relative merits of direct taxation and a tariff for revenue only. The majority was not ready to risk a clash with the Federal government by attempting to collect duties upon goods from other states or by admitting foreign goods free of duty. The Georgia Convention adopted an ordinance similar to that of South Carolina by a small majority, the minority wishing to allow the duties to be paid into the Federal treasury.[18] In other seceding states similar action was taken.[19]

The states in the Mississippi valley were much concerned about the navigation of the Mississippi river. They wished to continue their trade with the West, and they did not wish to antagonize states of the upper valley. Senator Slidell, of Louisiana, while yet in the United States Senate, promised free navigation of the Mississippi.[20] An ordinance recognizing the right of the free navigation of the Mississippi by all friendly nations bordering upon it was reported to the Louisiana Convention along with the ordinance of secession, and was adopted unanimously.[21] The Mississippi Convention adopted a resolution similar to the Louisiana ordinance, also by a unanimous vote.[22] The Alabama Convention

[17]Proceedings in *Journal of the Convention of South Carolina*, 45-47, 67, 83-88, 93-105; debate in New York *Herald*, Dec. 21, 25, 1860; *National Intelligencer*, Dec. 25.

[18]*Journal of the Convention of Georgia, 1861*, pp. 57, 83, 92, 123. The vote was 130-119.

[19]*Ordinances and Constitution of the State of Alabama . . . 1861*, p. 18, ordinance of Jan. 23, 1861; *Journal of the Proceedings of the Convention of the People of Florida . . . 1861*, p. 99; ordinance of Jan. 15, *Official Journal . . . of the Convention . . . of Louisiana*, 105, 106, 235, ordinances of Jan. 29. Mississippi, having no seaports, took no action. The Texas Convention took no action because it was expected that the Southern Convention at Montgomery would take the matter in hand in a few days.

[20]*Cong. Globe*, 36 Cong., 2 Sess., 137, 720.

[21]*Official Journal of the Convention of Louisiana*, 10, 18, 235.

[22]*Journal of the State Convention* [of Mississippi], 24, 68.

also declared that the navigation of the Mississippi should not be restricted.[23]

It was not an easy matter for the Provisional government of the Confederacy to fix upon a tariff and navigation policy. The commercial interests of the seceded states desired and expected free trade or an approximation thereto. Free trade, it was thought, would mean direct trade.[24] It would tend, too, to conciliate the North and make peaceful separation more possible. As early as December 5, 1860, Senator Iverson told the United States Senate that, if the Northern states would let the South go in peace, the new confederacy would treat them as a favored nation in the making of commercial treaties.[25] Free trade would make easier the settlement of the navigation of the Mississippi. It might also win sympathy for the Southern cause in England and France.[26] On the other hand the new government must be supported; the people were accustomed to indirect taxes, and the leaders hesitated to test their patriotism at the very start by a resort to direct taxation.[27] There were those who wanted a judicious tariff, because it would encourage manufactures. There were localities with interests to protect; Louisiana sugar interests demanded a tariff. Others wished to take advantage of the opportunity afforded to render the South independent of the North. When, in the Alabama Convention, W. R. Smith proposed that the South should continue free trade with states of the old Union, Yancey said that would reconstruct the "most material elements of the late Union into a Commercial Union."[28] The attitude of the border states was very important. One of the influences understood to be deterring Virginia, North Carolina, Tennessee, and other border states from secession was the fear that manufactur-

[23]Smith, *History and Debates of the Convention of the People of Alabama, 1861*, p. 184 f.; *Ordinances and Constitution of the State of Alabama*, 33, resolution of Jan. 25.

[24]William Porcher Miles to Howell Cobb, Jan. 14, 1861, G. B. Lamar to Cobb, Mar. 25, *Toombs, Stephens, Cobb Correspondence; National Intelligencer*, Dec. 20, quoting the Charleston *Mercury*.

[25]*Cong. Globe*, 36 Cong., 2 Sess., 12.

[26]G. B. Lamar to Howell Cobb, Feb. 9, 22, Mar. 9, 25, 1861, *Toombs, Stephens, Cobb Correspondence; DeBow's Review*, XXX, 93 ff.

[27]Junius Hillyer to Howell Cobb, Jan. 30, Feb. 9, 1861, *Toombs, Stephens, Cobb Correspondence.*

[28]Smith, *History and Debates of the Convention of Alabama, 1861*, p. 188.

ing, mining, and other interests there would be sacrificed to the free trade principles of the cotton states, and the people subjected to direct taxation.[29]

In various quarters duties upon exports were suggested. In his message of November 7, 1860, Governor Brown, of Georgia, suggested that the power to levy an export duty upon cotton would be a powerful support to the diplomacy of a Southern confederacy.[30] It would permit the Confederacy to raise ample revenue, and at the same time make her import duties so much lower than those of the North that either direct trade would be established, or the North would have to adopt free trade.[31] The possibilities of export duties as a protection to home industries were not overlooked. The chief consideration, however, in favor of export duties was the need of revenue. A small tax on cotton, for example, could be easily collected and would net a considerable sum.[32] In the border states the suggestion of export duties was welcomed because it relieved apprehension of direct taxation.[33]

The committee of the Montgomery Convention on a provisional constitution for the Confederate States reported a clause which forbade protective tariffs and prohibited duties in excess of 15 per cent, with the proviso that such import and export duties might be imposed "as may be expedient to induce friendly political relations" with nations pursuing unfriendly policies. The clause was rejected.[34] The Provisional Constitution as adopted contained a clause almost identical with the corresponding clause of the United States Constitution.[35] Export duties, however, were not prohibited. On February 9, 1861, the Provisional Congress passed

[29]Junius Hillyer to Howell Cobb, Jan. 30, Feb. 9, 1861, *Toombs, Stephens Cobb Correspondence; DeBow's Review*, XXX, 165; *National Intelligencer*, Nov. 27, 1860.

[30]Candler, *Confederate Records of the State of Georgia*, I, 52. Also Howell Cobb in the Provisional Congress, *Annual Cyclopedia*, I, 157; *DeBow's Review*, XXX, 564. See also *Correspondence of T. R. R. Cobb* (So. Hist. Assoc., *Publ.*, XI), letter to his wife, Feb. 21, 1861.

[31]*DeBow's Review*, XXX, 551-67.

[32]*Ibid.*, XXX, 565; Charleston *Courier*, Mar. 25, 1861.

[33]Richmond Correspondence, New York *Herald*, Feb. 3, 1861.

[34]*Senate Documents*, 58 Cong., 2 Sess., No. 234, Vol. I, *Journal of the Provisional Congress of the Confederate States of America*, p. 35.

[35]*Constitution for the Provisional Government of the Confederate States of America*, Art. I, 6, 1.

a bill continuing United States laws in force November 1, 1860, which were not inconsistent with the Provisional Constitution;[36] thus the United States tariff and navigation laws were adopted. February 18, Congress modified the tariff law to admit free of duty breadstuffs, provisions, agricultural products, living animals, and munitions.[37] By an act of February 28, an export tax of one-eighth cent a pound was levied on cotton.[38] On February 22, Congress unanimously passed a law establishing the free navigation of the Mississippi.[39] By an act of February 26, the United States navigation laws were virtually repealed, and the coastwise commerce of the Confederate states thrown open to the ships of all nations.[40] Another act, of March 15, authorized the transit of foreign merchandise through the Confederate States to points beyond their borders free of duties.[41] Regulations were at once made to put this act into effect.[42] Thus the Confederate government slowly took steps in the general direction of free trade.

Meanwhile, the Provisional government was engaged in drafting a permanent constitution for the Confederacy. On March 4 the clause relating to taxes was taken up. As reported from committee, it was almost identical with the corresponding clause of the United States Constitution. R. B. Rhett moved to add the proviso: "but no bounties shall be granted from the treasury; nor shall any duties or taxes on importations from foreign nations be laid to promote or foster any branch of industry." This amendment was adopted. Georgia, which had a small manufacturing interest, and Louisiana, which had the sugar industry to protect, voting in the negative.[43] The following day a clause was adopted which gave congress the power by a two-thirds majority to lay duties on exports.[44] Upon motion of Rhett, congress was denied

[36] *Statutes at Large of the Provisional Government of the Confederate States of America*, p. 27.

[37] *Ibid.*, 28.

[38] *Ibid.*, 42, Sect. 5.

[39] Approved, Feb. 25, *ibid.*, 36; *Annual Cyclopedia*, I, 157.

[40] *Statutes at Large of the Provisional Government of the Confederate States of America*, 38.

[41] *Ibid.*, 70.

[42] New York *Herald*, Mar. 19, 21; President Davis's Message of April 29, 1861, *Annual Cyclopedia*, I, 131, 618.

[43] *Journal of the Provisional Congress*, 853, 864, 865.

[44] *Ibid.*, 869. Art. I, 9, 6.

power to appropriate money in aid of internal improvements intended to facilitate commerce. The Texas delegation voted against this provision, and the Louisiana delegation was divided.[45] Texas was especially interested in the Pacific railroad, and Louisiana in the improvement of the navigation of the Mississippi. The Permanent Constitution was hailed generally in the South as the end of protectionism and special privilege of all kinds. Vice-President Stephens so described it.[46] The Charleston *Mercury* termed it, "the first acknowledgment in the fundamental law of any people, of the principle of just and equal taxation." It must be rightfully administered, however.[47] *DeBow's Review*, said, "The *protective system* receives its quietus thus: ..."[48] South Carolina free traders, however, feared the new Constitution left a loophole for protection, because it placed no maximum limit upon the duties congress might impose. This was one of the grounds upon which a number in the South Carolina Convention opposed ratification of the Constitution;[49] the Convention, however, ratified the Constitution by a large majority. The provision giving congress the power to lay duties on exports likewise did not give universal satisfaction.[50] In the North, too, a few were inclined to charge that the South had abandoned free trade principles. The South had claimed separate nationality, said one, "and it has proclaimed, not free trade, but a system of virtual, though covert, protection : . . What shall we say of their Chinese duty upon exports?"[51]

The early action of the Provisional Congress in continuing in force the United States tariff law, that is, the Tariff of 1857, was not generally satisfactory. The Augusta *Chronicle*, for example, thought Congress had done well in ignoring the fallacy of free trade (Augusta was a manufacturing town);[52] and the action seemed to have a good effect in the border states.[53] But many

[45] *Journal of the Provisional Congress*, 892. The provision made certain exceptions, Art. I, 9, 6.

[46] "Corner stone" speech. Moore, *Rebellion Record*, I, Doc. pp. 44-45.

[47] Mar. 5, 1861, quoted in New York *Herald*, Mar. 19.

[48] XXX, 484.

[49] *Journal of the Convention of South Carolina*, 207, 214, 253-60.

[50] *Ibid.*, 253; *DeBow's Review*, XXXI, 206, 305-13; G. B. Lamar to Howell Cobb, Feb. 9, 1861, *Toombs, Stephens, Cobb Correspondence*.

[51] Powell, *Notes on "Southern Wealth and Northern Profits,"* 29.

[52] Quoted in New York *Times*, Feb. 16.

[53] Report of H. P. Bell, Georgia commissioner to Tennessee, *Journal of the Convention of Georgia*, 369.

feared that it was not calculated to promote direct trade or win friends in Great Britain and France or conciliate the North and West. March 2 Mr. Harris, of Mississippi, moved to instruct the Committee on Finance of the Provisional Congress to enter upon a revision of the tariff with a view to a reduction of the duties and an enlargement of the free list. In explanation he said that when the tariff had been adopted, upon his motion an early revision had been promised "with a view to the future adoption of that policy which was to invite the great Northwest to other and cheaper markets than those to be found in Boston and New York, and also enable the merchants of the Confederate States to obtain their goods at lower rates than those purchased by the merchants of the United States, and consequently be enabled to undersell the latter. This policy would throw the evils of illicit traffic upon the shoulders of the Northern States, and put the crown of commercial supremacy upon the Confederate States—in other words, achieve one of the great positive advantages arising from our separation from the unfriendly States of North America—to wit: commercial independence."[54] William Porcher Miles, of Charleston, favored the resolution. He had always supposed the South was desirous of approaching as near free trade as possible. Judge Withers, of South Carolina, wanted to hold out free trade to Europe as an inducement to recognition of the South. A resolution was introduced in the Louisiana Convention, March 26, declaring for entire free trade with the Western states, both slave and free.[55] On May 17 a new tariff bill was passed in Congress over considerable opposition, chiefly from those who desired a measure calculated to produce more revenue.[56] The duties averaged about 5 per cent lower than those of the Tariff of 1857. Most manufactured goods bore duties of 15 per cent; most important raw materials bore duties of 10 per cent; the free list included provisions, breadstuffs, living animals, munitions and munitions materials, and ships. The bill was to go into effect August 31.[57] Plainly the measure repre-

[54]*Journal of the Provisional Congress,* 97; New York *Herald,* Mar. 9, debate on Harris's motion.
[55]*Annual Cyclopedia,* I, 431; New York *Herald,* Mar. 27.
[56]*Journal of the Provisional Congress,* 242, act·approved May 21.
[57]*Statutes at Large of the Provisional Government,* 127-35. The act was amended in minor particulars by act of Aug. 3. *Ibid.,* 171.

sented a compromise between the various views of a proper tariff policy.

Meanwhile the Congress of the United States had taken action highly satisfactory to the Confederacy when it enacted the Morrill tariff, approved March 2, 1861. The bill fixed moderately high duties to become effective April 1. The opposition press of the North represented the Morrill act as a stupendous piece of folly which would result in direct trade for the South, make it difficult to retain the border states in the Union, and alienate the sympathies of Great Britain and France.[58] The New York *Times*, a Republican paper, opposed it. The London *Times* represented it as a blunder on the part of the North.[59] In the South it was hoped the difference in the two tariffs would promote direct trade. Southern journals and representatives seized the opportunity afforded by the Morrill bill to play up, for the benefit of foreign opinion, the tariff as a cause of secession, and to present to foreign nations the view that it was to their interests to recognize the independence of a people which would continue to maintain as nearly free trade as its necessities would allow.[60] President Davis and Vice-President Stephens both announced that as near free trade as possible would be the policy of the government.[61] Secretary of State Toombs instructed Yancey, Rost, and Mann, commissioners to Europe, to point out the differing views of the North and South upon commercial policy, avoid discussion of slavery, and to assure European governments that the policy of the Confederacy would be an approximation of free trade.[62] Later in the year, Secretary Hunter in his instructions to J. M. Mason stated very forcibly the interest the British people had in the establishment of a free trade republic in America. He neglected, however, to emphasize differences over

[58]New York *Herald*, Feb. 1, 8, 18, 27, 28, Mar. 4, 15, 19, 23, 29; Carpenter, *Logic of History*, 146 f., quoting a number of Northern papers. There was little debate upon the tariff in Congress.

[59]Quoted in Carpenter, *op. cit.*, 147; to same effect in New York *Herald*, Mar. 23, 29, Apr. 6.

[60]*DeBow's Review*, XXXI, 69-77; Savannah *Republican*, May 22, in Moore, *Rebellion Record*, I, Diary p. 5.

[61]*Annual Cyclopedia*, I, 613; Moore, *Rebellion Record*, I, Doc. p. 48.

[62]Mar. 16, 1861. Richardson, *Messages and Papers of the Confederacy*, II, 3 ff.

commercial policy as a cause of separation; the Southern states had seceded when the government of the Union had threatened to "destroy their social system."[63] Yancey, Rost, and Mann presented with force and effect the advantages to European nations of an independent Southern confederacy dedicated to free trade.[64]

From the first there was a group in the Confederacy which wanted to make a bold bid for the support of Great Britain and France by granting them valuable commercial advantages for a long period of years, and this group was strengthened by the outbreak of the war. President Davis, however, believed the proper Southern policy to be to conciliate the North, if possible. In his inaugural address he said: "An agricultural people, . . . our true policy is peace, and the freest trade which our necessities will permit . . . There can be but little rivalry between ours and any manufacturing or navigating community, such as the northeastern States of the American Union."[65] Even after the war began President Davis promised the North treaties of amity and commerce if it would abandon coercion.[66] He relied upon their dependence upon the South for cotton to secure the good will, even aid, of European countries. Though, as we have seen, the commissioners to Great Britain and France had been instructed to represent that approximate free trade would be the policy of the Confederate government, they were not authorized to attempt any high diplomacy.[67]

On May 13, 1861, R. B. Rhett, chairman of the Committee on Foreign Relations, offered resolutions in Congress advising the negotiation of treaties guaranteeing a low maximum of duties for a long period of years. Mr. Cobb moved to amend by stipulating that such treaties should not extend beyond five years. The amendment was adopted; whereupon, on Mr. Rhett's motion the

[63]Sept. 23. Richardson, op. cit., II, 84 ff.
[64]Letters to Secretary Toombs, in ibid., II, 34, 42, 60. See also letter to the London Times, by John Lothrop Motley, in Moore, Rebellion Record, I, Doc. pp. 209-218; Callahan, Diplomatic History of the Southern Confederacy, 81, 109 ff.
[65]Annual Cyclopedia, I, 613.
[66]Ibid., I, 619, 139.
[67]Yancey, Rost, and Mann to Secretary of State, Toombs, Aug. 7, 1861, asking for new instructions, Richardson, op. cit., II, 56-59; DuBose, Yancey, 596.

whole matter was laid upon the table.[68] Congress acted upon the belief that the war would be short; there were perhaps still hopes that the North would abandon the war if assured that the Confederacy would not adopt a hostile commercial policy. The necessities of the South were not yet felt to be great; the Confederacy should hold herself free to adopt any commercial policy she might see fit. Twenty years of free trade with England would destroy the manufactures of the South. Secretary of State Toombs seems to have agreed with Mr. Rhett; but President Davis was in accord with the majority.[69] The representatives in Europe were given no new instructions. As the year wore on and the blockade of Southern ports tightened, the Administration showed a disposition to rely upon a shortage of cotton for the factories of England to bring about the intervention of that country. The exportation of cotton was forbidden except through Southern ports,[70] and Yancey, Rost, and Mann wrote Earl Russell that, "To be obtained it must be sought for in the Atlantic and Gulf ports of those States."[71]

From time to time through 1861 and the early part of 1862, efforts were made in Congress to admit all goods free of duty for a limited period except from the United States.[72] A bill to that effect passed the House April 3, 1862, by a large majority but was not acted upon in the Senate.[73] A convention of merchants and planters at Macon in October, 1861, had unanimously recommended the suspension of all duties and the adoption of free trade with all nations at peace with the Confederacy;[74] and sentiment favorable to the course was manifested elsewhere.[75] But in general public opinion supported the policy of the government. Confidence was still felt in the "cotton is king" argument.[76] Those who wished

[68]*Journal of the Provisional Congress*, 214, 253; Charleston *Mercury*, June 20, quoted in Moore, *Rebellion Record*, II, Diary p. 13; DuBose, *Yancey*, 598-602.

[69]*Ibid.*, 600-602.

[70]Act of May 21, *Statutes at Large of the Provisional Government*, 152.

[71]Richardson, *op. cit.*, II, 70.

[72]*Journal of the Provisional Congress*, 277, 290, 489, 547, 743, 820.

[73]Schwab, *Confederate States of America*, 246.

[74]*Ibid.*, 245.

[75]Gov. Brown, of Ga. Candler, *Confederate Records of Ga.*, II, 115; *DeBow's Review*, XXXI, 536 ff.

[76]*Ibid.*, XXXI, 400-404; 412 ff.

to make the South industrially independent of the North were disposed, 1861, to look upon the war and the blockade as a blessing in disguise. *DeBow's Review* reflected this disposition. In July, when the people were confident of an early peace, DeBow wrote: "Secession, disunion, will avail us nothing if we continue to have intercourse with the North and to trade with her .... there is danger, grave danger, that in making peace with the North we shall restore the old Union in all save the name."[77] In September, DeBow wrote: "The blockade will make us very independent at the South, and thank God for it. Every branch of manufactures is springing up. Our people need but this spur."[78] President Davis gave countenance to such an idea in his message of November 18, 1861: "If they [people] should be forced to forego many of the luxuries and some of the comforts of life, they will at least have the consolation of knowing that they are daily becoming more and more independent of the rest of the world."[79] As the war progressed the sentiment in favor of restrictions on imports and exports grew.[80] This was due chiefly, no doubt, to a desire to coerce foreign governments to recognize the Confederacy and raise the blockade; but in part it was the manifestation of a genuine protectionist sentiment.

The early tariff and navigation policies of the Confederacy, then, were determined mainly by the exigencies of the political situation; but there are sufficient indications that, could they have been worked out in peace and independence, they would have been adopted with expectations of great economic benefits to result therefrom. As to what the proper policies were, similar divisions would have occurred as among the secessionists *per se* before secession. The free traders would have won, at least temporarily; but the sentiment for protective measures would have been much stronger than the previous attitude of the Southern people on the tariff and navigation policies of the United States alone would have led one to expect.

When the cotton states seceded there was considerable discussion there as to what states would ultimately join the Confederacy,

---

[77]XXXI, 12. See also XXXI, 396.
[78]*DeBow's Review*, XXXI, 329, 518.
[79]*Annual Cyclopedia*, I, 624
[80]This subject is discussed in Schwab, *Confederate States*, 246-50.

and as to what states it was desirable should join. There was by no means a general desire that all the slaveholding states be included in the new confederation or that only slaveholding states be admitted to it. Consideration of other things than the best method of preserving slave institutions affected judgments upon the proper limits of the Confederacy.

There were many in the cotton states who preferred that the border states remain with the old Union; and the number would have been greater had there been assurance of peaceful secession.[81] Extreme advocates of reopening the slave trade, such as L. W. Spratt, preferred giving up the border states to abandoning their favorite project.[82] Extreme free traders and some of those who believed the best chance of winning independence to lie in enlisting the aid of Great Britain and France by commercial alliances, feared the protectionist propensities of the people of the border states.[83] Others believed that if the border states remained in the Union their influence would preserve the peace between the Confederacy and the Union.[84] The party in favor of leaving out the border states was quite strong in South Carolina. The great majority in the cotton states, however, considered it highly important to win the border states. In addition to a feeling of kinship and homogeneity of interests, there was a conviction on their part that the best chance for peaceful secession lay in forming a confederacy so strong that attack by the North would be hopeless of success.[85]

While many would have been glad to restrict the Confederacy to the cotton states alone, a considerably larger number would have welcomed accessions from the free states of the upper Mis-

---

[81]Jones, *Rebel War Clerk's Diary*, I, 41; New York *Herald*, Nov. 20, 1860, Washington Correspondence; Mar. 10, quoting Charleston *Mercury*, Mar. 6; *ibid.*, Mar. 26.

[82]L. W. Spratt's letter to Hon. John Perkins, Moore, *Rebellion Record*, II, Doc. pp. 357-65.

[83]G. B. Lamar to Howell Cobb, Mar. 25, 1861, *Toombs, Stephens, Cobb Correspondence.*

[84]The reference is to permanent policies. A greater number considered it good policy for the border states to remain in the Union and hold out a hope of reconstruction for the purpose of warding off conflict with the Federal government until the Confederate government should be firmly established.

[85]Address of Fulton Anderson, Mississippi commissioner, before the Virginia Convention, in *Journal of the State Convention* [of Mississippi], 219.

sissippi valley. The desire to strengthen the Confederacy against its enemies lent support to the hope of Western accessions, as did the wish to continue commercial relations with the Northwest without the obstacles of customs lines. The commerce between the West and South, it may be remarked again, was not considered indicative of "colonial vassalage" as was that between the East and South. There was yet surviving also an aspiration on the part of Southern seaports to supplant Eastern cities in exporting and importing for the upper Mississippi valley. The hope that Western states would sooner or later find it to their advantage to join the Confederacy was based chiefly upon an exaggerated idea of the dependence of those states upon the Mississippi river as an outlet for their commerce and of the value to the Western people of their Southern trade. The Southerners did not feel the degree of hostility toward the people of the West that they felt for the Yankees; and they believed the people of the West less strongly opposed to slavery than the people of the East. The opposition to seeking or accepting, should they be offered, accessions from the West was based upon the conviction that it had been and should be the object to establish a slaveholding confederacy; there should be no continuance of the discord between slave states and free states. In the Georgia, Mississippi, and Texas conventions ordinances were introduced which looked to the formation of a confederacy of slaveholding states only; but they were not adopted.[86] The Permanent Constitution of the Confederate States gave congress the power to admit new states by a two-thirds vote; it did not prohibit the admission of free states.[87] Serious objections to this clause were raised in the South Carolina Convention. President Davis, in his inaugural address, called attention to the clause; but he thought it to be the will of the people not to admit states which did not have interests homogeneous with theirs. Vice-President Stephens expressed a similar idea in his "Corner Stone" speech.[88]

[86] *Journal of the Convention of Georgia*, 68; *Journal of the Secession Convention of Texas, 1861*, p. 53; *Journal of the State Convention* [of Mississippi], 33.

[87] Stephens, Toombs, and Davis all favored leaving the door open. See Hull, "The Making of the Confederate Constitution," So. Hist. Assoc., *Publications*, IX, 284-85, letter of T. R. R. Cobb to his wife, Mar. 6, 1861; 290, Cobb's notes.

[88] The Constitution contained a "three-fifths clause" also. When the matter was being considered by the Provisional Congress, the three-fifths clause was

Without doubt the opinion was quite extensively held in the border states and in the North at the time of the secession of the cotton states that a chief object of secession was to reopen the African slave trade. The opinion was perhaps justified by knowledge of the agitation for renewal during the years 1856-1859. There are strong reasons, however, for believing that the importance of a desire to reopen the slave trade as a motive of secession was considerably exaggerated, perhaps purposely so.

The discussion of reopening the slave trade of a few years previous had made very clear that the people of the cotton states were badly divided upon the question. Disunionists had tried, and in a measure had succeeded, to silence the agitation because they found that it weakened the disunion movement. The discussion of those years had made it very clear, too, that the border states were very strongly opposed to reopening the slave trade. Disunionists understood also that the sentiment of European nations was against it. Cogent arguments had been presented before the election of 1860 to show the futility of expecting a Southern confederacy to reopen it. The prospect of reopening the trade was not held out to the electors as an inducement to go for secession during the brief campaign which preceded the election of delegates to the secession conventions. On the contrary, leaders early gave the assurance that it was not intended.[89]

The conventions of the three most populous cotton states adopted resolutions against reopening by great majorities and without hesitation. The Alabama Convention adopted, with only three dissenting votes, a resolution declaring the people of Alabama opposed to the reopening of the African slave trade on grounds of "public policy." The debate made it very clear that one of the chief grounds of "public policy" was a desire to win the border states.[90] The Mississippi Convention by a vote of 66 to 13 adopted a resolution declaring it not to be the purpose or policy of the

dropped upon the motion of Keith, of South Carolina. South Carolina, Florida, Mississippi, and Louisiana voted for the motion; Georgia, Alabama, and Texas against. Upon motion of A. H. Stephens the vote was reconsidered, and Mississippi reversed her vote. The states supporting the three-fifths provision, it may be said, were those having the largest white population in proportion to black. See *Journal of the Provisional Congress*, 861, 862, 889.

[89] *Southern Literary Messenger*, XXXII, 73.

[90] Smith, *op. cit.*, 194-211; 228-265.

people of Mississippi to reopen the slave trade.[91] The Georgia Convention unanimously adopted an ordinance prohibiting the African slave trade, and Georgia's commissioners to other states gave the assurance that the people of their state had no design to reopen it.[92] The Louisiana Convention, however, seemed to be in favor of reopening the trade. A resolution declaring the people of Louisiana opposed to reopening was rejected, 59 to 49; and another instructing the delegates to Montgomery to resist any and every attempt to reopen the slave trade and to secure a constitutional provision prohibiting it, was rejected, 83 to 28.[93] An analysis of these votes does not show that secessionists voted against them in greater proportion than opponents of secession. The conventions of South Carolina, Florida, and Texas seem to have taken no action on the matter.

The Provisional Congress put a prohibition of the foreign slave trade, except from the slaveholding states of the United States, in both the Provisional and the Permanent Constitution, only the South Carolina delegation voted, in each case, for a substitute giving Congress the power to prohibit the trade.[94] There was strong opposition in South Carolina to the prohibition. It was strongly criticized in the South Carolina Convention. The Charleston Mercury protested against the interdiction.[95] L. W. Spratt was irreconcilable. Much of the South Carolina opposition to the prohibitory clause, however, was made because it seemed to admit that slavery was in itself an evil; many of those opposed claimed not to favor the actual reopening of the foreign slave trade.[96] The Louisiana Convention refused to specifically approve the action of the Provisional Congress relative to the slave trade,[97] although it ratified both the Provisional and the Permanent Constitution of the Confederate states. Outside these two states there

[91]*Journal of the State Convention* [of Mississippi], 78, 84.
[92]*Journal of the Convention of Georgia*, 59, 363, 369.
[93]*Official Journal of the Convention of Louisiana*, 28, 29.
[94]*Journal of the Provisional Congress*, 35, 868.
[95]Mar. 15, 1861, quoted in New York *Herald*, Mar. 19.
[96]W. H. Russell, letter of April 30, 1861, on "The State of South Carolina," in Moore, *Rebellion Record*, I, Doc. p. 314 ff.
[97]*Official Journal of the Convention of Louisiana*, 60, 61.

seems to have been little dissatisfaction with the action of Congress. Surely if a desire to reopen the foreign slave trade had been a chief motive of secession, a constitutional prohibition of it would not have been acquiesced in so readily.

CHAPTER XI

ECONOMIC CONSIDERATIONS AFFECTING THE DECISION OF THE BORDER STATES

In the border states after the election of Lincoln, secessionists tried to show that the election of Lincoln, the Personal Liberty laws of Northern States, and the abolition agitation generally, justified secession; and the opponents of secession refuted their arguments. There were those who wished to make continuance in the Union contingent upon securing further guarantees for slavery; there were others who thought such guarantees unnecessary. The discussion of these points differed in no essential respect from the debate of similar propositions in the cotton states. Also, secessionists *per se* and unconditional Unionists advanced arguments to show that secession would affect advantageously or detrimentally the material interests (other than slavery) of their respective states. But it was understood from the start that the majority of the people of the border states preferred to remain in the Union if it could be saved intact; the initiation of secession must come from the cotton states. Ardent secessionists, therefore, devoted their first efforts after Lincoln's election to persuading the cotton states to take the initiative. Within the border states secessionists devoted their arguments chiefly to prove that it would be to the interest or honor of their respective states to join a Southern confederacy should one be formed—or, after the event, that it was to their interest or honor to join the Confederacy.

One alleged economic advantage of the secession of the border states, especially those east of the mountains, was that it would give an impetus to manufacturing. The moderate revenue duties imposed by the Confederate government would amply protect their manufacturing interests against Northern competition. In a Southern confederacy the Northern slave states would take the place of New England in manufacturing for the states farther south. Thomas L. Clingman described the manufactures of North Carolina, and said: "The result of only ten per cent duties in excluding products from abroad, would give life and impetus to mechanical and manufacturing industry throughout the entire South."[1] Senator Hunter, the author of the Tariff of 1857,

---

[1] *Cong. Globe*, 36 Cong., 2 Sess., 4.

promised the border states, especially Virginia, that in a Southern confederacy they would take the place of New England and other non-slaveholding states in manufacturing for the South. "Under the incidental protection afforded by a tariff, laid without other views than those for revenue purposes, there would be an un-exampled development of her vast capacity for mining, manu-facturing, agricultural and commercial production."[2] Randolph Tucker, Attorney General of Virginia, advanced a similar argu-ment.[3] The Georgia commissioners to Maryland, Delaware, and North Carolina urged in behalf of secession that the cotton states were agricultural, and the states named could manufacture for them. Said Mr. Hall, commissioner to North Carolina: "All your material interests must be promoted by your speedy union with us in the new government. The princely treasures which have been hitherto lavished with a generous hand upon ungrateful New England, will be poured into your lap."[4]

In the border states the free trade proclivities of the people of the cotton states were feared, and Unionists played upon this fear. They showed how free trade would injure manufacturing interests in the South, and how the tariff would be an apple of discord in a new confederacy as it had been in the old. Sherrard Clemens, of western Virginia, said: "It would be for the interest of the coast States to have free trade in manufactured goods; but how would that operate on the mechanical and manufacturing industry of Missouri, Kentucky, Virginia, Maryland and Delaware?"[5] Union-ists also showed that free trade would mean direct taxation. The Confederate Congress took cognizance of these speculations in border states when framing their early tariff legislation and the Provisional and the Permanent Constitution.[6] Their action was not entirely reassuring, however, since it included placing a pro-

<hr/>

[2]Letter on the Crisis, Nov. 24, 1860, New York *Herald*, Dec. 6; *DeBow's Review*, XXX, 115.

[3]In article, "The Great Issue: Our Relation to It," *So. Lit. Mes.*, XXXII, 187.

[4]*Journal of the Convention of Georgia*, 325, 330, 364.

[5]Speech in the House of Representatives, Jan. 22, 1861, in Moore, *Rebellion Record*, I, Doc. p. 25. See also Kennedy, *The Border States, their Power and Duty*, 23.

[6]H. P. Bell, Georgia Commissioner to Tennessee, reported that the adoption of the policy of raising revenue by duties on imports had strengthened the seces-sion movement in that state. *Journal of the Convention of Georgia*, 369.

hibition of protective tariffs in the Permanent Constitution. John P. Kennedy, of Maryland, referred to the belief of some that discriminatory duties would be laid on Northern goods with a view to the establishment of large manufacturing interests in the South. The Constitution, he said, had already put a veto upon protection. Once peace should be established, the South would become friends of the North, and would revert to free trade. Northern manufacturers could compete with the world in free trade, but Maryland's could not.[7]

Much was said of the commercial advantages which would accrue to cities of border states, particularly Norfolk, Richmond, and Baltimore, from their inclusion in a Southern confederacy. North Carolina had no seaport with prospects of becoming a New York under the stimulus of free trade and direct trade; it was understood that the trade of the old North State would have to contribute to the upbuilding of Charleston, Richmond, and Norfolk.[8] In Virginia, however, the commercial benefits of disunion were well canvassed. They were being discussed at Norfolk and Richmond shortly after Lincoln's election.[9] In the Union, said Tucker, Norfolk and Richmond would still be dependencies of New York. "With the command of the Southern trade, with her extended Southern connections, with her commercial facilities, Virginia would be the great commercial, manufacturing, and navigation State of the South. Her bottoms would replace those of New England—her merchants and factors those of New York—her factories those of the free States."[10] The efforts being made in Virginia to develop an extensive foreign trade by building railroads and canals and making arrangements in Europe, were represented as "utterly vain so long as our federal system continues."[11] Visions of commercial grandeur in a Southern confederacy explain in a measure the sympathy with secession manifested in Baltimore. Opponents of secession, however, were able to show the baselessness of these

[7]"An Appeal to Maryland," Moore, Rebellion Record, I, Doc. pp. 368-74. See also Journal and Proceedings of the Missouri Convention, Journal, 35, report of the Committee on Federal Relations.
[8]Clingman in the Senate, Cong. Globe, 37 Cong., Exec. Sess. of Sen., 1476.
[9]Norfolk and Richmond Correspondence, New York Herald, Nov. 28, Dec. 22, 1860.
[10]J. Randolph Tucker in article cited above.
[11]Willoughby Newton, National Intelligencer, Nov. 24, 1860.

expectations. Even should Southern independence change the course of Southern trade, which was highly problematical, what had Baltimore to hope from the change? they asked. "Will she import for the South, from the head of the Chesapeake, whilst Norfolk lies on the margin of the sea at its mouth . . . ?"[12] Even merchants of St. Louis were led to believe that, somehow, separation from the North would be conducive to her prosperity and make her the metropolis of the valley.[13]

But it was generally recognized that secession offered few or no positive advantages to the western border states. "Disunion on the slave line," said one, "carries such obvious and inevitable destructive results to Kentucky, Tennessee, and Missouri, that no Utopian projector of a Southern Confederacy has ever yet had the ingenuity to suggest even the plausible semblance of any compensating benefit to those three States."[14] As far as material interests other than slavery were concerned, the choice, in case of a disruption of the Union, between going with the South and remaining with the North was a choice between two evils. And in each of the border states the decision was affected more powerfully by considerations of which alternative would cause less disturbance and injury to *established* relations of trade and intercourse than it was by expectations of *positive* advantages to result from joining a Southern confederacy.

North Carolina was very slow to secede. Her people were conservative. (The state was often referred to as the Rip Van Winkle of the South.) Leaders of the secession movement had perfect confidence, however, that North Carolina would go out if Virginia did so; for, aside from questions of defense, the chief routes of trade and travel lay across the boundaries of Virginia and South Carolina. That portion of Virginia which lay between the mountains and the Chesapeake had important commercial connections with both the North and the South, but the routes of trade upon which Virginia cities depended for their prosperity were to the South and Southwest. The most important railroad, the Virginia

[12]John P. Kennedy, "An Appeal to Maryland," cited in note 7.

[13]*Journal and Proceedings of the Missouri Convention*, Proceedings, p. 86; New York *Herald*, Dec. 17, 1860, remarks of Mr. Grow in a meeting of the St. Louis Chamber of Commerce.

[14]*South Carolina, Disunion, and a Mississippi Valley Confederacy*, p. 6.

and Tennessee, ran via the southwest corner of the state in the
direction of Chattanooga, whence connection was had with Nashville, Memphis, and New Orleans. Another important road, the
Petersburg and Weldon, ran south, and conected with North and
South Carolina roads. The Shenandoah valley, however, and
much of Northern Virginia had been made commercially tributary
to Baltimore.

The commercial interests of Baltimore were an important
factor in the decision of Maryland. Baltimore was the commercial
center for central Maryland, much of northern Virginia, and to a
limited extent for the Susquehanna valley, in Pennsylvania. But
the most important connection was the Baltimore and Ohio railroad, which ran up the Potomac river to Cumberland and thence
to Wheeling, with a branch across western Virginia to Parkersburg. At Wheeling and Parkersburg connections were made with
the network of railroads in the old Northwest. The possession of
this western connection promoted Union sentiment in Baltimore,
especially because western Maryland and northwestern Virginia
showed strong Union tendencies. John P. Kennedy, of Maryland,
referred to the unfriendliness of eastern Virginia to Maryland's
internal improvement policy and the friendliness of the western
counties. "The true friends and allies of our policy are in the
West. At this moment that region is making its protest against
secession. It is a matter of deepest moment that we should wisely
appreciate this fact."[15]

One explanation of the strong union sentiment of western Virginia was the identity of economic interests with neighboring portions of Ohio, Pennsylvania, Kentucky, and Maryland rather than
with eastern Virginia. The trade of western Virginia went not
across the mountains to Richmond and Norfolk but to Cincinnati,
Pittsburgh, and other cities on the Ohio river, and by the Baltimore and Ohio railroad to Baltimore. Governor Pierpont said
secession would be fatal to the material interests of West Virginia.
"Secession and annexation to the South would cut off every outlet
for our productions."[16] It is quite possible that the failure to complete the Chesapeake and Ohio railroad and the James River and

[15]Moore, *Rebellion Record*, I, Doc. p. 373.
[16]*Ibid.*, II, Doc. p. 158. Also Virginia *Senate Journal and Documents*, Extra
Session, 1861, p. 20, message of Governor Letcher.

Kanawha canal before the Civil War was a deciding factor in the division of Virginia on the secession issue.[17] A desire to unify the state had been one of the motives of those who zealously supported these projects. It is possible, too, that, could the Chesapeake and Ohio railroad have been completed and successfully operated before 1861, the ties which bound Virginia to the Union would have been more difficult to break. It is not without significance that the leading and most persistent advocate of a Western connection, Joseph Segar, although a resident of the tidewater region, declined to go with his state in secession, and became an exile during the War.[18]

In the case of Tennessee, going South would without doubt cause the least disturbance and injury to established relationships of trade and intercourse.[19] Most of the cotton of Tennessee went via Memphis to New Orleans. A comparatively small amount went by rail to Charleston and Savannah. Still less, perhaps, went up the Mississippi and by other routes to the factories of the Ohio valley. Tennessee tobacco found an outlet chiefly by way of New Orleans. Mules, hogs, grain, and whiskey from the farming districts were sold to the planters of the cotton belt. With the opening of the Virginia and Tennessee railroad, the export of grain by way of Virginia began. Imports into Tennessee, however, came from all directions—from New Orleans, from Charleston and Savannah, to some extent from Virginia, and largely, from Cincinnati, Louisville, and St. Louis by rivers and railroads. It is noteworthy that while east Tennessee was about as firmly bound to the South by economic ties as any other part, yet no district in the South had a population more loyal to the Union. The explanation lies elsewhere than in such economic considerations as are here stated.

What has been said of the economic ties of Tennessee was true in greater degree of Arkansas. There were no railroads. Arkansas

[17]A Richmond correspondent wrote, in New York *Herald*, Nov. 22, 1860: "The facilities of intercommunication between Western and Eastern Virginia, and the frequent intercourses which result therefrom have procured a unity of sentiment between the people of both sections which no one could have anticipated ten years ago . . . . They are breaking up the associations of the people of the West with those of the border free states which were heretofore a necessity of trade."

[18]*Letter of Hon. Joseph Segar to a Friend in Virginia*, etc. (pamphlet, 1862).

[19]Cf. Fertig, *Secession and Reconstruction in Tennessee*, 13, 22.

products found an outlet chiefly by river routes. Memphis and New Orleans were the commercial centers. Governor Rector stated the situation concisely. Arkansas was disposed to be conservative as were Maryland, Virginia, Missouri, Kentucky, and Tennessee. But Arkansas was the natural ally of the cotton states. She was bound to them by the institution of slavery. Missouri might rid herself of it; Arkansas could not. "With the mart and channel of Southern commerce in the possession and control of the States of Louisiana and Mississippi, what would be the condition of Arkansas should she determine to adhere to the Union?"[20]

In Kentucky and Missouri it was generally recognized that as far as economic interests other than slavery were concerned, the states had much to lose and little to gain by seceding. Mr. Gamble, later governor of Missouri, put the matter tersely in the Missouri Convention: "Our interests as a State are bound up inseparably with the maintenance of the Union; our sympathies, our personal sympathies, in a large measure, are with the people of the South."[21] Most of the trade and intercourse of these states was with or by way of the free states of the North. They were dependent upon about the same markets as southern Illinois, Indiana, and Ohio. "It is true," wrote a pamphleteer, "that much the larger amount of the trade of the Northwest tends to the East, and not to the South, and if weighed in merely commercial scales the question of connection, as between the two, would preponderate in favor of the East."[22] The east and west railroads, built during the last decade or so, had reversed the outlet and outlook of these and other Western states; and of this the people were well aware. A correspondent of John J. Crittenden wrote him: "General Scott's plan would have worked twenty years ago. . . . but since railroads have intervened there can be no division between the people of the Mississippi valley north of Kentucky (including that state) and *all* East and Northeast—the 'railroad' tells the story."[23] Delegates in the Missouri Convention said St. Louis owed her greatness

[20]Message to the Legislature, New York *Herald*, Dec. 29, 1860.
[21]*Journal and Proceedings of the Missouri Convention*, Proceedings, p. 67. See also the Address of the Border State Convention to the people of the United States, Moore, *Rebellion Record*, I, Doc. p. 352.
[22]*South Carolina, Disunion, and a Mississippi Valley Confederacy*, 14.
[23]C. J. Davis to J. J. Crittenden, Jan. 1, 1861, *J. J. Crittenden MSS.*

to the Union, and nothing should be done to blast her progress.[24] They also gave consideration to the prospect that the route of the Pacific railroad would lie across the state. "And Missouri stands in the pathway of nations; over her soil this pathway must run, just as inevitably as fate."[25]

But if economic and commercial ties made it almost a necessity that Kentucky and Missouri remain with the North, their commercial relations with the South were so valuable that the destruction of the Union would be a great blow to their prosperity. St. Louis and Louisville each had a large Southern trade. Hemp and tobacco were sent South. Mules and horses, bacon, pork, and corn were shipped down the Mississippi or over the Louisville and Nashville railroad or by other routes to the cotton and sugar plantations. The people of the interior states, not only Kentucky and Missouri but Illinois, Iowa, Indiana, etc. as well, whose prosperity depended so largely upon the internal trade with the South and upon unimpeded access to the sea, felt that they had a greater interest in the maintenance of the Union than the people of any other section. Promises of the free navigation of the Mississippi and transit of foreign imports and exports across Southern territory free of duty were too insecure and inadequate to reconcile them to the establishment of a foreign power between them and the Gulf.[26] Governor MaGoffin, of Kentucky, who strongly sympathized with the secessionists, said that the "mouth and sources of the Mississippi river cannot be separated without the horrors of Civil War."[27] Such facts as these help to explain why the people of Kentucky and Missouri were so anxious for a compromise to save the Union.

But considerations of benefits or injuries to economic interests were by no means the only considerations determining the decision of border states. Others may be briefly summarized.

The question of the relation of slavery to secession in the border states presents several aspects peculiar to them. The people of those states were almost unanimously opposed to reopening the

[24]*Journal and Proceedings of the Missouri Convention*, Proceedings, 14, 86.
[26]*Ibid.*, Proceedings, 122.
[26]*Annual Cyclopedia*, I, 396.
[27]*Great Debates in American History*, V, 276. See also Coulter, E. M., "Effects of Secession upon the Commerce of the Mississippi Valley," *Miss. Val. Hist. Rev.*, III, 276-300.

African slave trade. Until it had been prohībited by the Constitution of the Confederate States, the fear that it might be reopened had been one of the chief influences retarding the secession
movement.[28]

The Constitution of the Confederate States gave congress the
power to prohibit the importation of slaves from the slaveholding
states of the United States. The provision was designed to bring
pressure to bear upon them to join the Confederacy;[29] and, although as a coercive measure it was resented in the border states,
it undoubtedly served the purpose for which it was intended. This
was especially true in the case of Virginia, where it was feared the
slave population would soon become redundant if the outlet for
the surplus should be cut off.[30]

Secessionists asserted that with seven slaveholding states out of
the Union the remaining would be in a hopeless minority. Constitutional guarantees would no longer suffice to protect slavery
therein, for the free states, then being three-fourths of all the
states, could amend the Constitution as they might see fit, even to
abolish slavery altogether. "If we do not go with the cotton states,"
said J. Randolph Tucker, "our $250,000,000 of slave property
would perish." The North would not tolerate it, and the South
would not buy.[31] Opponents, on the other hand, professed to
believe that secession would be destructive of slavery in the border
states. There would be no fugitive slave law; a fugitive who es-
caped across the line would be as surely beyond recovery as he
would be in Canada. In case of war the border states would be
invaded, and the slaves run off. Slave owners, in case of seces-

---

[28]Washington correspondence, New York *Herald*, Nov. 22, 1860; Raleigh correspondence, Jan. 12, 1861; *National Intelligencer*, Nov. 27, 29, Dec. 29, 1860,
Feb. 19, 1861; *So. Lit. Mes.*, XXXI, 472; XXXII, 73; *Journal of the Convention
of Virginia*, 67; speech of Sherrard Clemens, of Virginia, Moore, *Rebellion Record*, I, Doc. p. 24; *South Carolina, Disunion, and a Mississippi Valley Confederacy*, 4; Smith, *History and Debates of the Convention of Alabama*, 198,
208, 210, 251, 259; and see above, pp. 270-72.

[29]Smith, *History and Debates of the Convention of Alabama*, 236, 252, 258.
Yancey would have prohibited by constitutional provision the importation of
slaves from slaveholding states which did not join the Confederacy. P. 252.

[30]Willoughby Newton, *National Intelligencer*, Nov. 24, 1860.

[31]*So. Lit. Mes.*, XXXII, 187.

sion, would sell or carry their slaves South.[32] The dangers were particularly great in the case of Missouri, said Missourians, for the state was almost surrounded by free states.[33]

Among the most powerful arguments against secession in some of the border states were the difficulties of defending them against the North in case of war. The utter impossibility of defending the Eastern Shore of Maryland and Virginia against a power which could control the sea and the Chesapeake was pointed out.[34] Central Maryland would either be at once overrun by Northern troops, or would become a battle ground of the war.[35] The defenseless position of the trans-Alleghany portion of Virginia was a deterrent influence in that state;[36] and Unionists portrayed the destruction war would bring to eastern Virginia, perhaps with little effect. Kentuckians took account of the three free states which lay on her long northern boundary.[37] Missouri Unionists said secession could only lead to the military conquest of the state; for it was surrounded on three sides by free states which must have a highway across it.[38] Unionists demonstrated the folly of surrendering a position in the heart of a vast nation for one upon the frontier between two nations, which might find causes for frequent conflicts.[39] To these arguments the secessionists could only reply, before Sumter, that if all the slaveholding states would go out to-

[32] *Journal and Proceedings of the Missouri Convention*, Journal, p. 35; Proceedings, p. 88; Joseph Holt's "Letter on the Pending Revolution," in Moore, *Rebellion Record*, I, Doc. p. 290; *Annual Cyclopedia*, I, 442; *So. Lit. Mess.*, XXXII, 73, quoting M. F. Maury; *Cong. Globe*, 36 Cong., 2 Sess., 139, speech of Andrew Johnson.

[33] *Journal and Proceedings of the Missouri Convention*, Journal, 56, report of the Committee on the Commissioner from Georgia; Proceedings, 88.

[34] W. H. Collins, *Third Address to the People of Maryland*.

[35] Speech of Reverdy Johnson at Frederick, Md., *National Intelligencer*, May 11, 1861; message of Gov. Hicks, Moore, *Rebellion Record*, I, Doc. p. 159 ff.

[36] The Central Committee's address to the people of northwestern Virginia, *ibid.*, I, Doc. p. 328.

[37] *Ibid.*, I, Doc. p. 354, 73, 75.

[38] *Journal and Proceedings of the Missouri Convention*, Journal, 35, 52; Proceedings, 89.

[39] Moore, *Rebellion Record*, I, Doc. p. 289, 354; Collins, *Third Address*, etc.; *South Carolina, Disunion, and a Mississippi Valley Confederacy*, 13.

gether there would be no war; they would form a confederacy so powerful that the North would not dare attack it.[40]

Perhaps more effectual than the appeals to the fears of the people of the border states were the appeals to their sympathies, prejudices, and kinship. They were urged not to stand by and permit, or assist in, the subjugation of sister Southern states. The determination of the Federal government to maintain the Union by force of arms furnished the occasion for the secession of four states. In the cases of Virginia and Tennessee it is quite doubtful that secession would have occurred had the seceded states been permitted to depart in peace.[41] This was the view taken by an element in the South which wished to precipitate a conflict with the Federal government in order to insure the secession of the border states. Resistance to coercion was the issue which won over conservative Tennessee Whigs such as Bell, E. H. Ewing, Neil S. Brown, and John Callander.[42] It was the issue upon which the secessionists made their last stand in Maryland, Kentucky, and Missouri.

It is as difficult to identify the secessionists in the border states as it was the secessionists in the cotton states. In three, the people were given no opportunity to vote upon the issue until after the outbreak of war. It is impossible to state just what the issue was when the elections were held in the other five. It is certain that in no state did the majority favor secession if the Union could be preserved or reconstructed without war. In general, it would seem, about the same classes came, sooner or later, to favor seces-

[40]*So. Lit. Mess.*, XXXII, 182 ff.; *Annual Cyclopedia*, I, 730, quoting address of ten Virginia congressmen; *Letter of Hon. Joseph Segar to a Friend in Virginia*, 28.

[41]Cf. Fertig, *Secession and Reconstruction in Tennessee*, 20 ff; Rhodes, *History of the U. S.*, III, 344, 378, 383; Beverly Munford, *Virginia's Attitude toward Slavery and Secession;* J. M. Botts, *The Great Rebellion*, 205 ff. I do not name North Carolina in this connection. A large vote was cast for secession in January, when it was still believed a reconciliation could be effected. The House of Commons unanimously resolved in February that North Carolina would go with the South if reconciliation failed. *Annual Cyclopedia*, I, 538. This was the opinion of men in the cotton states. Report of Jacob Thompson, Commissioner from Mississippi to North Carolina, *Journal of the State Convention* [of Mississippi], 185. But see J. G. de Roulhac Hamilton, *Reconstruction in North Carolina*, 21 ff.; Wm. K. Boyd, "North Carolina on the Eve of Secession," Am. Hist. Assoc., *Rept.*, 1910, p. 177.

[42]Moore, *Rebellion Record*, I, Doc. pp. 72, 137.

sion which had supported the secession movements in the cotton states, namely, the people of the planting sections and of the cities and towns closely identified in interests with them. As in the cotton states, also, the opposition centered in districts in which the slave population was small in proportion to the white and in which farming rather than planting was the chief occupation of the people. Whigs, in general, were more adverse to secession than Democrats of the same districts.

In North Carolina a convention election of January 28 resulted in the choice of 85 constitutional Unionists and 35 secessionists. The opinion seems to have been quite prevalent at the time that the Union could yet be peacefully reconstructed; the issue, then, was neither strictly Union versus disunion, nor remaining with the North versus going with the South. Of 47 counties in the eastern part of the state, where the slave population was a high percentage of the total in most localities, 17 chose secession delegates, 30 Union delegates. Of the counties which went for secession 4 were normally Whig, 13 Democratic; of the counties which returned Union delegates 21 could be classed as Whig, 9 as Democratic. The secessionist counties were grouped pretty well in the southeast corner of the state. Of 38 counties in the western part of the state, in few of which the slaves constituted more than 25 per cent of the population, 11 selected secession, 27 Union delegates. Of the secession counties 6 were normally Whig, 5 normally Democratic; of the counties returning Union majorities, 23 were Whig, 4 Democratic. The counties which chose secession delegates were well grouped along the South Carolina border. Wilmington was strongly Democratic and secessionist; Wake county, in which Raleigh was located, was normally Democratic but strongly Unionist.[43]

In the Tennessee convention election of February 9, 91,803 votes were cast for Union, 24,749 for secession delegates. Virtually all of the secession votes were cast in west and middle Tennessee, but the majority in every section of the state was for Union.[44] At this time the people of Tennessee seem to have believed the

[43] I have used the classification of delegates made by H. M. Wagstaff, *State Rights and Political Parties in North Carolina*, 134.

[44] *Annual Cyclopedia*, I, 677; New York *Times*, Feb. 15, 1861.

Union could be peacefully reconstructed.[45] On June 8 the action of
the Tennessee Legislature declaring the state independent and
ratifying the Constitution of the Confederate States was submitted
to the people for their ratification. Overwhelming majorities in
west and middle Tennessee approved, but in east Tennessee the
vote was almost as strongly adverse.[46] The slave population of the
latter section was very small in comparison with the white.

An election was held in Virginia, February 4, to choose delegates
to a state convention. The result was considered a Union victory,
although the delegates could not be classified accurately as Unionists and secessionists. About 25 or 30 were considered unconditional secessionists.[47] No test vote was held in the Convention
upon a straight-out secession resolution until April 4, when such a
resolution was defeated by a vote of 90-45.[48] This was long after
it had become apparent that the Union could not be reconstructed
by agreement, but before it became certain that coercion was the
policy of the government. All but 3 of the 45 votes for secession
were cast by delegates from counties now in Virginia; all but 14 by
delegates from east of the Blue Ridge. All of the counties with
large slave population lay in the eastern section; it was the planting section. Of the 45 votes in favor of secession, 15 were cast by
delegates from counties normally Whig; 30 by delegates from
counties normally Democratic. The delegates from Richmond and
Petersburg, but not the delegate from Norfolk, voted for secession.
After Sumter the convention decided for secession by a vote of
79 to 64.[49] The delegates from northwestern Virginia, now West
Virginia, voted almost solidly against secession; those from east
of the Blue Ridge voted almost as solidly for it; those from the
intervening region were divided. This division in the Convention
reflected quite accurately the divisions among the people, as shown

[45]Report of H. P. Bell, Georgia Commissioner to Tennessee, *Journal of the
Convention of Georgia*, 369; Fertig, *Secession and Reconstruction in Tenn.*, 21.
[46]Moore, *Rebellion Record*, II, Doc. p. 169.
[47]Rhodes, *History of the U. S.*, III, 309; Tyler, *Letters and Times of the
Tylers*, II, 621; *Annual Cyclopedia*, I, 730.
[48]*Journal of the Committee of the Whole* [of the Convention of Virginia], 31.
[49]This is the test vote, not the vote upon the adoption of the ordinance of
secession. *Journal of the Secret Session*, p. 8.

by the popular vote on the ordinance of secession of May 23 and by the subsequent division of the state.[50]

Maryland and Kentucky declared, finally, for the Union, but there was strong sympathy in each with the secession movement. In Maryland the East Shore and the western part were strongly Unionist. Secession sentiment developed chiefly in the planting region of central Maryland, and was reflected in Baltimore. In Kentucky it was strongest in the Blue Grass region of the central part and the tobacco counties of the southwest. The delegates in the Missouri Convention who wished to resist coercion of the seceded states by the Federal government represented, with a few exceptions, counties along the Mississippi and Missouri rivers.[51] There were the districts which had a considerable slave population; there tobacco and hemp were grown.

The opposition of the non-slaveholding districts of the border states to secession did not, in general, signify hostility to slavery. It signified, however, a degree of indifference to the preservation of slavery and a disposition to remember that slavery was not the only important interest to be considered. This disposition found frequent expression. For example, Mr. Brodhead, in the Missouri Convention, said negro slavery was not the only great interest in Missouri. Slaves comprised less than one-ninth of the taxable property of the state. The white population was increasing four times as rapidly as the slave. The slaves were engaged in raising hemp and tobacco principally. There were mining, manufacturing, and commercial interests, to carry on which white labor was required. If Missouri seceded, the white laborers would not come, "when they know that, so far as our political power is concerned, we shall be subjected to the cotton lords of South Carolina and Louisiana."[52] Only in a few localities, such as St. Louis, which had a large German and Northern population, was there an active hostility to slavery. The Unionists of the border states entered the war with the understanding that it was a war to preserve the Union, not to destroy slavery.

---

[50] *Annual Cyclopedia*, 737 ff., 743; Rhodes, III, 387.
[51] An analysis of several divisions of the Convention.
[52] *Journal and Proceedings of Missouri Convention*, Proceedings, 122. See also *ibid.*, Journal, 35; Moore, *Rebellion Record*, I, 374.

In two, at least, of the border states, Tennessee and Virginia, the divisions of the people on the secession issue corresponded rather closely to long standing sectional divisions. Tennessee sectionalism was based largely upon social differences between the people of the east and those of the middle and west. The people of east Tennessee resented the political domination of the state by the planting society. While they did not hate slavery, they believed that the South should be a white man's country, and that one man was as good as another. They were not disposed to fight in support of a movement which they conceived to have been inaugurated to perpetuate and establish more firmly an aristocratic social system. Andrew Johnson was a typical representative of east Tennessee. "We find . . . " said he, "that the whole idea is to establish a republic based upon slavery exclusively, in which the great mass of the people are not to participate." And again, "We hold [in east Tennessee] that it is upon the intelligent free white people of the country that all governments should rest, and by them all governments should be controlled."[53] The old sectional division in Virginia had grown in part out of social differences similar to those in Tennessee, in part from separation by geographical barriers. Politically it had found expression in disputes over legislative apportionment, appropriations for and location of state aided internal improvements, and the apportionment of taxation. It is significant that the Virginia Convention submitted to the people of the state along with the secession ordinance, an amendment to the constitution providing that "Taxation shall be equal and uniform throughout the commonwealth, and all property shall be taxed in proportion to its value, . . . "[54] The purpose of the amendment was, of course, to insure the taxation of slaves at the same rate as other property; its proposal was a belated effort of the East to conciliate the West. The sectionalism of North Carolina was not so pronounced, but was not without bearing upon the alignment upon the secession issue. In North Carolina, too, the *ad valorem* issue was agitating the state upon the eve of secession. It is not possible within the limits of this

[53]Speech in the Senate, July 21, 1861, Moore, *Rebellion Record*, II, Doc. p. 425-6. See also speech of Dec. 19, 1860, *Cong. Globe,* 36 Cong., 2 Sess., 140 ff.

[54]*Journal of the Convention of Virginia*, 106, 134, 150; *Ordinances Adopted by the Convention of Virginia in Secret Session*, p. 21.

study to develop the subject of the relation of long standing sectional divisions within several Southern states to the divisions of the people upon the question of secession; but no study of the reasons for the attitude taken by the people in the largely non-slaveholding districts would be complete which does not take them into account.

The decision of the border states was slowly and carefully made. It was determined largely by fears for slavery, feelings of sympathy and kinship with the people of the cotton states, and considerations of their position in case of war; but the people of the border states were also powerfully influenced in their decision by their judgments as to the probable effect of secession upon the economic interests, slavery aside, of the localities involved. From this viewpoint, going with the South or remaining with the Union appeared as the choice of two evils. Only in eastern Virginia and in North Carolina did the people of the border states share to any considerable extent the expectations of great material benefits to follow secession and the formation of a Southern confederacy which the people of the cotton states entertained.

CHAPTER XII
SUMMARY AND CONCLUSIONS

In this study we have considered some of the economic aspects of Southern sectionalism during about twenty years prior to the Civil War. This period does not by any means include the beginning of such sectionalism.

During this period the people of the South, generally, were aware of a disparity between the North and South to the advantage of the former in material development—population, wealth, commerce, industry, financial strength, distribution of the comforts and conveniences of life. Although at intervals the Southern people were inclined to be satisfied with their degree of prosperity, their economic organization and methods, and the progress of their section, in general they felt that they did not enjoy the prosperity and were not making the material progress that the South's natural resources and their own efforts entitled them to expect. This dissatisfaction was not uniformly distributed throughout the South. It was greatest in the older states. It developed in the newer states only as conditions there approximated those of the older. It was greater in the planting than in the farming regions. It was greatly augmented because a political struggle between the sections, over slavery especially, called sharp attention to the relationship between material progress and political power.

The "decline" of the South was attributed to various causes by those who perceived it. One group persistently emphasized the alleged unequal operation of the Federal government upon the economic development of the sections. Somewhat earlier than the period of this study, Southern leaders, particularly of the planting regions, had come to hold widely different views from their colleagues in other sections as to the proper revenue, expenditure, and commercial policies to be followed by the Federal government. They opposed high tariffs, heavy governmental expenditures, aid to private enterprises, bounties, and special favors of all kinds, because they thought their section was not equally benefited thereby. As years went by, and they were not always able to make their views prevail, they, of the Calhoun school, came to attribute the decline of the South to policies which they had opposed. This group was strong in the cotton states.

Others attached comparatively little significance to governmental reactions upon economic development; they attributed Southern "decline" chiefly to a too exclusive devotion to undiversified agriculture attended, as it was, by industrial, commercial, and financial dependence upon the North and Europe, and by unsatisfactory methods of marketing and buying. These conditions had come about in a natural way; but because of them the Southern people produced wealth while others enjoyed it. Men of this class would have diversified agriculture; they pleaded for the introduction of cotton manufactures; they proposed plans for securing direct trade with Europe; they dreamed of railroad connections with the Northwest and with the Pacific which would rehabilitate Southern cities; they advocated various measures of a protective character on the part of state and local governments; they asked that sectional patriotism and pride take the form of developing the economic resources of the South.

These classes, generally, agreed that slavery was not the cause of the lagging prosperity of the section. They agreed, slaveholders and non-slaveholders, that slavery, the plantation system, and the production of great staples must remain fundamental features of the South's economic system. Some of them, to be sure, were aware that slavery had off-setting disadvantages in that it restricted the opportunities of white labor, deprived it of leadership, and, consequently, deprived the South of its full services, and acted as a bar to immigration. There was a class, also, in the South which opposed slavery, namely, non-slaveholders of the laboring class who came into competition with slave labor; but the class was only beginning to be numerous and vocal.

Not economic reasons only explain the determination of the great majority to maintain the institution of slavery. Aside from the fact that it constituted a vast vested interest, that it was established in the social organization, and social prestige attached to the owners of big plantations, was the firm conviction that a superior and an inferior race could not live side by side (the negroes were here to stay) without the greatest social disorders unless the inferior race were in bondage. Some of the staunchest defenders of the institution refused to support plans for the economic regeneration of the South, because they feared that, if successful, they would prove incompatible with the continued security of slavery. The majority, however, were either unaware of the incompatibility or unafraid. Like their fellow Americans in the other sections, most Southerners were not seeking a static society. They were willing to adapt themselves to changing circumstances. And, while progress and change may have been less rapid in the ante-bellum South than elsewhere in the Union, it is an error to regard Southern society as stationary.

Those who emphasized the unequal operation of the Federal government as a cause for Southern decline came early to believe that independent nationality would result in great material advantages. Many of those who advanced the various plans for regeneration mentioned above came eventually to believe that they could better be carried into effect in an independent republic. These views presented repeatedly to the Southern people convinced the great majority in the cotton states that, while secession might not be attended by any vast positive benefits, it would at least not be attended by any serious disadvantages; thus were they reconciled to a step which they were convinced was necessary to preserve slavery and maintain Southern honor. When the auspicious occasion came, the cotton states promptly went out of the Union. The people of the border states hesitated. With them slavery was not such a predominating interest. From an economic point of view they stood to lose whether they went out or stayed in. But confronted by a *fait accompli*, and war on one side or the other, they went with misgivings, where their sympathies, associations, or interests chiefly lay.

Now what basis had Southern sectionalism in actual economic facts? There can be no doubt of the divergent economic interests of the sections; one section was growing less rapidly in wealth and numbers, and was economically dependent upon the other. The divergence dated far back, even into colonial times. Fundamental causes lay in geography, climate, soil, and natural resources. Less important were conditions of settlement. The South had received a smaller proportion of thrifty, sturdy, middle class stock than had the North.

Slavery was both effect and cause. In days when slavery was considered no evil, natural conditions (soil and climate) explain why slavery was established and flourished chiefly below New Jersey. Once established, however, slavery, notwithstanding its great services in clearing forests, draining marshes, and growing great crops of staple products, was responsible for or tended to perpetuate some of the evils of the South's economic system. It *tended* to keep the South exclusively agricultural and to confine agriculture largely to the production of a few great staples, because it was best adopted to such an organization. It was largely responsible for a great mass of undirected, semi-productive white labor in the South.

But, not too much should be attributed to slavery. The South was vast in area; population spread easily and, perforce, remained sparse. In 1860 the oldest portions of the South still possessed characteristics of a frontier, and their business methods were appropriate thereto; they were still in the exploitation stage. The South was farther from Europe than the North. Her harbors were not so good as those of the North. Her mineral resources were less extensive and less accessible. Her soil, except in localities, was less productive than that of the Northwest. Her climate was more enervating than that of other sections.

The differing views of governmental policies grew out of different economic conditions. Northern states could be benefited by protective duties; they demanded them and at times secured them. There were more Northern enterprises and projects which were felt to be entitled to government aid; insistent demands were made for such aid and frequently secured. More Federal officials were required in the North; supplies and equipment for government needs could be more readily secured there; consequently most of the governmental expenditures were made in the North. There was justice in the Southern complaint that the South paid more in the form of taxes than she received back in disbursements, and that the difference was a drain upon Southern resources. But in those days Federal taxes were comparatively light, and governmental expenditures comparatively small; the operation of the Federal government would seem to have been of small consequence in determining the economic condition of sections as compared with other great economic forces of the time.

What shall be said of the remedies for Southern "decline?" Much more might have been accomplished than was had the plans advanced by the progressives been earnestly and intelligently carried out either by the state and local governments or the cooperative efforts of private citizens; for examples, commercial education, better banking laws, improved methods of marketing cotton. But the remedies lay chiefly in time and the natural order of events. Greater density of population would have come. Slavery or no slavery, capital would have come in or would have accumulated out of the profits of agriculture. White labor must have been put to work, first, perhaps, in cotton culture and later in other industries. Cotton manufactures would have sprung up as they promised to do in the forties, and as they did a few decades later. The Pacific railroad would have been built. The quantity of commerce would have become great enough to warrant direct trade with Europe. The development of the section's forest and mineral resources would have begun. But the South did not wait for time and the natural order of events. It is perhaps idle to speculate in regard to the economic future of the Southern states if they could have become an independent confederacy without war threatening national integrity. There is little likelihood that secession would have proved the magic proponents prophesied; about the same progress would have been made as in the Union. Slavery would have endured somewhat longer. The foreign slave trade would not have been reopened. Some industries might have been artificially stimulated. A measure of financial independence, as far as the actual transaction of business was concerned, would probably have been secured. But the economic advantages would have been off-set by the disadvantages of increased cost of government and the barriers imposed upon trade with states of the Union, with which trade had formerly been free.

The conditions were not right and the means not present for the formation among the Southern people of a thorough understanding of the great economic problems of the section. The press was poor and almost wholly partisan. *DeBow's Review,* after its founding in 1846, contained almost everything of value written on the economic conditions and problems of the South. The volumes were of very unequal merit; many of the articles were flimsy in character. DeBow himself, while a brilliant journalist, possessed of a vast fund of information, and a man of prodigious industry, was neither a man of broad grasp nor an impartial seeker after truth. Few books of value on economic subjects were published. Much as was said and written on the slavery question, for example, no considerable study of the economics of slavery of any value was produced. Too much that was written was based upon insufficient information and was speculative in character. A few men apparently did the thinking on economic questions for the vocal part of the population. The reading public was small; probably the thinking public also. The platform and the stump could and did contribute little to an understanding of economic problems. The schools had not yet become centers of study and research along economic lines, especially. Men of experience in large business affairs were comparatively too few, and seem to have written and talked too little. Much of the population was volatile and excitable. The bitter sectional quarrel over slavery was not conducive to calm thinking. After all, however, the remarkable thing is not how much intelligent consideration the Southern people gave to their economic conditions and problems but how little. Northerners and Englishmen contributed something to an understanding of these matters, but too much that they wrote was unsympathetic in character.[1]

And the Northern people as a whole did not have that sympathetic understanding of the complex social and economic problems of the South which was requisite to peace and amity between the sections and the eventual solution of those problems. The problems and interests of the sections were so different that serious conflict could be avoided only by mutual understanding, sympathy, and forbearance. The sections drifted into a war which was not inevitable.

[1]Notable for either breadth of understanding or sympathetic treatment or both were: Kettell, *Southern Wealth and Northern Profits;* Olmsted, *A Journey in the Seaboard Slave States; A Journey through Texas; A Journey in the Back Country; The Cotton Kingdom;* Weston, *The Progress of Slavery in the United States;* Russell, *North America* (English).

APPENDIX

TABLE I.—COMMERCE OF THE PRINCIPAL AMERICAN COLONIES AND COMMERCIAL STATES, 1760-1860.*

Year		New England / Massachusetts	New York	Pennsylvania	Maryland and Virginia / Maryland	Virginia	Carolina / So. Carolina	Georgia	Alabama	Louisiana
1760	Exports	£ 599,647	£ 480,106	£ 707,998	£ 605,882		£ 218,131	£ 12,198		
	Imports	37,802	21,125	21,754	504,451		162,769			
1774	Exports	562,476	437,937	625,652	528,738		378,116	57,518		
	Imports	112,248	80,008	69,611	612,030		432,302	37,647		
1791	Exports	$ 2,519,651	$ 2,505,465	$ 3,436,093	$ 2,239,691	$ 3,130,865	$ 2,693,268	$ 491,250		
1800	Exports	11,326,876	14,045,079	11,949,679	12,264,331	4,430,689	10,633,510	2,174,268		
1810	Exports	13,013,048	17,242,330	10,993,398	6,489,018	4,822,611	5,290,614	2,238,686		$ 1,899,592
1821	Exports	12,484,691	13,162,917	7,391,767	3,850,394	3,079,209	7,200,511	6,014,310	$ 108,960	2,272,172
	Imports	14,876,732	23,629,246	8,158,922	4,070,842	1,078,490	3,007,113	1,002,684		3,379,717
1830	Exports	7,213,194	19,697,983	4,291,793	3,791,482	4,791,644	7,627,031	5,336,626	2,294,594	15,488,692
	Imports	10,453,544	35,624,070	8,702,122	4,523,866	495,739	1,054,619	282,346	144,823	7,599,083
1840	Exports	10,186,261	34,264,080	6,820,145	5,768,768	4,778,220	10,036,769	6,862,956	12,854,690	34,236,936
	Imports	16,513,858	60,440,750	8,469,882	4,910,746	545,085	2,058,870	491,428	574,651	10,673,690
1845	Exports	10,351,030	36,175,298	3,574,363	5,221,977	2,104,581	8,890,648	4,557,435	10,538,228	27,157,495
	Imports	22,781,024	70,909,085	8,159,227	3,741,804	230,470	1,143,158	206,301	473,491	9,354,397
1850	Exports	10,681,763	52,712,789	4,501,606	6,967,353	3,415,646	11,447,800	7,551,943	10,544,858	38,105,350
	Imports	30,374,684	111,123,524	12,066,154	6,124,201	426,599	1,933,785	636,964	865,362	10,766,499
1855	Exports	28,190,925	113,731,238	6,274,338	10,395,984	4,379,928	12,700,250	7,543,519	14,270,565	55,367,862
	Imports	45,113,774	164,776,511	15,309,935	7,788,949	855,405	1,588,542	273,716	619,964	12,900,821
1860	Exports	17,003,277	145,555,444	5,628,327	9,001,600	5,858,024	21,205,337	18,483,030	58,670,183	108,417,798
	Imports	41,187,539	248,489,877	14,634,279	9,784,723	1,569,570	1,569,570	782,066	1,050,310	22,922,773

*DeBow, Compendium of the Seventh Census, 184, 186-7; Register of the Treasury, Commerce and Navigation, 1855, p. 330; 1860, p. 552.

TABLE II.—POPULATION OF NINE SEAPORTS AT TEN YEAR INTERVALS, 1790-1860*

SEAPORT	1790	1800	1810	1820	1830	1840	1850	1860
Boston.............	18,038	24,937	33,250	43,298	61,392	93,383	136,881	177,812
New York...........	33,131	60,489	96,373	123,706	202,589	312,710	515,547	803,653
Philadelphia........	42,520	69,403	91,874	112,722	161,410	220,423	340,045	585,529
Baltimore..........	13,503	26,114	35,583	62,738	80,625	102,313	169,054	212,418
Richmond..........	3,761	5,737	9,735	12,067	16,060	20,153	27,570	37,910
Norfolk............	......	6,916	9,193	8,478	9,814	10,920	14,326	14,620
Charleston.........	16,359	20,473	24,711	24,780	30,289	29,261	42,985	40,578
Savannah..........	......	5,166	5,215	7,523	7,776	11,214	15,312	22,292
Mobile.............	1,468†	......	......	1,500	3,194	12,672	20,515	29,258
New Orleans........	5,331†	8,056‡	17,242	27,176	46,310	102,193	116,375	168,675

*Seventh Census, *Appendix*, lii; Eighth Census, *Population*, Introduction, *passim*.
†1788.
‡1797.

TABLE III—REGISTERED AND ENROLLED AND LICENSED TONNAGE
IN STATES AND DISTRICTS OF THE UNITED STATES, 1793–1860*

STATE		1793	1810	CITY	1837	1850	1860
Massachusetts	Registered†	135,599	352,806	Boston...	127,955	270,510	411,410
	Enrolled‡	51,402	107,260		73,049	50,177	52,802
New York...	Registered	45,355	188,556	New York	191,322	441,336	838,449
	Enrolled	13,986	83,536		219,549	394,230	625,551
Pennsylvania	Registered	60,924	109,628	Philadelphia	39,156	64,205	67,094
	Enrolled	4,579	14,255		42,592	142,292	174,642
Maryland...	Registered	26,792	90,045	Baltimore.	34,954	90,669	114,185
	Enrolled	9,512	46,247		32,153	58,349	85,923
Virginia.....	Registered	23,997	45,339	Norfolk ...	1,864	10,542	10,452
	Enrolled	12,093	31,284		10,857	13,592	15,934
No. Carolina.	Registered	10,167	26,472	Wilmington	6,551	9,123	13,372
	Enrolled	2,764	10,562		2,088	6,074	10,335
So. Carolina..	Registered	12,998	43,354	Charleston	8,226	15,377	38,490
	Enrolled	2,058	9,449		12,957	17,915	26,934
Georgia.....	Registered	1,568	12,405	Savannah.	6,493	10,437	27,560
	Enrolled	283	3,107		6,414	9,293	12,280
Alabama....	Registered			Mobile ...	2,733	7,403	22,442
	Enrolled				7,585	16,753	30,314
Orleans Ty...	Registered		11,386	New Orleans	31,383	86,668	132,199
	Enrolled		1,326		60,992	165,040	96,043

Timothy Pitkin, *Statistical View of the Commerce of the United States*, pp. 397 ff.; *Commerce and Navigation, 1838*, p. 308; *1850*, Statement No. 15; *1860*, p. 658.
†Engaged in the foreign trade.
‡Including licensed. Engaged in the coastwise trade, etc.

TABLE IV—CONSUMPTION OF COTTON IN
THE UNITED STATES, 1840-1861*
(Bales of 500 lbs. each)

Year	North, including Maryland	South and West	South, including Virginia	West, including Kentucky
1839-1840	286,193	59,000		
1840-1841	282,288	70,000		
1841-1842	258,850	64,000		
1842-1843	315,782	70,000		
1843-1844	336,057	71,000		
1844-1845	374,506	80,000		
1845-1846	411,810	85,000		
1846-1847	417,476	91,000		
1847-1848	523,892	92,152	49,652	42,500
1848-1849	503,201	130,000	95,000	35,000
1849-1850	465,702	137,012	109,512	27,500
1850-1851	386,429	99,185	87,185	12,000
1851-1852	588,322	111,281	95,281	16,000
1852-1853	650,393	153,332	123,332	30,000
1853-1854	592,284	144,952	106,952	38,000
1854-1855	571,117	135,295	109,295	26,000
1855-1856	633,027	137,712	95,712	42,000
1856-1857	665,718	154,218	116,218	38,000
1857-1858	452,185	143,377	104,377	39,000
1858-1859	760,218	167,433	122,433	45,000
1859-1860	792,521	185,522	136,522	49,000
1860-1862	650,357	193,383	141,383	52,000

*The table was made from the estimates of the New York *Shipping List*, as quoted in *Hunt's Merchants' Magazine*, and E. J. Donnell's *History of Cotton*, and those of C. F. M'Cay, of Georgia, in *Hunt's Merchants' Magazine*, XXIII, 601.

BIBLIOGRAPHY

PUBLIC DOCUMENTS: FEDERAL AND CONFEDERATE

The Sixth Census of the United States: 1840.
The Seventh Census of the United States: 1850.
DE Bow, J. D. B. *Statistical View of the United States* . . . *Being a Compendium of the Seventh Census* . . . Washington, 1854.
KENNEDY, Jos. C. G. *Preliminary Report on the Eighth Census.* Washington, 1862.
The Eighth Census: 1860.
The Congressional Globe, 26th Congress to the 36th Congress.
Congressional Documents, 26th Congress to the 36th Congress.
COMMISSIONER OF PATENTS. *Annual Reports,* Agriculture, 1849-1861.
REGISTER OF THE TREASURY. *Reports* . . . *on the Commerce and Navigation of the United States* . . . , vols. for 1831-1836; 1837-1843; 1845-1847; 1849-1861.
U. S. Statutes at Large, 26th Congress to the 36th Congress.
MATHEWS, JAMES M. *The Statutes at Large of the Provisional Government of the Confederate States of America, from the Institution of the Government, February 8, 1861, to its Termination, February 18, 1862.* . . . Richmond, 1864.
Journal of the Provisional Congress of the Confederate States of America (*U. S. Senate Documents,* 58 Cong., 2 Sess., No. 234, Vol. I).

PUBLIC DOCUMENTS: STATE AND LOCAL

Journal, Acts, and Proceedings of a General Convention of the State of Virginia, Assembled at Richmond . . . *1850* . . . . Richmond, 1850.
Journal of the Acts and Proceedings of a General Convention of the State of Virginia, Assembled at Richmond . . . *1861.* Richmond, 1861.
Virginia House Journal and Documents, 1840-1861. Richmond.
Virginia Senate Journal and Documents, 1840-1861. Richmond.
Acts of the General Assembly of Virginia (published annually and biennially). Richmond.
The Convention of the People of North Carolina, Held on the 20th Day of May, A. D., 1861. Raleigh, 1862.
Journal of the State Convention of South Carolina, together with the Resolutions and Ordinances. Columbia, 1852.
Journal of the Convention of the People of South Carolina, Held in 1860, 1861, and 1862, together with Ordinances, Reports, and Resolutions, etc. Columbia, 1862.
Report of the Commissioners Appointed at the Last Session of the General Assembly to Inquire into the feasibility of improving the Channel of the Bar . . . *of Charleston* . . . . Columbia, 1852.
Report: Containing a Review of the Proceedings of the City Authorities from the 4th September, 1837, to the 1st August, 1838. . . . *By Henry L. Pinckney, Mayor.* Charleston, 1838.
A Digest of the Ordinances of the City of Charleston . . . *1783 to* . . . *1844, to which are annexed the acts of the Legislature which relate exclusively to the City of Charleston.*
Ordinances of the City of Charleston from . . . *August, 1844, to* . . . *September, 1851; and the Acts of the General Assembly relating to the City of Charleston.* 1854.

299

Ordinances of the City of Charleston . . . *1854, to the 1st December, 1859, and the Acts of the General Assembly* . . . *compiled by John R. Horsey* . . . *1859.*
Journal of the Georgia Convention held in Milledgeville in 1850. Milledgeville, 1850.
Journal of the Public and Secret Proceedings of the Convention of the People of Georgia, held in Milledgeville and Savannah in 1861, together with the ordinances adopted. Milledgeville, 1861.
HOTCHKISS, W. A. *Codification of the Statute Law of Georgia.* Savannah, 1845.
CANDLER, A. D. *The Confederate Records of the State of Georgia,* Vols. I-III. Atlanta, 1909-1910.
Ordinances and Constitution of the State of Alabama, with the Constitution of the Provisional Government and of the Confederate States of Amercia. Montgomery, 1861.
Acts of the General Assembly of Alabama, 1843-1860 (published annually and biennially). Tuscaloosa and Montgomery.
The Code of Ordinances of the City of Mobile,with the Charter and an Appendix. . . . *By the Hon. Alexander McKinstry.* 1859.
Journal of the Convention of the State of Mississippi, and the Act calling the same; . . . (1850). Jackson, 1851.
Journal of the State Convention and Ordinances and Resolutions adopted in January, 1861. . . . Jackson, 1861.
Proceedings and Debates of the Convention of Louisiana which assembled at . . . *New Orleans, January 14, 1845.* New Orleans, 1845.
Official Journal of the Proceedings of the Convention of the State of Louisiana. New Orleans, 1861.
Acts of the Legislature of Louisiana, 1840-1861 (published annually). New Orleans.
Digest of the Ordinances and Resolutions of the Second Municipality and of the General Council of the City of New Orleans, applicable thereto, January, 1848. By F. R. Southmayd, Sec'y.
TEXAS LIBRARY AND HISTORICAL COMMISSION. *Journal of the Secession Convention of Texas, 1861.* Austin, 1912.

MAGAZINES AND PERIODICALS

The American Review: a Whig Journal. . . . 16 vols. New York, 1845-1852.
DeBow's Commercial Review of the South and West. 38 vols. New Orleans, 1846-1870.
Hunt's Merchants' Magazine and Commercial Review. 63 vols. New York, 1839-1870.
Niles' Weekly (National) Register (Vols. L-LXXV). 75 vols. Baltimore and Philadelphia, 1811-1849.
The Southern Literary Messenger. 36 vols. Richmond, 1834-1864.
The Southern Quarterly Review. 26 vols. Charleston, etc., January, 1842 to January, 1856.
The United States Magazine and Democratic Review. 43 vols. Washington, 1838-1859.
The Western Journal and Civilian. 13 vols. St. Louis, 1848-1855.

NEWSPAPERS

New York *Herald,* January-June, 1854; July-December, 1857; January-June, 1859; July, 1860-June, 1861.
New York *Times,* 1861.
Baltimore *Sun,* July, 1852-June, 1853.

Daily National Intelligencer (Washington), 1844-1846; 1850-1851; 1856; 1860-1861.
Richmond *Daily Whig*, 1851.
Richmond *Daily Enquirer*, 1838, 1856, 1857.
Richmond *Semi-Weekly Enquirer*, 1850, 1852-1854.
Raleigh *Register*, 1839-1840.
Charleston (S. C.) *Daily Courier*, July, 1837-June, 1839; 1854-1856.
Charleston *Mercury*, July-December, 1838; 1858-1859.
Savannah *Daily Republican*, January-June, 1837; January-June, 1838; January-June, 1839; July-December, 1856.
Montgomery *Daily Confederation*, 1858-1859.
New Orleans *Picayune*, January-June, 1858.
New Orleans *Commercial Bulletin*, January-June, 1855.
New Orleans *Delta*, 1858.
New Orleans *True Delta*, 1859.
Memphis *Daily Eagle*, 1845.
Memphis *Eagle and Enquirer*, 1853.
Memphis *Daily Appeal*, January-June, 1853.
Republican Banner and Nashville Whig, July, 1856-December, 1857.

PAMPHLETS

MALLORY, FRANCIS. *Report on the Commercial Condition of the Commonwealth of Virginia. Presented to the Commercial Convention convened in Richmond, June 13, 1838.* Petersburg, 1838.
Convention of Merchants and Others for the Promotion of Direct Trade, 1839. Charleston, 1839.
DICKSON, SAMUEL H. *Address delivered at the Opening of the New Edifice of the Charleston Apprentices' Library Society, January 13, 1841.* . . . Charleston, 1841.
Southern State Rights, Free Trade and Anti-Abolition Tract No. 1. (Includes Letter of Langdon Cheves; Jackson's Letter on Texas; J. Q. Adams's Disunion Letter, etc.) Charleston, 1844.
A Reply to the Letter of the Hon. Langdon Cheves. By a Southerner. Charleston, 1844 (?).
GREGG, WILLIAM. *Essays on Domestic Industry; or an Inquiry into the Expediency of Establishing Cotton Manufactures in South Carolina.* Charleston, 1845.
———— *Inquiry into the Propriety of Granting Charters to the Manufacturers of South Carolina. By One of the People.* Charleston, 1845.
Journal of the Proceedings of the Southwestern Convention. . . . *Memphis* . . . *12th November, 1845.* Memphis, 1845.
HAMMOND, JAMES H. *Letters on Southern Slavery; Addressed to Thomas Clarkson, the English Abolitionist.* Charleston, 1848 (written in 1845).
ABBOTT, LAWRENCE. *Letters from the Hon.* . . . *to the Hon. William C. Rives of Virginia.* Boston, 1846.
A Voice from the South: Comprising Letters from Georgia to Massachusetts, and to the Southern States. Baltimore, 1847.
FISHER, ELLWOOD. *Lecture on the North and the South; Delivered before the Young Men's Mercantile Library Association of Cincinnati, Ohio, January 16, 1849.* Cincinnati, 1849.

Proceedings of the National Railroad Convention, which assembled in the City of St. Louis, on the fifteenth day of October, 1849. . . . St. Louis, 1849.

Minutes and Proceedings of the Memphis Convention assembled October 23, 1849. Memphis, 1849.

National Plan of an Atlantic and Pacific Railroad and Remarks of Albert Pike made thereon, at Memphis, November, 1849. Memphis, 1849.

JAMES, CHARLES T. *Practical Hints on the Comparative Cost and Productiveness of the Culture of Cotton, and the Cost and Productiveness of its Manufacture. Addressed to the Cotton Planters and Capitalists of the South.* 1849.

SMITH, HAMILTON. *Cannelton, Perry County, Indiana, at the Intersection of the Eastern Margin of the Illinois Coal Basin.* . . . Louisville, 1850.

Proceedings of the Convention in Favor of a National Road to the Pacific Ocean. . . . *Philadelphia, April 1st, 2nd and 3rd, 1850.* Philadelphia, 1850.

TRESCOTT, WILLIAM H. *The Position and Course of the South.* Charleston, 1850.

TOWNSEND, JOHN. *The Southern States; Their Present Peril and their Certain Remedy.* ———, 1850.

BRYAN, EDWARD B. *The Rightful Remedy. Addressed to the Slaveholders of the South.* Charleston, 1850.

GARNETT, MUSCOE R. H. *The Union, Past and Future: How It Works and How to Save It.* Washington, 1850.

DERBY, E. H. *Reality versus Fiction; a Review of a Pamphlet* . . . *entitled, "The Union, Past and Future. . . ."* Boston, 1850.

GRAYSON, W. J. *Letter to his Excellency, Whitemarsh B. Seabrook, Governor of . . South Carolina, on the Dissolution of the Union.* Charleston, 1850.

[MAGRATH A. G.] *A Letter of Southern Wrongs and Southern Remedies; addressed to the Hon. W. J. Grayson, in reply to his Letter to the Governor of South Carolina.* . . . Charleston, 1850.

CHEVES, LANGDON. *Speech of* . . . *Delivered before the* . . . *Nashville Convention,* . . . *November 15, 1850.* Columbia, 1850.

Southern Rights Association. Barnwell District, South Carolina, Meeting, January 6, 1851. ——— 1851.

Proceedings of the Meeting of Delegates from the Southern Rights Associations of South Carolina, held at Charleston, May, 1851. Columbia, 1851.

Proceedings of the Great Southern Co-operation and Anti-Secession Meeting, Held in Charleston, September 23, 1851. Charleston, 1851.

BARNARD, F. A. P. *Oration delivered before the Citizens of Tuscaloosa, Alabama, July 4, 1851.* Tuscaloosa, 1851.

ELLIOTT, HON. WILLIAM. *The Letters of Agricola.* Greenville, S. C., 1852. (First published, 1851.)

Address to the People of the Southern and Western States, and more particularly to those of La., Tex., Miss., Ala., Tenn., Ark., Ky., and Mo. (By a committee, in behalf of the New Orleans Railroad Convention, 1852). New Orleans, 1851.

Proceedings of the Southern and Western Commercial Convention, at Memphis, Tennessee, in June, 1853. . . . Memphis, 1854.

Graniteville Manufacturing Company. Report of the President and Treasurer for the Year 1854. (William Gregg, Pres.) Charleston, 1855.

CAREY, HENRY C.| *The North and the South.* (Reprinted from the New York Tribune.) 1854.

Journal of the Proceedings of the Commercial Convention of the Southern and Western States, . . . *Charleston* . . . *Commencing* . . . *10th April, 1854.* Charleston, 1854.

Two Tracts for the Times, the one entitled, "*Negro Slavery No Evil,*" *by B. F. Stringfellow, of Missouri; the other,* "*An Answer to the Inquiry, 'Is It Expedient to Introduce Slavery into Kansas?'* " *by D. R. Goodloe, of North Carolina.* Boston, 1855.

GREGG, WM. *Speech of* . . . *on the Bill* . . . *to authorize aid to the Blue Ridge Railroad Company in South Carolina.* Columbia, 1857.

WESTON, GEORGE M. *The Poor Whites of the South.* Washington, 1856.

BURWELL, WILLIAM. *True Policy of the South, with Suggestions for the Settlement of our Sectional Differences.* Washington, 1856.

Official Report of the Debates and Proceedings of the Southern Commercial Convention assembled at Knoxville, Tennessee, August 10, 1857. Knoxville, 1857. (An appendix contains the proceedings of the session at Savannah, December, 1856.)

Wealth, Resources and Hopes of Virginia. (From the *Daily Southern Argus.*) Norfolk, 1857.

FIELDER, HERBERT. *The Disunionist: a Brief Treatise upon the Evils of the Union* . . . *and the Propriety of a Separation and the Formation of a Southern United States.* ———, 1857.

HUGHES, HENRY. *Report* . . . *read before the Southern Commercial Convention at Vicksburg, May 10, 1859, on the subject of the African Apprentice System.* Vicksburg, 1859.

Third Annual Report of the Merchants' and Mechanics' Exchange of Norfolk, Virginia, January, 1860.

TOWNSEND, JOHN. *The South Alone Should Govern the South.* . . . Charleston. 1860.

——— *The Doom of Slavery in the Union: Its Safety out of It.* (2d ed.) Charleston, 1860.

ROBB, JAMES. *A Southern Confederacy. Letters by* . . ., *Late a Citizen of New Orleans to an American in Paris and the Honorable Alexander H. Stephens of Georgia.*

THORNWELL, J. H. *The State of the Country: An Article republished from the Southern Presbyterian Review.* New York, 1861.

Tracts for the Times in Relation to African Labor, the Future Supply of Cotton and Popular Government in North America (N. Y. *Herald* reprint). 1861.

ATKINSON, EDWARD. *Cheap Cotton by Free Labor, by a Cotton Manufacturer.* Boston, 1861.

COLWELL, STEPHEN. *The Five Cotton States and New York; or Remarks upon the Social and Economic Aspects of the Southern Political Crisis.* Philadelphia, 1861.

LORD, DANIEL. *The Effect of Secession upon the Commercial Relations between the North and South and upon each Section* (New York *Times* reprint). 1861.

POWELL, SAMUEL. *Notes on "Southern Wealth and Northern Profits."* Philadelphia, 1861.

COLLINS, WILLIAM H. *Third Address to the People of Maryland, by* . . . *of Baltimore.* Baltimore, 1861.

——— *Address to the People of Maryland by* . . . *of Baltimore.* Baltimore, 1861.

HOLT, JOSEPH. *Letter from Hon.* ——— *to J. F. Speed, Esq.* ——— 1861.

CLARKE, JAMES FREEMAN. *Secession, Concession, or Self-Possession, Which?* Boston, 1861.

KENNEDY, JOHN P. *The Border States, their Power and Duty in the Present Disordered Conditions of the Country.* ————, 1860.

South Carolina, Disunion, and a Mississippi Valley Confederacy [by a Kentuckian]. ————, 1861.

SEGAR, JOSEPH. *Letter . . . to a Friend in Virginia in Vindication of his Course in Declining to follow his State into Secession.* Washington, 1862.

OWEN, ROBERT DALE. *The Future of the Northwest in Connection with the Scheme of Reconstruction without New England.* Philadelphia, 1863.

TRENHOLM, W. L. *The Centennial Address before the Charleston Chamber of Commerce, 11th February, 1884.* . . . Charleston, 1884.

PUBLISHED DIARIES, SPEECHES, AND CONTEMPORARY CORRESPONDENCE

BROWN, AARON V. *Speeches, Congressional and Political, and other Writings.* Nashville, 1854.

CALHOUN, JOHN C. *Correspondence of John C. Calhoun.* Edited by J. F. Jameson. (Amer. Hist. Assoc., *Report,* 1899, Vol. II.) Washington, 1900.

———— *Works of John C. Calhoun.* Edited by R. K. Cralle. 6 vols. New York, 1854-1855.

CAPERS, HENRY D. *Life and Times of C. G. Memminger.* Richmond, 1893.

CHITTENDEN, L. E. *A Report of the Debates and Proceedings in the Secret Sessions of the Conference Convention, for proposing Amendments to the Constitution of the United States. Held at Washington, D. C. in February, A. D. 1861.* New York, 1864.

CLAIBORNE, J. F. H. *Life and Correspondence of John A. Quitman.* 2 vols. New York, 1860.

CLEVELAND, H. *Alexander H. Stephens in Public and Private.* Philadelphia, 1866.

CLINGMAN, THOMAS L. *Speeches and Writings.* Raleigh, 1878.

COBB, T. R. R. *Correspondence of . . . , 1860-1862* (So. History Assoc., *Publ.,* XI, 147-86; 233-61; 308-28.) Richmond, 1907.

COLEMAN, MRS. CHAPMAN. *The Life of John J. Crittenden, with Selections from his Correspondence and Speeches.* 2 vols. Philadelphia, 1871.

COLTON, CALVIN. *Life, Correspondence and Speeches of Henry Clay.* 6 vols. New York, 1854.

FIELDER, H. *Life, Times, and Speeches of Joseph E. Brown.* Springfield, Mass., 1883.

HAMILTON, J. G. DE R. *The Correspondence of Jonathan Worth.* 2 vols. Raleigh, 1909.

———— *The Papers of Thomas Ruffin; Collected and Edited by* ————. 2 vols. Raleigh, 1918.

HILL, BENJAMIN H., JR. *Senator Benjamin H. Hill of Georgia, His Life, Speeches and Addresses.* Atlanta, 1891.

HILLIARD, HENRY W. *Speeches and Addresses.* New York, 1855.

HULL, A. L. "The Making of the Confederate Constitution," So. Hist. Assoc., *Publ.,* IX, 272-92 (Letters of T. R. R. Cobb).

HUNTER, ROBERT M. T. *Correspondence of* . . . . Edited by C. H. Ambler. (American Hist. Assoc., *Report*, 1916, Vol. II.) Washington, 1918.

JOHNSTON, R. M., and BROWNE, W. H. *Life of Alexander H. Stephens.* Philadelphia, 1878.

JONES, JOHN B. *A Rebel War Clerk's Diary at the Confederate States' Capital.* 2 vols. Philadelphia, 1866.

MASON, VIRGINIA. *The Public Life and Diplomatic Correspondence of James M. Mason with Some Personal History by* . . . *his daughter.* Roanoke, Va., 1906.

PHILLIPS, U. B., ed. *The Correspondence of Robert Toombs, Alexander H. Stephens and Howell Cobb.* (Amer. Hist. Assoc., *Report*, 1911, Vol. II.) Washington, 1913.

QUAIFE, M. M. *The Diary of James K. Polk.* 4 vols. Chicago, 1910.

ROWLAND, DUNBAR, ed. *Jefferson Davis, Constitutionalist: his Letters, Papers and Speeches.* 10 Vols. Jackson, Miss., 1923.

SEWARD, WILLIAM H. *An Autobiography from 1801-1834; with a Memoir of his Life, etc., 1832-1872, by Frederick W. Seward.* 3 vols. New York, 1891.

SMITH, WILLIAM R. *The History and Debates of the Convention of the People of Alabama, begun and held in the City of Montgomery, on the seventh day of January, 1861.* . . . Montgomery, 1861.

TYLER, LYON G. *Letters and Times of the Tylers.* 3 vols. Richmond and Williamsburg, 1884-1896.

UNPUBLISHED CORRESPONDENCE, DIARIES, AND PAPERS[1]

William Burwell Papers.
J. J. Crittenden Papers.
J. H. Hammond Papers.
M. F. Maury Papers.
Edmund Ruffin's Diary.
Whitemarsh B. Seabrook Papers.

MEMOIRS AND REMINISCENCES

BENTON, THOMAS H. *Thirty Years' View, or a History of the Workings of the American Government for Thirty Years, from 1820 to 1850.* 2 vols. New York, 1854.

BOTTS, JOHN M. *The Great Rebellion: Its Secret History, Rise, Progress, and Disastrous Failure.* New York, 1866.

BROWNLOW, W. G. *Sketches of the Rise, Progress and Decline of Secession; with a Narrative of Personal Adventures among the Rebels.* Philadelphia, 1862.

BUCHANAN, JAMES. *Mr. Buchanan's Administration on the Eve of the Rebellion.* New York, 1866.

CHESNUT, MARY B. *A Diary from Dixie* . . . . New York, 1916.

CLAIBORNE. J. F. H. *Mississippi as a Province, Territory, and State.* Jackson, 1880.

FOOTE, HENRY S. *Casket of Remininiscences.* Washington, 1874.

———— *War of the Rebellion; or, Scylla and Charybdis.* New York, 1866.

GARRETT, WILLIAM. *Reminiscences of Public Men in Alabama for Thirty Years.* Atlanta, 1872.

GREEN, DUFF. *Facts and Suggestions, Biographical, Historical, Financial and Polical.* New York, 1866.

----

[1]Preserved in the Library of Congress.

HILLIARD, HENRY W. *Politics and Pen Pictures at Home and Abroad.* New York, 1892.

HOLDEN, W.W. *Memoirs of* . . . . Edited by Wm. K. Boyd. (John Lawson Monographs of the Trinity College Hist. Soc.) Durham, N. C., 1911.

PERRY, B. F. *Biographical Sketches of Eminent American Statesmen, with Speeches, Addresses and Letters.* Philadelphia, 1887.

PRYOR, MRS. ROGER A. *Reminiscences of Peace and War.* New York, 1905.

SARGENT, NATHAN. *Public Men and Events from the Commencement of Mr. Monroe's Administration, in 1817, to the close of Mr. Fillmore's Administration, in 1853,* Vol. II. 2 vols. Philadelphia, 1875.

BOOKS OF TRAVEL OR DESCRIPTION, STATISTICAL WORKS, AND DIRECTORIES

BANCROFT, JOSEPH. *Census of the City of Savannah, together with Statistics relating to the Trade, Commerce, Mechanical Arts, and Health of the same;* . . . 2d ed. Savannah, 1848.

BUCKINGHAM, J. S. *The Slave States of America.* 2 vols. London, 1842.

CAMPBELL, JOHN P. *The Southern Business Directory and General Commercial Advertiser.* . . . Charleston, 1854.

CHASE, HENRY and SANBORN, C. H. *The North and the South: A Statistical View of the Condition of the Free and the Slave States.* New York, 1856.

CIST, CHARLES. *Sketches and Statistics of Cincinnati in 1851.* Cincinnati, 1851.

———— *Sketches and Statistics of Cincinnati in 1859.* Cincinnati, 1859.

DAWSON, J. L., and DeSAUSSURE, H. W. *Census of the City of Charleston, South Carolina for the year 1848;* . . . . Charleston, 1849.

FEATHERSTONHAUGH, GEORGE W. *Excursion through the Slave States.* New York, 1844.

FORREST, WILLIAM S. *The Norfolk Directory, for 1851-1852* . . . . Norfolk, 1852.

KEMBLE, MRS. FRANCES ANNE. *Journal of a Residence on a Georgia Plantation in 1838-1839.* New York, 1863.

LYELL, SIR CHARLES. *A Second Visit to the United States.* 2 vols. London, 1849.

MACKAY, CHARLES. *Life and Liberty in America; or Sketches of a Tour in the United States and Canada in 1857-1858.* New York, 1859.

PITKIN, TIMOTHY. *Statistical View of the Commerce of the United States.* 2d ed. New York, 1817.

ROBERTSON, JAMES. *A Few Months in America* . . . . London, 1865.

RUSSELL, ROBERT. *North America; Its Agriculture and Climate,* . . . . Edinburgh, 1858.

RUSSELL, WILLIAM H. *Pictures of Southern Life, Social, Political, and Military.* New York, 1861.

STIRLING, JAMES. *Letters from the Slave States.* London, 1857.

TUCKER, GEORGE. *Progress of the United States in Wealth and Population.* New York, 1843.

WHITE, GEORGE. *Statistics of the State of Georgia, Including an Account of Its Natural, Civil and Ecclesiastical History.* . . . Savannah, 1849.

CONTEMPORARY MONOGRAPHS, SPECIAL WORKS, AND BOOKS OF A CONTROVERSIAL CHARACTER

ADAMS, REV. NEHEMIAH. *A Southside View of Slavery, or Three Months at the South.* Boston, 1854.

BATCHELDER, S. *Introduction and Early Progress of Cotton Manufacture in the United States.* Boston, 1863.

BLEDSOE, ARTHUR TAYLOR. *An Essay on Liberty and Slavery.* Philadelphia, 1856.

CAIRNES, J. E. *The Slave Power. Its Character, Career and Probable Design.* 2d. ed. London, 1863.

CARPENTER, S. D. *The Logic of History.* Madison, Wis. 1864.

CHRISTY, DAVID. *Cotton is King, and Its Relation to Agriculture, Manufactures, and Commerce,* . . . . 2d. ed. New York, 1856.

COBB, T. R. R. *An Inquiry into the Law of Negro Slavery.* Philadelphia, 1858.

DAVIS, JEFFERSON. *Rise and Fall of the Confederate Government.* 2 vols. New York. 1881.

ELLIOTT, E. N., ed. *Cotton is King and Pro-Slavery Arguments, Comprising the Writings of Hammond, Harper, Christy, Stringfellow, Hodge, Bledsoe, and Cartwright* . . . . Augusta, 1860. (These writings can be found separately.)

FITZHUGH, GEORGE. *Cannibals All, or Slaves without Masters.* Richmond, 1856.

———— *Sociology for the South, or the Failure of Free Society.* Richmond, 1854.

GOODLOE, DANIEL R. *An Inquiry into the Causes which have Retarded the Accumulation of Wealth and Increase of Population in the Southern States* . . . . Washington, 1846.

GOODELL, WILLIAM. *Slavery and Anti-slavery; a History of the Great Struggle in both Hemispheres,* . . . . New York, 1852.

GREELEY, HORACE. *The American Conflict.* 2 vols. Hartford, 1864.

HARPER, WILLIAM. *The Pro-Slavery Argument as Maintained by the Most Distinguished Writers of the Southern States, containing the several essays on the subject, of Chancellor Harper, Dr. Simms, and Professor Dew.* Philadelphia, 1852.

HELPER, HINTON R. *The Impending Crisis of the South, How to Meet It.* New York, 1857.

HILDRETH, RICHARD. *Despotism in America.* Boston, 1854.

HODGSON, JOSEPH. *The Cradle of the Confederacy; or, the Times of Troup, Quitman, and Yancey.* Mobile, 1876.

KETTELL, THOMAS PRENTICE. *Southern Wealth and Northern Profits, as exhibited in Statistical Facts and Official Figures.* New York, 1860.

LUNT, GEORGE. *The Origin of the Late War; Traced from the Beginning of the Constitution to the Revolt of the Southern States.* New York, 1866.

OLMSTED, FREDERICK LAW. *A Journey in the Seaboard Slave States, with Remarks on their Economy.* New York, 1856, New York (Putnam's, 2 vols.), 1904.

———— *A Journey through Texas.* . . . New York, 1857.

———— *A Journey in the Back Country.* 2 vols. New York (Putnam's), 1907.

———— *The Cotton Kingdom, a Traveller's Observations on Cotton and Slavery.* 2d ed. 2 vols. New York, 1862.

POLLARD, E. A. *The Life of Jefferson Davis, with a Secret History of the Southern Confederacy.* . . . Philadelphia, 1869.

———— *The Lost Cause; a New Southern History of the War of the Confederates.* New York, 1867.

RUFFIN, EDMUND. *Anticipations of the Future to Serve as Lessons for the Present Time*. Richmond, 1860.

RUSSELL, WILLIAM H. *My Diary North and South*. Boston, 1863.

[SCOTT, JOHN]. *The Lost Principle; or the Sectional Equilibrium; How It Was Created—How Destroyed—How It May be Restored. By "Barbarossa."* Richmond, 1860.

STEPHENS, ALEXANDER H. *A Constitutional View of the Late War Between the States*. 2 vols. Philadelphia, 1868-1870.

TUCKER, BEVERLY. *The Partisan Leader*. Washington, 1836, New York, 1861.

VAN EVRIE, DR. JOHN H. *Negroes and Negro Slavery*. New York, 1853.

WARE, N. A. *Notes on Political Economy, as Applicable to the United States, by a Southern Planter*. New York, 1844.

WESTON, GEORGE M. *The Progress of Slavery in the United States*. Washington, 1858.

WILSON, HENRY. *History of the Rise and Fall of the Slave Power in America*. 3 vols. Boston, 1872-1877.

WOLFE, S. M. *Helper's Impending Crisis Dissected*. Philadelphia, 1860.

COLLECTIONS OF SOURCES

AMES, HERMAN V. *State Documents on Federal Relations*. Philadelphia, 1906.

American Annual Cyclopedia and Register of Important Events, Vols. I and II. (Appleton's) New York, 1862 ——.

CALLENDAR, G. S. *Selections from the Economic History of the United States, 1756-1860*. Boston, New York, 1909.

CLUSKY, MICHAEL W. *The Political Text Book, or Encyclopedia*. Philadelphia, 1858.

COMMONS, J. R., et al. *A Documentary History of American Industrial Society*, Vols. I and II: *Plantation and Frontier*. Edited by U. B. Phillips. Cleveland, 1909.

DEBOW, J. D. B. *Industrial Resources, etc., of the Southern and Western States*. 3 vols. New Orleans, 1852-1853.

Great Debates in American History, Vol. V: *State Rights, 1798-1861, Slavery, 1858-1861*. M. M. Miller, ed. New York, 1913.

HAMBLETON, JAMES P. *A Biographical Sketch of Henry A. Wise, with a History of the Political Campaign in Virginia in 1855*. Richmond, 1856.

McPHERSON, EDWARD. *The Political History of the United States of America during the Great Rebellion*. 3d ed. Washington, 1876.

MOORE, FRANK. *The Rebellion Record: A Diary of American Events with Documents, Narrative, Illustrative Incidents, etc.*, Vols. I and II. (Putnam's) New York.

PIKE, JAMES S. *First Blows of the Civil War. The Ten Years of Preliminary Conflict in the United States*. New York, 1879.

POORE, B. P. *Federal and State Constitutions, Colonial Charters and Other Organic Laws of the United States*. Washington, 1877.

RICHARDSON, JAMES D. *Compilation of the Messages and Papers of the Presidents*, Vols. III-VI. 10 vols. Washington, 1896.

—— *A Compilation of the Messages and Papers of the Confederacy, Including the Diplomatic Correspondence, 1861-1865*. 2 vols. Nashville, 1905.

RECENT MONOGRAPHS AND SPECIAL ARTICLES AND WORKS[2]

*AMBLER, CHARLES H. *Sectionalism in Virginia from 1776-1861.* Chicago, 1910.
———— *Thomas Ritchie: A Study in Virginia Politics.* Richmond, 1913.
BALLAGH, J. C. *A History of Slavery in Virginia* (Johns Hopkins Univ., *Studies*, Sup. Vol. XXIV). Baltimore, 1902.
———— *Southern Economic History: Tariff and Public Lands* (Amer. Hist. Assoc., *Report*, 1898). Washington, 1899.
BATES, WILLIAM W. *American Navigation; the Political History of its Rise and Ruin.* Boston and New York, 1902.
BOGART, E. L. *The Economic History of the United States.* New York, 1907.
BOLLES, A. S. *Industrial History of the United States.* . . . Norwich, Conn., 1879.
*BOUCHER, CHAUNCEY S. *The Nullification Controversy in South Carolina.* Chicago, 1916.
*———— *The Ante-Bellum Attitude of South Carolina towards Manufactures and Agriculture* (Washington Univ. Humanistic Studies, Vol. III, Pt. II, No. 2). St. Louis, 1916.
BOUCHER, CHAUNCEY S. *The Secession and Co-operation Movements in South Carolina, 1848 to 1852* (Washington Univ. Humanistic Studies, Vol. V, Pt. II, No. 2). 1918.
———— *South Carolina and the South on the Eve of Secession, 1852-1860* (Washington Univ. Humanistic Studies, Vol. VI, Pt. II, No. 2). 1919.
BOYD, WILLIAM K. "North Carolina on the Eve of Secession," Amer. Hist. Assoc., *Report*, 1910, pp. 167-77. Washington, 1912.
BROWN, WILLIAM GARROTT. *The Lower South in American History.* New York, 1902.
CALLAHAN, JAMES MORTON. *The Diplomatic History of the Southern Confederacy.* Baltimore, 1910.
———— "The Mexican Policy of Southern Leaders under Buchanan's Administration," Amer. Hist. Assoc., *Report*, 1910, pp. 135-51.
CALLENDER, G. S. "Early Transportation and Banking Enterprises of the States," *Quar. Jour. of Econ.*, XVII, 111-162. Boston, 1902.
CLARK, VICTOR S. *History of Manufactures in the United States, 1607-1860.* Washington, 1916.
*COLE, ARTHUR C. *The Whig Party in the South.* Washington, 1913.
———— "The South and the Right of Secession in the Early Fifties," *Miss. Val. Hist. Rev.*, I. Cedar Rapids, 1914.
COLLINS, WINFIELD H. *The Domestic Slave Trade of the Southern States.* New York, 1904.
COTTERILL, R. S. "Southern Railroads and Western Trade," *Miss. Val. Hist. Rev.*, III, 427-441.
———— "Memphis Railroad Convention, 1849," *Tenn. Hist. Mag.*, IV, 83-94.
COULTER, E. M. "Effects of Secession upon the Commerce of the Mississippi Valley," *Miss. Val. Hist. Rev.*, III, 276-300.

[2]No attempt has been made to list all the monographs and special articles and works which have bearing upon the subject, but only those are listed that have proved of some assistance in the preparation of this thesis. The most valuable are starred.

DAVIS, WILLIAM WATSON. *Ante-Bellum Southern Commercial Conventions* (Ala. Hist. Soc., *Transactions*, V, 153-202). Montgomery, 1904.

DAVIS, JOHN P. *The Union Pacific Railway: A Study in Railway Politics, History, and Economics.* Chicago, 1894.

DEWEY, DAVID R. *Financial History of the United States.* New York, 1915.

DILL, JACOB S. "Life Story of Commander Matthew Fontaine Maury," *Jour. Am. Hist.*, IV, 319-29.

DONNELL, E. J. *Chronological and Statistical History of Cotton.* New York, 1872.

DUBOIS, W. E. B. *The Suppression of the African Slave Trade to the United States of America, 1638-1870* (Harvard *Historical Studies*, Vol. I). New York, 1896.

ELLIS, HENRY G. "The Influence of Industrial and Educational Leaders on the Secession of Virginia," *So. Atlan. Quar.*, IX, 372-76.

FERTIG, J. W. *Secession and Reconstruction of Tennessee.* Chicago, 1898.

FICKLIN, JOHN ROSE. *History of Reconstruction in Louisiana, through 1868* (Johns Hopkins Univ. *Studies*, Series XXVII, No. 1). 1910.

FISH, CARL RUSSELL. "The Decision of the Ohio Valley," Amer. Hist. Assoc., *Report*, 1910, pp. 153-64.

FLEMING, WALTER T. "Immigration to the Southern States," *Pol. Sci. Quar.*, XX, 276-297. New York, 1905.

GARNER, JAMES W. "The First Struggle over Secession in Mississippi," Miss. Hist. Soc., *Publ.*, Vol. IV. Oxford, Miss., 1901.

HAMER, PHILIP MAY. *The Secession Movement in South Carolina, 1847-1852.* Allentown, Pa., 1918.

HAMILTON, J. G. DE R. *Reconstruction in North Carolina* (Columbia Univ. *Studies*, Vol. LVIII, No. 141). New York, 1914.

*HAMMOND, M. B. *The Cotton Industry: An Essay in American Economic History, Part I: The Cotton Culture and the Cotton Trade.* New York, 1897.

HEARON, CLEO. *Mississippi and the Compromise of 1850* (Miss. Hist. Soc., *Publ.*, XIV). Oxford, Miss., 1914.

HOUSTON, D. F. *A Critical Study of Nullification in South Carolina* (Harvard *Historical Studies*, Vol. III). New York, 1896.

*INGLE, EDWARD. *Southern Sidelights: A Picture of Social and Economic Life in the South a Generation before the War.* New York, 1896.

———— "Two Southern Magazines," So. Hist. Assoc., *Publications*, I. Washington, 1897.

JACK, T. H. *Sectionalism and Party Politics in Alabama, 1819-1842.* Menasha, Wis., 1919.

JACOBSTEIN, MEYER. *The Tobacco Industry in the United States* (Columbia Univ. *Studies*, Vol. XXVI, No. 3). 1907.

MAYES, EDWARD. "Origin of the Pacific Railroads, and especially of the Southern Pacific" (Miss. Hist. Soc., *Publ.*, Vol. VI). Oxford, Miss., 1902.

MILLION, JOHN W. *State Aid to Railways in Missouri.* Chicago, 1896.

MUNFORD, B. B. *Virginia's Attitude toward Slavery and Secession.* New York, 1909.

PAGE, THOMAS NELSON. *The Old South: Essays Social and Political.* New York, 1896.

———— *Social Life in Virginia before the War.* New York, 1898.

*PHILLIPS, ULRICH B. *American Negro Slavery; a Survey of the Supply, Employment, and Control of Negro Labor as Determined by the Plantation Regime*. New York, 1918.

*———— *Georgia and State Rights* (Amer. Hist. Assoc., *Report*, 1901, Vol. II). Washington, 1902.

———— *A History of Transportation in the Eastern Cotton Belt to 1860*. New York, 1908.

———— "The Origin and Growth of the Southern Black Belts," *Amer. Hist. Rev.*, XI, 798-815. New York, 1906.

———— "The Economic Cost of Slaveholding," *Pol. Sci. Quar.*, XX, 257-75. 1905.

———— "The Slave Labor Problem in the Charleston District," *Pol. Sci. Quar.*, XXII, 416-439. 1907.

———— "The Decadence of the Plantation System," *An. of the Amer. Acad. of Pol. and Soc. Sci.*, XXXV, 37-41. Philadelphia, 1910.

———— "The Literary Movement for Secession," *Studies in Southern History and Politics*, ch. II. New York, 1914.

RAMSDELL, CHARLES W. "The Frontier and Secession," *Studies in Southern History and Politics*, ch. III.

REED, J. C. *The Brothers War*. Boston, 1905.

RINGWALT, JOHN L. *Development of Transportation Systems in the United States*. Philadelphia, 1888.

*SCHAPER, W. A. *Sectionalism and Representation in South Carolina* (Amer. Hist. Assoc., *Report*, 1900, Vol. I). Washington, 1901.

*SCHWAB, J. C. *The Confederate States of America, 1861-1865*. New York, 1901.

SCOTT, W. A. *Repudication of State Debts* . . . New York, 1893.

SIOUSSAT, ST. GEORGE L. "Tennessee, the Compromise of 1850, and the Nashville Convention," *Miss. Val. Hist. Rev.*, II, 313 ff.

———— "Memphis as a Gateway to the West," *Tenn. Hist. Mag.*, 1917, pp. 1-27, 77-114.

*STONE, A. H. "The American Factorage System of the Southern States," *Amer. Hist. Rev.*, XX, 557 ff. 1914-1915.

———— "Some Problems of Southern Economic History," *Amer. Hist. Rev.*, XIII, 779-97. 1907-1908.

TAUSSIG, WILLIAM. *The Tariff History of the United States*. New York, 1914.

THOMPSON, HOLLAND. *From Cotton Field to Cotton Mill. A Study of the Industrial Transition in North Carolina*. New York, 1906.

TILLINGHAST, J. A. *The Negro in Africa and America*. New York, 1902.

*TREXLER, H. A. *Slavery in Missouri, 1804-1865* (Johns Hopkins Univ. *Studies*, Series XXXII, No. II). 1914.

WAGSTAFF, H. M. *State Rights and Political Parties in North Carolina, 1776-1861* (Johns Hopkins Univ. *Studies*, Series XXIV). 1906.

WEAVER, C. C. *Internal Improvements in North Carolina previous to 1860* (Johns Hopkins Univ. *Studies*, Series XXI, Nos. III and IV). 1903.

BIOGRAPHIES AND BIOGRAPHICAL SKETCHES

BASSETT, JOHN S. *The Life of Andrew Jackson*. 2 vols. New York, 1911.

BUTLER, PIERCE. *Judah P. Benjamin*. Philadelphia, 1907.

CALDWELL, J. W. "John Bell of Tennessee," *Amer. Hist. Rev.*, IV, 651-64. 1899.
COLTON, CALVIN. *The Life and Times of Henry Clay.* 2 vols. New York, 1846.
DAVIS, MRS. VARINA H. *Jefferson Davis, Ex-President of the Confederate States: a Memoir.* 2 vols. New York, 1890.
DODD, WILLIAM E. *Jefferson Davis.* Philadelphia, 1907.
DUBOSE, J. W. *Life and Times of W. L. Yancey.* Birmingham, 1892.
ELLIS, H. G. *Edmund Ruffin, His Life and Times (Branch Historical Papers*, Vol. III, 100-23). Richmond, 1903.
HALL, CLIFTON R. *Andrew Johnson, Military Governor of Tennessee.* London, 1916.
HUNT, GAILLARD. *John C. Calhoun.* Philadelphia, 1908.
JERVEY, THEODORE. *Robert Y. Hayne and his Times.* New York, 1909.
MAYES, EDWARD. *Lucius Q. C. Lamar: His Life, Times and Speeches, 1825-1893.* Nashville, 1896.
PHILLIPS, ULRICH B. *The Life of Robert Toombs.* New York, 1913.
STOVALL, P. A. *Robert Toombs: Statesman, Speaker, Soldier, Sage.* New York, 1892.
TRENT, W. P. *William Gilmore Simms.* Boston and New York, 1892.
WHEELER, JOHN H. *Reminiscences and Memoirs of North Carolina and Eminent North Carolinians.* Columbus, 1884.
WISE, BARTON H. *Life of Henry A. Wise.* New York, 1899.

STATE AND LOCAL HISTORIES

AVERY, ISAAC. *The History of the State of Georgia from 1850 to 1881;* . . . New York, 1881.
BROWN, WILLIAM G. *A History of Alabama.* New York, 1900.
BURTON, H. W. *The History of Norfolk.* Norfolk, 1877.
CABLE, GEORGE W. *History and Present Condition of New Orleans (Tenth Census*, XIX, Pt. II, 213-95).
CARR, LUCIEN. *Missouri, A Bone of Contention (American Commonwealths* series). Boston, 1888.
CORDOZA, J. N. *Reminiscences of Charleston.* Charleston, 1866.
FORREST, WILLIAM S. *Historical and Descriptive Sketches of Norfolk and Vicinity.* . . . Philadelphia, 1853.
FORTIER, ALCÉE. *The History of Louisiana*, Vol. IV. 4 vols. New York, 1904.
GARRISON, GEORGE P. *Texas (American Commonwealths* series). Boston, 1903.
GAYARRÉ, CHARLES. *History of Louisiana*, Vol. IV, *The American Domination.* 4 vols. New Orleans, 1903.
HAMILTON, PETER J. *Mobile of the Five Flags, the Story of the River Basin and Coast about Mobile from the Earliest Times to the Present.* Boston, 1913.
HOWISON, ROBERT R. *A History of Virginia from Its Discovery and Settlement by Europeans to the Present Time.* 2 vols. Philadelphia, 1848.
MCELROY, R. M. *Kentucky in the Nation's History.* New York, 1909.
MOORE, J. W. *History of North Carolina.* 2 vols. 1880.
ROWLAND, DUNBAR, ed. *Encyclopedia of Mississippi History.* 2 vols. Madison, 1907.
SHALER, N. S. *Kentucky (American Commonwealths* series). Boston, 1885.

GENERAL HISTORIES

Of the many general histories covering the period, the following have especially valuable chapters or sections dealing with topics discussed in this thesis:

The American Nation: A History, A. B. Hart, ed. 27 vols. New York, 1906—.
    Vol. 16, Hart, A. B., *Abolition and Slavery*, especially, chs. I-X.
    Vol. 17, GARRISON, GEORGE P., *Westward Extension*, ch. XII.
    Vol. 18, SMITH, T. C., *Parties and Slavery*, chs. IV, V, XIII, XIX, XX.
    Vol. 19, CHADWICK, F. E., *Causes of the Civil War*, chs. I-IV, IX.
The Chronicles of America Series, ALLEN JOHNSON, ed. 50 vols. New Haven, 1918—.
    Vol. 24, STEPHENSON, N. W., *Texas and the Mexican War*, especially ch. IX.
    Vol. 27, DODD, WILLIAM E., *The Cotton Kingdom*.
    Vol. 29, STEPHENSON, N. W., *Abraham Lincoln and the Union*, especially chs. I-VI.
    Vol. 30, STEPHENSON, N. W., *The Day of the Confederacy*, especially chs. I-IV.
DODD, W. E. *Expansion and Conflict*, chs. VII-XIV (Vol. III of the *Riverside History of the United States*). Boston, 1915.
HOLST, HERMAN E. VON. *Constitutional and Political History of the United States*, especially Vol. I, chs. IX, X; Vol. III, ch. XVII; Vol. VII, chs. VII, VIII. 8 vols. Chicago, 1877-92.
McMASTER, JOHN B. *A History of the People of the United States*, Vols. VII and VIII, *passim*. 8 vols. New York, 1888-1913.
RHODES, JAMES FORD. *History of the United States from the Compromise of 1850*, especially Vol. I, chs. I, IV; Vol. II, chs. XII-XV; Vol. III. 7 vols. New York, 1896-1906.
The South in the Building of the Nation, by J. A. C. Chandler, *et al.*, Vols. I-V, especially Vol. IV, Pt. III, ch. II. Richmond, 1909-13.
THORPE, FRANCIS NEWTON. *The Civil War: The National View*, chs. I-IV (Vol. XV of the *History of North America*, GUY CARLETON LEE, ed.). Philadelphia, 1906.

VITA

Robert R. Russell was born on a farm near Galva, Kansas, September 27, 1890. He attended rural school and later a two years high school in a near-by town. In 1906 he entered the Academy Department of McPherson College, McPherson, Kansas; he received his A.B. from that institution in 1914. The summer of 1914 and year 1914-1915 he did graduate work in the University of Kansas, receiving the A.M. degree in June. The subject of his thesis was "Early Projects for a Railroad to the Pacific." The two following years he did graduate work in the University of Illinois. He held fellowships in history during the three years of graduate study. He was elected a member of the Illinois Chapter of Phi Beta Kappa, 1917. Before graduation from college he taught three years in the grades and in high school. For two quarters, 1919, he was Assistant in History in the University of Illinois. For three years he was Professor of History in Ottawa University, Ottawa, Kansas. He is now teaching history in Western State Normal School, Kalamazoo, Michigan. During the War he served fifteen months in the United States Army.

INDEX

secession, 243, 251; project for steamship line to Europe, 256

New Orleans *Delta*, on Southern Commercial Convention, 132, 138; disunionist, 180

New Orleans *Picayune*, on panic of 1857, 103; on Southern Commercial Convention, 149; Union not detrimental to South, 192; against reviving slave trade, 223; on Southern progress, 230

Newton, Willoughby, Calhoun Democrat, 92; on economic benefits of secession, 184; on slavery and secession, 281

New York City, importance of Southern trade, 21; financial concentration, 101; finances movement of Southern staples, 101 f.; advantages over Southern cities, 110 ff.; steamship lines, 114, 117, 122; Southern expectations of effect of secession on, 188, 249

New York *Herald*, on Southern Commercial Convention, 144; on economic effects of secession, 192; represents business interests, friendly to South, 209; on causes of secession, 254

New York *Times*, on causes of secession, 253; opposes Morrill Tariff, 264

Non-intercourse with North discussed, 157-58, 175-76

Non-slaveholding whites, attitude toward slavery and slaveholders, 11, 53-54, 218-20, 223, 290; attitude toward secession, 239-43, 283-88; *see also* labor *and* poor whites

Norfolk, direct trade convention, 18; advantages and aspirations, 96; yellow fever, 112n.; proposed steamship lines, 116 ff.; and secession, 275, 285

North, advantages of union with South, 20 ff., 46, 48-49, 80 ff., 94-96, 104, 115, 182, 188, 190-91, 196-97, 207-10; North and South compared, 24, 33, 47-49, 205-6, 227-29; imports from South, 12, 108, 190; exports to South, 12, 24, 109, 190; commercial policy of Confederacy toward North considered by disunionists, 181, 183-84; formulated, 258-59, 261, 263, 265-67; relations of East and West and East and South compared, 186, 202; effects of secession on North considered, 188, 190-92, 194, 208, 235, 248-49, 253; class of Northerners encourage disunionists, 189-92; Northern opin-

ions of disunionist sentiment in South, 195-98; Northern views of causes of secession, 252-54; *see also* capital, commerce, manufactures, tariff

North Carolina, little interest in direct trade in 1830s, 31; agricultural depression, 34; growth of cotton manufactures, 41, 44, 227; disunion sentiment, 73, 74, 79n.; disunion arguments refuted, 88; people regret commercial dependence on Virginia and South Carolina, 97; tariff and discriminatory taxation questions, 161-62; state aid to railroad, 172-73; agricultural conditions, 203; ad valorem issue, 219, 287; sectionalism, 220, 287; secession defeated, 233; considerations affecting final decision for secession, 273-75, 276, 283n., 284, 287

Northerners and foreigners in South, as merchants, factors, etc., 19, 28, 198; in New Orleans and Mobile, 31; attitude toward slavery, 57, 220; merchants in cities and towns, 99-100

Nullifiers, in direct trade conventions, 17; on causes of commercial dependence, 22; origin, 65; party affiliations, 66; political principles 67-68; become disunionists, 68-72, 88-92; not satisfied by Tariff of 1846, 70, 162; for free trade and direct taxation, 163-65; *see also* Democratic party

Olmsted, F. L., on Southern imports, 108; on domestic slave trade, 211; and white labor in cotton industry, 221

Pacific railroad, 14, 94, 97, 290, 293; conventions at Memphis, St. Louis, and Philadelphia, 126; becomes sectional issue, 127, 135; considered in Southern Commercial Convention, 130, 132-36, 138, 139, 148; and railroad across Tehuantepec, 132; and Gadsden Purchase, 135; disunionists consider, 181; Texas interested, 262; and secession in Missouri, 280

Panic, of 1837, 16; specie payments suspended, 27; general stagnation of business, 30, 93; in Southwest, 31; effects of panic of 1857, 102-4, 199; South weathers better than North, 205

Seabrook, W. B., Governor of South
Carolina, and secession movement,
73-74; and state aid to manufactures,
155, 161
Secession movement, attitude of diversificationists, 58; disunionist views of
economic value of Union, 68-69, 72;
Bluffton movement and, 69-70;
growth of disunion sentiment, 70-73;
Nashville Convention and, 73-76;
contests over acceptance of compromise of 1850, 76-77; disunionist arguments, 77-88; secessionists (in 1850)
identified, 88-92; disunionists in
Southern Commercial Convention,
137-44, 149-50, 179; George Fitzhugh
and, 177; growth of disunion sentiment, 179; methods of propagating,
180; issue sought, 181; every aspect
considered, 181-82; various motives,
182; economic arguments for secession, 182-89, 291, 293; class of Northern writers encourages disunionism,
189-92; secessionists refuted in South,
192-95; Northern opinions of movement, 195-98; secessionists agitate
slave trade question, 213-14, 216,
270; secession of cotton states, 231-
33; secession delayed in border states,
233; arguments of secessionists, 234-
35, 236-38; of Unionists, 235-36, 237;
secessionists identified, 238-43; statements of causes, 243-48; expectations of economic benefits, 248-49;
border state views of causes, 249-52;
Northern views, 252-54; causes as
shown by economic policies of Confederacy, 255-70; desire to reopen
slave trade not the cause, 270-72;
considerations affecting decision of
border states, 273-88, 291; secessionists identified in, 283-86
Sectionalism, in Alabama, 220, 232, 241;
in Tennessee, Virginia, and North
Carolina, 220, 277, 287
Seward, W. H., effects of secession on
North, 196; on causes of secession,
252
Shipping and shipbuilding in South
12, 16, 25, 147, 227; Louisiana bonus,
170
Slavery, basis of sectionalism, 11, 13;
question little discussed in direct
trade conventions, 30; as cause of
Southern "decline," 47, 196-98, 290-
92; responsibility for poor whites,
53, 198, 223, 292; hostility toward in
South, 53-54, 218-20, 223, 286-88;

quarrels over augment interest in
manufactures, commerce, etc., 55-58,
98; struggles over cause growth of
disunion sentiment, 68, 71-76, 179,
182, 195, 197; Southern defense,
68, 72, 98, 176, 206-10, 290; quarrel
reaches bitter stage, 128; leads to
threats of commercial retaliation,
157-61, 169-70, 175; West becoming
hostile, 187; attitude of Northern
business interests, 189-92, 196, 209-
10; fears for as cause of secession,
234-36, 239-48, 250, 254, 269, 273,
281, 283-86, 291; in Confederate
Constitution, 269
Slaves, distribution, 11; employment in
factories suggested, 41, 54-55; tried,
55, 62, 210, 222; redundancy of labor,
55, 210; considered necessary to cotton industry, 207, 290; prices rise,
210; shift to black belts, 210-11;
foreign slave trade revived, 211, 215;
demand outrunning supply, 212, 220
ff.
Slave trade, movement to reopen the
foreign, discussed in Southern Commercial Convention, 139, 141, 143-44,
150, 213-15; disunionists and the
agitation, 181; origin and development of movement, 212-16; motives
and arguments of advocates and opponents, 216-24; attitude of border
states, 224; strength of movement,
224-25; desire to reopen as cause of
secession, 248, 250-51, 253, 270-72;
fears of revival delay secession of
border states, 280
Smith, Hamilton, advocates manufactures in Ohio valley, 43-46; suggests
export duty on cotton, 154
South Carolina, distress in agriculture,
34, 36, 41; agitation in behalf of
manufactures, 37 ff.; Bluffton movement, 37-40, 69-70; hostility of white
labor to slaves, 53, 219; nullification
in, 66; party divisions, 66 f.; disunion
movement (1849-52), 72-74, 76, 77,
82-85, 89; question of aid to manufactures, 155; discriminatory taxation, 156, 160; and tariff, 166; aid to
railroads, 172; agriculture, 203; and
revival of slave trade, 213, 215, 217,
225; manufactures, 227; secession,
231, 239, 243-45, 250-51; projects for
direct trade, 256; and Confederate
Constitution, 262, 269, 271
Southern Commercial Convention, origin, 123-29; objects and proceedings,